Ben Curry

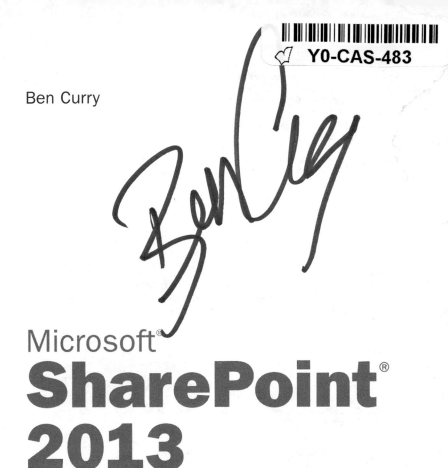

Microsoft®
SharePoint® 2013

Pocket Guide

SAMS | 800 East 96th Street, Indianapolis, Indiana 46240 USA

Microsoft® SharePoint® 2013 Pocket Guide

ISBN-13: 978-0-672-33698-0
ISBN-10: 0-672-336987
Library of Congress Control Number: 2013941410
Printed in the United States of America
First Printing September 2013

Trademarks

All terms mentioned in this book that are known to be trademarks or service marks have been appropriately capitalized. Sams Publishing cannot attest to the accuracy of this information. Use of a term in this book should not be regarded as affecting the validity of any trademark or service mark.

Warning and Disclaimer

Bulk Sales

Sams Publishing offers excellent discounts on this book when ordered in quantity for bulk purchases or special sales. For more information, please contact

U.S. Corporate and Government Sales
1-800-382-3419
corpsales@pearsontechgroup.com

For sales outside of the U.S., please contact

International Sales
international@pearsoned.com

Editor-in-Chief
Greg Wiegand

Executive Editor
Neil Rowe

Development Editor
Box Twelve Communications

Managing Editor
Kristy Hart

Project Editor
Andy Beaster

Copy Editor
Barbara Hacha

Indexer
Erika Millen

Proofreader
Megan Wade-Taxter

Technical Editor
Neil Hodgkinson

Editorial Assistant
Cindy Teeters

Cover Designer
Anne Jones

Compositor
Nonie Ratcliff

Contents at a Glance

Table of Contents

About the Author

Ben Curry (CISSP, MVP, MCP, MCT) is an author and enterprise architect specializing in knowledge management, BPM, ECM, and collaborative technologies. Ben is a founding Partner at Summit 7 Systems, a company focused on the next generation of Microsoft products, and has been awarded the Most Valuable Professional (MVP) by Microsoft six years in a row.

Ben's philosophy is that the best solutions are inspired by the best ideas, and he encourages his team to continuously generate and share ideas. His numerous publications embody his philosophy. Ben enjoys sharing his ideas as an instructor, both in the IT world and in the marine world. Ben is a Master Scuba Diver Trainer with a passion for diving and spearfishing.

Ben's other life passions include driving his Shelby around the countryside in his hometown of Huntsville, Alabama, and coaching his daughter's softball team. Ben is happily married to Kimberly and is the proud father of their children, Madison and Bryce.

About the Coauthors

Jason Batchelor (MCP) is an information architect and technology strategist who works to bring a balanced approach toward successful system deployments. Jason has been able to leverage core technology strengths in the areas of knowledge management, collaboration technologies, and enterprise content management toward the creation and implementation of successful system designs ranging from large and small enterprises to local and state governments. Jason is a senior consultant and the manager of Professional Services at Summit 7 Systems, a company focused on the next generation of Microsoft products. Jason has more than 11 years of experience in information system design and information architecture. Understanding the balanced need between technology and business, Jason has been instrumental in efforts utilizing SharePoint as a foundation for business process automation and reengineering through the use of tools such as Lean and Six Sigma. Outside of his professional passions, Jason enjoys coaching both high school and travel soccer in his hometown of Madison, Alabama, where he lives with wife, Patricia, and their three children, Zachary, Caila, and Jacob. Jason is a graduate of the University of Alabama in Huntsville where he obtained both his BSBA and MS in management information systems.

Jay Simcox (MCSE Security, MCTS, MCITP) is a respected IT professional and educator with more than 12 years of information technology experience. Jay is a manager and senior consultant with Summit 7 Systems, where his background in network and systems administration, SharePoint architecture and administration, and end user support and training are utilized by government agencies seeking to make better use of the tools they are provided. Jay holds an A.A.S. in network engineering and a B.S. in management information systems; he has five years of instructional experience related to information technology. He is a native of Havelock, North Carolina, and currently lives in Huntsville, Alabama, with his beautiful wife, Anna, and their two children, Joey and Allyson. In his spare time Jay enjoys playing golf, reading, and supporting University of North Carolina Tar Heel basketball.

Shane King (CISSP, MCTS) is a senior consultant with Summit 7 Systems, specializing in the strategy, design, and implementation of business critical information systems. He has more than 14 years of experience in aerospace and systems engineering, which allows him to bring a holistic approach to solution design and solving business problems. Shane completed his masters of accountancy (MAcc) in December 2008 and is a part-time instructor, teaching accounting information systems and business process management. Shane is a native of Huntsville, Alabama, where he enjoys spending his time off-roading in his Jeep and volunteers as a karate instructor, teaching young adults and youth self-defense. Shane is a loving father to his three children, Noah, Evie, and Blake.

Jason Cribbet (MCPD and MCITP) is a senior developer at Summit 7 Systems, with more than 12 years of information technology experience serving commercial, government, and nonprofit organizations. Jason has developed within the Microsoft technology stack since the early days of the .NET framework and has been working with SharePoint-related technologies since 2007. He is a graduate of the University of Central Florida with a B.S. in computer engineering. A native of South Florida, Jason lives in Huntsville, Alabama, with his wife, Lori, and their three children, Ellie, Alexa, and Jason.

Joy Curry is an information technologist who has spent more than 5 years working with Microsoft SharePoint. She comes from a government contracting background where she was responsible for both SharePoint 2007 and SharePoint 2010 farms. Her experience includes all aspects of creating SharePoint-based solutions, from determining initial vision with senior stakeholders, through requirements, design, and finally, implementation. Joy has also spent considerable time doing internal training of critical users as well as working with executive and senior management to realize their goals for SharePoint. When not working with SharePoint, Joy enjoys hiking and off-roading with her husband, James, and their two spoiled dogs.

Dedication

I want to dedicate this book to my best friend and brother, Jim Curry. Jim—you've stood by me my entire life without waiver. I love you, bro.
—Ben Curry

I want to thank my wife, Patricia (P.J.), for your love, infinite support, and continual motivation. You inspire me. For these reasons, and so much more, this book is dedicated to you.
—Jason Batchelor

I dedicate this book to my kids Blake, Evie, and Noah King who are my inspiration.
—Shane King

For my family, near and far, without your love and support I would not be the person I am today. I love you all.
—Jay Simcox

Acknowledgments

I first want to thank the crew at Summit 7 Systems for supporting questions throughout the writing of the book and your patience with me when I delayed answers to your questions during this project. I also want to thank my business partner and friend, Scott Edwards. He has always been a great support during large projects, and this one was no exception.

There were many new features in this product that made it impossible for a single person to write a book in a reasonable amount of time. Thanks first of all to the coauthors: Jason Batchelor, Shane King, and Jay Simcox. They each wrote a substantial portion of the book and really poured their heart and soul into the project. I also want to say a big thank-you to my technical editor, Neil Hodgkinson from Microsoft. He's one of the best guys you'll ever meet and a heck of a SharePoint MCM as well! Thanks, Neil.

I also had three contributing authors: Daniel Webster (one of the best Enterprise Search people you'll find), Joy Curry (site collection guru), and Jason Cribbet. Jason wrote most of the developer content, and if you ever get a chance to work with him, you'll learn a lot and be glad to know him.

Thanks to all the staff at Pearson for believing in the project and helping to bring this book to market. Last, thanks to Jeff Riley, who was a very patient and understanding editor. He helps make us look like we know what we're doing! Thanks, Jeff.

We Want to Hear from You!

As the reader of this book, *you* are our most important critic and commentator. We value your opinion and want to know what we're doing right, what we could do better, what areas you'd like to see us publish in, and any other words of wisdom you're willing to pass our way.

We welcome your comments. You can email or write to let us know what you did or didn't like about this book—as well as what we can do to make our books better.

Please note that we cannot help you with technical problems related to the topic of this book.

When you write, please be sure to include this book's title and author as well as your name and email address. We will carefully review your comments and share them with the author and editors who worked on the book.

Email: consumer@samspublishing.com

Mail: Sams Publishing
           ATTN: Reader Feedback
           800 East 96th Street
           Indianapolis, IN 46240 USA

Reader Services

Visit our website and register this book at www.informit.com/title/ for convenient access to any updates, downloads, or errata that might be available for this book.

Introduction

From the beginning of the project, this book was written to be a concise and easy-to-reference guide that you can use when you have questions about SharePoint Server 2013 administration. A thorough index has been provided to help you quickly find the information you need. This is a guide you will want close by when working with the new versions of SharePoint products and technologies.

This book provides administrative procedures, quick answers, tips, and tested design examples. In addition, it covers some of the most difficult tasks, such as scaling out to a server farm and implementing disaster recovery. It also covers many of the new Windows PowerShell commands now needed for building and maintaining SharePoint Server. The text contains illustrative examples of many advanced tasks required to implement a SharePoint Products solution for almost any size organization.

Who Is This Book For?

SharePoint Server 2013 Administrator's Guide covers SharePoint Server 2013 Standard and SharePoint Server 2013 Enterprise editions. This book is designed for the following:

- Administrators migrating from SharePoint Server 2007 and SharePoint Server 2010
- Administrators who are experienced with Windows Server 2008 and Internet Information Services
- Current SharePoint Foundation 2013 and SharePoint Server 2013 administrators
- Administrators who are new to Microsoft SharePoint Technologies
- Technology specialists, such as site collection administrators, search administrators, and web designers

Because this book is limited in size and I wanted to give you the maximum value, I assumed a basic knowledge of Windows Server 2012, Active Directory, Internet Information Services

(IIS), SQL Server, and web browsers. These technologies are not presented directly, but this book contains material on all these topics that relate to the administrative tasks of SharePoint Products.

How Is This Book Organized?

This book was written to be a daily reference for administrative tasks. The capability to quickly find and use information is the hallmark of this book. For this reason, the book is organized into job-related tasks. It has an expanded table of contents and an extensive index for locating relevant answers. In addition, there is an appendix for many of the new SharePoint Server Windows PowerShell cmdlets. If you are looking for a comprehensive guide to implementing SharePoint Products, you should consider purchasing the *SharePoint 2013 Unleashed* book, by Sams Publishing, because this pocket guide has been stripped to the bare essentials required to complete a task. Michael and Colin do a fantastic job with that book, and you'll be glad you own it as well.

I really hope you find the *SharePoint Server 2013 Administrator's Guide to be* useful and accurate. I have an open door policy for email at *bcurry@summit7systems.com*. Because my inbox stays quite full, please be patient; replies sometimes take a week or longer.

PART I

DEPLOYING

IN THIS PART

CHAPTER 1

Installing SharePoint Server 2013

- Preparing for Installation
- Farm Topologies
- Installing the First SharePoint Foundation 2013 Server in the Farm
- Installing the First SharePoint 2013 Server in the Farm
- Post-Installation Configuration
- Advanced Installation Options

Before inserting SharePoint Server 2013 installation media and clicking Next, it is important that you take time to understand the different options available in the setup wizard. Making the wrong selection during setup could result in the need to do a complete uninstall and reinstall of the binaries. Moreover, making good choices in the beginning will make it considerably easier to scale Microsoft SharePoint products in the future:

- **Choose a SQL Server Type**—During installation you have the option to select the type of server installation you want to perform. You can either install all components on a single server—this includes Microsoft SQL Server Express 2008 R2 SP1—on the single computer, or you can select a dedicated SQL Server installation for the databases. Choose the SQL Server Express option only when you are sure that you will not scale to a server farm in the future. Although scaling to a server farm is technically possible, migrating SharePoint products from SQL Server 2012 Express to SQL Server 2012 Enterprise or Standard is a tedious task.

- **Use Assigned IP Addresses**—Host headers ease installation and reduce administrative overhead. Also, assigning IP addresses may strengthen your overall security posture by simplifying Intrusion Detection rules and logs. Assigning an individual IP address for every web application simplifies your logs, prepares for load balancing, and allows for separate firewall rules.

- **Process Security Isolation**—Depending on the level of security your organization requires, you can choose to install with one or several accounts for Microsoft Internet Information Services (IIS) application pools and database access. It is much easier to install with separate accounts in the beginning than it is to change and isolate application pools later. Be aware that the more application pools you create, the greater the amount of memory that is required.

- **Assign Administrators**—You must define the administrative roles and separation of duties. If you want to granularly define administrative roles, pay close attention to the details of service accounts and groups. If you are in a small organization, consider using a dedicated farm account for all administrative tasks.

- **Select a Site Template for the Web Application Root**—When creating your first web application, it is wise to create a site collection in the root managed path. This site can be modified, but the site template cannot be changed, so give careful consideration to the template used.

This chapter covers Microsoft SharePoint Foundation 2013 and SharePoint Server 2013 deployments, when using IIS host headers alone or with assigned IP addresses. When neither Microsoft SharePoint Foundation 2013 nor SharePoint Server 2013 is specified, the material applies to both software products.

Note

Although this book is focused on SharePoint Server 2013, many developers and beginning administrators install SharePoint Foundation 2013 early on in their education with SharePoint 2013 products. Therefore, the installation chapter covers both products.

Preparing for Installation

At a minimum, before proceeding with installation, sketch out your design, including IIS configuration, SQL Server databases, accounts, administrator, and any other pertinent data you will need. Microsoft Office Visio is a very helpful tool when designing and maintaining server farms, IIS servers, and SQL Server databases. In addition to planning layout, verify that your servers meet the minimum hardware requirements. If using Active Directory for authentication, you will use service accounts for the server farm prior to beginning the installation wizard. You want to make sure that any needed Active Directory accounts have been created prior to beginning installation.

Understanding Hardware and Software Requirements

The single biggest change in the minimum hardware requirements for SharePoint 2013 is in the memory requirements for web servers, application servers, and single-server installations.

Table 1.1 details the minimum hardware requirements.

Table 1.1   **Minimum Hardware Requirements for Web Servers, Application Servers, and Single Server Installations**

Component	Minimum Requirement
Processor	64-bit, dual processor, 4 cores.
RAM	8GB for development/evaluation instance of SharePoint Foundation 2013.
	24GB for development/evaluation instance of SharePoint Server 2013. (This assumes all components will be on a single machine.)
	12GB for pilot, user acceptance test, or production deployment of SharePoint Server 2013. (This assumes SQL Server will be hosted on a different machine.)
Hard disk	80GB free space.

The basic hardware requirements for Microsoft SQL Server database servers supporting SharePoint 2013 remain the same as those for SharePoint 2010.

Table 1.2 details the minimum hardware requirements for database servers.

Table 1.2   Minimum Hardware Requirements for Database Servers

Component	Minimum Requirement
Processor	64-bit, 4 cores for small deployments 64-bit, 8 cores for medium deployments
RAM	8GB for small deployments 16GB for medium deployments
Hard disk	80GB free space

Considerations

Make sure you take the following items into consideration when planning your hardware environment:

- The 80GB hard disk requirement identified in Tables 1.1 and 1.2 is specific to the system drive of the server and is intended to accommodate system updates and patches. This requirement does not take into account storage space for SharePoint 2013 log files or content storage within the database.

- The memory requirements identified in Tables 1.1 and 1.2 apply to small and medium deployments only.
  http://technet.microsoft.com/en-us/library/cc298801.aspx.

The minimum requirements for each server in a farm have changed, and at the time of this writing they require the installation of a variety of available hotfixes. Those hotfixes are called out separately in the Note following Table 1.3.

Table 1.3   Minimum Software Requirements

Environment	Minimum Requirement
Server operating system	64-bit edition of Windows Server 2012 Standard or Datacenter
	64-bit edition of Windows Server 2008 R2 Service Pack 1, Standard, Enterprise, or Datacenter
Database server in a farm	64-bit edition of Microsoft SQL Server 2012
	64-bit edition of Microsoft SQL Server 2008 R2 Service Pack 1

Environment	Minimum Requirement
Standalone server	SQL Server 2008 R2 Express x64 with SP1
	Web Server (IIS) role
	Application Server role
	Microsoft .NET Framework 4.5
	SQL Server 2008 R2 SP1 Native Client
	Microsoft WCF Data Services 5.0
	Microsoft Information Protection and Control Client (MSIPC)
	Microsoft Sync Framework Runtime v1.0 SP1 (x64)
	Windows Management Framework 3.0, which includes Windows PowerShell 3.0
	Windows Identity Foundation (WIF) 1.0 and Microsoft Identity
	Extensions (previously named WIF 1.1)
	Windows Server App Fabric
	Cumulative Update Package 1 for Microsoft AppFabric 1.1 for Windows Server (KB 2671763)
Front-end Web/Application servers in a farm	Web Server (IIS) role Application Server role
	Microsoft .NET Framework 4.5
	SQL Server 2008 R2 SP1 Native Client
	Microsoft WCF Data Services 5.0
	Microsoft Information Protection and Control Client (MSIPC)
	Microsoft Sync Framework Runtime v1.0 SP1 (x64)
	Windows Management Framework 3.0, which includes Windows PowerShell 3.0
	Windows Identity Foundation (WIF) 1.0 and Microsoft Identity Extensions (previously named WIF 1.1)
	Windows Server App Fabric
	Cumulative Update Package 1 for Microsoft AppFabric 1.1 for Windows Server (KB 2671763)

Table 1.3   Minimum Software Requirements (continued)

Environment	Minimum Requirement
Client computer	Windows 7
	Microsoft Silverlight 3.0
	A supported browser
	Silverlight 3
	Office 2013
	Microsoft Office 2010 with Service Pack 1
	Microsoft Office 2007 with Service Pack 2
	Microsoft Office for Mac 2011 with Service Pack 1
	Microsoft Office 2008 for Mac version 12.2.9

Considerations

Make sure you take the following into consideration and apply the appropriate hotfixes where necessary when preparing your server environment for your SharePoint 2013 installation:

- The SharePoint parsing process crashes in Windows Server 2008 R2. To address this issue, apply KB 2554876.

- IIS 7.5 configurations are not updated when you use the ServerManager to commit configuration changes. This is addressed by applying KB 2708075.

- An issue in the .NET Framework 4.5 has been identified where the IIS worker process may crash or experience a deadlock when running in an integrated pipeline mode. This issue is addressed by applying the following hotfixes:
  - For Windows Server 2008 R2 SP1—KB 2759112.
  - For Windows Server 2012—KB 2765317.

Installing Prerequisites

The following prerequisites can be automatically downloaded and installed from the SharePoint Server 2013 Start page:

- Web Server (IIS) role
- Application Server role

- Microsoft .NET Framework version 4.5
- SQL Server 2008 R2 SP1 Native Client
- Microsoft WCF Data Services 5.0
- Microsoft Information Protection and Control Client (MSIPC)
- Microsoft Sync Framework Runtime v1.0 SP1 (x64)
- Windows Management Framework 3.0, which includes Windows PowerShell 3.0
- Windows Identity Foundation (WIF) 1.0 and Microsoft Identity Extensions (previously named WIF 1.1)
- Windows Server AppFabric
- Cumulative Update Package 1 for Microsoft AppFabric 1.1 for Windows Server (KB 2671763)

You may find that security requirements for your customer prohibit web access from the servers you are planning to install on SharePoint 2013. In this case the prerequisites can be downloaded and either installed manually or using Windows PowerShell. More information on how to script the installation of the prerequisites can be found in the "Advanced Installation Options" section of this chapter.

Note

Links to all the prerequisites for your SharePoint 2013 installation can be found on Microsoft TechNet at the following link:
http://technet.microsoft.com/en-us/library/cc262485.aspx#section4

Identifying Service Accounts

One of the most important aspects of planning for deployment is to identify the service accounts that will be needed. Several accounts must be specified, even for the most basic farm topologies. Other accounts will be required depending on the additional functionality deployed.

Table 1.4 lists the accounts that are required for all SharePoint 2013 installations, and Table 1.5 lists other service accounts that may be necessary for a fully functional farm.

Table 1.4   **Required Service Accounts**

Account	Purpose	Requirements
SQL Server service account	Run SQL Server processes service account	Either a local system account or domain account.
		Ensure that this account has access to any external resources used to back up or restore. If using a local system account (Network Service or Local System), grant access to domain_name\SQL_hostname$.
Setup user account	Run installation and SharePoint Products and Technologies Configuration Wizard	Domain account.
		Member of the Administrators group on each server where setup is run.
	Run Windows PowerShell commands	SQL Server login on database server.
		Member of securityadmin and dbcreator server roles.
		If using Windows PowerShell, you must be a member of the dbowner fixed role on the database.
Server farm account/ database access account	Application pool identity for Central Administration website	Domain account.
		Additional permissions are also granted on Web front-end and application servers because they are added to the farm.
	Run SharePoint Foundation Timer Service	This account is also added to the following SQL Server roles on the farm database server:
		dbcreator fixed server role
		securityadmin fixed server role
		db_owner fixed database role on all SharePoint databases for the farm

Table 1.5 lists other service accounts that may be required to enable or configure specific service applications or functionality within the farm.

Table 1.5   **Other Service Accounts**

Account	Purpose	Requirements
Search Service account	Run Search Service.	This account defaults to the farm should administrator account, but you specify a different account for security purposes.
Content Access account	Used to access content sources for crawling. Defaults to Search Service account.	Domain account with read access to content to be crawled.
Web Application pool accounts	Used for running IIS Web applications that host SharePoint site collections.	Can be a local system account or domain account.
Service Application pool accounts	Used for running SharePoint Service applications that provide specialized functionality to the farm.	Can be a local system account or domain account. This will vary depending on the service application the account is intended for use with.

Farm Topologies

Farm topologies vary widely based on a number of factors, including number of users, redundancy requirements, scalability requirements, and service applications being used. Aside from a database server and one or more web servers, there can be any number of servers hosting one or more service applications.

The recommendation is to use the concept of "server groups" to group services with similar performance characteristics onto a single server and then add servers based on the needs of those particular services. For instance, Search is implemented as a service application in SharePoint 2013, and small farms might start out using a single dedicated server. As search usage increases, a server might be added to the search "group" to maintain the required level of performance. Using this model to group servers in your farm into logical collections can be a helpful tool in the planning process. Note that this is simply a planning method—you won't find the term "server group" used in Central Administration.

This section provides an overview of some standard topologies for farms of varying sizes.

Single-Server Farm

A single-server farm, as shown in Figure 1.1, is ideal for evaluation or development purposes, or for a very small (fewer than 100) number of users. This farm consists of a single server performing all roles, including the database role. If SQL Server is not installed prior to running the SharePoint 2013 installer, SQL Server 2008 Express will be installed and used.

All roles on one server, including SQL server.

FIGURE 1.1
A single-server farm consists of SQL Server Express, Standard, or Enterprise and all product binaries.

Two-Server Farm

For a user base between 100 and approximately 10,000 users, a two-server farm might be sufficient. As shown in Figure 1.2, this farm consists of a database server and a single web server that performs all application server roles. For high-availability requirements in a farm with more than 1,000 users, a second clustered or mirrored database server is recommended.

All Web and application server roles.

Databases

FIGURE 1.2
A two-server farm offloads the database processing.

Two-Tier Small Farm

For an environment with 10,000 to 20,000 users with low service usage, a two-tier small farm is recommended. This farm consists of a database server and two web servers, with one of the web servers performing all the application server roles as well. Figure 1.3 shows an example of a two-tier small farm. Note that the Search components may need to be arranged differently depending on your requirements.

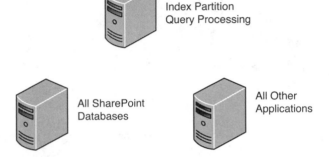

SPF Web
Index Partition
Query Processing

All SharePoint
Databases

All Other
Applications

FIGURE 1.3
A two-tier small farm provides additional process for applications.

Three-Tier Small Farm

The three-tier small farm is the same as a two-tier farm, except that a dedicated application server is added between the presentation tier and the data tier to handle moderate service usage. A commonly implemented topology is implementing the SharePoint Foundation Web Application service and Query Processing component on the same servers, and all other applications on dedicated application server, as shown in Figure 1.4.

Medium Farm

The medium farm is a three-tier farm. The first tier consists of two or more web servers. A general rule for planning is 10,000 users per web server. The middle tier consists of two servers dedicated to crawling content, content processing, search administration, and search analytics, and one or more servers for other service applications. As service applications grow in number or usage, more servers can be added to the middle tier to handle the growth. As shown in Figure 1.5, the third tier uses dedicated servers for the search databases, with one or more servers used for all other SharePoint databases.

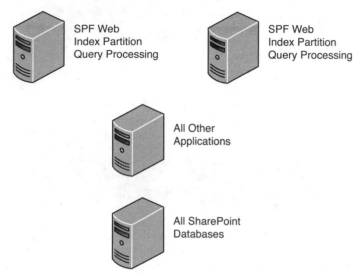

FIGURE 1.4
Three-tier small farm allows for great search performance and processing.

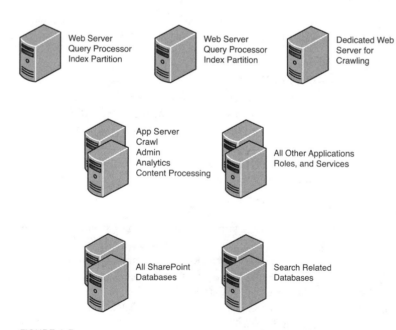

FIGURE 1.5
A three-tier medium farm provides substantial process power for an enterprise.

Large Farm

The large farm builds on the server group concept used in the medium farm. For example, you can have a dedicated group of servers for handling incoming requests and one or more separate servers for crawling and administration. Most large farms have two or more dedicated Search servers for crawling, content processing, index partitions, analytics, and administration. Figure 1.6 is an example of what a large farm might look like, but large farm architecture will greatly depend on the technical and functional requirements. For example, if you had 100K users executing queries on 1 million indexed items, the query processing component would need to be robust. Inversely, if you had 10 users querying a dynamic index of 10 million items, you'd need to increase the performance for crawling and content processing. After you have decided your search topology, you then would need one or more servers for other service applications, and possibly one or more isolated servers for running sandboxed code and dedicated timer jobs. In the data tier, the search databases and content databases will have dedicated servers, with another server handling all other SharePoint databases. Figure 1.6 shows an example of a large farm.

Web Servers

Web Server Group 1

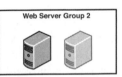
Web Server Group 2

Web Servers for Handling All
Incoming Requests

Dedicated Web Server(s) for Crawling and
Administration

Application Servers

Application Server
Group 1

Application Server
Group 2

Application Server
Group 3

Application Server
Group 4

Query Processing
Index Partition

All Other Search Components

All Other Sevices Including
Central Administration

Servers for Miso Services
and Dedicated Timer Job
Servers

Database Servers

Database group 1

Database group 2

Database group 1

Content and Configuration
Databases

Search Databases

All Oher SharePoint
Databases

FIGURE 1.6
A large server farm can service thousands of simultaneous requests.

Installing the First SharePoint Foundation 2013 Server in the Farm

After carefully reviewing hardware and software requirements and creating or obtaining the necessary service accounts, you are ready to begin the installation process for SharePoint Foundation 2013. This chapter covers the installation of the initial server in the farm. If you are planning a multiserver deployment, see Chapter 5, "Scaling Web and Service Applications," for detailed information regarding adding servers to the farm.

> **Note**
>
> When you install SharePoint Server, SharePoint Foundation is installed automatically during the installation process. Although it is possible to install SharePoint Foundation manually before installing SharePoint Server, you are not required to do so.

Running the SharePoint Products and Technologies Preparation Tool

The SharePoint Products and Technologies Preparation tool helps to ensure that all prerequisites have been installed on your server before you proceed with installation. You must have an Internet connection to automatically install prerequisites; otherwise, prerequisites will have to be installed manually.

To run this tool, complete the following steps:

1. If you are using a downloadable installer, double-click SharePoint.exe. If you are using installation media, select Setup.exe from the media.

2. On the SharePoint Foundation 2013 Start page, select Install Software Prerequisites, as shown in Figure 1.7.

3. On the Welcome to the Microsoft SharePoint Products and Technologies Preparation Tool page, click Next.

4. On the License Terms for Software Products page, review the terms and conditions, select the check box verifying that you agree to the terms and conditions, and click Next.

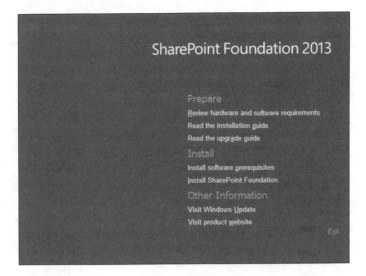

FIGURE 1.7
Install software prerequisites before installing the binaries.

Note

As shown in Figure 1.8, the preparation tool provides feedback as it automatically installs and configures the necessary prerequisite components to ensure a successful installation. It is possible that a reboot might be required. In the event of a required reboot, the installation wizard automatically starts when you log on after the reboot.

---

5. On the Installation Complete page, review the components that were automatically installed, configured, or both, and click Finish.

Note

Information about installing the SharePoint 2013 prerequisites manually or using a Windows PowerShell script can be found in the "Advanced Installation Options" section of this chapter.

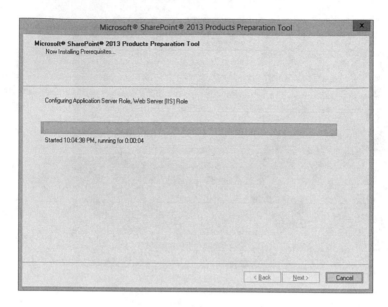

FIGURE 1.8
The preparation tool might take several minutes to complete.

Installing the SharePoint Foundation 2013 Binaries

Be sure that you've either installed the software prerequisites using the preparation tool or that you've manually installed them. After the prerequisites have been installed, you can install the SharePoint Foundation 2013 binaries by doing the following:

1. On the SharePoint Foundation 2013 Start page (shown in Figure 1.9), click Install SharePoint Foundation.

2. Review the Read the Microsoft Software License Terms page, select the box verifying that you have read and understand the terms, and then click Continue.

3. On the Server Type Tab, choose the default option Complete, as shown in Figure 1.10, when using SQL Server Standard or Enterprise. Click Install Now to perform the setup.

4. When setup completes, leave the Run the SharePoint Products Configuration Wizard Now check box selected, as shown in Figure 1.11, and click Close.

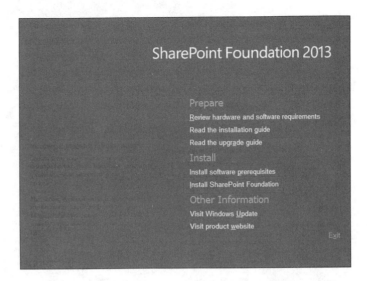

FIGURE 1.9
Install SharePoint Foundation after installing the software prerequisites.

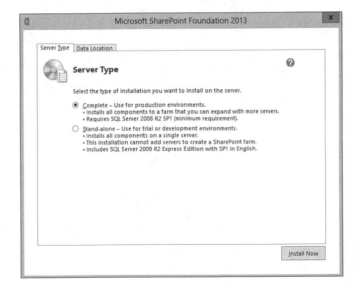

FIGURE 1.10
Click Complete when using SQL Server Standard or Enterprise.

FIGURE 1.11
Select Close to begin the Configuration Wizard.

> **Tip**
>
> If setup fails for any reason, you can check the log files in the TEMP
> folder of the current user. Click the Start menu and type **"%temp%"** into
> the search box. If this resolves to a location ending in **1** or **2**, you might
> have to navigate up one directory to find the log file, which is named
> Microsoft Windows SharePoint Services 4.0 (<timestamp>).

Running the SharePoint 2013 Products Configuration Wizard

At this point you've installed the SharePoint Foundation binaries, but you
haven't provisioned a server farm. A server farm is defined as a configuration database. The SharePoint Products Configuration Wizard will guide
you through the process of provisioning the farm:

1. If the SharePoint 2013 Products Configuration Wizard does not
   launch automatically, you can find it located at Start, All Programs,
   Microsoft SharePoint 2013 Products.

2. On the Welcome to SharePoint Products page, click Next.

3. A dialog box, as shown in Figure 1.12, appears and states that some services might need to be restarted during configuration. Click Yes to proceed.

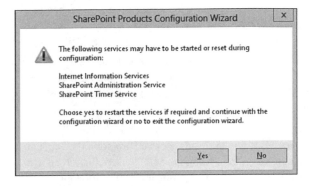

FIGURE 1.12
Click Yes to continue configuration.

4. On the Connect to a Server Farm page, shown in Figure 1.13, choose Create a New Server Farm, and then click Next.

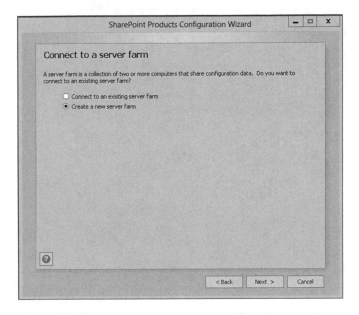

FIGURE 1.13
Select Create a New Server Farm, and then click Next.

5. The Specify Configuration Database Settings page allows you to
    provision a configuration database. You should enter the following
    values:

    ■ In the Database Server box, type the server name of the data-
       base server.

    ■ In the Database Name box, type a name for the configuration
       database. If the database server is hosting multiple farms, you
       should type a name that uniquely identifies the farm you are
       configuring; otherwise, you can keep the default value of
       SharePoint_Config.

    ■ In the Username box, type the server farm administrator
       account name. If you are using Active Directory, the account
       name should be in the format DOMAIN\username, as shown
       in Figure 1.14. Remember that this account will be given
       special access to the relevant SQL Server databases and will
       be the application pool identity for the Central Administration
       website.

    ■ In the Password box, type the account password.

FIGURE 1.14
Verify all information and then click Next.

6. On the Specify Farm Security Settings page, shown in Figure 1.15, type a phrase into the Passphrase box, and click Next. This passphrase should be guarded, and it must be entered any time a server is joined to the farm. It is used to encrypt credentials of SharePoint accounts. This passphrase uses your default domain password security policy. By default, the passphrase must meet the following criteria:

    ■ It should be eight characters in length.

    ■ It should contain three of the following four character types:

        English uppercase letters (A through Z)

        English lowercase letters (a through z)

        Numerals (0 through 9)

        Nonalphanumeric characters (such as "!","*","#", and so on)

FIGURE 1.15
Be sure to document the farm passphrase.

7. The Configure SharePoint Central Administration Web Application page allows you to specify the settings for the website used to perform administrative tasks in SharePoint.

   ■ Specify a port number for the Central Administration Web site or use the default as seen in Figure 1.16.

   ■ Choose the NTLM or Negotiate (Kerberos) option for authentication. Most administrators choose NTLM and change to Kerberos later if required.

   ■ Click Next.

FIGURE 1.16
If unsure, do not specify a port number.

8. On the Completing the SharePoint Products Configuration Wizard page (see Figure 1.17), review your specified settings and click Next to begin configuration. SharePoint configures the farm according to your specifications, providing feedback during each step of the process.

9. On the Configuration Successful page, shown in Figure 1.18, be sure to document all settings on the final page of the SharePoint Products Configuration Wizard, and then click Finish.

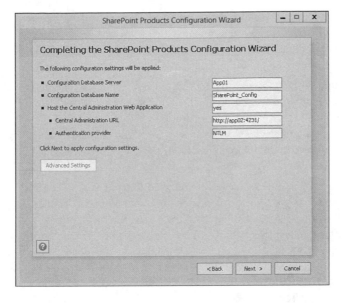

FIGURE 1.17
Be sure to document all settings after a successful configuration.

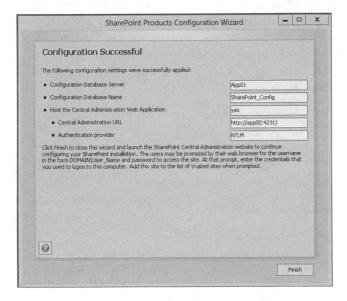

FIGURE 1.18
Be sure to document all settings after a successful configuration.

If the configuration fails, you can check the PSCDiagnostics files located on the drive where SharePoint is installed, in the %CommonProgramFiles%\Microsoft Shared\Web Server Extensions\ 15\Logs folder.

If the configuration is successful, Internet Explorer is launched and the Central Administration website is opened. If you are prompted for credentials, you should add the Central Administration URL to your Local Intranet Zone or, alternatively, to your Trusted Sites list and ensure that Internet Explorer is configured to automatically pass user credentials to sites in that list.

If you see a proxy server error message, you need to make sure to configure your browser to bypass the proxy server for local addresses. In Internet Explorer, this setting can be configured on the Tools, Internet Options menu, under the Connections tab. Click LAN Settings to access the proxy server configuration settings.

Using the SharePoint Foundation 2013 Configuration Wizard

If you are an experienced SharePoint products administrator, you probably will not want to use the Farm Configuration Wizard because it limits your installation options. However, using it does make initial farm configuration easier. If you are new to SharePoint Foundation 2013, using the Farm Configuration Wizard is an acceptable method to begin with, but you are strongly encouraged not to use it for production deployments.

After you run the SharePoint 2013 Products Configuration Wizard, the farm is provisioned, but it must be configured.

To use the Farm Configuration Wizard, do the following:

1. Open the Central Administration site (shown in Figure 1.19) and click Configuration Wizards. To go directly to the page, browse to http://servername:4231/default.aspx.

2. Choose Launch the Farm Configuration Wizard.

3. Decide whether you'll automatically send information to Microsoft on the Help Make SharePoint Better page. Enter your choice, and then click OK.

4. On the Configure Your SharePoint Farm page choose Yes, Walk Me Through the Configuration of My Farm Using This Wizard, and then click Start the Wizard.

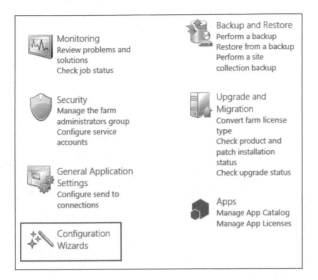

FIGURE 1.19
Click Configuration Wizards to see the available farm product wizards.

5. In the Service Account section, specify the service account you want to use to configure your services, as shown in Figure 1.20. It is recommended that you choose an account other than the farm administrator account for security purposes.

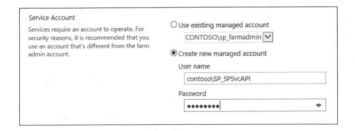

FIGURE 1.20
Verify that the account exists in Active Directory before continuing.

6. Decide whether you'll use the service applications available by default in SharePoint Foundation (see Figure 1.21):

■ **App Management Service**—Allows you to add SharePoint Apps from the SharePoint Store or App Catalog.

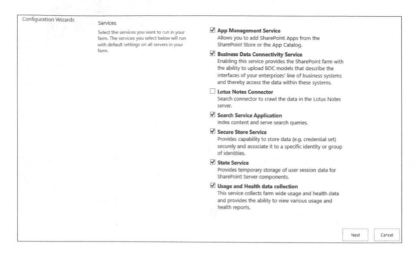

FIGURE 1.21
Choose the appropriate service applications.

- **Business Data Connectivity Service**—Enables access to structured data from various line-of-business systems, such as Siebel, SAP, or custom databases.

- **Lotus Notes Connector**—Search connector to crawl data in the Lotus Notes server.

- **Search Service Application**—Index content and serve search queries.

- **Secure Store Service**—Allows you to store credentials and use it for data access purposes.

- **State Service**—Provides the capability to set credentials securely and associate those credentials with a specific identity or group of identities.

- **Usage and Health Data Collection**—Collects farmwide usage and health data and provides the capability to view various usage and health reports.

7. Click Next.

8. On the Configure Your SharePoint Farm page, select which template you'll use and then click OK.

9. On the wizard summary page, click Finish to complete the initial configuration.

Understanding Databases Created During Installation

After installation, you see several databases that are created in SQL Server and need to be added to your SQL Server maintenance plan:

- **SharePoint Configuration**—The SharePoint configuration database (config DB) holds all your server farm configuration data and is akin to the Windows Server System Registry. Any server that uses this installation's config DB is considered a member of the same server farm.

- **Central Administration content**—Because the Central Administration web application is a custom site collection in a dedicated web application, it has a corresponding content database. Rebuilding this web application is not a simple task and should be avoided by correctly backing up the server for future restoration.

The preceding databases are installed by default in all SharePoint 2013 deployments. There will be additional databases created as service and web applications are created, configured, and deployed in the farm. More information regarding the databases created for service applications can be found in Chapter 2, "Configuring Farm Operations."

Installing the First SharePoint Server 2013 Server in the Farm

The SharePoint Server 2013 product installation process is similar to the SharePoint Foundation 2013 process. This is understandable because the SharePoint Server product is built on the SharePoint Foundation platform. After reviewing the requirements for hardware and software listed earlier in this chapter and obtaining or creating the necessary service accounts, you can proceed to install SharePoint Server 2013.

Running the Microsoft SharePoint Products and Technologies Preparation Tool

The SharePoint Products and Technologies Preparation Tool helps to ensure that all prerequisites have been installed on your server before you proceed with installation. You must have an Internet connection to automatically install prerequisites; otherwise, prerequisites will have to be installed manually. Complete the following steps to run the SharePoint Products and Technologies Preparation Tool:

1. Launch the setup executable for SharePoint Server 2013.

2. On the SharePoint Server 2013 Start page, click Install Software Prerequisites, as shown in Figure 1.22.

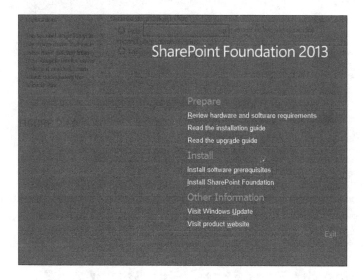

FIGURE 1.22
Install software prerequisites before installing the product binaries.

3. On the Welcome to the Microsoft SharePoint Products Preparation Tool page, click Next.

4. On the License Terms for Software Products page, review the terms and conditions, select the check box verifying that you agree to the terms and conditions, and click Next.

5. On the Installation Complete page, click Finish.

Installing the SharePoint Server 2013 Binaries

Now that all prerequisites have been installed, you can install SharePoint Server 2013 by doing the following:

1. On the SharePoint Server 2013 Start page, click the Install SharePoint Server as shown in Figure 1.23.

2. On the Enter Your Product Key page, type your product key and click Continue.

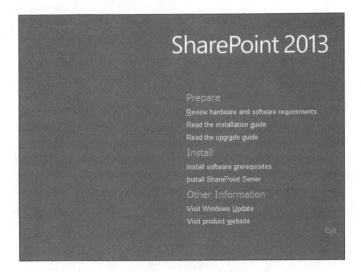

FIGURE 1.23
Install SharePoint Server after you have installed the software prerequisites.

3. On the Read the Microsoft Software License Terms page, review the terms and conditions, select the check box verifying that you agree to the terms and conditions, and click Continue.

4. On the File Location tab, enter the installation and search index data folder locations, and then click the Server Type tab. This tab is used to identify custom installation and log file locations for the farm in the event that you do not want to use the default locations.

5. On the Server Type tab, shown in Figure 1.24, select the type of installation you want to perform. In this case we will choose Complete, which allows you to add additional servers to the farm at a later date.

6. Click Install Now to proceed with the installation.

7. When setup completes, leave the Run the SharePoint Products Configuration Wizard Now check box selected and click Close, as shown in Figure 1.25.

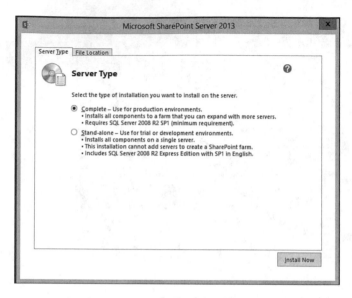

FIGURE 1.24
Click Complete when using SQL Server Standard or Enterprise.

FIGURE 1.25
Click Close to begin the farm provisioning process.

Running the SharePoint Products Configuration Wizard

At this point, you've installed the SharePoint Server 2013 binaries, but you haven't created a configuration database. It is important to note that a farm is defined by a configuration database. Provisioning a farm is the same as provisioning a new configuration database. The SharePoint 2013 Products Configuration Wizard guides you through the process of provisioning the farm:

1. If the SharePoint 2013 Products Configuration Wizard does not launch automatically, you can find it by clicking Start, All Programs, Microsoft SharePoint 2013 Products.

2. On the Welcome to SharePoint Products page, click Next.

3. A dialog box appears, stating that some services might need to be restarted during configuration. Click Yes to proceed.

4. On the Connect to a Server Farm page, click Create a New Server Farm, and then click Next.

5. On the Specify Configuration Database Settings page, make the following changes:

   - In the Database Server box, type the server name of the database server.

   - In the Database Name box, type a name for the configuration database. If the database server is hosting multiple farms, you should type a name that uniquely identifies the farm you are configuring; otherwise, you can keep the default value of SharePoint_Config.

   - In the Username box, type the server farm administrator account name. If you are using Active Directory, the account name should be in the format DOMAIN\username. Remember that this account must have SQL permissions of Database Creator and Security Administrator defined before installation of SharePoint Server 2013. This account will also be the application pool identity for the Central Administration website, and it will have access to all server farm databases. Thus, be sure to protect this account's credentials.

   - In the Password box type the account password.

   - Click Next.

6. On the Specify Farm Security Settings page, type a passphrase and click Next. This passphrase must be entered any time a server is joined to the farm and is used to encrypt credentials of SharePoint

accounts. By default, it is constrained by your Active Directory minimum password complexity requirements. If it is the default, the passphrase must meet the following criteria:

- It must be eight characters in length.

- It must contain three of the following four character types:

    English uppercase letters (A through Z)

    English lowercase letters (a through z)

    Numerals (0 through 9)

    Nonalphanumeric characters (such as !, *, #)

7. The Configure SharePoint Central Administration Web Application page allows you to specify the settings for the website used to perform administrative tasks in SharePoint:

    - Specify a port number for the Central Administration website or use the default.

    - Choose NTLM or Negotiate (Kerberos) for authentication.

    - Click Next.

8. On the Completing the SharePoint Products Configuration Wizard page, review your specified settings and click Next to begin configuration.

9. On the Configuration Successful page, click Finish.

Note

If the configuration fails, you can check the PSCDiagnostics files located on the drive where SharePoint is installed, in the %CommonProgramFiles%\Microsoft Shared\Web Server Extensions\15\Logs folder.

If the configuration is successful, Internet Explorer is launched and the Central Administration website is opened. If you are prompted for credentials, you should add the Central Administration URL to your trusted sites list and ensure that Internet Explorer is configured to automatically pass user credentials to sites in that list.

If you see a proxy server error message, you need to make sure to configure your browser to bypass the proxy server for local addresses. In Internet Explorer, this setting can be configured on the Tools, Internet Options menu, under the Connections tab. Click LAN Settings to access the proxy server configuration settings.

Using the SharePoint 2013 Farm Configuration Wizard

If you are an experienced SharePoint Server administrator, you probably will not want to use the Farm Configuration Wizard because it limits your installation options. However, using it does make initial farm configuration easier. If you are new to SharePoint Server 2013, using the Farm Configuration Wizard is an acceptable method to begin with.

> **Note**
>
> When you are manually configuring the farm, there isn't necessarily one correct way of accomplishing success. But, during the writing of this book, the following order of creating and configuring web and service applications was followed:
>
> 1. Create the primary web application.
> 2. Create the My Site Provider (web application).
> 3. Create the Content Type Hub web application (optional).
> 4. Create and configure the Search Service application.
> 5. Create and configure the User Profiles Service application.
> 6. Create and configure the Managed Metadata service application.
> 7. Create the SPState Service application.
> 8. Start services for relevant service applications.
> 9. Verify the association of service applications to web applications.

If you are using the Configuration Wizard to install SharePoint Server 2013, do the following:

1. Open the Central Administration site (as shown in Figure 1.26) and click Configuration Wizards. To go directly to the page, browse to http://servername:29514/default.aspx.

2. Click Launch the Farm Configuration Wizard.

3. On the How Do You Want to Configure Your SharePoint Farm page, choose Yes, Walk Me Through the Configuration of My Farm Using This Wizard, and then click Start the Wizard.

4. In the Service Account section, select the service account you want to use to configure your services. You should choose an account other than the farm administrator account for security purposes, and it should be in the format DOMAIN\username, as shown in Figure 1.27.

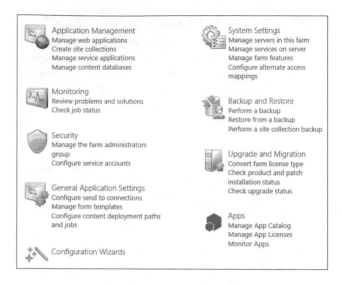

FIGURE 1.26
Click Configuration Wizards to continue.

FIGURE 1.27
Enter the account name previously created in Active Directory.

5. Many more services are available by default in SharePoint Server 2013 than in SharePoint Foundation 2013. The decision about which services to use doesn't have to be made at this point. You can rerun the configuration wizard again later and install additional services. Select which services to enable, or accept the defaults for these services and click Next.

6. On the Create Site Collection page, click Skip. You can create the first site collection here, but you will probably want to have more control over the initial web application creation and configuration, so

it is best to skip this step for now. Creating the initial web application for hosting sites is covered in the "Post-Installation Configuration" section.

7. On the Farm Configuration Wizard summary page, click Finish to complete the initial configuration.

Post-Installation Configuration

Even though the Farm Configuration Wizard created and configured the basic applications required for your farm, additional configuration steps will probably be required depending on the specific functionality you want to provide your users. Some functionality within new web applications might be missing until the appropriate configuration is performed.

The vast majority of configuration actions performed for a SharePoint farm are performed in the Central Administration website. This site should have been installed on at least one of the farm servers when the farm was provisioned and can be used to configure all farmwide and web application-level settings.

Configuring the Farm Administrators Group

You can add or remove farm administrators by going to Central Administration, Security, Manage the Farm Administrators Group and adding or deleting users. Members of the Farm Administrators group have full access to all settings across the entire farm and can take ownership of any site in the farm. This group should be carefully managed and limited to as few individuals as possible.

Configuring Outgoing Email Settings

Outgoing email must be configured for users to receive alerts from SharePoint. The Simple Mail Transport Protocol (SMTP) service must be set up on a server accessible to the SharePoint farm, and it must be configured to allow anonymous messages. You must be a member of the Farm Administrators group to modify these settings:

1. In Central Administration, click System Settings.

2. On the System Settings page, in the Email and Text Messages (SMS) section, choose Configure Outgoing Email Settings.

3. In the Mail Settings section of the Outgoing Email Settings page, type the SMTP server name for outgoing email in the Outbound SMTP Server box.

4. Enter the From Address and Reply-To Address to be used. The From address will appear in the From field of any email messages sent by SharePoint. The Reply-To address will be used for replies to any email messages sent by SharePoint.

5. In the Character Set drop-down list, select the appropriate character set.

6. Click OK to save the settings.

Creating a Web Application to Host Site Collections

As in previous versions of SharePoint, all SharePoint sites are rendered via Internet Information Services. To create a web application for hosting site collections, perform the following steps:

1. In Central Administration, click Manage Web Applications in the Application Management section.

2. Click the New button on the left side of the ribbon.

3. Enter the following values for the new web application:

   - **IIS Website**—Choose Create a New IIS Web Site. Give it a descriptive name. Ensure that the Port value is 80 and that the host header value uses the FQDN, as shown in Figure 1.28. Leave the default value for Path unless you have specific requirements to do otherwise.

Note

If you choose a path other than C:\, be sure that path exists on all current and future members of the farm. Otherwise, the server addition to the farm will fail.

   - **Security Configuration**—Leave the default values selected, as shown in Figure 1.29.

   - **Public URL**—Enter the base URL that will be used to access the website, and leave the Zone set to Default. You do not have to include the TCP port number with the URL when on a standard port, such as TCP 80 (:80). Figure 1.30 shows an example of a web application on TCP port 80.

Create New Web Application   ✕

Warning: this page is not encrypted for secure communication. User names, passwords, and any other
information will be sent in clear text. For more information, contact your administrator.

| | | | | OK | Cancel |

IIS Web Site

Choose between using an
existing IIS web site or create a
new one to serve the Microsoft
SharePoint Foundation
application.

If you select an existing IIS web
site, that web site must exist on
all servers in the farm and have
the same name, or this action
will not succeed.

If you opt to create a new IIS
web site, it will be automatically
created on all servers in the
farm. If an IIS setting that you
wish to change is not shown
here, you can use this option to
create the basic site, then
update it using the standard IIS
tools.

○ Use an existing IIS web site

    Default Web Site   ▼

◉ Create a new IIS web site
  Name

    SharePoint - Portal

Port

    80

Host Header

    app01.contoso.com

Path

    C:\inetpub\wwwroot\wss\VirtualDirectories\app

Security Configuration

If you choose to use Secure
Sockets Layer (SSL), you must
add the certificate on each

Allow Anonymous

○ Yes
◉ No

FIGURE 1.28
Use the FQDN for the first Host Header if possible.

Security Configuration

If you choose to use Secure
Sockets Layer (SSL), you must
add the certificate on each
server using the IIS
administration tools. Until this
is done, the web application will
be inaccessible from this IIS web
site.

Allow Anonymous

○ Yes
◉ No

Use Secure Sockets Layer (SSL)

○ Yes
◉ No

Claims Authentication Types

Choose the type of
authentication you want to use
for this zone.

Negotiate (Kerberos) is the
recommended security
configuration to use with
Windows authentication. If this
option is selected and Kerberos
is not configured, NTLM will be
used. For Kerberos, the
application pool account needs
to be Network Service or an
account that has been
configured by the domain
administrator. NTLM

☑ Enable Windows Authentication
   ☑ Integrated Windows authentication

    NTLM   ▼

   ☐ Basic authentication (credentials are sent in clear text)

☐ Enable Forms Based Authentication (FBA)
  ASP.NET Membership provider name

  ASP.NET Role manager name

FIGURE 1.29
You can change the Claims Authentication Type to Kerberos later, if necessary.

FIGURE 1.30
The default URL should use the FQDN.

- **Application Pool**—Select Create New Application Pool and choose the account to be used to run the application pool, as shown in Figure 1.31.

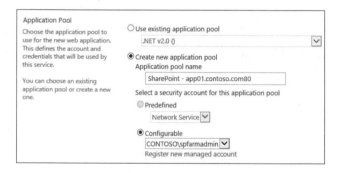

FIGURE 1.31
Create a new application pool for isolation and security.

- **Database Name and Authentication**—The database server defaults to the server where the configuration database resides. If needed, you can specify another database server, as shown in Figure 1.32. Choose a database name to distinguish this content database from other databases on the server. Using Windows Authentication to connect to the database is highly recommended. The use of SQL Authentication requires an in-depth knowledge of the SharePoint Server 2013 architecture and SQL Server architecture as well. The use of SQL Authentication will result in an increased level of manual configuration.

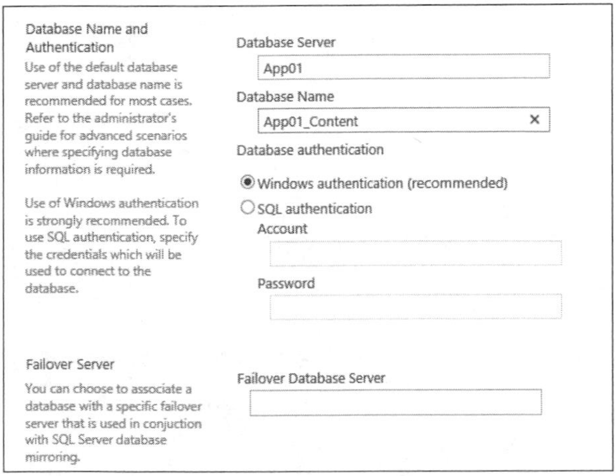

Database Name and Authentication	Database Server
Use of the default database server and database name is recommended for most cases. Refer to the administrator's guide for advanced scenarios where specifying database information is required.	App01
	Database Name
	App01_Content ✕
	Database authentication
Use of Windows authentication is strongly recommended. To use SQL authentication, specify the credentials which will be used to connect to the database.	⦿ Windows authentication (recommended)
	◯ SQL authentication
	Account
	Password
Failover Server	Failover Database Server
You can choose to associate a database with a specific failover server that is used in conjuction with SQL Server database mirroring.	

FIGURE 1.32
Enter the database server and database name.

- **Failover Server**—You can specify a failover database server name to be used with SQL Server database mirroring. Note that this only makes SharePoint 2013 Products mirroring aware; you must still configure database mirroring in SQL Server.

- **Search Server**—This value is used exclusively in a SharePoint Foundation 2013–only environment. If you are using SharePoint Server 2013, this option is not applicable.

- **Service Application Connections**—You can accept the default service application settings as shown in Figure 1.33, or you can choose to customize the settings for the new web application.

4. Click OK to create the new web application.

FIGURE 1.33
Select which service applications to associate, or select the default group.

Configuring Usage and Health Collection

Usage and Health Data collection settings are farm-level settings and cannot be configured for a specific server. The user configuring these settings should be a member of the Farm Administrators group:

1. On the home page of Central Administration, click Monitoring.

2. In the Reporting section of the Monitoring page, click Configure Usage and Health Data Collection.

3. In the Usage Data Collection section of the Configure Usage and Health Data Collection page, enable usage data collection by selecting the Enable Usage Data Collection check box.

4. In the Event Selection list, choose the events to log by clicking the corresponding check boxes as shown in Figure 1.34. Keep in mind that logging uses system resources and can affect performance. Therefore, in a new installation you might consider setting the event and trace log thresholds to Critical and Unexpected, respectively.

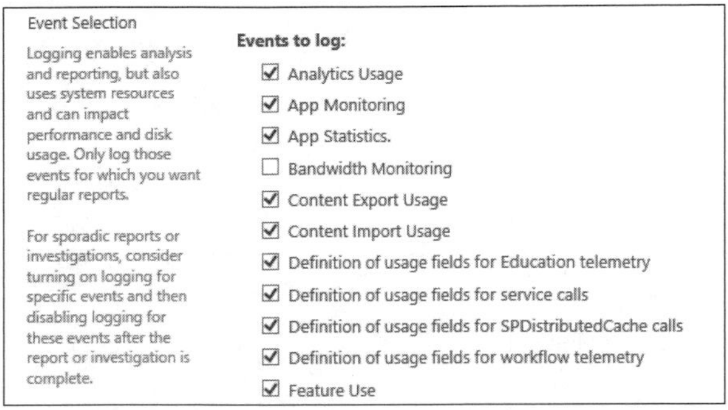

Event Selection

Logging enables analysis
and reporting, but also
uses system resources
and can impact
performance and disk
usage. Only log those
events for which you want
regular reports.

For sporadic reports or
investigations, consider
turning on logging for
specific events and then
disabling logging for
these events after the
report or investigation is
complete.

Events to log:

☑ Analytics Usage
☑ App Monitoring
☑ App Statistics.
☐ Bandwidth Monitoring
☑ Content Export Usage
☑ Content Import Usage
☑ Definition of usage fields for Education telemetry
☑ Definition of usage fields for service calls
☑ Definition of usage fields for SPDistributedCache calls
☑ Definition of usage fields for workflow telemetry
☑ Feature Use

FIGURE 1.34
Select what events you'll log.

5. In the Usage Data Collection Settings section, enter the path where
    usage and health data should be written in the Log File Location
    box. This path must exist on all farm servers, and you should ensure
    that sufficient disk space exists on the destination drive. The follow-
    ing example, shown in Figure 1.35, uses the C:\ volume. If your log
    files will be very large, consider using a different volume.

Note

The Log File Location value must exist on every server in the farm. If a
server does not have the specified drive, the server will not successfully
be added to the farm.

Usage Data Collection
Settings

Usage logs must be saved
in a location that exists on
all servers in the farm.
Adjust the maximum size
to ensure that sufficient
disk space is available.

Log file location:

C:\Program Files\Common Files\Microsoft Shared\Web Server Extensions\15\LOGS\

FIGURE 1.35
Verify that space exists in the log file location.

6. In the Health Data Collection section, select the Enable Health Data
    Collection check box, as shown in Figure 1.36. To change the sched-
    ule or disable any health-related timer jobs, click Health Logging
    Schedule for a list of jobs, and then click the job to change its
    settings.

FIGURE 1.36
If needed, enable health data collection.

7. To change the schedule or disable any usage log-related timer jobs, in the Logging Collection Schedule click Log Collection Schedule for a list of jobs, and then click the job to change its settings.

8. In the Logging Database Server section, select the appropriate authentication mechanism. Windows authentication is recommended. The logging database server or database name can be changed only with Windows PowerShell.

9. Click OK to save the settings.

Configuring Diagnostic Logging

Diagnostic logging for the SharePoint farm is highly configurable and can be performed through Central Administration. You should consider minimizing diagnostic logging in a new installation. You must be a member of the Farm Administrators group to perform these actions:

1. On the Home page of Central Administration, click Monitoring.

2. In the Reporting section of the Monitoring page, click Configure Diagnostic Logging.

3. In the Event Throttling section of the Diagnostic Logging page are the following options for configuring Event Throttling:

    ■ For all categories:

        ■ Select the All Categories check box.

        ■ Select the event log level from the least critical event to report to the event log list.

        ■ Select the event log level from the least critical event to report to the trace log list.

- For one or more categories:

  - Select the check boxes for the categories you want to configure.

  - Select the event log level from the least critical event to report to the event log list.

  - Select the event log level from the least critical event to report to the trace log list.

- For one or more subcategories:

  - Click (+) next to the category to expand the subcategories.

  - Select the check box next to the subcategory.

  - Select the event log level from the least critical event to report to the event log list.

  - Select the event log level from the least critical event to report to the trace log list.

- To restore the defaults for all categories:

  - Select the All Categories check box.

  - Select Reset to Default from the least critical event to report to the event log list.

  - Select Reset to Default from the least critical event to report to the trace log list.

4. In the Event Log Flood Protection section, select the Enable Event Log Flood Protection check box. This prevents the same event from being logged excessively, further degrading performance.

5. In the Trace Log section, enter the path to the folder where the logs should be written in the Path box.

6. Specify the number of days for log files to be kept (from 1 through 366) in the Number of Days to Store Log Files box, as shown in Figure 1.37.

7. The disk space used by log files can be restricted by selecting the Restrict Trace Log Disk Space Usage check box and entering the maximum number of gigabytes (GB) the log files should be allowed to use. When this limit is reached, older files are automatically deleted.

8. Click OK to save the settings.

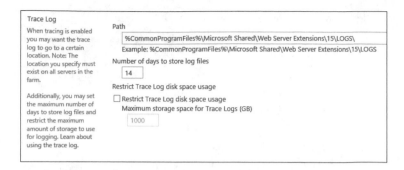

FIGURE 1.37
Restrict log disk space usage when using the C:\ volume.

Assigning IP Addresses to Web Applications

Many administrators will need to assign IP addresses to their web applications to meet organizational and regulatory compliance requirements. This is a multistep process that cannot be performed solely within a SharePoint Server 2013 administration tool. To assign IP addresses to your web applications, follow these steps:

1. Add a host (A record) in the DNS Management Console.

2. Add the associated IP address to your Windows Server.

3. After an IIS reset, assign the IP address to the web application in website bindings. Figure 1.38 shows an example of an Internet Information Services configuration.

FIGURE 1.38
Enter the host name and port number for the web application.

4. Click the existing binding, and click Edit.

5. If desired, choose the IP address to assign to this web application from the IP Address drop-down list.

6. Enter the URL from the A record in step 1 in the Host Name box.

7. Click OK to save the binding.

8. Open Central Administration and on the Home page, in the System Settings section, click Configure Alternate Access Mappings.

9. Click the name of the web application, and verify that the URL for the default zone is set correctly. An example is shown in Figure 1.39.

FIGURE 1.39
Verify that the internal URL is defined in DNS.

Advanced Installation Options

In some situations you may want to automate some or all of your SharePoint Server 2013 installation. This may be driven by a customer security policy that prohibits servers from having Internet access, or you have a large number of servers to install and configure. In either case, it is possible to use Windows PowerShell to accomplish this task in an efficient manner.

> **Note**
>
> The changes you are making in this section would be considered configuration, or bit-level, changes to the application. It is recommended that you are logged in using your SharePoint Farm Administrator account when attempting to execute these commands.

Installing the Prerequisites Offline

To install the prerequisites for installing SharePoint 2013, you first have to download them and save them locally or to a network share for installation either manually or through the use of a Windows PowerShell script. A link to the complete list of prerequisite downloads can be found in the "Installing Prerequisites" section earlier in this chapter.

After the prerequisites have been downloaded and stored locally to the network or server, there are three ways to install those executable files:

1. Install each prerequisite manually by double-clicking the executable file.

2. Install the prerequisites from the command line:

   - Navigate to the SharePoint 2013 source directory.

   - Install each file individually from the command line using the appropriate switch and path to the filename. For example, to install the Native SQL client alone, you would enter the following from the command line:

     ```
     prerequisiteinstaller.exe /SQLNCLi:
     "\\o15-sf-admin\SP_prereqs\sqlncli.msi"
     ```

3. Create a Prerequisites.installer.txt file to install the prerequisites:

   - This file must have all the switches and paths in one long string with no line beaks in order to work correctly.

   - The file must be named Prerequisites.arguments.txt.

   - The file must be located in the same folder or file share as the prerequisitesinstaller.exe application.

   An example of the prerequisitesinstaller.arguments.txt is shown in Figure 1.40.

```
Untitled - Notepad

File  Edit  Format  View  Help

/PowerShell:"<path>\WINDOWS6.1-KB2506143-x64.msu" /NETFX:"<path>\dotNetFx45_Full_x86_x64.exe" /IDFX:"<path>
\Windows6.1-KB974405-x64.msu" /sqlncli:"<path>\sqlncli.msi" /Sync:"<path>\Synchronization.msi" /AppFabric:"<path>
\setup.exe" /IDFX11:"<path>\Microsoft Identity Extensions.msi" /MSIPCClient:"<path>\msipc.msi"
/WCFDataServices:"<path>\WcfDataServices.exe" /KB2671763:"<path>\AppFabric1.1-RTM-KB2671763-x64-ENU.exe
```

FIGURE 1.40
An example of the prerequisites.arguments.txt file.

Installing the prerequisites manually from the command line, or using Windows PowerShell, does not change the fact that the server will have to reboot a number of times to complete the installation. If you are installing the prerequisites using Windows PowerShell, the script should resume executing when the server returns to a running state.

Considerations

The following issues must be addressed after your manual or scripted has completed:

- The SharePoint parsing process crashes in Windows Server 2008 R2. To address this issue, apply KB 2554876.

- IIS 7.5 configurations are not updated when you use the ServerManager to commit configuration changes. This is addressed by applying KB 2708075.

- An issue in the .NET Framework 4.5 has been identified where the IIS worker process may crash or experience a deadlock when running in an integrated pipeline mode. This issue is addressed by applying the following hotfixes:
  - For Windows Server 2008 R2 SP1—KB 2759112.
  - For Windows Server 2012—KB 2765317.

Scripting Installations of the SharePoint Binaries

Scripting the installation of the SharePoint 2013 binaries is slightly different from the processes used for the prerequisites. In this case we are going to use a config.xml file to provide SharePoint 2013 with the parameters necessary to install the SharePoint 2013 binaries on the server.

Microsoft has provided the basic answer file we need to script the installation in the file structure of the installation media. If you look in the root of your installation media, you will see a folder named Files. In that folder are six more folders, each of which represents a different installation option:

- **Setup**—Performs a standalone installation of the farm using SQL Server Express.
- **Setupfarm**—Performs a complete server farm installation.
- **Setupfarmsilent**—Performs a silent installation of a complete server farm.
- **Setupfarmupgrade**—Performs an upgrade installation from SharePoint Foundation 2013 to SharePoint Server 2013.
- **Setupsilent**—Performs a silent installation of a standalone farm.

- **Setupsingleupgrade**—Performs a silent upgrade of a standalone farm using SQL Server Express.

Each folder contains a config.xml file that resembles Figure 1.41.

```
                                                config - Notepad
File  Edit  Format  View  Help
<Configuration>
        <Package Id="sts">
                <Setting Id="LAUNCHEDFROMSETUPSTS" Value="Yes"/>
        </Package>

        <Package Id="spswfe">
                <Setting Id="SETUPCALLED" Value="1"/>
        </Package>

        <Logging Type="verbose" Path="%temp%" Template="SharePoint Server Setup(*).log"/>
        <!--<PIDKEY Value="Enter Product Key Here" />-->
        <Setting Id="SERVERROLE" Value="APPLICATION"/>
        <Setting Id="USINGUIINSTALLMODE" Value="1"/>
        <Setting Id="SETUPTYPE" Value="CLEAN_INSTALL"/>
        <Setting Id="SETUP_REBOOT" Value="Never"/>
</Configuration>
```

FIGURE 1.41
Sample config.xml file for a scripted installation of the SharePoint 2013 binaries.

In this XML file you will need to make two changes: add the PID key and uncomment that line within the file and save it. After you have made those changes, the XML file will look similar to Figure 1.42.

```
                                                config - Notepad
File  Edit  Format  View  Help
<Configuration>
        <Package Id="sts">
                <Setting Id="LAUNCHEDFROMSETUPSTS" Value="Yes"/>
        </Package>

        <Package Id="spswfe">
                <Setting Id="SETUPCALLED" Value="1"/>
        </Package>

        <Logging Type="verbose" Path="%temp%" Template="SharePoint Server Setup(*).log"/>
        <PIDKEY Value="xxxxx-xxxxx-xxxxx-xxxxx-xxxxx" />
        <Setting Id="SERVERROLE" Value="APPLICATION"/>
        <Setting Id="USINGUIINSTALLMODE" Value="1"/>
        <Setting Id="SETUPTYPE" Value="CLEAN_INSTALL"/>
        <Setting Id="SETUP_REBOOT" Value="Never"/>
</Configuration>
```

FIGURE 1.42
An example of the edited config.xml.

To run the SharePoint 2013 setup, enter the following in the address bar of Windows Explorer from the Run Command:

```
<path>\setup.exe /config <path>\config.xml
```

The two preceding path parameters refer to the path to location of the SharePoint 2013 binaries. Note that the config.xml file must be in the same folder as the setup.exe file that executes to initiate the installation.

Note

For more information on unattended and silent installations of SharePoint 2013, see the Microsoft TechNet article at http://technet.microsoft.com/en-us/library/ff806334(v=office.14).aspx.

CHAPTER 2

Configuring Farm Operations

- Introducing Central Administration
- System Settings
- Database Management
- Configuring Send To Connections

Core Operations refers to farm-level settings and applications such as Central Administration, server services, settings, and email configuration. Items such as service applications, search, and web applications are such large and important topics that they have dedicated chapters. This chapter will cover the core farm operations not covered elsewhere in the book. Much of this chapter will show you how to set up farm operations that are configured only once, such as Short Messaging Service (SMS) mobile services. Although the interaction with other Microsoft SharePoint Server functional areas will be discussed, you should reference the chapter for each of those functional areas for detailed information.

Introducing Central Administration

At the heart of every server farm is the configuration database. This database stores the majority of your core server farm configuration. The association of Service Applications, configuration of Web Applications and content databases, email settings, server services architecture, farm solutions, and farm features are stored in this database. To manage all this configuration data, you need a tool. Central Administration is the primary administrative tool available to you. How you access the Central Administration website will depend on what operating system is running on your SharePoint server.

Accessing Central Administration

To access the Central Administration website on a SharePoint server running Windows 2008 R2 SP 2, click through the following path: Start, All Programs, Microsoft SharePoint 2013 Products, SharePoint 2013 Central Administration.

To access the Central Administration website on a SharePoint server running Windows Server 2012, take the following steps:

1. Access the Start page either by using the icon on the right side of the desktop or using the pop-up menu in the lower-left corner.

2. On the Start page find the SharePoint 2013 Central Administration tile and click it. If you do not see the tile, start typing **Share** and it will search for the application.

Figure 2.1 shows Central Administration as installed out of the box.

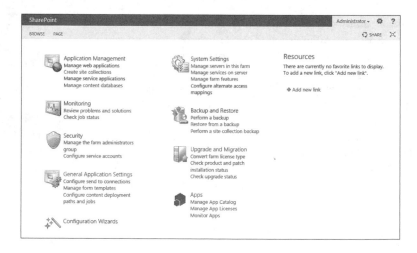

FIGURE 2.1
Central Administration is the primary administrative interface for SharePoint Server 2013.

In addition to Central Administration, much of the SharePoint farm configuration can be managed through the use of Windows PowerShell and STSADM.exe. In fact, as you read through this book, in several situations the use of Windows PowerShell is required. This is because there are certain configuration tasks that cannot be performed through the Central Administration user interface (UI).

To access the Windows PowerShell console on a SharePoint server running Windows Server 2008 R2 SP2, navigate through the following path: Start, All Programs, Microsoft SharePoint 2013 Products, SharePoint 2013 Administration Shell.

To access the Central Administration website on a SharePoint server running Windows Server 2012, take the following steps:

1. Access the Start page either by using the icon on the right side of the desktop or using the pop-up menu in the lower-left corner.

2. On the Start page find the SharePoint 2013 Management Shell and right-click it.

3. In the taskbar find the icon to Run as Administrator and click it. This runs the management shell with elevated permissions.

Additionally, the stsadm.exe command still exists in SharePoint Server 2013 and can be used where appropriate. We do not recommend using stsadm.exe except in those situations where you may have no other choice or are unable to get Windows PowerShell to perform as desired.

Tip

You can find stsadm.exe in C:\Program Files\Common Files\Microsoft Shared\Web Server Extensions\15\bin. You can either include this directory in your system path or create a shell script to navigate to the directory to make it easier to execute. It can also be executed from the SharePoint Server Management Shell.

Central Administration Architecture

It's important to understand that Central Administration is a site collection contained in a dedicated web application. As such, it has an associated content database for the web application. If you use the SharePoint 2013 Products Configuration Wizard, by default the content database will be named SharePoint_AdminContent_<GUID>, as shown in Figure 2.2. Although it's not difficult, you need to detach the content DB, rename, and reattach if you want to rename it later. Therefore, if you want a different name for your Central Administration content database, it's simpler to create your server farm using Windows PowerShell.

FIGURE 2.2
You can view your Central Administration content database using Microsoft SQL Server Management Studio.

Because Central Administration requires write access to your server farm configuration database, you should never use this web application or associated application pool for collaborative web applications. Doing so could provide a hacker with potential write access through another web application. Central Administration was created automatically when you ran the SharePoint 2013 Products Configuration Wizard and should not be modified. Although Central Administration is technically just another site collection and can be modified as such, a best practice is to leave it in the default state. Only administrators access the site collection, so branding and customization shouldn't be an issue.

As shown in Figure 2.1, Central Administration has nine primary areas:

- **Application Management**—Hosts administrative links to web applications, site collections, service applications, and databases. Chapter 3, "Creating Web Applications and Content Databases," explains this section and associated tasks in depth.

- **System Settings**—Contains your server and server service management, email and text messaging, and other farm management settings. Most of the functionality discussed in this chapter can be found in System Settings.

- **Monitoring**—This area has been greatly expanded in SharePoint Server 2013 and includes Reporting, Analytics, Timer Jobs, Health Analyzer, and Usage information. Chapter 16, "Configuring Sites and Site Collections," covers Reporting and the Health Analyzer in detail. Only the server farm timer jobs are discussed in this chapter.

- **Backup and Restore**—The location where both farm and granular backups and restores are performed. Chapter 14, "Backing Up and Restoring SharePoint 2013," provides more information.

- **Security**—Includes links to manage the farm administrators group, configure farm accounts, manage passwords for those accounts, define blocked file types, configure antivirus settings, manage Web Part security, and control Information Management Policies global settings.

- **Upgrade and Migration**—Upgrade-specific information can be found in Chapter 17, "Upgrading from SharePoint Server 2010."

- **General Application Settings**—Includes external service connections, document conversions, InfoPath forms services, site directory, SharePoint Designer, farm-scoped search settings, and content deployment.

- **Apps**—Includes links to specific configuration and functionality options for the Apps store.

- **Configuration Wizards**—Contains configuration wizards for your installation. Depending on additionally installed products, this screen can present multiple options for the automated configuration of your farm.

As you manage a SharePoint Server 2013 farm, you will perform administrative tasks on a regular basis. Remember that Central Administration is a web-based interface, so you can create favorites in your web browser to save time. Additionally, you will see multiple locations to manage the same item, such as web application general settings, within Central Administration.

Working with the Central Administration Web Application

Although Central Administration is a SharePoint Server web application, it differs from others because you don't create and deploy the web application. Because the deployment of other web applications is done from Central Administration, the provisioning of Central Administration itself is performed at either the command line or via the SharePoint 2013 Products Configuration Wizard. To deploy Central Administration to a server other than the one on which you first installed SharePoint Server, you must install the SharePoint Server binaries and run the SharePoint 2013 Products Configuration Wizard. You can run this wizard using one of the two following methods, depending on the operating system running on your SharePoint server.

To access the SharePoint 2013 Products Configuration Wizard on a SharePoint server running Windows Server 2008 R2 SP2, navigate through the following path: Start, All Programs, Microsoft SharePoint 2013 Products, SharePoint 2013 Products Configuration Wizard.

To access the Central Administration website on a SharePoint server running Windows Server 2012, take the following steps:

1. Access the Start page either by using the icon on the right side of the desktop or using the pop-up menu in the lower-left corner.

2. On the Start page find the SharePoint 2013 Management Shell and right-click it.

3. In the taskbar, find the icon to Run as Administrator and click it. This runs the management shell with elevated permissions.

Be very careful not to disconnect from the server farm, which can be specified with the option shown in Figure 2.3.

After you click Next once, select the Advanced Settings to provision the Central Administration website. Select Use This Machine to Host the Web Site, as shown in Figure 2.4.

You can also use the SharePoint 2013 Products Configuration Wizard to repair a broken Central Administration, assuming it is an Internet Information Services (IIS) configuration error causing the fault. To deprovision Central Administration, choose Yes, I Want to Remove the Web Site from This Machine. You should wait a few minutes to allow the farm configuration to update and also to allow time for the local IIS configuration to update. When the web application is no longer visible from IIS, you can rerun the SharePoint 2013 Products Configuration Wizard to reprovision the Central Administration on that server.

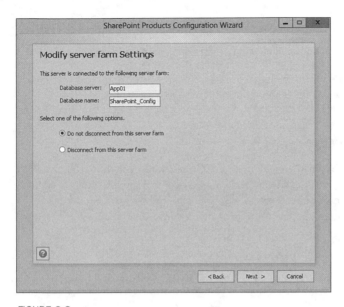

FIGURE 2.3
If provisioning Central Administration, be sure not to disconnect from the server farm.

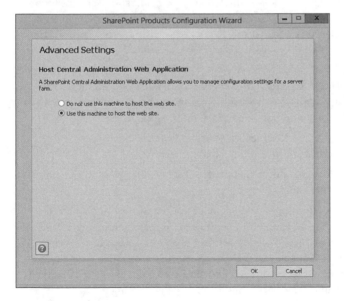

FIGURE 2.4
Select Use This Machine to Host the Web Site, and click OK.

> **Note**
>
> A web application problem with Central Administration might require you to make a technical support call. The actual content of Central Administration is contained in the associated content database, and farm configuration is contained in the configuration database.

System Settings

The System Settings area of Central Administration contains crucial settings that you need to plan and carefully control modification of. Most of the system settings affect all web applications and associated users in your server farm. System Settings is divided into three sections:

- Servers
- Email and Text Messages (SMS)
- Farm Management

Servers

The Servers section of System Settings gives you, at a glance, visibility into your server farm topology, including your application services topology. It also provides the SharePoint configuration database version and SQL Server name(s).

Servers in Farm

From the Manage Servers in This Farm link, you can see all the servers in your farm, as contained in the configuration database. You'll see five headings beneath the configuration database information:

- **Server**—Lists all servers in your server farm. You can click the Server text itself to sort the list alphabetically.

- **SharePoint Products Installed**—Displays the relevant SKU information about that server.

- **Services Running**—A valuable tool when discovering and troubleshooting a SharePoint Server farm. You are able to quickly see where specific application services are provisioned. If you were troubleshooting the User Profile Service, for example, you could find what server or servers were processing that data. You can then go to the relevant server and begin troubleshooting.

Farm Information

Configuration database version: 15.0.4420.1017
Configuration database server: App01
Configuration database name: SharePoint_Config

Server	SharePoint Products Installed	Services Running	Status	Remove Server
APP01	Microsoft SharePoint Server 2013	Access Database Service 2010 Access Services App Management Service Business Data Connectivity Service Central Administration Claims to Windows Token Service Distributed Cache Excel Calculation Services Machine Translation Service Managed Metadata Web Service Microsoft SharePoint Foundation Database Microsoft SharePoint Foundation Incoming E-Mail Microsoft SharePoint Foundation Subscription Settings Service Microsoft SharePoint Foundation Web Application Microsoft SharePoint Foundation Workflow Timer Service Secure Store Service Visio Graphics Service Word Automation Services Work Management Service	No Action Required	Remove Server
APP02	Microsoft SharePoint Server 2013	Access Database Service 2010 Access Services App Management Service Business Data Connectivity Service Central Administration Claims to Windows Token Service Distributed Cache Excel Calculation Services Machine Translation Service	No Action Required	Remove Server

FIGURE 2.5
All farm members and started services can be seen on the Services on Server management page.

Note

Figure 2.5 shows the services provisioned on a server and not necessarily the current status. It's possible that a service is nonfunctional and still shows as running on this screen. It's also possible that a server is completely offline because that status is not displayed.

- **Status**—Displays whether a server action is required or is being performed. Examples of this are service packs, language packs, and platform additions such as Project Server.

- **Remove Server**—Use this option if you want to remove a server's entry in the configuration database. Use this option with caution because it is irreversible. You should need to remove a server using Central Administration only if that server is no longer operational. The best way to remove a server from a farm is using the SharePoint 2013 Products Configuration Wizard on the server you want to remove and then selecting to disconnect it from server farm.

Manage Services on Server

The Manage Services on Server page is used to stop and start farm server services. These services are not Windows Server services. Although turning one of these services on or off in the configuration database might result in a Windows Service being turned on or off, the consequences of mistakenly stopping a SharePoint service are much worse than stopping a Windows Server service. For example, turning off the SharePoint Server Search service will update the configuration database and remove all entries related to that search server. Therefore, all relevant search content, such as the index, will be deleted, and the associated Windows Server service will be stopped. Basically, everything you start or stop in this screen is making configuration database changes. The timer job will subsequently pick up those changes from the database and modify application services accordingly.

The Manage Services on Server page also controls where processing of information is performed in your server farm. For example, you could have multiple servers in your farm performing the task of Managed Metadata Services. This allows for scalability of processing because it allows each server in the farm to process different server farm services. To stop or start services, you can select the Start or Stop hyperlink. If configuration is required to start, you will be automatically taken to the configuration screen. Don't confuse these services with service applications. Although service applications might use a service on a server, service applications apply across a server farm and exist at a level above services on the server. Always verify you are modifying the correct server, as shown in Figure 2.6.

FIGURE 2.6
Verify you are configuring the correct farm before starting or stopping services.

Email and Text Messages

SharePoint Server 2013 provides many ways to communicate via email and mobile text messaging. Pay close attention to the configuration of both incoming email messages and text messages (SMS). There are possible cost and security issues associated with external, automated farm communications.

Outgoing Email Settings

Outgoing email is primarily used for system alerts. Alerts allow users to be updated when an object changes, such as a list or a document. Depending on the users' choice, they can be alerted immediately, daily, or weekly. Additionally, the system generates messages for workflows and other system content that leverages outgoing email. To configure outgoing email, you need to specify an outbound Simple Mail Transfer Protocol (SMTP) server, as shown in Figure 2.7.

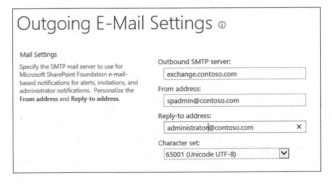

FIGURE 2.7
The From address and Reply-To address values can be different.

Although the From and Reply-To addresses can be different, they usually are not. Allowing a different From address might help you with current Unsolicited Commercial Email (UCE) whitelists, for example. You can also change the character set if needed for a different language. Be sure both the SharePoint Foundation 2013 and SharePoint Server 2013 language packs are loaded for the selected language.

> **Note**
>
> SharePoint Server 2013 cannot send credentials for outbound SMTP. Therefore, you must allow relaying on your SMTP server from SharePoint Server 2013 servers that will send mail. Always confirm that the required TCP ports and DNS entries are correct before troubleshooting a problem with SharePoint Server 2013 outgoing email.

Incoming Email Settings

Configuring incoming email is more complex than configuring outgoing email and requires changes to both your Windows servers and Active Directory configuration. First, you must have an SMTP server loaded on the servers that will accept incoming email. SharePoint Server 2013 does not include an SMTP service, but the default Windows Server SMTP server should work quite well. In Windows Server 2008 and Windows Server 2012, you add the SMTP server from Server Manager, Features.

> **Note**
>
> You must install and configure the SMTP service prior to configuring incoming email. See the steps at the following link: http://technet. microsoft.com/en-us/library/cc262947.aspx#section2

After you have installed the SMTP service, or identified an external SMTP server to use for incoming email and have created and delegated permissions in Active Directory, you can proceed with configuring your farm's Incoming Email settings. If you have enabled the Directory Management Service, distribution lists can be created automatically when enabled for SharePoint Server sites. Creating distribution lists automatically creates a distribution list in Active Directory and keeps it synchronized from SharePoint Server to Active Directory. Doing so allows users to easily send email to SharePoint Server groups when needed.

> **Note**
>
> The Directory Management Service is a one-way service. In other words, users are added to the Active Directory distribution list when they are added to a SharePoint group, but users are not added to the SharePoint group when they are added directly to the Active Directory distribution list.

An additional function of the Directory Management Service is that it automatically creates an Active Directory contact when email–enabling a list or library. Although it is not required or always desired, you can have the email address available in the Global Address List (GAL) after email-enabling a list. If you have not enabled the Directory Management Service, you must manually, or through a custom process, create an entry for each mail-enabled document library and list you want to receive email.

> **Note**
>
> Advanced mode is necessary only when you are not using the SMTP service to get incoming email.

To configure incoming email, navigate to the Incoming Email Settings page at Central Administration, System Settings, Configure Incoming Email Settings:

1. Select Yes to enable sites on this server to receive email.

2. Select Automatic unless you are using an SMTP server other than the native Windows Server SMTP Service. If you are using a third-party SMTP server, be sure to define the email drop folder at the bottom of the page. Be aware that many third-party SMTP servers will not integrate with SharePoint Server 2013.

3. Select Yes to create a distribution group or contact, or select Use Remote if you already have an existing Directory Management Service. If you select Yes *and* you use Exchange Server, you must take additional configuration steps outside of SharePoint 2013:

   - You must delegate permissions to an Active Directory OU to be used for the storage and management of SharePoint Server 2013 contacts and distribution lists.

   - You must ensure that an A record for your SharePoint 2013 server exists in your organization's DNS configuration.

   - You must add an SMTP connector on the Exchange Server. For more information on adding an SMTP connector, see the following link: http://technet.microsoft.com/en-us/library/cc262947.aspx#AddSMTPconnector

4. Specify the Active Directory OU where new distribution lists and contacts will be stored. In this example we have created an OU named SharePointDMS in our Active Directory. Use the distinguished name of the container in the text box: OU=SharePointDMS, DC=contoso, DC=com. Figure 2.8 shows an example of the OU and SMTP server settings.

5. Enter the name of the SMTP server where you will accept incoming email. This server must be a member of the server farm. The Microsoft SharePoint Foundation Timer on this SMTP server monitors the default email drop folder. When it discovers an email with a corresponding incoming email address in SharePoint Server 2013, it routes the email constrained by the list or library settings.

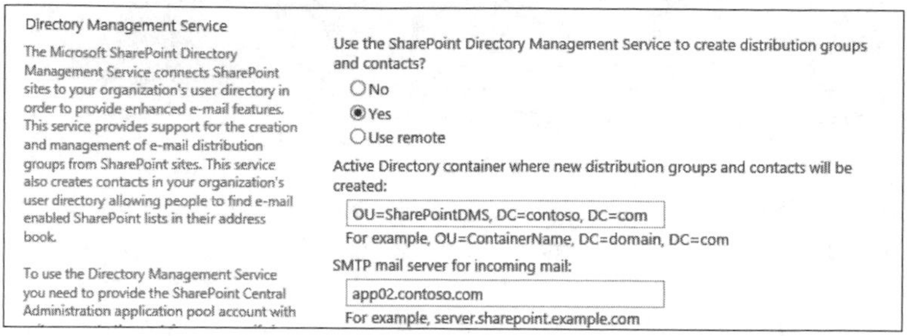

FIGURE 2.8
Carefully enter the path to the container specified for the Directory Management Service.

6. You must decide whether to accept messages from authenticated users or all users. If you decide to accept messages from authenticated users, a Send-To email address must match that of a user with write access on the destination list or library.

7. Select whether to allow the creation of distribution lists. You can configure SharePoint Server 2013 to create contacts in Active Directory without creating distribution lists for synchronization with SharePoint Groups. If you decide to create distribution lists, you also need to decide what level of scrutiny the list names will have. You have four options when managing the creation and modification of distribution groups:

   - Create New Distribution Group
   - Change Distribution Group Email Address
   - Change Distribution Group Title and Description
   - Delete Distribution Group

   Note that there is no approval option when creating contacts. Approval settings exist only for distribution groups.

Note

Give careful consideration to selecting any of the options to make changes to distribution groups. Changes made to existing distribution groups will cause emails sent to those distribution lists to be returned when replied to.

---

8. You can also define the incoming email server display address. Figure 2.9 shows an example of setting the value. Be aware that only defining the display address will not route email correctly. In this example, the server name is app02.contoso.com, but the display address is contoso.com. Care must be taken to correctly route the email from the SMTP server servicing the contoso.com domain.

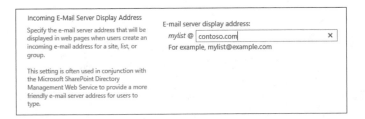

FIGURE 2.9
Verify that you have the routing rule on the SMTP server configured correctly to reflect the incoming email display address.

9. Verify that that DNS has the correct records for routing email. SMTP and SharePoint Server 2013 both need to have the correct DNS configuration before incoming email will function correctly.

10. If you are using Automatic mode, you should configure the Safe Email Servers settings. This setting can force incoming email to route through your safe mail servers that perform antivirus and anti-spam scanning. It can also reduce the surface area for Internet-based attacks. To specify a safe server, enter the IP address—for example, 10.1.1.200. Entering the fully qualified domain name (FQDN) of the mail server will not work.

11. Click OK to complete the configuration.

Incoming email is now configured and can be enabled on your SharePoint 2013 lists and libraries. Figure 2.10 shows an example of the incoming email configuration settings for a document library on a team site.

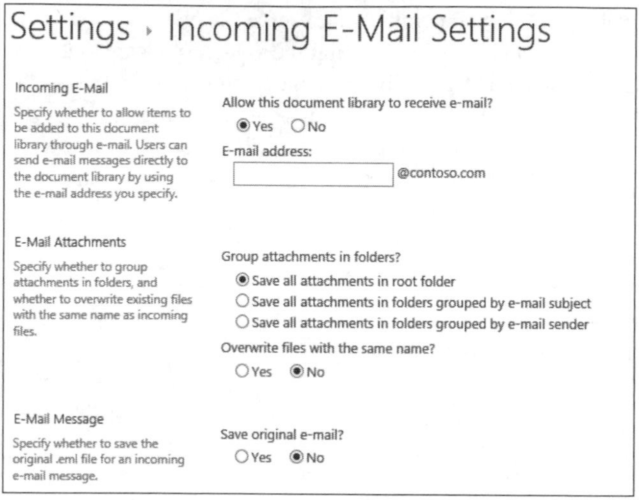

Settings ‣ Incoming E-Mail Settings

Incoming E-Mail

Specify whether to allow items to be added to this document library through e-mail. Users can send e-mail messages directly to the document library by using the e-mail address you specify.

Allow this document library to receive e-mail?

◉ Yes   ○ No

E-mail address:

[   ] @contoso.com

E-Mail Attachments

Specify whether to group attachments in folders, and whether to overwrite existing files with the same name as incoming files.

Group attachments in folders?

◉ Save all attachments in root folder
○ Save all attachments in folders grouped by e-mail subject
○ Save all attachments in folders grouped by e-mail sender

Overwrite files with the same name?

○ Yes   ◉ No

E-Mail Message

Specify whether to save the original .eml file for an incoming e-mail message.

Save original e-mail?

○ Yes   ◉ No

FIGURE 2.10
The incoming email configuration settings of a list or library.

Configuring Mobile Accounts

The Mobile Alert feature allows users to subscribe to alerts with their mobile phones. The idea behind the functionality is that many professionals prefer to get important alerts via mobile text (SMS) rather than via email. Not all users have smart phones or smart phones that are compatible with their corporate email system. Configuring mobile alerts allows notification to almost any cellular telephone. The feature does come with some drawbacks, however. First, you must have a subscription with a third-party SMS provider. The SMS provider acts as a "man in the middle" to relay mobile messages to cellular providers. This comes at a cost. Although the future of this space is widely unknown, current prices range from $.02 USD to $.06 USD per message. You can find a list of SharePoint Server 2013–compatible providers at http://messaging.office.microsoft.com/HostingProviders.aspx?src=O14&lc =1033. There is a constantly changing list, and your costs will vary based on your geographic location and volume of prepaid SMS alerts.

To configure SharePoint 2013 to support mobile accounts using Windows PowerShell, take the following steps:

1. Confirm that the farm account has permissions to access the Internet to send alerts.

2. Obtain the root certificate for the service provider's HTTPS web address.

3. Import the service providers root certificate and create a trusted root authority using Windows PowerShell:

  - Import a trusted root certificate:

    - Click Start, Run, and enter **MMC**; then click Enter.

    - In the Microsoft Management Console, click the File tab and select Add/Remove Snap-in.

    - Select Available Snap-ins, Certificates, Add.

    - In the Certificates Snap-in Wizard, select Computer account and click Next.

    - Click Local Computer.

    - Click Finish.

    - In the Add or Remove Snap-ins Wizard, click OK.

    - In the console tree, expand the Certificates node.

    - Right-click the Trusted Root Certificate Authorities store.

    - Click All Tasks, Import.

    - In the Certificate Import Wizard, click Next.

    - Browse to the location of your trusted root authority certificate, and click Next.

    - Select the option button for Place All Certificates in the Following Store, and browse to the Trusted Root Authority; click Next.

    - Click Finish to complete the wizard.

  - Create the trusted root authority by clicking Start, All Programs, Microsoft SharePoint Server 2013 Products, SharePoint 2013 Management Shell:

    - Right-click Run as Administrator.

  - To get the root certificate, enter the following command:

    ```
    $cert = Get-PfxCertificate <ObtainedCertificatePath>
    ```

  - Create the trusted root authority using the following command at the Windows PowerShell command prompt:

    ```
    New-SPTrustedRootAuthority -Name <Name> -Certificate <$cert>
    ```

- <Name> = name of the trusted root authority you want to create.

- <ObtainedCertificatePath> = location of the root certificate file.

- Set the mobile account using Windows PowerShell:

```
Set-SPMobileMessagingAccount -Identity sms -
WebApplication http://portal.contoso.com -ServiceURL
https://yoursmsprovider.com/omsservice.asmx -UserId
user@contoso.com -Password password1
```

To configure a mobile account from Central Administration, take the following steps:

1. Import the trusted root certificate of your service provider using Windows PowerShell as described earlier in step 3a.

2. Create the trusted root authority as described in step 3b.

3. Navigate to the Mobile Account Settings page in Central Administration at Central Administration, System Settings, Configure Mobile Account.

4. Click the Microsoft Office Online link for a list of messaging providers, and select your wireless provider's country and region.

5. Select a service provider from the list. After you have selected the provider you want to use, you will be directed to the provider's website.

6. In the username and password box, type the username and password that you received from the SMS service provider.

7. Click Test Service to verify that the text service is running as expected.

8. Click OK to complete the configuration.

Farm Timer Jobs

The Microsoft SharePoint Foundation Timer service runs on each server in the farm and is the master process for all timer jobs. It is not configurable—that is, it cannot be started and stopped from within Central Administration. It can, however, be restarted if you suspect a problem by going to Windows Server services from Start, All Programs, Administrative Tools, Services. It is listed as SharePoint 2013 Timer. You should not directly modify the logon account or other settings directly from Windows Server. You should restart only if necessary.

Timer jobs are created and deleted by SharePoint Server 2013 features or by developers via custom code. If your developers will deploy timer jobs to support custom code, be sure to test on an environment other than your production servers, and test for 24 hours or longer. Many timer jobs do not immediately display errors. Only time will show if the custom timer job has a problem. Third-party products that create timer jobs should be tested to the same level as custom code. Be sure to test any custom timer jobs before a major service pack or SharePoint Server 2013 version change.

To see the currently defined timer jobs, browse to Central Administration, Monitoring, Review Job Definitions and look at the job definitions. When viewing the Service Job Definitions page, you'll notice approximately 180 timer job definitions in your fully configured SharePoint Server 2013 server farm. This number will vary depending on the number of web applications, configured service applications, and the configuration of core operations. Figure 2.11 shows a portion of the timer jobs in the Server Job Definitions page.

Job Definitions

View: All ▾

Title	Web Application	Schedule Type
Analytics Event Store Retention		Weekly
Analytics Timer Job for Search Service Application Search Service Application		Minutes
App Installation Service		Minutes
App State Update		Hourly
Application Addresses Refresh Job		Minutes
Application Server Administration Service Timer Job		Minutes
Application Server Timer Job		Minutes
Audit Log Trimming	SharePoint - MySites	Monthly
Audit Log Trimming	SharePoint - portal.contoso.com80	Monthly
Autohosted app instance counter		Weekly
Bulk workflow task processing	SharePoint - MySites	Daily
Bulk workflow task processing	SharePoint - portal.contoso.com80	Daily
CEIP Data Collection		Daily
Cell Storage Data Cleanup Timer Job	SharePoint - MySites	Daily
Cell Storage Data Cleanup Timer Job	SharePoint - portal.contoso.com80	Daily

FIGURE 2.11
Every web application you create will instantiate several timer jobs.

Some of these timer job definitions will be minutes, whereas others are hourly, daily, weekly, or monthly. The capability to easily change the timer job's schedule from the user interface is still available, although caution should be used when modifying the default schedule because it can affect server farm and application functionality. For the most part, you should leave the timer jobs in the default state. For some timer job definitions, such as the Content Type Hub and Content Type Subscriber, you will be very tempted to increase the frequency of the timer job. Although this action will make enterprise content types available sooner and give the subscribing site collections more frequent updates, it comes with a compromise in performance. Timer jobs take both processor power and memory, so you need to weigh the benefits with the performance penalty. Figure 2.12 shows an example of changing the Content Type Subscriber frequency. Also notice that you can click Run Now. This option often negates the need for increasing the frequency of a timer job because you can force an update manually.

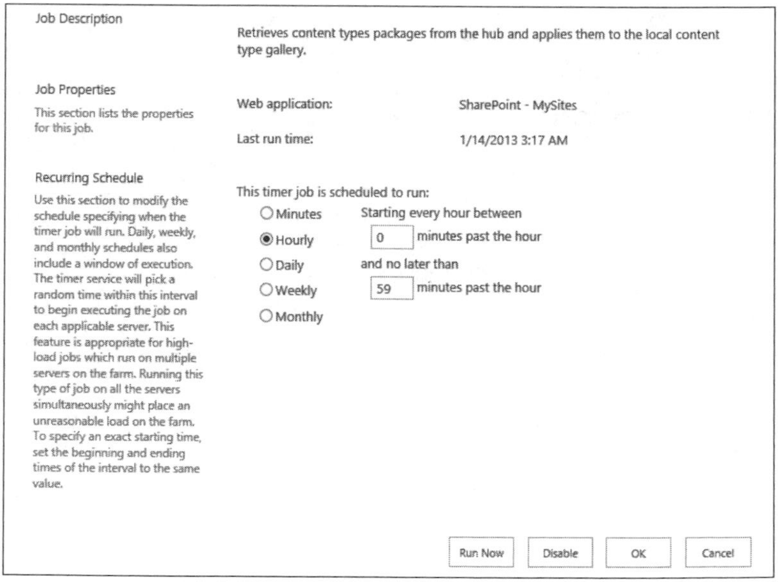

Job Description

Retrieves content types packages from the hub and applies them to the local content type gallery.

Job Properties

This section lists the properties for this job.

Web application: SharePoint - MySites

Last run time: 1/14/2013 3:17 AM

Recurring Schedule

Use this section to modify the schedule specifying when the timer job will run. Daily, weekly, and monthly schedules also include a window of execution. The timer service will pick a random time within this interval to begin executing the job on each applicable server. This feature is appropriate for high-load jobs which run on multiple servers on the farm. Running this type of job on all the servers simultaneously might place an unreasonable load on the farm. To specify an exact starting time, set the beginning and ending times of the interval to the same value.

This timer job is scheduled to run:
- Minutes   Starting every hour between
- Hourly   [0] minutes past the hour
- Daily   and no later than
- Weekly   [59] minutes past the hour
- Monthly

[Run Now] [Disable] [OK] [Cancel]

FIGURE 2.12
Click Run Now to manually start a timer job.

> **Note**
>
> Be careful when creating multiple web applications. Although it is often necessary to create multiple web applications for requirements such as My Sites and the Content Type Hub, keeping your web applications to a minimum will increase system performance. Every web application you create automatically generates many timer jobs that consume system resources. So, in addition to the memory space used by the application pool and associated management overhead, you now also have more timer jobs and potential issues with the SharePoint Foundation Timer service.

Although timer jobs run on every server in the farm by default, you can select a preferred server to execute timer jobs on per-content-database basis. Workflows are one of the driving factors to include this functionality. Using this example of workflows will help you understand why server timer job affinity is important.

SharePoint Server 2013 executes workflow actions on the web server that the client was connected to when started. If this workflow must wait to continue because of a scheduled time delay or inaction by the user, the SharePoint 2013 Timer service will handle the workflow execution. In a multiple web server configuration, you can set the preferred server for executing the workflow via the content database that hosts the site collection in question. To set the preferred server for timer jobs, do the following:

1. Browse to the Manage Content Database page, Central Administration, Application Management, Databases, Manage Content Databases.

2. Select the database you want to modify.

3. Select the physical server you want to associate as the preferred server. See Figure 2.13 for an example of setting affinity.

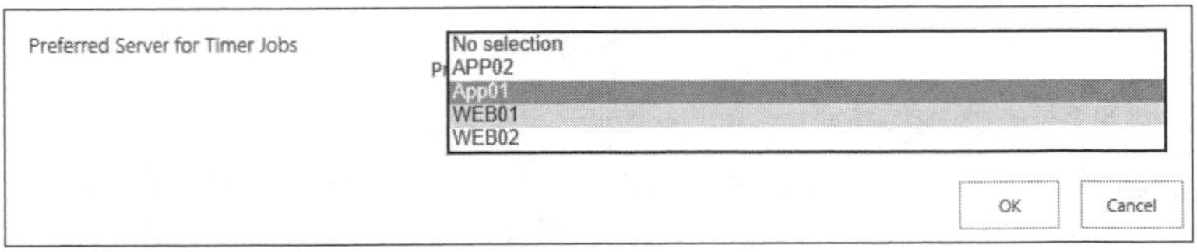

FIGURE 2.13
You can select any server farm member to be the preferred server for a content database.

> **Note**
>
> If the preferred server is unavailable, another will be selected automatically until the preferred server is back online.

In addition to managing the timer job, you can also check the job status from Central Administration, Monitoring, Timer Jobs, Check Job Status (see Figure 2.14).

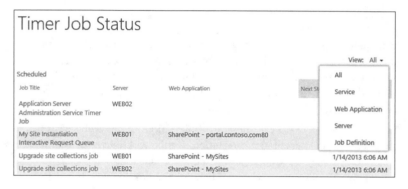

FIGURE 2.14
The Timer Job Status page.

The Timer Job Status page allows you to view the status of scheduled jobs, see running jobs, and view timer job history. You'll find this page useful when troubleshooting problems within your farm. Hung processes, such as workflows or backup and restore, can be deleted to allow for future instances. It is recommended that you not delete timer jobs when you are not sure of the consequences of that action. There is no option for you to delete platform-level jobs; this action would have dire consequences. Instead, they have replaced the delete option with a disable option. Always document your action for future reference if you delete or disable a timer job.

Farm Management

The Farm Management area, located under System Settings, is essentially a bucket for items that are associated with the configuration database or didn't fit neatly elsewhere. The Farm Management functional areas are as follows:

- **Alternate Access Mappings**—Details about this configuration option can be found in Chapter 4, "Creating and Configuring Service Applications."

- **Manage Farm Features, Manage Farm Solutions, and Manage User Solutions**—Details on these options are presented in Chapter 15, "Managing Apps and Solutions."

- **Configure Privacy Options**—This configuration option allows you to decide whether your server farm will automatically connect to Microsoft for the Customer Experience Improvement Program (CEIP), error reporting, and external web-based help. Be careful when turning these on if you are in a secure environment. Many times, servers in a secure environment will not have outbound HTTP enabled. If that is the case, web-based help will not function.

Database Management

The bulk of SharePoint Server 2013 content is almost entirely contained in SQL Server. As such, a properly designed and managed SQL Server infrastructure is critical to a well-running SharePoint Server environment. Because SQL Server has many books dedicated to the product, you'll be introduced only to the topics every SharePoint Server administrator should know in this section. Database management is contained in the Application Management section of Central Administration. The majority of Application Management deals with web applications, service applications, and site collections. Although databases are used with all three of these, there is a dedicated section for database management, as shown in Figure 2.15.

Content Databases

There are many farm-level settings and configuration options you should be aware of with content databases. When the first content database is created during web application creation, it includes several default options. The following configuration options should be taken into consideration when managing content databases:

- Size of the content database

- Number of site collections per content database

- Status of content databases

- Read-only content databases

- Location on the SQL Server physical disk

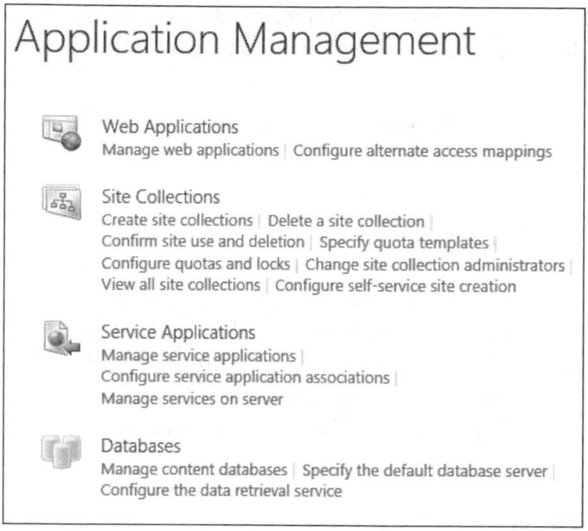

Application Management

 Web Applications
Manage web applications | Configure alternate access mappings

 Site Collections
Create site collections | Delete a site collection |
Confirm site use and deletion | Specify quota templates |
Configure quotas and locks | Change site collection administrators |
View all site collections | Configure self-service site creation

 Service Applications
Manage service applications |
Configure service application associations |
Manage services on server

 Databases
Manage content databases | Specify the default database server |
Configure the data retrieval service

FIGURE 2.15
Databases are contained in the Application Management grouping.

Controlling Database Sizes

SharePoint Server 2013 does not provide direct functionality to limit the
content database size. Although SQL Server can provide this option, it is
generally recommended that you control the content database sizes with
SharePoint Server 2013 site quotas. First, you need to know that site
quotas are actually site collection quotas. There is no native method to
limit site quotas. Second, you can limit the number of site collections in a
database, but you cannot limit the number of sites. Again, the Central
Administration interface is ambiguous on sites versus site collections.
When we're discussing items within Central Administration, the word
"sites" always references site collections. To limit the size of a content
database using SharePoint Server options, you need to combine the following three SharePoint Server 2013 settings:

- **Maximum Number of Sites That Can Be Created in This
  Database**—This setting is found in Central Administration,
  Application Management, Manage Content Databases, after select-
  ing a content database.

- **Quotas of the Sites (site collections) Contained in the Database**—
  These settings can be found in Central Administration, Application
  Management, Configure Quotas and Locks.

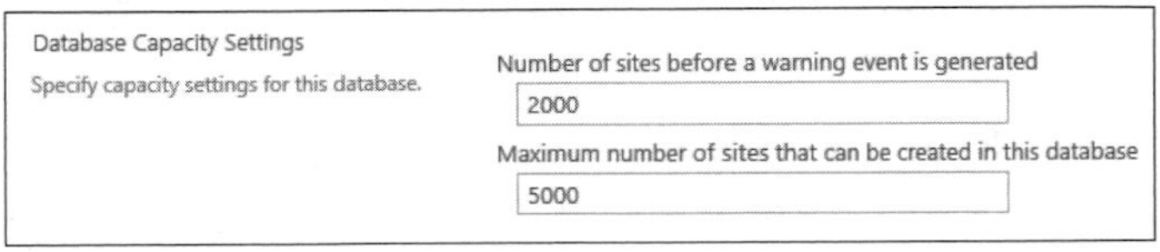

Database Capacity Settings
Specify capacity settings for this database.

Number of sites before a warning event is generated

2000

Maximum number of sites that can be created in this database

5000

FIGURE 2.16
The Database Capacity Settings in Central Administration enables you to limit the
number of sites in each content database.

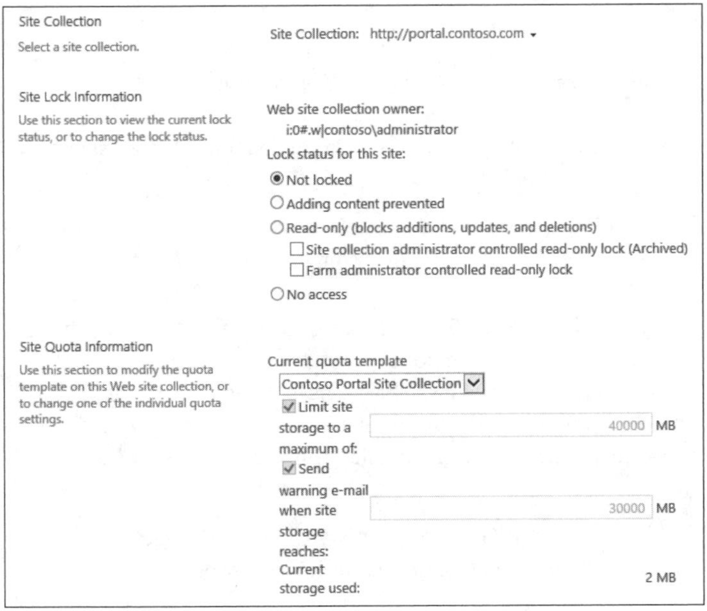

Site Collection
Select a site collection.

Site Collection: http://portal.contoso.com ▾

Site Lock Information
Use this section to view the current lock
status, or to change the lock status.

Web site collection owner:
    i:0#.w|contoso\administrator
Lock status for this site:
⦿ Not locked
◯ Adding content prevented
◯ Read-only (blocks additions, updates, and deletions)
    ☐ Site collection administrator controlled read-only lock (Archived)
    ☐ Farm administrator controlled read-only lock
◯ No access

Site Quota Information
Use this section to modify the quota
template on this Web site collection, or
to change one of the individual quota
settings.

Current quota template
Contoso Portal Site Collection ☑
    ☑ Limit site
    storage to a   40000 MB
    maximum of:
    ☑ Send
    warning e-mail
    when site   30000 MB
    storage
    reaches:
    Current   2 MB
    storage used:

FIGURE 2.17
Site collection quota settings in the Site Collections and Locks section found in
Central Administration, Application Management, Configure Quotas and Locks.

■ **Percent of Site (site collection) Used for the Second-Stage
    Recycle Bin**—These settings are located in Central Administration,
    Manage Web Applications, General Settings on the Web
    Applications tab.

```
Recycle Bin

Specify whether the          Recycle Bin Status:
Recycle Bins of all of the    ● On    ○ Off
sites in this web
application are turned on.    Delete items in the Recycle Bin:
Turning off the Recycle        ● After [              30 ] days
Bins will empty all the
Recycle Bins in the web        ○ Never
application.
                             Second stage Recycle Bin:
The second stage Recycle       ● Add [              50 ] percent of live site quota for
Bin stores items that end    second stage deleted items.
users have deleted from        ○ Off
their Recycle Bin for easier
restore if needed. Learn
about configuring the
Recycle Bin.
```

FIGURE 2.18
Configuring the Recycle Bin settings for the web application.

Using the settings just shown, you define the maximum database size by using the following formula:

$$(\text{Maximum number of sites}) \times (\text{site quota}) \times$$
$$(1 + \% \text{ of live site quota for second stage})$$

Configuring the Number of Site Collections per Content Database

The default number of sites (site collections) per content database should almost assuredly be changed. The default settings of thousands of sites as the maximum is entirely a fail-safe mechanism in the product. Using the formula previously mentioned, here is the result for a 15,000-site maximum:

$$15,000 \text{ sites} \times 10\text{GB site quota} \times 1(.50 \text{ second stage}) =$$
$$\text{possible database size of 219 terabytes}$$

A more likely scenario is this:

$$20 \text{ sites} \times 10\text{GB site quota} \times 1(.20 \text{ second stage}) =$$
$$\text{possible database size of 250GB}$$

The maximum database size recommended is somewhere between 200GB and 300GB. Your databases can be much larger in theory, but the practical daily management becomes difficult beyond the recommended limit.

Note

You should be very careful with maximum site collection sizes (the site quota settings). Large, busy site collections are likely to have SQL locking/blocking errors. A general rule is to have large site collections and a few users or small site collections with a large user population.

If you must have large content databases, try to isolate very busy site collections in a dedicated content database. This gives you the flexibility of managing the disk I/O of the site collection at the SQL level.

Configuring Content Database Status

The Content Database Status can be set to either Ready or Offline. The status of Offline is a bit confusing because the real purpose of taking a content database offline is to not allow more site collections to be created therein. In fact, site collections contained in an offline content database can still be seen and written to. The safest way to limit the number of site collections in a content database is by following these steps:

1. Turn off warning events by setting the threshold to zero.

2. Set the maximum number of site collections to the current number listed in the user interface. Be sure to create a new content database before creating a site collection; otherwise, the creation will fail.

Configuring Read-Only Content Databases

SharePoint Server 2013 also supports read-only SQL Server content databases. When you set a content database to Read-Only, the permissions in all site collections will automatically be reflected in the users' web browsers. For example, Figure 2.19 shows an example of a document library contained in a read/write content database, and Figure 2.20 is the same document library after setting the content database to Read-Only.

FIGURE 2.19

This is an example of a document library contained in a Read/Write database.

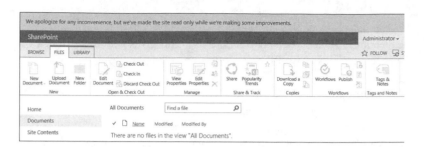

FIGURE 2.20
When the hosting database is set to Read-Only, no editing commands are available, and there will be an informational message across the top of the site.

You can see the current state of a content database by browsing to Central Administration, Application Management, Manage Content Databases, and selecting the relevant database. SharePoint Server 2013 displays only the status, however, and cannot be used to set the database state. To set a database to Read-Only, you must do so from SQL Server Management Studio. To configure a database to be Read-Only, do the following on the SQL Server console:

1. Open SQL Server Management Studio. (Its location will vary based on your version and edition of SQL Server.)

2. Locate the SQL Server database you want to modify, right-click, and select Properties.

3. Select the Options page, and under Other Options scroll down until you see the State options.

4. Locate Database Read-Only and click False, as shown in Figure 2.21.

5. Change the status from False to True, and click OK.

6. Restart the SharePoint Servers in the farm.

Setting the Database Location on a SQL Server Physical Disk

Although SharePoint Server 2013 can create databases and perform a minimal SQL Server database setup, you still want to do basic configuration of the databases on the SQL Server physical disks. Maintenance plans and recovery models can be quite extensive and are not covered in this section. It is recommended that you leave the recovery model as it is set by the SharePoint Server Configuration Wizard, unless you have advanced SQL Server experience and can verify that you'll be in a supported configuration.

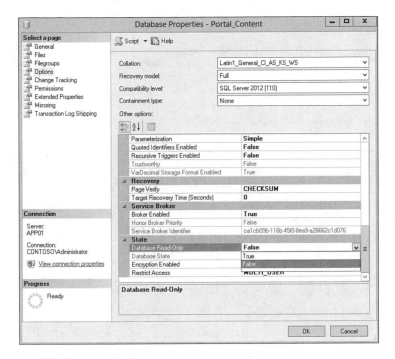

FIGURE 2.21
Select the down-arrow to the right of False to change the database state to Read-Only.

Note

For more information on SQL Server maintenance plans and system configuration, see http://technet.microsoft.com/sqlserver. However, some aspects for regular SQL maintenance do not apply to SharePoint Serve 2013. An example is *autocreate statistics*. SQL DBAs should validate any maintenance plan changes with the SharePoint Administrator before implementation.

If your SQL Server content must be highly available, service a significant number of requests, or both, you should separate the transaction log files and data files. Content is always written to the transaction log first, regardless of the recovery model. This allows the database to be brought back into a consistent state if you need to recover the database using SQL Server restore tools. Next, a SQL Server checkpoint process runs at regular intervals and writes the transactions to the data file.

Note

In the Full Recovery model, transaction logs are retained until you back up the database, at which time the transaction logs are truncated.

When users are viewing your web applications, they are almost always consuming the data file on SQL Server. By contrast, write actions are processed in the transaction log. Therefore, it is safe to assume that in a read-only server farm, the data file physical disk will be the most utilized. Because of the nature of SharePoint Server transactions, the transaction log and data file are usually equally used in a collaborative environment.

By default, SQL Server places both the data files and transaction logs on the same volume on SQL Server. You can change this default behavior by modifying the default SQL Server settings. To change the default location for new databases, do the following on your SQL Server console:

1. Open SQL Management Studio.
2. Right-click the server name and select Properties.
3. Select Database Settings.
4. In the Database Default Locations Settings, choose a previously created volume.

Note that if multiple volumes share the same physical disks, you will not see a performance increase. If possible, you should separate the transaction logs and the data files on separate physical disks and not on the system volume. Figure 2.22 shows an example of changing the data file location to the D: volume and the transaction logs to the L: volume.

Note

For current best practice information on separating the disk location of transaction log files and data files, browse to http://technet.microsoft.com/en-us/library/bb402876.aspx.

Note

For information on testing the SQL Server I/O subsystem, browse to http://technet.microsoft.com/en-us/library/cc966412.aspx.

FIGURE 2.22
You can change the database default locations in SQL Server Properties.

Changing the Default Database Server

When you installed SharePoint Server 2013, you selected a database server
for the configuration database. The SQL Server you selected became the
default content database server. You can change this default at any time
from Central Administration, Application Management, Specify the
Default Database Server. Unless you are in a specialized environment, do
not use SQL Server authentication. Windows Authentication is almost
always the correct choice. Do not fill in the Database Username and
Password fields when using Windows Authentication. SharePoint Server
2013 automatically configures the SQL Server permissions when using
Windows Authentication.

Configuring Data Retrieval Service

The Data Retrieval Service was first introduced in Windows SharePoint
Services 2.0 and allowed for a connection to internal or external data
sources via web services. SharePoint Server 2013 continues to build on the

service, and it can be configured for the entire server farm or on a per–web application basis. For the most part, you leave this configuration set to default unless you are requested to change it by a designer or developer. For example, you might need to change it when requiring access to stored procedures on a non–SharePoint Server database, external content source (OLEDB), or XML and SOAP web services from within SharePoint Server 2013.

Configure the Data Retrieval Service

To configure the Data Retrieval Service, browse to Central Administration, Application Management, Configure the Data Retrieval Service. There are seven configuration options:

- **Web Application**—Be sure you are selecting the correct web application before continuing. Note that the user interface refers to Global Settings—those are also selected in the web application drop-down menu, as shown in Figure 2.23. By default, the global settings for the Data Retrieval Service load when you access the page. If you select a web application from the drop-down list, you are given the option to inherit the global settings.

FIGURE 2.23
Select Change Web Application or Global Settings using the drop-down menu.

- **Customize Web Application**—If you want to use web-application scoped settings, clear this option. If you want to override prior web-application changes, you can also select this box to reapply the global settings. This is useful if you made a mistake configuring a specific web application.

- **Enable Data Retrieval Services**—Be careful when deciding whether to turn off this option. Both SharePoint Designer 2013 and Visual Studio 2012 might leverage these services via web parts and custom code. Check with your development team before disabling these services.

- **Limit Response Size**—Unless directed by your development team, the default OLEDB response size should be selected. You should monitor your server's memory utilization if you increase the defaults, and you should do so over a period of several days. Large OLEDB queries can quickly use server memory.

- **Update Support**—This option is disabled by default, but many developers will want to enable this option. A common reason for doing so is that custom code might call a stored procedure in a non–SharePoint Server 2013 database. This is often more efficient than bringing the data into .NET for processing.

- **Data Source Time-Out**—Unless you are calling data sources over a wide area network (WAN), the default timeouts should be sufficient.

- **Enable Data Source Controls**—Data Source Controls allow controls to bind to other controls without the need for custom code. This option is usually enabled.

Configuring Send to Connections

This section walks you through the configuration options of an external service connection in Central Administration and shows you how to connect to a site collection for the purpose of publishing a document.

Before you can use Send to Connections in a site collection, you must first configure the service in Central Administration. The connection is valid for an entire web application, but you must configure an entry to each site collection you want to connect to. In the following example, the destination site collection is http://portal.contoso.com/sites/ISO.

To begin configuration, browse to Central Administration, General Application Settings, External Service Connections, Configure Send to Connections. Always verify you are configuring the correct web application before continuing.

Configuring Site Subscription Settings

SharePoint Server 2013 allows for multitenancy and is primarily targeted at SharePoint Server hosting providers. This allows for isolation of hosted site collections, as well as the capability to consume service applications at the site collection level. This segmentation is known as a *site subscription*. Although most readers will not have their implementations configured in such a fashion because of the complexity involved, you can limit the ability of these tenants to create connections beyond their environment. If you do not have multitenancy configured, this option can be left as the default. If you do have multitenancy enabled, you must decide whether to allow connections between tenants. This decision is a business, process, and security decision.

Configuring the Content Organizer in the Destination Site

Before you can configure Central Administration for Send to Connections, you must first enable the Content Organizer feature in the destination site. The Content Organizer feature allows settings and rules to route inbound files to the site. Based on the defined settings and rules, the destination site will sort and route files to the appropriate library or even to other site collections.

Enable the Content Organizer in the Destination Site

To enable the Content Organizer in the destination site, do the following:

1. Browse to the site you want files routed to.
2. Select Settings, Site Settings.
3. Under the Site Actions Grouping, select Manage Site Features.
4. Activate the Content Organizer feature.
5. Click Settings, Site Settings, Site Administration, configure Content Organizer Settings and Rules.

Note

For more details on configuring the Content Organizer, see Chapter 9, "Configuring Document Management."

Configuring Multiple Send to Connections

You can configure multiple Send to Connections and even create multiple connections to the same site using different rules. If this is your first connection, just continue completing the form. If this is a subsequent connection, either choose New Connection or select one for editing. Note that you can select the Add Connection control if you want to configure multiple Send To Connections. This prevents the configuration screen from closing and allows you to immediately add another connection. Figure 2.24 shows an example of the Send to Connections configuration page while adding the http://portal.contoso.com/sites/ISO connection.

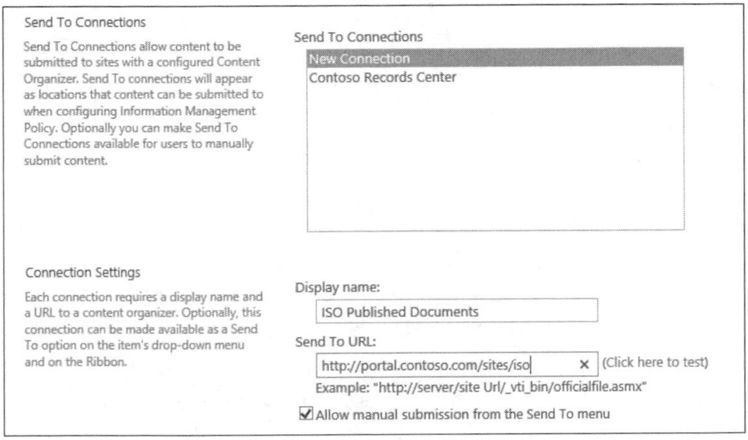

FIGURE 2.24
Highlight New Connection when creating a new Send to Connection.

Note

Before you can add a new Send to Connection, you must first activate the Content Organizer feature in the destination site.

Allowing Manual Submissions

A commonly configured option is to Allow Manual Submissions from the Send To menu, as shown in Figure 2.24. Selecting this option allows users to manually send to the destination site from the user menu in a library. If you do not select this option, you'll have to use another mechanism, such as custom code or SharePoint Designer 2013, to enable the file transfer. If you select to allow manual submissions, the user experience is similar to that shown in Figure 2.25.

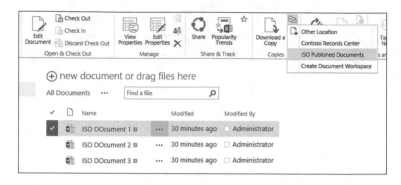

FIGURE 2.25
Select the Send To location from the Copies section of the document library ribbon.

CHAPTER 3

Creating Web Applications and Content Databases

- Web Application Architecture
- Creating and Managing Content Databases
- Creating and Extending Web Applications
- Configuring and Managing Web Applications
- Alternate Access Mappings

Web applications are a fundamental part of any Microsoft SharePoint Server 2013 implementation. They exist at the top of the Information Architecture hierarchy and serve as the primary point of interaction with end users. SharePoint Server 2013 web applications differ from most websites in that content exists in a database, not in or on the local file system of the web server. Only the minimal content required to connect an Internet Information Services (IIS) server to the database exists on a SharePoint server. The logical structure of a web application is stored entirely in Microsoft SQL Server databases. A web application's configuration is stored in the configuration database, and the user content web is stored in one or many content databases.

From a physical architecture perspective, web applications represent a specific IIS website and application scope, providing users the ability to interact with content via a Uniform Resource Locator (URL). The end user does not have a visual representation of the web application—it is completely managed at the farm level with either Microsoft Windows PowerShell or the

Central Administration website. The stsadm.exe administrative tool can still be used in some cases but is being phased out. Transitioning to the use of Windows PowerShell is highly encouraged.

Using Windows PowerShell provides administrators and developers with a variety of functionality. Routine tasks can be scripted and run using the Windows Task Scheduler; administrators can access information not available in the user interface, as well as easily leverage application programming interfaces (APIs).

Web Application Architecture

A web application can be created from Central Administration in the User Interface (UI) or by using Windows PowerShell. When a web application is created, IIS and ASP.NET will create an IIS website associated with the web application. The IIS website provides a channel that addresses the processing of the user request. The processing of the request includes handling the authentication and authorization of the user's identity, providing the response to the request, and logging the request. The IIS website also provides a container to hold the framework of virtual directories that map to the file structure folders in the 15 hives that provide the built-in functionality of SharePoint Server 2013.

In addition to IIS and ASP.NET creating the IIS website, SharePoint Server 2013 creates at least one content database on your SQL Server implementation. The content database is used to contain the settings and information around the site collections that will be hosted in the web application.

In the event that either the website or the content database is not created, you would not be able to create any site collections within the web application.

Remember, a new web application is an empty shell and contains no Site Collections by default. If you try to navigate to a web application before the Site Collection has been created, you will see an HTTP 404 Page Not Found error.

> **Note**
>
> IIS creates an IIS website for each web application created in SharePoint. SharePoint creates the Site Collections within SharePoint web applications.

If you use the Farm Configuration Wizard, the wizard guides you through the steps necessary to create the first web application as well as its first Site Collection. Figure 3.1 shows the relationship between web applications, Site Collections, and content databases.

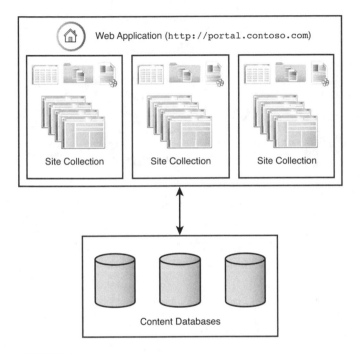

FIGURE 3.1
The relationship between web applications, Site Collections, and Content Databases.

Managing a Web Application

Web applications can be managed using Central Administration. There are two links to the Manage Web Applications page. The first is located in the Central Administration page under the Application Management section, as shown in Figure 3.2.

The Manage Web Applications link can also be found in Central Administration under the Application Management section. Listed on the Application Management page is the Web Applications grouping, as shown in Figure 3.3.

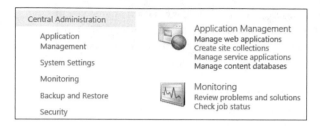

FIGURE 3.2
The Manage Web Applications link is located on the Central Administration home page.'

FIGURE 3.3
The Manage Web Applications link is also located in the Application Management section.

Application Pools

An IIS application pool is an isolated memory space that is routed to one or more worker processes within the security context of a user. A worker process (w3wp.exe) runs web applications and handles requests sent to a server for a specific application pool. A web application with its own application pool will not be affected by problems with other applications in separate application pools. In Figure 3.4, two web applications (https://extranet.contoso.com and http://portal.contoso.com) are using the same application pool. Sharing an application pool in this fashion reduces the memory footprint, but it introduces the risk of both web applications crashing in the event one of them crashes from poorly written code or a compromised server.

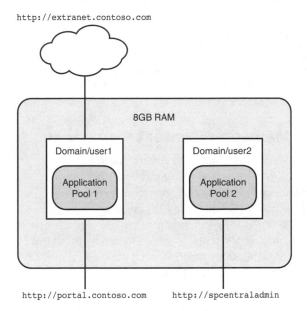

FIGURE 3.4
Application pools hosting web applications in memory.

> **Note**
>
> The use of web gardens in conjunction with SharePoint 2013 is not recommended. Web gardens are an IIS functionality that allows application pools to be supported by multiple worker processes. Configuring SharePoint 2013 to leverage web gardens could have a negative impact on page output caching.

Implementing a different application pool and username (identity) for each web application strengthens your overall security stance, but every additional web application pool requires more memory.

The decision to use multiple application pool identities depends on the level of security your organization requires. Generally, web applications with the same level of security share an application pool identity. Otherwise, you can choose to create web applications with one or several accounts for the corresponding IIS application pools and SQL Server databases. It is much easier to use separate accounts from the beginning than it is to change and isolate application pools later.

> **Note**
>
> The software boundaries and limits identified for SharePoint Server 2013 limit the supported number of application pools to 10 per web server. Those limits can be viewed at http://technet.microsoft.com/en-us/library/cc262787(v=office.15).aspx.

Creating and Managing Content Databases

Content databases contain all Site Collection content, including most customizations performed in the browser and SharePoint Designer. By default, a single content database is created per web application. You should create additional content databases to limit the size of your content databases and for isolation on the SQL Server physical disk. For example, if your Site Collection quota is 10GB and you want to limit your content database size to 100GB, you need to create a content database for every 10 Site Collections in the associated web application.

It is important to consider the configurations of the Recycle Bin and audit logs when planning your content database sizing. By default the second-stage Recycle Bin has a limit of 50% of the live site quota. If the site does not have a quota set, there will be no limit to the amount of space that the second-stage Recycle Bin can consume. Audit logs are also stored in the content database and are limited by the settings identified in Diagnostic Logging settings of the SharePoint Server 2013 farm.

> **Note**
>
> Limiting the size of your content databases is a key component of your disaster recovery plans. By limiting the content database size, you will be able to restore a database from backup much more quickly. You can also set priorities for the order in which the content databases will be restored from backup and brought back online.

> **Note**
>
> A content database completely contains a Site Collection. A content database associated with Web Application1 can be removed and associated with Web Application2. All Site Collections in this content database will then be available in Web Application2 under its original managed path. The exception is when the URL is already in use, such as the root managed path. This functionality is made possible because a mapping of

the information associated with a content database and the Site Collections it contains are stored in the sitemap table in the SharePoint Server 2013 farm configuration database. When a content database is attached or removed, the information in the sitemap table is updated to reflect those changes.

Content databases can be created and managed several ways; when creating a web application, you can use Central Administration or Windows PowerShell.

Creating a Content Database in the New Web Application

Creating the content database as a part of the Create New Web Application process is very simple. This method will be used whenever you create new web applications and will not provide you with the full set of content database management functions. If you want to configure other options on the content database, such as Status, you can do so after web application creation.

In the Database Name and Authentication section, enter the name of your database server and a name for your content database, as shown in Figure 3.5.

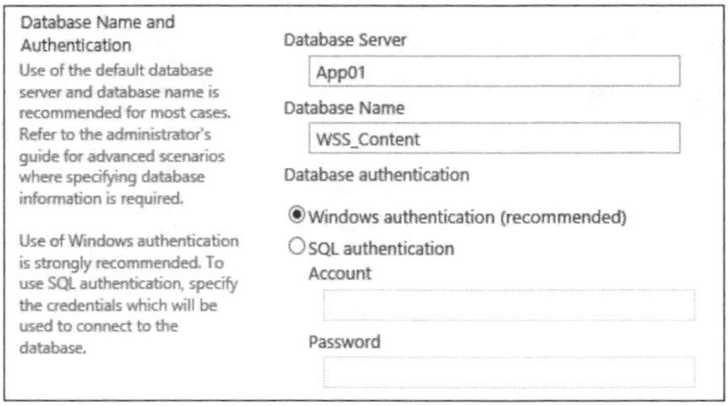

FIGURE 3.5
The Database Server and Database Name field in the Create New Web Application modal window.

Tip

Always give your databases meaningful names, and do not leave them as the default WSS_Content. Attempting to attach a database named WSS_Content can result in unexpected failures.

Creating a Content Database in Central Administration

To use Central Administration to create a new content database or manage existing content databases, from Central Administration browse to Application Management, Databases, Manage Content Databases, as shown in Figure 3.6.

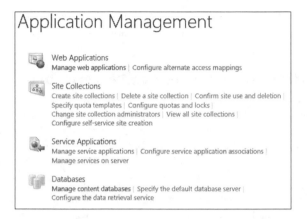

Application Management

Web Applications
Manage web applications | Configure alternate access mappings

Site Collections
Create site collections | Delete a site collection | Confirm site use and deletion |
Specify quota templates | Configure quotas and locks |
Change site collection administrators | View all site collections |
Configure self-service site creation

Service Applications
Manage service applications | Configure service application associations |
Manage services on server

Databases
Manage content databases | Specify the default database server |
Configure the data retrieval service

FIGURE 3.6
Location of the Manage Content Databases link in Central Administration.

From the Manage Content Databases link you can add, remove, or manage content databases, as well as view information about a content database, as shown in Figure 3.7.

Add a content database			Web Application: http://portal.contoso.com/ ▾			
Database Name	Database Status	Database Read-Only	Current Number of Site Collections	Site Collection Level Warning	Maximum Number of Site Collections	Preferred
WSS_PortalContent	Started	No	0	2000	5000	

FIGURE 3.7
The Manage Content Databases interface.

There are six primary properties for each content database:

- **Database Information**—Shows the Database server name, SQL_Server database name, Database status, and Database Read-Only status. Changing the status to Offline prevents new Site Collections from being created in that content database. It also shows the type of authentication that was defined during the associated web application creation when it is the first content database, or during content database creation for subsequent databases.

- **Database Versioning and Upgrade**—Enables you to verify the Database Schema Version and upgrade status of your content databases. Each line in this section identifies the Current Schema Version and the Maximum Schema Version. If the Current Schema Version is less than the Maximum Schema Version, you should upgrade your databases as soon as possible.

- **Failover Server**—Introduced in SharePoint Server 2010 to support SQL database mirroring. Configuring this setting does not configure database mirroring. It only makes SharePoint Server 2013 mirroring-aware. To successfully finish the configuration, you must configure database mirroring in SQL Server Management Studio.

- **Database Capacity Settings**—You should make an educated decision about what values to use for the Number of Sites before a warning event is generated and the maximum number of sites that can be created in the database settings. For example, if you do not want your content databases to be larger than 200GB and your site quotas are set to 1GB, you need to change the maximum number of sites to 200. The default settings are almost always too high and should be changed. Note that the settings in this section refer to Site Collections, not subsites.

- **Remove Content Database**—Removing a content database disassociates the database from a web application; it does not delete the database from SQL Server. There are few reasons to remove a content database without removing the entire web application. You might do so when taking sensitive data offline immediately or reassociating a content database with a new web application. When removing a content database, all data remains in the database and can be attached to another web application for access. Reassociating content databases to another web application should be done only after thorough testing in a lab environment.

- **Preferred Server for Timer Jobs**—Supports the separation of services on different servers. This can be especially useful when troubleshooting issues with a timer job that is not running as expected in a multiple-server environment and you want to isolate the issue to assess it. You could also offload timer jobs associated with a specific web application to a specific server for performance reasons.

Creating a Content Database Using Windows PowerShell

Before you can create or manage a content database using PowerShell, you must be logged in to the SharePoint Server 2013 server using an account that has security admin and db_creator on the SQL Server instance and is a member of the local administrators group on the SharePoint Server 2013 server.

Create a Content Database Using Windows PowerShell

After you have logged in, access the Start page on the server and find the SharePoint 2013 Management Shell icon. Right-click and select the Run as Administrator icon in the taskbar, as shown in Figure 3.8.

FIGURE 3.8
Click the Run as Administrator link in the taskbar.

At the Windows PowerShell command prompt, type the following command:

```
PS C:\> New-SPContentDatabase -Name <ContentDBName> -
WebApplication <WebApplicationName>
```

<ContentDBName> is the name of the content database you are creating.

<WebAppName> is the name of the web application that your new content database is being attached to.

You can specify additional parameters with the following parameters as a part of the New_SPContentDatabase command:

- **DatabaseServer**—Identifies the name of the SQL Server instance for the new content database.

- **MaxSiteCount**—Sets the maximum number of sites that can be created in the new content database.
- **WarningSiteCount**—Sets the number of websites that can be created before a warning event is generated by the system.

For example:

```
PS C:\> New-SPContentDatabase -Name SiteContentDB
-WebApplication
SharePoint-portal.contsos.com80 -MaxSiteCount 200 -
WarningSiteCount 180
```

You can use several other actions for managing content databases using PowerShell:

- **Get-SPContentDatabase**—Returns information about the content databases in your SharePoint Server 2013 farm.
- **Dismount-SPContentDatabase**—Detaches a content database from a web application.
- **Mount-SPContentDatabase**—Attaches a content database to a web application. This command is most often used when doing a database attach upgrade.
- **Remove-SPContentDatabase**—Detaches a content database from the web application and drops it from SQL Server.
- **Set-SPContentDatabase**—Sets content database properties such as MaxSiteCount, WarningSiteCount, and Status.
- **Test-ContentDatabase**—Verifies whether the customizations referenced in a content database are present in the web application it is being attached to. It is often used as a part of the database attach upgrade process.

Creating and Extending Web Applications

A web application provides the interface that users interact with from their browsers. A web application is a combination of an IIS virtual server, a specific URL, an authentication method, an associated content database, and entries for these items in the SharePoint configuration database.

Creating a Web Application

Prior to creating a web application, you should review the initial configuration for accuracy. Many settings, such as those for the host header or application pools, cannot be easily changed after the web application has been created. Although you can modify the web application settings directly in IIS, SharePoint stores permissions and configuration settings in many locations, making it very difficult to manually make these changes. The recommended way to make changes to an existing web application is either through the Central Administration site or by using PowerShell.

In addition, all configuration settings in Central Administration are written to the configuration database and are referenced anytime you add a new server to the SharePoint farm or restart the services on the server. If you make changes to your web applications directly in IIS, those changes are not written to the configuration database and will force you to manually update your server configurations each time you restart the Microsoft SharePoint Foundation Web Application service.

There are two recommended methods of creating a new web application:

- Central Administration
- PowerShell

Create a Web Application Using Central Administration

Using the Central Administration site to create a new web application allows a certain amount of control over the process, but without any automation. The creation of a new web application using the Central Administration site will create and configure only the most basic parameters necessary for the web application to function. Additional steps will be required to fully configure settings like time zones, throttling, SharePoint Designer usage, and so on.

To create a web application using Central Administration, follow these steps:

1. Browse to Central Administration, Application Management, Manage Web Applications, and then click New on the ribbon as shown in Figure 3.9.

2. Configure authentication for this web application. This is one of the most important changes in SharePoint Server 2013. Claims-based authentication is now the default authentication method, and Classic authentication has been deprecated and removed from Central Administration. Web applications using Classic authentication can still be created using PowerShell:

FIGURE 3.9
Create a new web application.

- **Claims Authentication Types**—In SharePoint 2013, both Claims and Classic authentication are still supported, but the default roles have been reversed. Claims authentication is now the default authentication type with Classic authentication being deprecated and removed from the UI. Web applications using Classic authentication can still be created and managed using Windows PowerShell, but their use is not recommended.

- Claims authentication is a flexible framework based on the Windows Identity Framework (WIF) that allows users to authenticate across Windows-based systems as well as systems that are not Windows-based. Examples of the available Claims providers in SharePoint Server 2013 are Windows Active Directory, forms-based authentication, and Security Assertion Markup Language (SAML) token issuers. An SAML token issuer is also known as a security token service, or STS.

> **Tip**
>
> If you are migrating a classic-mode SharePoint Server 2010 web application to SharePoint Server 2013, you should convert the web application to a claims-based web application within the SharePoint 2010 product and then migrate it to SharePoint Server 2013. Although it is recommended that the conversion from Classic authentication to Claims be done prior to migration, the task can also be accomplished using PowerShell after the migration is complete.

3. Create a new IIS website. If you select Use an Existing IIS Web Site, the web application will read the IIS configuration of the server running Central Administration. This setting is rarely used for new web applications; it's usually used to fix a broken web application. For this example, select Create a New IIS Web Site. Enter a name that is easily identified in IIS Manager. The IIS Web Site, Port, Host Header, and Path options are shown in Figure 3.10.

IIS Web Site	
Choose between using an existing IIS web site or create a new one to serve the Microsoft SharePoint Foundation application.	○ Use an existing IIS web site
	Default Web Site
	◉ Create a new IIS web site
	Name
If you select an existing IIS web site, that web site must exist on all servers in the farm and have the same name, or this action will not succeed.	SharePoint - 80
	Port
	80
If you opt to create a new IIS web site, it will be automatically created on all servers in the farm. If an IIS setting that you wish to change is not shown here, you can use this option to create the basic site, then update it using the standard IIS tools.	Host Header
	Path
	C:\inetpub\wwwroot\wss\VirtualDirectories\8(

FIGURE 3.10
The IIS Web Site configuration default settings.

4. Define the port number it will use. This is usually port 80 for HTTP and port 443 for HTTPS.

5. Define the host header for your new web application. The host header will usually be the fully qualified domain name (FQDN) for the web application. This can be changed later in IIS on every server in the farm, but it cannot be changed in the configuration database. The host header must be configured correctly when creating the web application.

Warning

Only one host header can be defined during web application creation. If you require multiple host headers, such as http://portal.comtoso.com and http://portal, you must add the latter in IIS on every server in the farm.

---

6. Define the path for the website. Unless you are directed to use settings other than the defaults, the default settings should work very

well. If you must change the path, verify that the drive letter and path exist on every web server in the farm. Otherwise, the creation of the web application will fail on servers that do not have that drive letter and path. This is because when SharePoint creates the web application it will replicate that creation to the other servers in the farm using the same drive letter and path. If the drive letter and path do not exist, SharePoint will not be able to complete the action.

7. Select your choices for the Security Configuration of the web application. There are individual options here for Allow Anonymous and Use Secure Sockets Layer (SSL):

- **Allow Anonymous**—Unless you are serving content for public consumption, you should not allow anonymous access. Although enabling anonymous access is allowed for collaborative Site Collections via its web application, it is generally a bad practice to enable it. Keep in mind that enabling anonymous access for a web application doesn't allow anonymous access by itself. A Site Collection administrator must also enable anonymous access at the site level.

- **Use Secure Socket Layer (SSL)**—If your organization plans to collaborate via an Internet-facing web application, enabling SSL is recommended for security. You must still add an SSL certificate in IIS Manager if choosing SSL.

8. Configure the Claims Authentication Types. There are three authentication types available for your new web application: Windows Authentication using NTLM or Kerberos, Forms-Based Authentication, and Trusted Identity Providers.

- **Enable Windows Authentication**—The use of Windows Integrated Authentication appears to be the same as it was in previous versions of SharePoint Server. In fact, under the hood is some very different behavior. When SharePoint Server 2013 is configured for Windows Integrated Authentication, the sign-in happens using the Negotiate (NTLM/Kerberos) authentication challenge. At the time the user signs in to SharePoint, an identity object is created representing the Windows user. SharePoint Server 2013 converts that identity object into a claims identity. The converted claims identity becomes the user's token used by SharePoint Server 2013 to determine authentication.

9. Kerberos is the recommended security configuration for your farm. Kerberos is similar to NTLM but requires more in-depth planning and configuration in comparison to NTLM and, as a result, is more difficult to implement. The most challenging aspect of configuring Kerberos is the configuration of the Service Principal Names (SPNs). SPNs are unique identifier strings that are associated with a service running on a server. Each SPN is registered with the active domain Key Distribution Center (KDC), which uses the SPN to determine whether a ticket should be granted to allow a request for access to a service. If any miscommunication occurs between the SPN and the KDC, the request will fail and access will be denied:

   - **Enable Forms-Based Authentication (FBA)**—Supply the ASP.NET Membership provider name and ASP.NET Role manager name to enable FBA. These are usually provided to you by your development team.

   - **Trusted Identity Provider**—The Trusted Identity Provider allows for federated users in the web application. Your development team will usually create and deploy the Trusted Identity Provider for you.

   - **Sign-In Page URL**—The Sign-In Page URL allows you to designate a custom sign-in page for your farm. This will be required if you are using Forms-based authentication. The custom form will be deployed by your designers or developers.

10. Enter the public URL. The public URL should be the one most likely to be visited by your users, usually an FQDN. Unless you are selecting a nonstandard HTTP port, remove the :80 from the URL, as shown in Figure 3.11. Be sure to modify your Domain Name Server (DNS) server to include the new web application.

Note

A Domain Name Server (DNS) translates domain names into IP addresses. Because domain names are easier for us to remember and the Internet is based on IP addresses, or numbers, we rely on DNS to translate the names of the sites we are attempting to access into the number universally recognized as associated with that name.

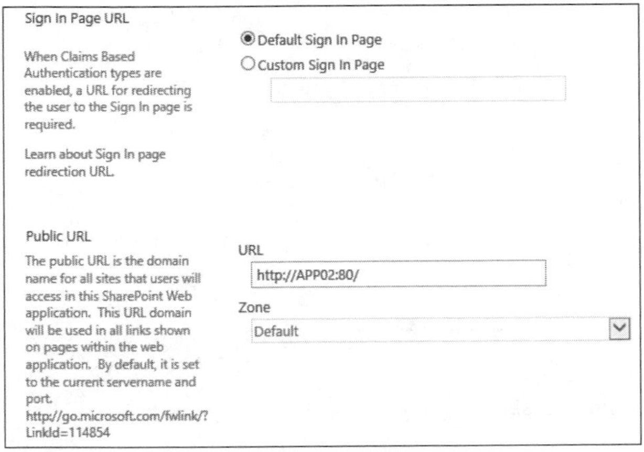

Sign In Page URL

When Claims Based
Authentication types are
enabled, a URL for redirecting
the user to the Sign In page is
required.

Learn about Sign In page
redirection URL.

◉ Default Sign In Page
○ Custom Sign In Page

Public URL

The public URL is the domain
name for all sites that users will
access in this SharePoint Web
application. This URL domain
will be used in all links shown
on pages within the web
application. By default, it is set
to the current servername and
port.
http://go.microsoft.com/fwlink/?
LinkId=114854

URL

http://APP02:80/

Zone

Default

FIGURE 3.11
The Public URL configuration settings.

> **Note**
>
> SharePoint Server 2013 gives users the capability to differentiate incoming traffic based on zones. Zones can help sort incoming traffic to different extended web applications with matching URLs. The URL entered in the user's browser is mapped to the correlating zone, allowing greater flexibility in isolating and directing incoming traffic. All web applications must be created initially on the Default zone.

11. Decide whether you'll use an existing application pool or create a new application pool. If security and process isolation are important to your organization, you should consider creating an application pool for each web application. Creating an application pool requires additional resources, such as memory and administrative time. In the 64-bit environment mandated by SharePoint Server 2013, multiple application pools are more appealing because you do not have the 32-bit memory restrictions. To create a new application pool, provide an easily identifiable name, as shown in Figure 3.12.

12. Select the managed account for the application pool identity, or register a new managed account. Note that you'll have to reenter all previous information on the page when creating a new managed account.

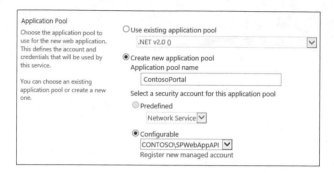

FIGURE 3.12
Configuring Application Pool settings.

13. Enter the database server and database name as shown in Figure 3.13.

```
Database Name and                Database Server
Authentication
Use of the default database        App01
server and database name is      Database Name
recommended for most cases.
Refer to the administrator's        WSS_Content_Portal
guide for advanced scenarios
where specifying database        Database authentication
information is required.
                                 ◉ Windows authentication (recommended)
Use of Windows authentication    ○ SQL authentication
is strongly recommended. To          Account
use SQL authentication, specify
the credentials which will be
used to connect to the           Password
database.
```

FIGURE 3.13
Configuring the Database Name and Database Authentication Settings.

- **Database Server**—For most installations, use the default SQL server that was specified during the configuration of the farm. You might select a different SQL server (instance) if you have several large web applications that require dedicated, isolated content databases. If you are using named instances, use this format: <SERVERNAME\instance>.

- **Database Name**—Always change the default database name to correlate to the web application name. For example, if the web application is http://sales.contoso.com, use WSS_Content_Sales for the database name. Intelligent naming of web applications, application pools, and databases greatly eases the management of medium to large SharePoint Server 2013 implementations.

■ **Authentication Type**—The recommended authentication type is Windows Authentication. Use SQL authentication only when working in a workgroup environment and when you have selected SQL authentication for all database connections, including the configuration database. The user logged on to Central Administration must also have the ability to create SQL Server databases.

14. Optionally, define a failover database server. This was a new feature in SharePoint Server 2010 to support SQL database mirroring. SQL database mirroring allows a database to fail over from one server to another or to another instance. The principle server is the original instance, and when it fails, SharePoint automatically retries the connection with the failover server every 15 seconds (the default setting). The SharePoint content database will need to be configured in SQL Server mirroring to have a partner database on the failover server. Setting the name of the failover server in SharePoint does not configure the SQL mirroring. See Figure 3.14 for a view of the Failover Server configuration section.

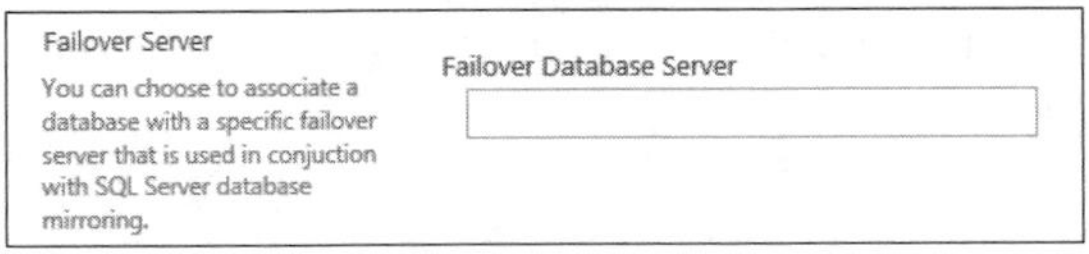

Failover Server

You can choose to associate a database with a specific failover server that is used in conjuction with SQL Server database mirroring.

Failover Database Server

FIGURE 3.14
The Failover Database setting.

15. Optionally, change the default Service Application Connections settings. Most implementations will not require a change. If you have custom service application proxy groups, you need to configure the service applications for this web application. In the drop-down menu, the default is set, which automatically configures the services selection. From the drop-down menu, select Custom to configure the server application connections for the web application. The configuration area is shown in Figure 3.15.

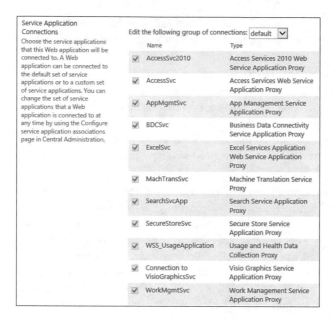

FIGURE 3.15
Configuring Service Application settings.

16. Select Yes or No to participate in Microsoft's Customer Experience Improvement Program. The overhead of this feature is minimal, but it still has an impact.

17. Click OK.

Create a Web Application Using Windows PowerShell

You also have the capability to create a new web application using Windows PowerShell. Because of the changes to the default authentication type in SharePoint Server 2013, there are additional steps that must be taken in your Windows PowerShell script.

To create a Web Application using Windows PowerShell, do the following:

Before we can call the New-SPWebApplication parameter in our Windows PowerShell script, we have to specify the authentication provider parameter we want to use. We do that by using the New-SPAuthenticationProvider parameter. Our final script will look like the following:

```
PS C:\> $ap = New-SPAuthenticationProvider -
UseWindowsIntegratedAuthentication -DisableKerberos
```

```
PS C:\> New-SPWebApplication -Name "Contoso Portal PS" –
ApplicationPool "ContosoPortal" -HostHeader
portalps.contoso.com
-Port 80 -Url http://portalps.contoso.com -AuthenticationMethod
NTLM -AuthenticationProvider $ap -DatabaseName
"WSS_Content_PortalPS"
```

This script will create a web application named ContosoPortalPS on port 80 with a host header of *http://portalps.contoso.com*. The web application will use Windows Integrated Authentication as the authentication provider and NTLM as the authentication method.

Extending a Web Application

Extending web applications allows the same content databases to serve content for multiple IIS websites via zones. An example of this is an organization that needs to serve content internally via http://portal using Windows Integrated Authentication but also serve the same content externally via https://portal.contoso.com using Forms authentication over SSL for security.

Tip

If the URL needs to be accessed both internally and externally, consider using the most available URL as the default URL. This approach allows system-generated email messages using the default URL to be available, whether they are internal or external. Using the previous example, the default URL is https://portal.contoso.com.

Extend a Web Application Using Central Administration

To extend a web application, do the following:

1. Browse to Central Administration, Application Management, Web Applications, Manage Web Applications, and select the web application to extend.

2. Click Extend on the ribbon, as shown in Figure 3.16.

3. Select Create a New IIS Web Site. Enter a name that is easily recognizable in IIS Manager.

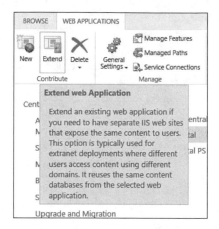

FIGURE 3.16
The Extend button on the Web Applications tab on the ribbon.

4. Define the port number. If you are using HTTP, this is usually port 80. As with web application creation, this information is written to the configuration database but can be changed manually in IIS Manager on every web server in the farm. It is best to correctly define it when creating the zone.

5. Enter the host header. The host header is usually the FQDN of the zone, such as portal.contoso.com, as shown in Figure 3.17. You should type information in the Host Header text box, even if you'll assign IP addresses in Internet Information Services Manager.

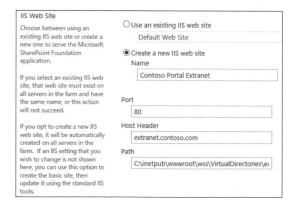

FIGURE 3.17
Always use intelligent names for IIS websites.

Note

If you are using host headers, the description changes automatically to the host header plus the TCP port number.

Tip

If you plan to assign IP addresses to web applications, you should enter the host header information at this point and change the port to 80. Additional host headers can be added using IIS Manager. It is important to understand that changes made manually in this manner are not written to the configuration database and may be lost the next time the server is updated or possibly even when the server is rebooted. As was previously mentioned, the use of PowerShell to accomplish this task is highly recommended.

6. Decide whether you'll use NTLM, Kerberos, or Basic authentication. If you need to use Basic authentication, select NTLM and configure authentication providers after you finish extending the web application. If you use Kerberos, don't forget to register the SPN for the Default zone's web application pool identity. Security configuration options are shown in Figure 3.18.

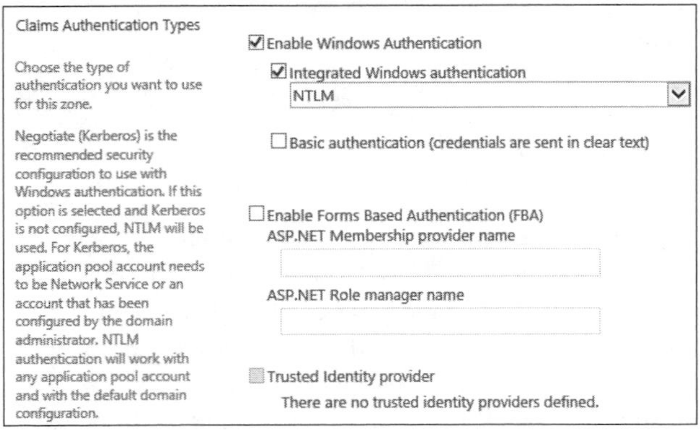

FIGURE 3.18
Extending the web application security configuration.

> **Caution**
>
> You are not given the option to create another web application pool. Doing so would break the functionality of the web application extension. Therefore, never change the application pool of an extended site in IIS Manager.

7. If you are extending the configuration to leverage the security of SSL, be sure to select that option here. Although this setting can be changed later, it is easier to do it now. Note that you must configure a certificate for this site in IIS Manager after creation before it can successfully serve content via SSL. SharePoint Server 2013 does not bind the certificate to the IIS website.

> **Note**
>
> SSL certificates and assigned IP addresses are not stored in the configuration database. If you must restore a web server for any reason, you will need to reconfigure the web applications using SSL or assigned IPs. Alternatively, you can restore IIS from the last backup.

8. Define the public URL. The URL can be set to a previously defined Domain Name System (DNS) hostname for this web application, or it can be set to a DNS hostname for a Network Load Balancing (NLB) IP address.

9. Select the zone.

10. Click OK.

Extend a Web Application Using Windows PowerShell

To extend a web application using Windows PowerShell, use the New-SPWebApplicationExtension command. Because you are actually extending an existing web application, we will tell Windows PowerShell to get the web application we want to extend first by using the Get-SPWebApplication command. The command to extend the Contoso Portal web application will look like the following:

```
PS C:\> $ap = New-SPAuthenticationProvider –
UseWindowsIntegratedAuthentication -DisableKerberos
PS C:\> Get-SPWebApplication –Identity
http://portal.contoso.com
```

```
New-SPWebApplicationExtension -Name Contso Portal -HostHeader
portal.contoso.com -Zone Extranet -URL
http://extranet.contoso.com -Port 80 -AuthenticationProvider
$ap
```

Deleting a Web Application

You should exercise caution when deleting a web application. Before deleting a web application, always have a verified farm backup.

Delete a Web Application Using Central Administration

To delete a web application, do the following:

1. Browse to Central Administration, Application Management, Manage Web Applications.

2. Select the web application you want to delete, and click Delete on the ribbon.

3. If you want to delete the content databases, select Yes. Otherwise, leave the default settings as shown in Figure 3.19.

FIGURE 3.19
The options available when deleting a web application.

4. To delete the IIS website, select Yes. It is possible to delete the definition of the web application in the configuration database while retaining both the content database or databases and the IIS website.

5. Click Delete.

Delete a Web Application Using Windows PowerShell

You can also delete web applications using Windows PowerShell by using the Remove-SPWebApplication command. The following command will delete the Contoso Portal web application, its associated IIS website, and any associated content databases. Using the Confirm parameter in this command will require that you confirm deleting the web application:

```
PS C: \> Remove-SPWebApplication http://portal.contoso.com -
Confirm -DeleteIISSites -RemoveContentDatabases
```

Deleting an Extended Zone

Deleting an extended zone is much like deleting a web application, with the exception that you can select the IIS website associated with the zone but not the content database. If you choose to remove SharePoint from an existing IIS website, be very careful when selecting the option from the ribbon. Do not click the Delete button, which is the primary option to delete—you need to click the down arrow on the Delete button to select the Remove SharePoint from IIS Web Site option, as shown in Figure 3.20.

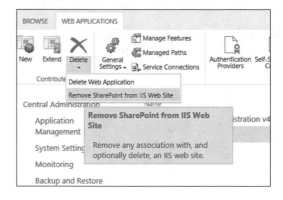

FIGURE 3.20
Delete a web application, or remove it from IIS.

Delete an Extended Zone Using Central Administration

To delete an extended zone, do the following:

1. Browse to Central Administration, Application Management, Manage Web Applications.

2. Select the web application with the associated zone that you want to delete.

3. On the ribbon, click the down arrow to display the drop-down menu for Delete, and select Remove SharePoint from IIS Web Site.

4. Click the drop-down arrow to display the menu under Select IIS Web site and zone to remove it, as shown in Figure 3.21.

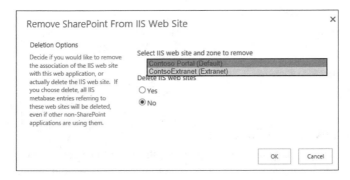

Remove SharePoint From IIS Web Site   ✕

Deletion Options

Decide if you would like to remove   Select IIS web site and zone to remove
the association of the IIS web site
with this web application, or   Contoso Portal (Default)
actually delete the IIS web site. If   ContsoExtranet (Extranet)
you choose delete, all IIS   Delete IIS web sites
metabase entries referring to
these web sites will be deleted,   ○ Yes
even if other non-SharePoint
applications are using them.   ● No

                                                        OK   Cancel

FIGURE 3.21
Select the IIS website and zone to remove.

5. Select Yes and click OK.

Caution

Exercise caution when deleting or removing SharePoint from an IIS website. The default zone of the web application is displayed by default and if deleted will break all zones.

Delete an Extended Zone Using Windows PowerShell

To delete an extended zone using Windows PowerShell, we will modify the command we used to delete a web application. Before the extended zone can be deleted, you have to tell Windows PowerShell which web application and zone you want to delete. To delete the extended Extranet zone we created earlier, use the following command:

```
PS C:\> Get-SPWebApplication http://portal.contoso.com ¦
Remove-
SPWebApplication -Zone "Extranet" -Confirm
```

Configuring and Managing Web Applications

The management and configuration of common tasks in SharePoint Server 2013 can be performed using the management ribbon from Central

Administration, Application Management, Manage Web Applications. When a web application is selected, the ribbon changes to display configuration options relevant to managing your web applications. The ribbon is divided into four specific areas:

- Contribute
- Manage
- Security
- Policy

Configuring Web Applications

After you create a web application, many tasks still need to be completed. The process of creating a web application accomplishes only the minimum requirements for defining a web application in the configuration database, which includes configuring IIS and creating the first associated content database.

To manage a web application, you need to set the focus of the ribbon to the web application. In the example shown in Figure 3.22, Contoso Portal has been selected as the web application to configure.

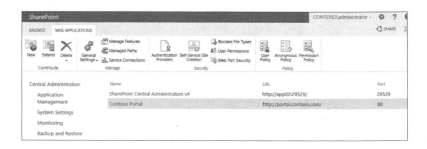

FIGURE 3.22
The Web Application Management page in Central Administration.

Each web application has individual settings that affect all sites and Site Collections hosted in that web application. Figure 3.23 shows the General Settings menu, which includes different options from those contained in the primary General Settings tab.

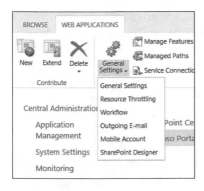

FIGURE 3.23
The General Settings drop-down menu in the Web Application Management page.

Configure General Settings

The General Settings page contains the most common web application settings. Although it's not mandatory to do so, most administrators change one or many of the following items:

- **Default Time Zone**—By default, each web server uses the time zone of the operating system. If you need to set the web application to another time zone, configure it here. It is generally a good idea to manually set the time zone to prevent inconsistencies in a load-balanced server farm.

- **Default Quota Template**—Each web application can have a suggested quota template for Site Collections created therein. New Site Collections will display this template by default, but the quota can be changed by the administrator creating the Site Collection. You must have previously created a quota template from Central Administration, Application Management, Specify Quota Templates.

> **Note**
>
> If you have existing Site Collections in this web application, changing the quota template will not affect those Site Collections. Site (Site Collection) quotas are used only when creating Site Collections. If you want to change a Site Collection quota after creation, you must set an individual quota. Individual quotas are configured in Central Administration, Application Management, Configure Quotas and Locks.

- **Person Name Actions and Presence Settings**—Presence settings are used to configure whether you'll allow the display of the online status and additional actions for users in SharePoint Server 2013. The presence status is displayed next to a user's name wherever the user's display name appears. Additional actions appear when a user right-clicks a member name. When this option is disabled, presence information and additional actions will no longer appear for users of the site. By default, it is enabled for all web applications.

- **Alerts**—Users are allowed to create alerts on all sites they have access to in a given web application if this setting is enabled. The default limit is 500, which is a reasonable limit for most organizations. However, you might need to increase or decrease this number based on your requirements. Be careful not to raise the limit too high because a user might subscribe to thousands of alerts and the resulting effect could be both SharePoint Server 2013 and Exchange Server performance degradation.

- **RSS Settings**—Really Simple Syndication (RSS) feeds allow users to subscribe to lists and libraries for sites with a compatible RSS reader, such as Microsoft Outlook 2013. By default, this is enabled for the web application and is available to many web parts. Note that it must be manually enabled for many lists and libraries.

- **Blog API Settings**—This is enabled by default and allows usernames and passwords to be sent via the Blog API. One of the most common uses of the Blog API is using Microsoft Office Word 2013 to compose blogs and then publish directly to a SharePoint Server 2013 blog site.

- **Browser File Handling**—When users upload files to SharePoint Server 2013 or you have custom code in lists, libraries, or the SharePoint Root, you can define how those files are executed. Unless you have a controlled environment, you should leave the default setting of Strict. This prevents attacks, such as cross-site scripting, from compromising the integrity of your server farm. The Strict setting forces the code to be executed on the client browser, not on the physical SharePoint Server 2013 web server.

- **Web Page Security Validation**—This property will automatically cease a session for sites in the web application if the session has been idle for a specific amount of time. By default, the time setting is 30 minutes. If users attempt to access a page in a site after being idle for more than the set amount of time, the page will have to be refreshed or the connection will have to be reestablished. This is most useful when a web application is using Forms-based authentication. If a client logs on from a public computer, the session is authenticated for only 30 minutes. This minimizes the risk of a SharePoint Server 2013 session browser being used for an indefinite period of time. If you are using Windows Authentication with Internet Explorer's automatic logon with current username and password, the revalidation of security will happen transparently to the user.

■ **Send User Name and Password**—In email this functionality is used only when SharePoint Server 2013 is installed in Active Directory account creation mode. This mode is for Internet Service Providers and is rarely used for organizational SharePoint Server 2013 server farms. If you did not select the advanced installation option of Active Directory account creation mode, this setting has no effect on your web application, regardless of the setting.

Tip

Although this setting probably doesn't affect your web application for better or worse, many administrators set this to No to reduce concerns from the Information Assurance auditor.

■ **Master Page Setting for Application _Layouts Pages**—If you do not enable this setting, all _layouts pages for this web application will use the application.master page in the SharePoint Root directory. This is usually unacceptable because pages, such as the Site Settings page, use a different master page than the rest of the site. Figure 3.24 shows the Site Settings page.

■ **Recycle Bin**—First, turning off the Recycle Bin on an active web application will empty both the first and second stages on all Recycle Bins, and that action is not easily reversed. Second, the time-based expiration setting is a global setting. Therefore, items do not expire from the first stage to the second stage. When the time-based limit is reached, the item is expunged. Think of it this way: if the time-based setting was 90 days and a user emptied her Recycle Bin 60 days after initially deleting an item, the item will remain in the second stage for 30 days. Third, if you turn off time-based expiration and do not use site quotas, the second stage will have no limit. Because the second stage is based on the site quota, Site Collections without quota will essentially have no second-stage storage limit. As you can see, the Recycle Bin configuration should be carefully thought out.

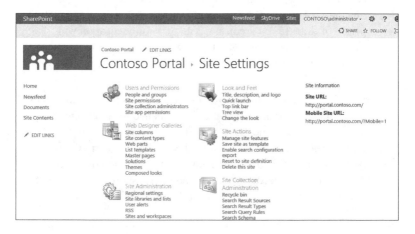

FIGURE 3.24
Site Settings is an example of a page using _layouts.

- **Maximum Upload Size**—The maximum upload size limits the size of single files or the aggregate size of multiple files in a single upload action. The latter option is often misunderstood or unknown to administrators. The default setting is 250MB. For most network infrastructures, 400MB to 500MB is the upper limitation unless there will be no Internet access or wide area network (WAN) access by users. If you begin to get timeouts on uploads, you might need to decrease the maximum upload size setting.

- **Customer Experience Improvement Program**—The overhead of this feature is minimal, but it still has an impact. It is not recommended for Internet-facing sites.

- **Usage Cookie**—The usage cookie provides SharePoint the capability to gather usage data related to anonymous users on all sites within the web application. If you are not allowing anonymous access, this setting can be left as Off.

Use Resource Throttling

Resource throttling allows you to configure options for throttling server resources on large lists for each web application. Throttling is a performance control designed to limit users' ability to negatively affect server performance and to control resource utilization during peak usage. Server resources monitored by default are CPU, Memory, Requests in Queue, and Wait Time. SharePoint Server 2013 checks resources every 5 seconds, and a throttling period will be initiated by the server if three checks are returned that exceed the defined threshold for a resource. This throttling period will end with a successful check. During a throttle period, HTTP GET requests and Search Robot requests generate a 503 error and are logged in the event viewer. No new timer jobs will start during a throttling period.

To configure Resource Throttling, follow these steps:

1. On the General Settings tab, select Resource Throttling.

2. Enter values for the List View Threshold option. This option limits queries within a list to guard against performance degradation with too many list items. In SharePoint Server 2013, a list can support up to 30 million items. If a list contains a large number of items, queries with too many results will be very slow. If a user tries an action that would hit a throttle limit, a message will appear, listing alternative methods that will not affect farm performance. The accepted performance limit in SharePoint Server 2013 is 2000 items in a view. Increasing the limit beyond 2000 items can have negative performance implications for your web servers and database servers. The default setting is 5000.

3. Allow or disallow object model override. This allows users with the correct permissions to programmatically override the List View Threshold setting for specific queries. Custom code will most often communicate directly with the object model.

4. Set the List View Threshold for auditors and administrators.

5. Define the List View Lookup Threshold. The default of 8 generally works in new implementations. List view lookups can often go beyond six fields. In this event, you need to increase the limit. Queries that have many lookup fields can significantly decrease database performance.

6. The Daily Time Window for Large Queries. This allows you to specify a daily time window to run large queries against your lists. If possible, this daily window should be outside of normal business hours to minimize the impact to end users.

7. Define the List Unique Permission Threshold. This option is rarely changed.

8. Turn Backward-Compatible Event Handlers on or off. By default, this is off. If you have a large amount of development work in SharePoint Server 2007 or 2010 that leveraged event handlers for lists or libraries, you should turn this on. Check with your developers if you are upgrading from SharePoint Server 2007 or 2010.

9. Configure HTTP Request Monitoring and Throttling. This job provides monitoring of front-end web server performance related to HTTP requests. If this setting is enabled and an overload of HTTP requests is detected, the server will reject, or throttle, low-priority requests.

10. Define the Change Log constraints. By default, SharePoint Server 2013 deletes entries from the change logs after 60 days. Caution should be used when reducing this setting because it may negatively impact services that rely on history information for sites contained in the web application.

11. Click OK.

Modify Workflow Settings

From the General Settings drop-down menu, select Workflow. Workflows are enabled by default for all web applications. You can modify the global workflow settings from the Workflow Settings option in Central Administration. In the web application Workflow Settings management interface, you can enable or disable workflows for a web application and modify task notifications. Here are the options in that interface:

■ **Enable User-Defined Workflows**—When set to Yes, this option allows users to create and deploy SharePoint Server 2013 declarative workflows. Users will need at least the design permission level on the site in a particular web application. These are not code-centric workflows deployed to the server as compiled code.

■ **Alert Internal Users Who Do Not Have Access**—You can decide whether to alert internal users who do not have site access but have been defined as a workflow participant. This notification is enabled by default. Upon selecting the embedded hyperlink emailed to them, users can request permission to access the site. Selecting No allows workflow tasks to be assigned only to users who have prior permission on the target item of the workflow.

■ **Allow External Users to Participate in Workflow**—You can enable documents to be emailed to external participants in a workflow. This feature is disabled by default, and if security is paramount in your organization, it should be left disabled.

Configure Outgoing Email

At a minimum, you should select outgoing mail settings, or alerts will not function. The SMTP Relay Server, From Address, and Reply To Address settings must be defined for outgoing email to work.

To configure outgoing email, follow these steps:

1. From the General Settings drop-down menu, select Outgoing Email.

2. Define the outgoing SMTP server. This can be any SMTP-compliant server that SharePoint can connect to using TCP port 25.

3. Define the From address. This address will appear as the sender of the email message.

4. Define the Reply-To address. This does not need to be the same as the From email address, which allows the email to be sent to a different address.

5. Select the character set. This will be the character set of the email being sent. The default is UTF-8, which is most commonly used for email, and allows for characters being used in all languages Unicode supports.

Warning

The SMTP server specified in SharePoint Foundation 2013 and SharePoint Server 2013 for outgoing email must allow relaying by IP address. SharePoint products do not authenticate outbound email. You must use another method for high availability because neither SharePoint Foundation 2013 nor SharePoint Server 2013 allows for multiple SMTP server addresses.

Configure Mobile Access

The mobile alert feature allows users to subscribe to alerts with their mobile phones. The idea behind the functionality is that many professionals prefer to get important alerts via mobile text (SMS) rather than via email. Not all users have smart phones, or smart phones that are compatible with their corporate email system. Configuring mobile alerts allows notification to almost any cellular telephone. The feature does come with some drawbacks, however. First, you must have a subscription with a third-party SMS provider. The SMS provider acts as a "man in the middle" to relay mobile messages to cellular providers. This comes at a cost. Although the future of this space is widely unknown, current prices range from $.02 USD to $.06 USD. You can find a list of SharePoint Server 2010–compatible providers at http://messaging.office.microsoft.com/HostingProviders.aspx?src=O14&lc=1033. There is a constantly changing list, and your costs will vary based on your geographic location and volume of prepaid SMS alerts.

Note

There is no method to throttle alerts at the web application level. If you have a user who subscribes to hundreds of alerts or you have a system error, you could quickly increase the costs associated with your third-party provider. Most administrators will want to configure throttling with the third-party provider to mitigate these risks.

To configure the Text Message (SMS) service, follow these steps:

To configure the Text Message (SMS) service, do the following:

1. Subscribe to an online SMS provider, and note the URL and user name/password given by the provider.

2. Browse to Central Administration, System Settings, Configure Mobile Account.

3. Enter the URL provided by the SMS provider.

4. Enter the username and password given to you by the SMS provider.

5. Test account settings.

Manage SharePoint Designer Governance

To manage SharePoint Designer 2013 policies, browse to Central Administration, Application Management, Manage Web Applications and select the web application to configure. Select SharePoint Designer from the General Settings drop-down menu in the management ribbon, as shown in Figure 3.25.

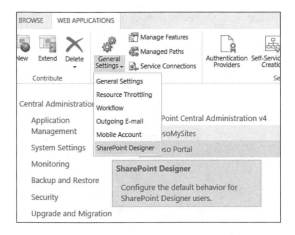

FIGURE 3.25
Select SharePoint Designer from the General Settings menu.

The following options are available to control SharePoint Designer 2010 users:

- Allow SharePoint Designer to Be Used in This Web Application
- Allow Site Collection Administrators to Detach Pages from the Site Template
- Allow Site Collection Administrators to Customize Master Pages and Layout Pages
- Allow Site Collection Administrators to See the URL Structure of the Web Site

Site Collection administrators can further delegate SharePoint Designer permission to site owners. To delegate permissions to site owners, browse to a Site Collection. From Site Actions, Site Settings, select SharePoint Designer Settings in the Site Collection Administration grouping. Site Collection administrators can then control the same options shown in Central Administration.

Manage Features

In a SharePoint Server 2013 farm, there are different levels where features can be installed: Farm, Web application, Site Collection, and Site. In Central Administration, Application Management, you can deactivate and activate installed features that are scoped to the web application. To activate or deactivate features, click Manage Features on the ribbon. Be sure you select the correct web applications before modifying, as shown in Figure 3.26.

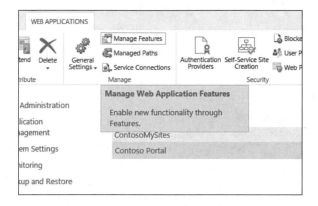

FIGURE 3.26
The Manage Features option on the web application ribbon.

Configure Managed Paths

From the Manage area of the ribbon on the Web Applications tab, click Managed Paths, as shown in Figure 3.27.

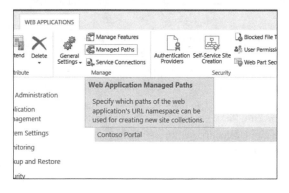

FIGURE 3.27
The Managed Paths option on the web application ribbon.

A managed path is defined as the path in the Uniform Resource Identifier (URI) that is managed by SharePoint products. If you have a medium-scale or larger implementation, give serious consideration to extending the default set of managed paths. For example, sites is the managed path in http://portal.contoso.com/sites/madison. Managed paths cannot be limited for use by specific security groups, nor can they be targeted directly with audiences. They are simply a way to organize a large quantity of Site Collections. When using managed paths, you can have two Site Collections with the same name—for example, http://portal.contoso.com/HR/Meetings and http://portal.contoso.com/Sales/Meetings.

When adding a new path, you have the option either to include only that path (explicit inclusion) or to specify that path and all subordinate paths (wildcard inclusion). If the path http://portal.contoso.com/sites was specified as an explicit inclusion, content can still be served from the WFE file system at http://portal.contoso.com/sites/path. When creating an explicit-inclusion managed path, you can then create a single Site Collection in the root of that path. If http://portal.contoso.com/sites was specified as a wildcard inclusion, multiple named Site Collections can be created under that path.

Alternate Access Mappings

Alternate Access Mappings is the second option in the Web Application area of Application Management in Central Administration. See Figure 3.28.

FIGURE 3.28
The Web Application section of Application Management in Central Administration.

Accessing Alternate Access Mappings

To access alternate access mappings, follow these steps:

1. The account logged in to Central Administration must be a member of the farm Administrator's group.

2. From Central Administration, select Application Management.

3. Under Web Applications, you will find two links: Manage Web Applications and Configure Alternate Access Mappings. Select the second link, Configure Alternate Access Mappings. Figure 3.29 shows the Alternate Access Mappings configuration page.

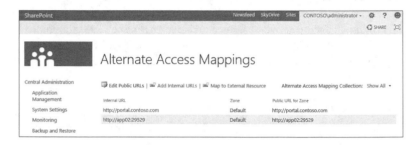

FIGURE 3.29
The Alternate Access Mappings page.

Alternate access mappings (AAMs) provide a way to change your web application URLs, configure Network Load Balancing web applications, and add URLs for alternative access. For example, if you served content from a single web application via multiple host headers for security, you would need to map the additional host headers with alternate access mapping URLs. Figure 3.30 shows an example of the web application http://portal.contoso.com being served securely and externally as https://external.contoso.com.

In this example the internal URL already exists, but you must add an AAM for the external URL. If you do not add the alternate access mapping URL, the host field returned in an external user's browser will be incorrect. Therefore, an external user would be returned http://portal.contoso.com when in fact, the user should be returned https://external.contoso.com. In addition, the embedded URLs in alert emails would be sent incorrectly.

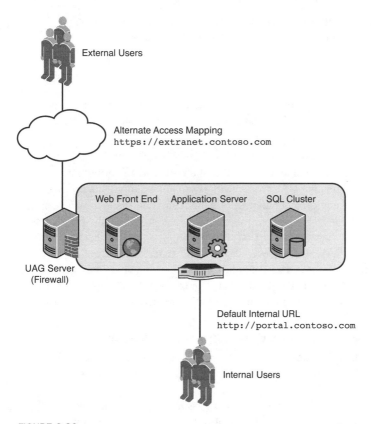

External Users

Alternate Access Mapping
https://extranet.contoso.com

Web Front End   Application Server   SQL Cluster

UAG Server
(Firewall)

Default Internal URL
http://portal.contoso.com

Internal Users

FIGURE 3.30
You must configure an alternate access mapping for each additional URL that you
configure for a web application.

Caution

Absolute, or hard-coded, URLs (URLs that are hard-coded on a web page or
document) cannot be mapped by the SharePoint 2013 AAM feature.
Examples of where this might be seen would be Content Editor Web Parts
(CEWP) that have links or contain HTML content or web parts that aggregate information from other locations.

Configuring Alternate Access Mappings

You can edit the public URLs from the Configure Alternate Access
settings under Web Applications found in the Application Management

section of Central Administration. There are three choices when modifying AAMs: Edit Public URLs, Add Internal URL, and Map to External Resources.

Edit Public URLs

You can edit public URLs from the Alternate Access Mappings page shown in Figure 3.29. By default there is no AAM collection selected; this feature is for your protection.

After selecting a collection, you have several options for defining the public URLs. For public URLs, fill in the URL and authority to correspond with the originating URL from the browser. For example, if a user types http://portal.contoso.com, that will be the return address in the browser. Conversely, if a user types https://external.contoso.com in the browser, the user will be directed to that URL. If the user types a URL that does not exist as an AAM, the request will fail. For example, if you are using two different IIS virtual servers to publish the same content database or databases, and your default internal URL is http://portal and your extranet URL is https://external.contoso.com, you configure alternate access URLs as follows:

- The default internal URL is http://portal.contoso.com.

- Either the Internet, Extranet, or Custom URL setting should be https://portal.contoso.com.https://external.contoso.com.

When users visit http://portal, they are assumed to be on the internal network and will be returned content to http://portal.contoso.com. Conversely, if they visit https://portal.contoso.com, it is assumed that they are coming from an external network and are returned to https://external.contoso.com as the correct address. This being the case, your security should not rely on AAM and zones because they merely supplement your firewall and router policies.

Add an Internal URL

To edit the default URL, choose to Add Internal URL; select the AAM collection; and change the URL protocol, host, and port. Do not change the zone. Alternatively, you can select the hyperlink of the web application to reach the same interface.

Mapping to External Resources

In addition to mapping server farm URLs, you can also map URLs to external resources. Most installations do not use this feature, but it can be enabled to allow access through SharePoint to other IIS web applications.

CHAPTER 4

Creating and Configuring Service Applications

- Service Application Architecture
- Managing Service Applications
- Deploying Service Applications

Service applications in SharePoint Server 2013 represent a further evolution of the changes implemented in SharePoint Server 2010. That evolution does not include any changes in the underlying architecture of Service applications; in fact, the architecture is identical to the SharePoint Server 2010 Service application architecture. The changes that SharePoint farm administrators and architects will see revolve around the exclusion of a number of the Service applications found in SharePoint Server 2010, enhanced functionality in others, and new Service applications making their debut in SharePoint Server 2013.

SharePoint Server 2013 continues to provide an extensible, pluggable Service Application model allowing web applications to consume services provided by the local farm as well as services published from remote farms. The functionality enhancements provided by the addition of new Service applications and re-engineering or removal of others only increases the flexibility of the SharePoint Server 2013 Service application architecture.

Service Application Architecture

Service applications are just that: distinct applications providing a specific service, such as Search, User Profiles, or Business Data Connectivity. They are deployed to an application or web server in a SharePoint Server 2013 farm and then accessed through a web server connection. This web server may or may not be the same physical server as the application server.

Service applications will consist of some or all of the following components:

- **Application bits**—One or more processes with associated Windows Communication Foundation (WCF) Services.

- **Administrative interface**—One or more web pages used to configure and administer the service.

- One or more databases.

- **One or more service application pools**—Application pools provide the context within which a service application operates. Application pools can be also be used to isolate service applications from each other.

Understanding Service Application Topologies

The service application topology has been designed with the greatest flexibility and scalability in mind and consists of five components:

- **Service Instance**—The actual implementation of the application binaries that provide the desired functionality. This could include configuration settings, Registry entries, or Windows services. As a part of the installation process, these bits are deployed to every server in the farm. This can be seen in the status notifications when you run PSConfigUI.exe on the servers in the farm.

- **Service Machine Instance**—These are the servers in the farm running a specific service. For example, if you were to configure the Excel Services Application to run on two out of three Application Servers in the farm, those two servers would be the Service Machine Instance of that service application. When more than one server is functioning as a service machine instance, software round-robin load balancing is provided. This provides the redundancy that was mentioned earlier, where if one server was to go offline, requests for the service are still answered by the server remaining online.

- **Service Application Endpoint**—On any server running a service machine instance that has an associated service application, there will be an IIS Virtual Application created within the SharePoint Web Services IIS Web Site on that server. The IIS virtual application will include the Service Application Endpoint, which could be either a WCF or ASMX file type. Every service application must have an associated service application endpoint that will not be created until the associated service machine instance is started using Central Administration, System Settings, Manage Services on Server, or via Windows PowerShell.

> **Note**
>
> Windows PowerShell provides SharePoint Administrators a greater degree of control over creating and managing service applications. Some service applications require that Windows PowerShell be used to manage their configurations.

- **Service Application**—This is the implementation and configuration of a specific service in the farm and includes the management features of the service application. These could be the database(s), administration pages, and so on.

- **Service Application Proxy**—Resides on the web server(s) and provides an interface between the web application and the service application. The interface also provides a way for a web application to consume applications and services that are capable of leveraging the software round-robin load-balancing scheme. The service application proxy also provides the capability to share services across multiple farms.

The simplest service application topology is a single server deployment. In the case of a single server deployment, all service applications and associated service application proxies exist on the same physical server. This can be seen in Figure 4.1.

This configuration is easily implemented and convenient to manage but does not provide redundancy. If you are running a single application server and that server goes offline, service applications will be unavailable. This approach might be considered acceptable in some small, simple environments but will not be acceptable in larger enterprise environments. Most organizations will implement application servers in redundant sets of two or more.

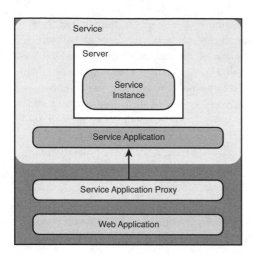

FIGURE 4.1
Single-server topology.

As mentioned earlier, a single logical service application can consist of multiple service instances running on different application servers. This arrangement provides redundancy and can support more users than the single-service approach. Figure 4.2 shows a topology with multiple service instances for a single logical service application, with one of the services installed but not running on the application server.

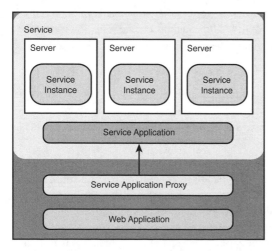

FIGURE 4.2
Service application topology with multiple service instances.

There are countless variations of these topologies that can be put into practice. The same service application could be exposed as multiple endpoints to provide isolation between groups, such as providing the finance department a separate search service from the rest of the company. These diagrams represent only a single service application, but a single application server could host many service applications. Also, some service applications can be federated, or shared, across multiple farms. This approach allows expensive and maintenance-intensive services to be hosted in a central location, thus providing access to the service without incurring the overhead of maintaining the service for each farm that wants to consume it.

Managing Service Applications

Service applications can be deployed automatically using the Farm Configuration Wizard, manually using the Manage Service Applications page of Central Administration, or using Windows PowerShell. With several exceptions, when a service application is deployed using Central Administration it can added to the farm's group of default service application connections by leaving the available check box selected. This behavior can be overridden by deploying the new service application using Windows PowerShell or by unchecking the box to add the new service application to the farm's default proxy list.

The following list of service applications do not have an option to add the service application to the default proxy list at the time of creation:

- Business Data Connectivity Service
- Machine Translation Service
- PerformancePoint Service Application
- Search Service Application
- Secure Store Application
- Work Management Service

Editing Service Application Connections for a Web Application

Web applications connect to service applications through membership in a service application connection group, also called an application proxy group. To manage application connection groups, you must be a member of the Farm Administrators group.

Edit an Application Connection Group

The following steps should be performed to edit an application connection group:

1. Go to Central Administration, Application Management.

2. On the Application Management page, in the Service Applications section, click Configure Service Application Associations.

3. On the Service Application Associations page, Select Web Applications from the View drop-down list.

4. In the list of Web Applications, in the Applications Proxy Group column, click the name of the service application connection group you want to change.

5. In the Configure Service Application Associations dialog box, shown in Figure 4.3, use the check boxes to add or remove service application proxies from the application proxy group.

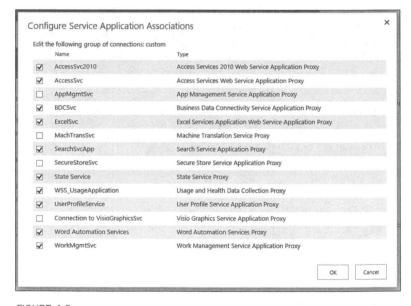

FIGURE 4.3
The Configure Service Application Association dialog box.

6. Click OK to save the application proxy group settings.

Manage Administrators of a Service Application

You must be a member of the Farm Administrators group to manage service application administrators:

1. Go to Central Administration, Application Management and click Manage Service Applications.

2. On the Manage Service Applications page, click the row of the service application that you want to manage the administrators of.

3. On the management ribbon, in the Operations section, click the Administrators icon.

4. In the Administrators dialog box, add or remove users or groups.

5. For users or groups, use the check boxes to configure permissions.

6. Click OK to save the settings.

Delete a Service Application

You must be a member of the Farm Administrators group to delete a service application:

1. Go to Central Administration, Application Management and click Manage Service Applications.

2. On the Manage Service Applications page, click the row of the service application you want to delete.

3. On the management ribbon, in the Operations section, click the Delete icon.

4. In the confirmation dialog box, click the Delete Data Associated with the Service Application check box if you want to delete the associated database, or in some cases multiple databases. In addition, if you are deleting the search service application, this action will delete the search indexes associated with that specific search service application.

5. Click OK to delete the service application.

Deploying Service Applications

In addition to providing the service application framework, both SharePoint Foundation and SharePoint Server provide some default service application implementations out of the box. SharePoint Foundation provides the more basic service applications, such as Business

Connectivity Services and Usage and Health Data Collection Service. SharePoint Server adds many more, such as the following:

- Access Services
- Access Services 2010 (new in SharePoint Server 2013)
- App Management Service (new in SharePoint Server 2013)
- Excel Services
- Machine Translation Service (new in SharePoint Server 2013)
- Managed Meta Data Service
- PerformancePoint Services
- Search Service
- Secure Store Service
- Visio Graphics Service
- Word Automation Service
- Work Management Service (new in SharePoint Server 2013)

Configuring Access Services

Access Services has been completely redesigned for SharePoint Server 2013. It now provides subject matter experts the capability to create data-driven applications for their businesses using Access 2013 and then easily deploy those applications to SharePoint Server 2013. After the application has been deployed, SharePoint Server 2013 hosts the application front end and provides authentication, authorization, and security for the Access 2013 applications. Your on-premise SQL database instance will provide the data storage technology and a location to store and manage the Access 2013 application tables, views, macros, and queries SQL Azure serves as the default location for Access Services databases deployed in an Office 365 environment.

Configure Access Services

Perform the following steps to configure access services:

1. Go to Central Administration, Application Management, and in the Service Applications section click the link to Manage Service Applications.

2. On the Manage Service Applications page, click the Access Services link for the service application (not the service application proxy). See Figure 4.4.

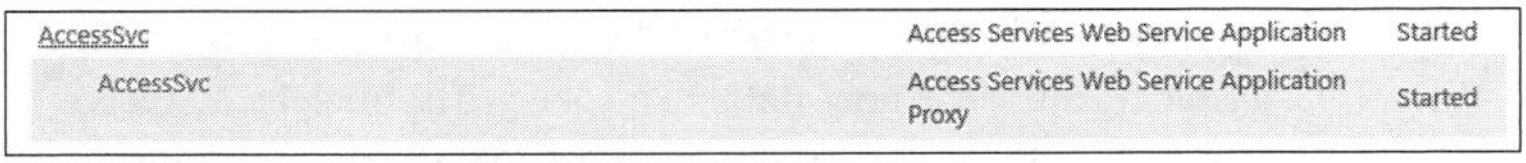

| AccessSvc | Access Services Web Service Application | Started |
| AccessSvc | Access Services Web Service Application Proxy | Started |

FIGURE 4.4
The Access Services item on the Manage Service Applications page.

3. On the Manage Access Services page, in the Session Management section, configure the following values:

■ **Maximum Request Duration**—Enter the maximum duration (in seconds) allowed for a request from an application. The default setting is 30 seconds.

■ **Maximum Sessions Per User**—Enter the maximum number of sessions allowed per user. If a user has the maximum number of sessions and starts a new one, the user's oldest session is deleted. The default setting is 10.

■ **Maximum Sessions per Anonymous User**—The maximum number of sessions allowed per anonymous user. If this maximum is hit, the oldest session will be deleted when a new session is started. The default setting is 25.

■ **Cache Timeout**—The maximum time (in seconds) that a data cache can remain available, as measured from the end of each request for data in that cache. The default setting is 300 seconds.

■ **Query Timeout**—Maximum time in seconds for a database command or query to execute before it is cancelled. The default is 60 seconds.

4. In the Memory Utilization section configure the following value:

■ **Maximum Private Bytes**—The maximum number of private bytes (in MB) allocated by the Access Services process. The default setting is –1, which means the limit should be 50 percent of the amount of physical memory on the server.

5. In the New Application Database Server section the following values are available if you want to specific a new location to store your Access service apps:

■ **Application Database Server**—Specify the name of a new database server.

- **Application Database Authentication**—Specify the authentication type for the new database server. If you select SQL authentication, you will also have to specify the Account and Password to use.

Note

Additional information on configuring Access Services for SharePoint Server 2013 is available at http://technet.microsoft.com/en-us/library/jj714714.aspx.

Configuring the App Management Service

The App Management Service in SharePoint Server 2013 manages the licensing information related to SharePoint apps you have purchased from Microsoft Marketplace; it manages the farms App Catalog, monitors apps, and sets app permissions. After the App Management Service has been created and configured, a new link displays under the Central Administration heading, as shown in Figure 4.5.

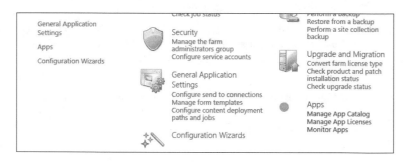

FIGURE 4.5
The App Management settings on the Central Administration page.

Clicking the Apps link in the Quick Launch navigation takes you to the Apps page where you can access Microsoft Marketplace, download or purchase apps, manage app licenses, manage the app catalog, and set app permissions.

> **Note**
>
> Some apps may require certain functionality in the farm before you can download or install them. For example, apps you download that are used for project management functionality may require an existing instance of Microsoft Project Server in the farm.

Before the App Management Service can be created, there are some DNS configuration changes that have to be put into place. When apps are deployed into the SharePoint Server 2013 farm, each app will have its own isolated URL. Deploying apps in this manner helps prevent cross-site scripting between your SharePoint site where the app is deployed and the app itself. Those isolated URLs are enabled by creating a domain or subdomain in DNS.

> **Note**
>
> Additional information on configuring DNS to host SharePoint Server 2013 apps is available at the following link: http://technet.microsoft.com/en-us/library/fp161236(v=office.15).

Configure the App Management Service

To configure the App Management Service, perform the following steps:

1. Verify that the Subscription Settings Service application is running. If not, you will need to create it using PowerShell. Configuring the Subscription Settings Service must be done using PowerShell; there is no user interface to do this. More information on creating the Subscription Setting Service can be found at this link: http://msdn.microsoft.com/en-us/library/fp179923(v=office.15).

2. Go to Central Administration, Apps, Configure App URLs.

3. On the Configure App URLs page, configure the following settings:

   ■ **App Domain**—Specify the domain that will host the apps purchased for your farm. For example, in my test farm my App domain is contosoapps.com.

   ■ **App Prefix**—The app prefix is prepended to the subdomain of the app URLs. In my test farm I have entered app.

4. Click OK to save your settings and continue.

After these steps have been completed, you are prepared to deploy apps into your SharePoint Server 2013 farm. There are number of things to be aware of:

- Host header web applications will not work with app domain URLs. The app domain redirect will attempt to use IIS to resolve the app URL, which will not work. To use host headers for your web applications and leverage the App Management Service, you will have to create another web application using port 80 or 443 that does not have a host header. Stop the default website and any redirect coming in. The new host header should now be able to work using the new web application.

- As an alternative to the creation and configuration of an additional web application to act as a listener, you could create your web applications without host headers and use Host Header Site Collections.

> **Note**
>
> Host Header Site Collections must be created using Windows PowerShell.

> **Note**
>
> Additional information on configuring App Management Services for SharePoint 2013 can be found at the following link: http://technet.microsoft.com/en-us/library/fp161236.aspx.

Configuring Access Services 2010

Access Services 2010 provides backward compatibility for SharePoint Server 2010 Access applications. This backward compatibility allows for the continued maintenance of existing SharePoint Server 2010 Access service applications using both Access 2010 and Access 2013. You cannot create new Access 2010 applications for use in SharePoint Server 2013.

Configure Access Services 2010

To configure Access Services 2010, perform the following steps:

1. Go to Central Administration, Application Management, Manage Service Applications.

2. On the Manage Service Applications page, click the Access Services 2010 link for the service application (not for the service application proxy). See Figure 4.6.

| Access Services 2010 | Access Services 2010 Web Service Application | Started |
| Access Services 2010 | Access Services 2010 Web Service Application Proxy | Started |

FIGURE 4.6
The Access Services 2010 item on the Manage Service Applications page.

3. On the Manage Access Services 2010 page, in the Lists and Queries section, configure the following values:

- **Maximum Columns Per Query**—Enter the maximum number of columns that can be referenced in a query. Note that some columns may automatically be referenced by the query engine and will be included in this limit. The default setting is 32.

- **Maximum Rows Per Query**—Enter the maximum number of rows that a list used in a query can have or that the output of the query can have. The default setting is 25000.

- **Maximum Sources Per Query**—Enter the maximum number of lists that may be used as input to one query. The default setting is 12.

- **Maximum Calculated Columns Per Query**—Enter the maximum number of inline calculated columns that can be included in a query, either in the query itself or in any subquery on which it is based. Calculated columns in the underlying Microsoft SharePoint Foundation list are not included. The default setting is 10.

- **Maximum Order By Clauses Per Query**—The maximum number of Order By clauses in the query. The default setting is 4.

- **Allow Outer Joins**—Check the box to allow left and right outer joins in a query. Inner Joins are always allowed. The default setting is "Outer Joins Allowed".

- **Allow Non Remotable Queries**—Check the box to allow queries that cannot be remoted to the database tier to run. The default setting is "Remotable Queries Allowed".

- **Maximum Records Per Table**—Enter the maximum number of records that a table in an application can contain. The default setting is 500000.

4. In the Application Objects section, enter the maximum number of records an Access Services 2010 Application can contain. The default setting is 3000.

5. In the Session Management section, configure the following values:

   ■ **Maximum Request Duration**—Enter the maximum duration (in seconds) allowed for a request from an application. The default setting is 30 seconds.

   ■ **Maximum Sessions Per User**—Enter the maximum number of sessions allowed per user. If a user has the maximum number of sessions and starts a new one, the user's oldest session is deleted. The default setting is 10.

   ■ **Maximum Sessions Per Anonymous User**—Enter the maximum number of sessions allowed per anonymous user. If this maximum is hit, the oldest session will be deleted when a new session is started. The default setting is 25.

   ■ **Cache Timeout**—Enter the maximum time (in seconds) that a data cache can remain available, as measured from the end of each request for data in that cache. The default setting is 1500 seconds.

   ■ **Maximum Session Memory**—Enter the maximum amount of memory (in MB) that a single session can use. The default setting is 64MB.

6. In the Memory Utilization section, enter the maximum number of private bytes (in MBs) allocated by the Access Services process. The default setting is –1, which means the limit should be 50 percent of the amount of physical memory on the server.

7. In the Templates section, enter the maximum allowed size (in MBs) for Access 2010 Templates (ACCDT). The default setting is 30MB.

8. Click OK to save the settings.

Note

Additional information on configuring Access Services 2010 for SharePoint Server 2013 is available at the following link: http://technet.microsoft.com/en-us/library/ee748653.aspx.

Configuring Business Connectivity Services

Business Connectivity Services (BCS) in SharePoint Server 2013 represents the next version of the Business Data Catalog (BDC). BCS remains baked into the platform, and new enhancements further extend the capabilities of the service to new and more powerful methods of interacting with, and surfacing, internal and external data.

As in past versions of BCS, external data connections can be built and managed using SharePoint Designer 2013. New in this version of BCS is the capability of Office 2013 client applications to directly interact with BCS. These client-side solutions require installation of the following prerequisites:

- MS SQL Server Compact 4.0.

- Microsoft .NET Framework 4.0.

- WCF Data Services 5.0 for OData V3.

- Office 2013 applications can interact with external data, but there are some limitations to be aware of.

- Word 2013 supports only read-only BCS connections to online data.

- Access 2013 supports BCS connections that can utilize a full range of Create, Read, Update, Delete, and Query (CRUDQ) operations to online data.

- Visio 2013 supports only read-only BCS connections to online and offline data.

- InfoPath 2013 will support BCS connections that can utilize a full range of Create, Read, Update, Delete, and Query (CRUDQ) operations to online and offline data.

- Excel 2013 supports BCS connections that can utilize a full range of Create, Read, Update, Delete, and Query (CRUDQ) operations to online data.

- Outlook 2013 supports BCS connections that can utilize a full range of Create, Read, Update, Delete, and Query (CRUDQ) operations to online and offline data.

Configure Business Connectivity Services

Follow these steps to configure Business Connectivity Services:

1. Go to Central Administration, Application Management, Manage Service Applications.

2. On the Manage Service Applications page, click the Business Connectivity Services link.

3. On the Edit tab in the ribbon of the View BDC Application page are several configuration options:

- On the BDC Models tab, the Import options allows you to import a BDC model file that provides the definition of an external content type and its related external systems, connection settings, and authentication mode. After uploading, you can use the external content types defined by the model file in external lists, user profiles, client applications, and custom applications.

- There are two types of BDC Model Definition file that can be imported, the Model file and the Resource file:

  - Model Definition files contain the base XML metadata for a system.

  - Resource Definition files provide the capability to import or export localized Names, Properties, and Permissions resources of a BDC application. The import of these resources is managed in the Advanced Settings page of the Import BDC Model page.

- On the Permissions tab are options to Set Object Permissions and Set Metadata Store Permissions:

  - Set Object Permissions allows you to configure permissions on an external content type. To set object permissions take the following steps:

    1. Click the Browse button, select the account you want to grant object permissions to, and click Add.

    2. Set the appropriate permissions for the account you are adding. The available options are Edit, Execute, Selectable in Clients, and Set Permissions.

    3. Check the box to propagate the changes you are making to all BDC Models, External Systems and External Content Types in the BDC Metadata Store. Checking this box will overwrite any existing permissions:

  - Set Metadata Store Permissions allows you to set permissions on the BDC Metadata Store. To set metadata store permissions, take the following steps:

1. Click the Browse button, select the account you want to grant object permissions to, and click Add.

2. Set the appropriate permissions for the account you are adding. The available options are Edit, Execute, Selectable in Clients, and Set Permissions.

3. Check the box to propagate the changes you are making to all BDC Models, External Systems, and External Content Types in the BDC Metadata Store. Checking this box will overwrite any existing permissions:

■ On the Manage tab, you can delete existing external content types.

■ On the Profile Pages tab, you can create, upgrade, and configure external content type profile page hosts. It is recommended that you use a dedicated SharePoint site to host all your external content type profile pages.

Configuring Excel Services

Excel Services was introduced in SharePoint 2007 as a way to manage, publish, and share Excel 2007 data connected workbooks across an organization securely using SharePoint as the medium. In SharePoint Server 2013, that functionality is continued and improved upon again. The tighter integration of PerformancePoint, PowerView, and PowerPivot with Excel 2013 brings more robust business intelligence and reporting capabilities to SharePoint Server 2013.

Note

Excel Services is available only in the Enterprise edition of SharePoint Server 2013.

Configure Excel Services

Take the following steps to configure Excel Services:

1. Go to Central Administration, Application Management, Manage Service Applications.

2. On the Manage Service Applications page, click the Excel Services Application link.

3. On the Manage Excel Services Application page, click Global Settings to define those settings that apply to the behavior of Excel Services across the farm.

4. In the Security section of the Excel Services Applications Settings page, set the following values:

   ■ **File Access Method**—Enter the authentication method used by Excel Calculation Services to retrieve workbook files from all non-Microsoft SharePoint Foundation trusted file locations. The default setting is Impersonation.

   ■ **Connection Encryption**—This setting determines whether connection encryption is required between client computers and front-end components of Excel Services Application. The default setting is Not Required.

   ■ **Allow Cross-Domain Access**—This setting determines whether selected files from one HTTP domain can be displayed on a page in a different HTTP domain. The default setting is Unchecked or to not allow cross-domain access.

5. Under the Load Balancing section, choose a load-balancing scheme for sessions across Excel Calculation Services (ECS) processes:

   ■ **Workbook URL**—The Workbook URL is the default setting for the load-balancing scheme. This setting uses a URL in the workbook to determine which ECS process opens the workbook.

   ■ **Round-Robin**—Uses the round-robin load-balancing scheme to determine the ECS process to be used to open a workbook.

   ■ **Local**—Determines whether an ECS process is local to the computer where the workbook is being opened. If so, that process is used. If a local ECS process is not available, the round-robin load-balancing scheme is used.

6. In the Session Management section, enter the value for the Maximum Sessions per User. If this maximum is hit, the oldest session will be deleted when a new session is started. The default setting is 25; for unlimited sessions set the value to −1.

7. In the Memory Utilization section, configure the following settings:

- **Maximum Private Bytes**—This setting determines the maximum number of private bytes (in MBs) allocated by the Excel Calculations Services process. The default setting is -1, which is the equivalent of 50 percent of the physical memory on the server.

- **Memory Cache Threshold**—This setting controls the percentage of the Maximum Private Bytes that can be allocated to inactive objects. When the memory cache threshold is exceeded, cached objects that are not currently in use are released. The default setting is 90.

- **Maximum Unused Object Age**—This setting controls the maximum time (in minutes) that inactive objects remain in the memory cache. The default setting is -1, which is the equivalent of no maximum.

8. In the Workbook Cache section, configure the following settings:

- **Workbook Cache Location**—This setting determines the local file system location of the workbook file cache. If there is no value, the workbook cache location will be a subdirectory in the system's temporary directory. The default setting is blank.

- **Maximum Size of Workbook Cache**—This setting controls the maximum amount of disk space (in MBs) that can be allocated to workbooks that are currently in use by Excel calculation Services. This value includes the maximum disk space that can be allocated for recently used files that are not open. The default setting is 40960 (40GB).

- **Caching of Unused Files**—Selecting the check box enables caching of files that are no longer in use by Excel Calculation Services sessions. By default, this check box is unchecked.

9. In the External Data section, configure the following settings:

- **Connection Lifetime**—This setting controls the maximum time (in seconds) for a connection to remain open. Older connections are closed and reopened for the next query. The default setting is 1800 seconds.

■ **Analysis Services EffectiveUserName**—This setting determines whether the EffectiveUserName connection string property will be used as an alternative to Windows delegation for allowing users secure access to Analysis Services data. The default setting for this check box is blank.

> **Note**
>
> This setting impacts only external data connections based on Analysis Services workbook connections with an authentication setting of Use the Authenticated User's Account.

■ **Unattended Service Account**—This setting designates a single account in the Secure Store Service that all workbooks can use to refresh data.

> **Note**
>
> An unattended service account is required when the workbook connections specify the Use the Unattended Service Account without using Windows Credentials.

■ **Secure Store Service Association**—This section allows you to specify an existing Unattended Service Account or create a new one.

10. Click OK to save the settings.

Add a Trusted File Location

To add a Trusted File Location, perform the following steps:

1. Go to Central Administration, Application Management, Manage Service Applications.

2. On the Manage Service Applications page, click the Excel Services Application link.

3. On the Manage Excel Services Application page, click Trusted File Locations.

4. On the Trusted File Locations page, click Add Trusted File Location.

5. In the Location section, configure the following settings:

■ **Address**—This can be a Microsoft SharePoint Foundation website, a network file share via a UNC path, or an HTTP web folder.

■ **Location Type**—Select the appropriate option button based on the address chosen in the Location settings. The default setting is Microsoft SharePoint Foundation.

■ **Trust Children**—This setting determines whether the trusted file location will trust files stored in child libraries or directories of the chosen location. By default this check box is blank, indicating that child libraries or directories will not be trusted.

■ **Description**—The description text box is optional. However, a description of the trusted file location and its purpose is highly recommended.

6. In the Session Management section, configure the following settings:

■ **Session Timeout**—This setting determines the maximum time (in seconds) that an Excel Calculation Services session can remain open and inactive before it is shut down, as measured from the end of each request. The default setting is 450 seconds. To set the session timeout to No Timeout enter the value –1.

■ **Short Session Timeout**—This setting determines the maximum time (in seconds) that an Excel Services Application session can remain open and inactive, prior to any user interaction, before it is shut down. Short Session Timeout duration is measured from the end of the initial Open request. The default setting is 450 seconds. To set the short session timeout to disabled, enter a value of –1.

■ **New Workbook Session Timeout**—This setting determines the maximum time (in seconds) that an Excel Calculation Services session for a new workbook can remain open and inactive before it is shut down, as measured from the end of each request. The default setting is 1800 seconds. To set the new workbook session timeout to No Timeout, enter a value of –1.

■ **Maximum Request Duration**—This setting determines (in seconds) the maximum duration of a single request in a session. The default setting is 300 seconds. To set the maximum duration request to No Limit, enter a value of –1.

■ **Maximum Chart Render Duration**—This setting determines the maximum amount of time (in seconds) spent rendering any single chart. The default setting is 3 seconds. To set the maximum chart render duration to No Limit, enter a value of –1.

7. In the Workbook Properties section, configure the following settings:

   ■ **Maximum Workbook Size**—This setting determines the maximum size (in MBs) of a workbook that can be opened by Excel Calculation Services. The default setting is 10MB. The maximum setting for this value is 2000MB.

   ■ **Maximum Chart or Image Size**—This setting determines the maximum size (in MBs) of a chart or image that can be opened by Excel Calculation Services. The default setting is 1MB.

8. In the Calculation Behavior section, configure the following settings:

   ■ **Volatile Function Cache Lifetime**—This setting determines the maximum time (in seconds) that a computed value for a volatile function is cached for automatic recalculations. The default setting is 300 seconds.

   ■ **Workbook Calculation Mode**—This setting determines the Calculation mode of workbooks in Excel Calculations Services. The default setting for this value is File, which does not override the workbook settings. The other three options, Manual, Automatic, Automatic Except Data Tables, all override the workbook settings.

9. In the External Data section, configure the following settings:

   ■ **Allow External Data**—This setting specifies which data connections to allow. The default setting is Trusted Data Connection Libraries and Embedded.

   ■ **Warn on Refresh**—This setting determines if a warning will be displayed before refreshing external data for files in this location. The default setting is to display the warning.

   ■ **Display Granular External Data Errors**—This setting determines if granular error messages for external data failures will be displayed. The default setting is to display the errors.

   ■ **Stop When Refresh on Open Fails**—This setting determines if the open operation on a file in this location stops under specific circumstances. Those circumstances are when the file contains a Refresh on Open data connection and the file cannot be refreshed or when the user does not have Open Item permissions to the workbook. The default setting is set to stop when enabled.

- **External Data Cache Lifetime**—This setting determines the maximum time (in seconds) that the system can use external data query results:

  - **Automatic Refresh (periodic/on-open)**—The default setting is 300 seconds.

  - **Manual Refresh**—The default setting is 300 seconds. To set the manual refresh to never refresh after the first query, enter the value –1.

- **Maximum Concurrent Queries Per Session**—This setting determines the maximum number of external data queries that can execute concurrently in a single session. The default setting is 5.

- **Allow External Data Using REST**—This setting determines if the REST API can refresh external data connections. This setting has no effect if the Allow External Data is set to None. The default setting is disabled.

10. In the User-Defined Functions section, configure the Allow User-Defined Functions setting to allow user-defined functions to be called from workbooks in the trusted location. The default setting is to not allow user-defined functions.

11. Click OK to save the trusted file location.

Add a Trusted Data Connection Library

To add a trusted data provider, perform the following steps:

1. Go to Central Administration, Application Management, Manage Service Applications.

2. On the Manage Service Applications page, click the Excel Services Application link.

3. On the Manage Excel Services Application page, click Trusted Data Providers. A trusted data provider is an external data provider that workbooks opened in Excel Services Applications are permitted to use.

4. On the Excel Services Application Trusted Data Providers page, click Add Trusted Data Provider.

   - **Provider ID**—Give the trusted data provider an identifier.

■ **Provider Type**—Select the provider type for the trusted data provider. The default setting is OLE DB. Other options are ODBC and ODBC DSN.

■ **Description**—Give your trusted data provider a description. Entering the details of the provider type would be helpful here.

Add a Trusted Data Connection Library

Perform the following steps to add a trusted data connection library:

1. Go to Central Administration, Application Management, Manage Service Applications.

2. On the Manage Service Applications page, click the Excel Services Application link.

3. On the Manage Excel Services Application page, click Trusted Data Connection Libraries.

4. On the Trusted Data Connection Libraries page, click Add a Trusted Data Connection Library.

   ■ **Address**—Enter the address of the trusted data connection library.

   ■ **Description**—Enter the description of the trusted data connection library.

   ■ Click OK to save the new trusted data connection library.

Register User-Defined Function Assemblies

User-defined functions can be defined in assemblies (dynamic-link libraries, or DLLs) that can then be referenced from Excel Services. All such assemblies must be registered with the Excel Services application to let SharePoint know that the assembly is safe:

1. Go to Central Administration, Application Management, Manage Service Applications.

2. On the Manage Service Applications page, click the Excel Services Application link.

3. On the Manage Excel Services Application page, click User Defined Function Assemblies.

4. On the User-Defined Functions page, click Add User-Defined Function Assembly.

   ■ **Assembly**—Enter the Strong Name or full path of an assembly that contains user-defined functions, which Excel Calculation Services can call.

   ■ **Assembly Location**—Enter the location of the user-defined assembly. The default setting for this is the Global Assembly Cache (GAC). You can also enter the file path to the assembly.

   ■ **Enable Assembly**—This setting determines if the user-defined assembly can be loaded and used by Excel Calculation Services. The default setting is Assembly Enabled.

5. Click OK to save the new user-defined assembly.

Configure Data Model Settings

The Data Model Settings allows the registration of SQL Server Analysis Services servers that Excel Services Applications can use for advanced data analysis. Follow these steps to add a new data model:

1. Go to Central Administration, Application Management, Manage Service Applications.

2. On the Manage Service Applications page, click the Excel Services Application link.

3. On the Manage Excel Services Application page, click Data Model Settings.

4. On the Data Model Settings page, click Add Server to add a new server.

   ■ **Server Name** —Add the identifier for the SQL Server Analysis Services server in the SERVERNAME\INSTANCE format.

   ■ **Description**—Add a description of the new server.

Note

This server must be running SQL Analysis Services 2012 SP 1 or higher in SharePoint Deployment mode.

> **Note**
>
> Additional information on configuring Excel Services for SharePoint Server 2013 can be found at the following link: http://technet.microsoft.com/en-us/library/jj219698.aspx.

Configuring the Machine Translation Service

New to SharePoint Server 2013, the Machine Translation service allows SharePoint to be configured to automatically provide machine translation of files, files within a document library or a site using Microsoft's online translation service. To successfully configure the machine translation service, the following prerequisites must be configured and in place:

- App Management service application.
- Server-to-server authentication and app authentication.
- User Profile service application proxy in the default proxy group for the farm.
- User Profile service application must be started and configured by using Central Administration or Windows PowerShell.
- The server performing the translation service must have an Internet connection.

Configure the Machine Translation Service

After verifying that the prerequisites are in place, perform the following steps to configure the Machine Translation service:

1. Go to Central Administration, Application Management, Manage Service Applications.
2. On the Manage Service Applications page, click the Machine Translation Services Application link.
3. On the Machine Translation Service management page, configure the following settings:
    - **Enabled File Extensions**—This section allows you to identify the specific file extension you would like the machine translation service to handle. It includes files related to four specific parsers: Microsoft Word Document Parser, HTML Parser, Plain-text Parser, and XLIFF Parser. The default setting of this section is that all file extensions are selected:

■ **Item Size Limits**—This section allows you to set the maximum file sizes and character count for the service to achieve better performance.

■ **Maximum File Size for Binary Files in KB**—Microsoft Word documents are binary files. This setting allows you to set the maximum file sizes for binary files to be translated. The default setting is 51200.

■ **Maximum File Size for Text Files in KB**—Plain-text, HTML, and XLIFF documents are text files. This setting allows you to set the maximum file sizes for text files to be translated. The default setting is 5120.

■ **Maximum Character Count for Microsoft Word Documents**—Allows you to set the maximum character count for Microsoft Word documents. The default setting is 500000.

4. In the **Online Translation Connection** section, you specify the web proxy server used by the service application to communicate with the online translation service.

5. In the **Translation Processes** section, you set the number of translation processes available on each server available to the service application. By default this is set to 1.

6. In the **Translation Throughput** section, configure the settings that determine how often translations are started and how many will be included in each batch:

   ■ **Frequency with which to Start Translations (minutes)**— This setting determines how often the translation jobs will run. The default setting is 15 minutes.

   ■ **Number of Translations to Start (per translation process)**—This setting determines the number of translations to start with each run of the translation job. The default setting is 200.

7. In the **Maximum Translation Attempts** section you can set the number of times the translation job will attempt to run. The default for this setting is 2.

8. The **Maximum Synchronous Translation Requests** provides the capability to set the maximum number of synchronous translation attempts that can be processed at one time on each server available to the service application. The default setting is 10.

9. In the **Translation Quota**, configure the following sections to limit the usage of the service's queue mode to ensure high throughput:

   * **Maximum Number of Items Which Can Be Queued Within a 24-hour Period**—The default is No Limit, although you do have the capability to specify the maximum number of items that can be queued in a 24 hour period.

   * **Maximum Number of Items Which Can Be Queued Within a 24-hour Period per Site Subscription**—The default is No Limit, although you do have the capability to specify the maximum number of items that can be queued in a 24-hour period.

10. In the **Completed Job Expiration Time section**, specify the amount of time the completed job history is retained. The default setting is 7 days. To retain a history of all completed jobs, select the No Expiration option button.

11. In the **Recycle Threshold** section, specify the number of documents translated by the translation process before it is restarted. The default setting is 100.

12. In the **Office 97-2003 Document Scanning** section, disable or enable Office 97-2003 document scanning. Enabling this setting adds additional checks against the document before they are opened. Enabling this setting can have an impact on server performance. The default setting is No.

13. Click OK to save your settings.

Note

Additional information on configuring the Machine Translation Service for SharePoint Server 2013 can be found at http://technet.microsoft.com/en-us/library/jj553772.aspx.

Configuring the Managed Metadata Service

Managed metadata in SharePoint Server 2013 refers to a hierarchical collection of terms used to describe various types of items, such as documents and list items. The terms can be managed using the Term Store Management tool and then exposed, along with content types, via the Managed Metadata Service in applications, lists, and libraries. This allows multiple site collections, web applications, and even farms to share terms and content types. SharePoint Server 2013 has simplified the process, allowing the use of managed metadata to drive navigation within the farm. This type of navigation can be enabled in the Navigation settings at the Site collection level.

> **Note**
>
> The Managed Metadata Service application will be discussed in more detail in Chapter 8, "Configuring Enterprise Content Types and Metadata".

> **Note**
>
> Additional information on the Managed Metadata Service can be found at http://social.technet.microsoft.com/wiki/contents/articles/12713.sharepoint-2013-how-to-configure-managed-metadata-service.aspx.

Configuring PerformancePoint Services

PerformancePoint Services provides tools to easily manage and analyze data stored in back-end systems. Those tools include dashboards, key performance indicators (KPIs), filters, and analytic reports. Originally, PerformancePoint was a standalone product built on IIS; the product was built in to SharePoint with the Server 2010 release, and with the introduction of the SharePoint Server 2013 product, it provides better reports, iPad support, and a more closely integrated authentication model with the SharePoint Server 2013 platform.

Manage the PerformancePoint Services Application

Perform the following steps to configure or manage the PerformancePoint Services application:

1. Go to Central Administration, Application Management, Manage Service Applications and click the link for the PerformancePoint Services Application.

2. On the Manage PerformancePoint Services page, click the link for PerformancePoint Services Application Settings.

3. On the PerformancePoint Service Application Settings page, configure the following settings:

- **Secure Store and Unattended Service Account**—In this section, set the following:

  - **Secure Store Service Application**—Identify the secure store application you want to use with the PerformancePoint service.

  - **Unattended Service Account**—Set the username and password for the unattended service account or the target application ID for the Unattended Service Account Target Application ID.

- **Comments**—Users with appropriate permissions can annotate scorecard cells in both Dashboard Designer and on a deployed SharePoint site. Multiple comments can be made per annotation:

  - **Enable comments**—Checked by default.

  - **Maximum Number of Annotated Cells per Scorecard**—Default setting is 1000.

- **Cache**—The cache allows the system to temporarily store frequently accessed items. This behavior decreases load times for future requests.

  - **KPI Icon Cache**—Set the maximum amount of time (in seconds) an item may remain in cache. The default setting is 10 seconds.

- **Analysis Services EffectiveUserName**—This setting provides the capability to use a managed account to access PerformancePoint services.

  - Enabling this setting applies to all Analysis Services data sources configured for per-user authentication.

  - Using EffectiveUserName requires that the PerformancePoint managed account is an administrator in Analysis Services.

  - EffectiveUserNames is *not* supported for PowerPivot use over https.

- **Data Sources**—This section allows you to set the duration of the response before a data source query is canceled. The default setting is 300 seconds.

- **Filters**—This section allows you to specify how long user-selected filters persist and how often to clear them when they *expire.* You can also specify the maximum number of items to retrieve into a filter of type tree.

- **Remember User Filter Selections For**—This setting is in days and defaults to 90.

- **Maximum Number of Items to Load in Filter Tree**— Identify the maximum number of items that will be allowed to load into a filter tree. The default setting is 5000 items.

- **Identify the Search Results Limit.** Allows you to set a limit on the number of items returned as part of a search query. The default setting is 100 items.

- **Select Measure Control**—Set the maximum number of measures to retrieve into a dashboard. By default, the maximum measure to load into Select Measure Control is 1000.

- **Show Details**—This section allows you to limit the number of rows returned when a user clicks Show Details.

  - Initial retrieval limit is 1000 rows.

  - Maximum retrieval limit can be

  - Fixed limit with a default of 10000 rows

  - Limit controlled by Analysis Services

- **Decomposition Tree**—This section allows you to set the maximum number of individual items, per level, returned to the decomposition tree visualization. The maximum number for this setting is 1,000,000.

4. Click OK to save and continue.

Configure Trusted Data Source Locations

By default all SharePoint locations are trusted. To specify that only certain locations be trusted, take the following steps:

1. Go to Central Administration, Application Management, Manage Service Applications and click the PerformancePoint Services link.

2. On the Manage PerformancePoint Services page, click the Trusted Data Source Locations link.

3. Select the Only Specific Location option button; when the setting is applied, you will see the Add Trusted Data Location link activate.

4. In the modal dialog box, enter the URL of the SharePoint location you are going to use as your trusted data source location; then select the Location Type, add a description, and click OK.

5. Click OK to save your changes and continue.

Configure Trusted Content Locations

By default all SharePoint locations are trusted. To specify that only certain locations be trusted, take the following steps:

1. Go to Central Administration, Application Management, Manage Service Applications and click the PerformancePoint Services link.

2. On the Manage PerformancePoint Services page click the Trusted Content Locations link.

3. Select the Only Specific Location option button; when the setting is applied, you will see the Add Trusted Data Location link activate.

4. In the modal dialog box enter the URL of the SharePoint location you are going to use as your trusted data source location; then select the Location Type, add a description, and click OK.

5. Click OK to save your changes and continue.

> **Note**
>
> Additional information on configuring PerformancePoint Services can be found at http://technet.microsoft.com/en-us/library/ee748644.aspx.

Configuring Search Services

SharePoint Server 2013 introduces many changes to how search manages and displays results. The most important aspect of those changes is the consolidation of all three SharePoint-related search entities. In the past, where there has been SharePoint Foundation Search, SharePoint Server Search, and possibly FAST Search for SharePoint 2010, there is now just SharePoint Server Search. By combining the search engines and their underlying technologies, SharePoint Server 2013 provides a much more powerful and flexible search tool.

> **Note**
>
> The Search Services application is discussed in more detail in Chapter 8.

Add a Content Source

You must be a service application administrator for the Search Service Application to add a new content source;

1. Go to Central Administration, Application Management, Manage Service Applications and click the link for the Search Service Application.

2. On the Search Administration page, go to the Crawling section in the left navigation pane, and click Content Sources.

3. On the Manage Content Sources page, click New Content Source.

4. On the Add Content Source page, in the Name section, type a name for the content source in the Name text box.

5. In the Content Source Type section, choose the type of content to be crawled.

6. In the Start Address section, type the URLs the crawler will initiate from in the Type Start Addresses Below (one per line) box.

7. In the Crawl Settings section, select the desired crawling behavior.

8. In the Crawl Schedules section, select or define a schedule for full crawls and incremental crawls. Full crawls crawl all content defined by the content source, whereas incremental crawls crawl only content that has changed since the last crawl.

9. In the Content Source Priority section, select the priority for the content source.

10. Click OK to save the new content source.

Add a Crawl Rule

You must be a service application administrator for the search service application to add a crawl rule:

1. Go to Central Administration, Application Management, Manage Service Applications and click the link for the Search Service Application.

2. On the Search Administration page, in the Crawling section in the left navigation pane, click Crawl Rules.

3. Click New Crawl Rule.

4. On the Add New Crawl Rule, in the Path section, type the path to which the crawl rule will apply.

5. To use regular expressions instead of wildcard characters in the path, select the Use Regular Expression Syntax for Matching This Rule check box.

6. In the Crawl Configuration section, choose between the following:

   ■ Choose Exclude All Items in This Path to exclude items in the path from crawls. Choose the Exclude Complex URLs (URLs That Contain Question Marks (?)) option if you want to exclude URLs that have parameters that use the question mark notation.

   ■ Choose Include All Items in This Path to include items in the path in crawls.

   ■ Choose the Follow Links on the URL Without Crawling the URL Itself option to omit the starting URL from crawls.

   ■ Choose the Crawl Complex URLs (URLs That Contain Question Marks (?)) option to include URLs that have parameters that use the question mark notation in crawls.

   ■ Choose the Crawl SharePoint Content as HTTP Pages option to use the HTTP protocol to crawl SharePoint content rather than the special protocol normally used. If you choose this option, item permissions for crawled content will not be stored.

7. In the Specify Authentication section (if available), choose the authentication mechanism. You have the following choices:

   ■ Specify a Different Content Access Account

   ■ Specify Client Certificate

   ■ Specify Form Credentials

   ■ Use Cookies for Crawling

   ■ Anonymous Access

8. Click OK to save the new crawl rule.

Start a Full Crawl

Perform the following steps to start a full crawl of a content source:

1. Go to Central Administration, Application Management, Manage Service Applications and click the link for the Search Service Application.

2. On the Search Administration page, in the Crawling section in the left navigation pane, click Content Sources.

3. On the Manage Content Sources page, point to the content source you want, click the arrow that appears, and then choose Start Full Crawl.

You can start an incremental crawl, pause a crawl, resume a crawl, or stop a crawl by following the preceding steps and choosing the appropriate option from the content source context menu.

Note

Additional information on configuring the Search Service can be found in Chapter 10, "Enterprise Search.

Configuring Secure Store Services

The Secure Store service stores and manages credentials used to access a variety of external data stores securely. Those credentials are typically in the form of usernames and passwords, but depending on the target application the use of other authorization types could be required:

- PIN number
- Key
- Certificate
- Certificate password

All credentials and their application ID mappings are stored in an encrypted database.

Create and Configure a New Target Application ID

To create and configure a new Target Application ID, take the following steps:

1. Go to Central Administration, Application Management, Manage Service Applications, and click the link for the Secure Store service application.

2. On the Secure Store Service Application page, click the Edit tab in the ribbon at the top of the page.

3. In the Manage Target Application section, click New.

4. On the Create New Secure Store Target Application page, configure the following sections:

- **Target Application ID**—Set a unique identifier for the target application. This cannot be changed after you have created the target application.

- **Display Name**—Set an easily identifiable display name for the target application.

- **Contact E-mail**—Set the contact email of the person responsible for the target application for notification purposes.

- **Target Application Type**—Identify the type of credential mapping the target application will use. The two primary types of mappings are

  - **Individual mappings**—Each individual requiring access to the target application is mapped to a unique set of credentials. This is especially useful when auditing of the target application is a requirement but may come at the expense of server performance.

  - **Group mapping**—All members of a domain group are mapped to the same set of credentials. Group mappings are easier to manage and maintain. Anytime members must be added or removed, they are simply added to the group and no additional credential mapping has to occur.

- **Target Application Page URL**—The options available here will vary based on the target application type you identified previously:

  - **Group and Group Restricted**—The target application page URL will default to None. You can use a custom page but cannot use the default page.

- **Group Ticket**—The target application page URL will default to None. You do have the same options listed in Group and Group Restricted as well as the option to set a ticket timeout (in minutes).

  - **Individual and Individual** Restricted—You may use any of the three options: User Default Page, Use Custom Page, or None.

  - **Individual Ticket**—Has the capability to leverage all three options as listed in the Individual and Individual Restricted section, in addition to the capability to set a ticket timeout on the target application.

5. Click Next to continue the target application creation process.

6. In the next screen of the target application creation process, configure the credentials that will be used for the target application:

   ■ In the Field Name section, enter the labels that will be displayed on the authentication page. Typically these labels would match the field type you select.

   ■ In the Field Type section, select the field type for the credentials to be used.

   ■ In the Masked section, check the box to mask the text that users will enter in the credentials boxes.

7. Click Next to continue the target application process.

   ■ **Target Application Administrators**—In this section use the People Picker to identify those individuals that will be administrators of the target application.

   ■ **Members**—(Available only when the target application type is a group.) Add individuals to the group membership using the People Picker. The People Picker allows you to add Active Directory security groups here.

8. Click OK to complete the target application creation process.

Note

Additional information on configuring the Secure Store Service Application can be found at the following link: http://technet.microsoft.com/en-us/library/ee806866.aspx.

Configuring the State Service

The State Service is used by multiple components of SharePoint Server 2013 to store temporary user data across related HTTP requests in a SQL Server database. The State Service is required for use with InfoPath Forms Services 2013 and workflows within the SharePoint Server 2013 farm. The state service can be created using the Farm Configuration Wizard or Windows PowerShell. Using Windows PowerShell gives you more control over database and service names than using the Farm Configuration Wizard.

Take the following steps to configure the State Service using Windows PowerShell:

1. Start the Windows PowerShell interface in Administrative mode:

   ■ In Windows Server 2012, access the Start page and find the tile for SharePoint 2013 Management Shell. Right-click the tile and in the taskbar at the bottom of the screen select Run as Administrator.

   ■ In Windows Server 2008 R2, go to Start, All Programs, SharePoint 2013; right-click the SharePoint 2013 Management Shell; and select Run as Administrator.

2. To create the actual service application, type the following Windows PowerShell command:

```
$ServiceApp = NewSPStateServiceApplication -Name
"<StateServiceName>"
```

3. The new State Service will require that a State Service database be created and associated with the new State Service application:

```
New-SPStateServiceDatabase -Name
"<StateServiceDatabase>" -ServiceApplication
$serviceApp
```

4. Create a State Service application proxy and associate it with the server's default proxy group using the following command:

```
New-SPStateServiceApplicationProxy -Name
<ProxyApplicationName> -"Servic3Application"
$serviceApp -DefaultProxyGroup.
```

Configuring the Visio Graphics Service

The Visio Graphics Service in SharePoint Server 2013 offers significant upgrades and improvements over the past versions, including the capability to easily build workflows that support stages, steps, and loops; embed comments directly into Visio diagrams from the browser; refresh data from BCS external lists and SQL Azure; and render as PNG or Silverlight.

To configure the Visio Graphics Service, take the following steps:

1. Go to Central Administration, Application Management, Manage Service Applications, and click the link for the Visio Graphics service application.

2. On the Manage the Visio Graphics Service page, access the Global Settings heading.

   ■ **Maximum Web Drawing Size, in MBs**—Set the maximum size allowed for a web drawing. It is important to make sure this setting is large enough to allow complicated drawings to render while not negatively impacting server performance.

   ■ **Minimum Cache Age, in minutes**—A shorter cache age will increase the CPU and memory usage on the server but will allow for more frequent data refresh operations.

   ■ **Maximum Cache Age, in minutes**—Longer cache ages decrease file I/O and CPU load but will increase memory usage on the server.

   ■ **Maximum Recalc Duration, in seconds**—Determines how long a data refresh operation will run before timing out.

   ■ **Maximum Cache Size, in MBs**—Larger size limits could result in the services using more disk resources, whereas smaller limits may have a negative impact on performance.

   ■ **External Data**—Identify and set the Application ID used by the Secure Store Service to reference unattended account credentials. These credentials are required when connecting to external data sources such as SQL.

3. On the Manage the Visio Graphics Service page, access the Visio Graphics Service Trusted Data Providers heading. This page allows you to create and manage trusted data providers for the Visio Graphics Service. New trusted data types must be one of the following types:

   ■ OLE DB

   ■ SQL

   ■ ODBC

   ■ ODBC with DSN

   ■ SharePoint Lists

   ■ Custom Data Provider

   ■ To add a New Trusted Data Provider, take the following steps:

      1. Click the link for Add a New Trusted Data Provider.

      2. Enter a value for the Trusted Data Provider ID.

      3. Enter a value for the Trusted Data Provider Type.

   4. Enter a value for the Trusted Data Provider Type
      Description.

■ To edit a Visio Graphics Service Trusted Data Provider, take
  the following steps:

   1. In the list of trusted data providers, select the trusted data
      provider you want to edit, click the drop-down menu, and
      select Edit Trusted Data Provider.

   2. Edit the fields of the trusted data provider type.

   3. Click OK to save your changes.

■ To Delete a Visio Graphics Service Trusted Data Provider
  type, take the following steps:

   1. In the list of trusted data providers, select the trusted data
      provider you want to edit, click the drop-down menu, and
      select Delete Trusted Data Provider.

   2. In the dialog box warning, click OK if you want to delete
      the item from the configuration.

Configuring the User Profile Service

The User Profile Service application provides a centralized store for user
information. Table 4.1 describes the functions of the User Profile Service
in more detail.

Table 4.1   User Profile Service Application

Feature	Description
User Profiles	Used to store information about users and to import and synchronize from various sources. It is highly customizable and searchable.
Organization Profiles	Used to store information about an organization.
Audiences	Used to target content to users based on user profile information.
My Sites	Used to create personal sites where users can store data such as documents and links, connect with colleagues, and update profile information.
Social Tags and Notes	Used to provide users with the capability to add tags to items in SharePoint or to external items such as web pages, blog posts, and so forth. Notes can also be posted to any type of SharePoint page. Administrators have the ability to remove tags and notes for a user or to disable them altogether.

> **Note**
>
> The User Profile Service application is highly configurable and will be discussed in more detail in Chapter 13, "Configuring the Social Experience."

Configuring the Word Automation Service

The Word Automation Service provides unattended, server-side conversion of documents into formats that are supported by the Microsoft Office Word client application. Tasks that used to require the Word client can now be automated on the server without having to install the client at all. The Word Automation Service supports the following file formats:

- Open XML Format (.docx, .docm, .dotx, .dotm)
- Word 97-2003 files (.doc, .dot)
- Rich Text files (.rtf)
- Single-file web pages (.mht, .mhtml)
- Word 2003 XML documents (.xml)

The Word Automation Service can save files in all the formats listed, as well as the Portable Document Format (.pdf) and XML Paper Specification (.xps) formats. New functionality in SharePoint Server 2013 includes the following items:

- On-demand document conversion.
- **Stream support**—Developers will be able to leverage Word Automation services on files stored outside of SharePoint Server 2013.
- Notifications or update of items in SharePoint Server 2013 after document conversion has been completed.

Configure the Word Automation Service

You must be a member of the Farm Administrators group to configure the Word Automation Service:

1. Go to Central Administration, Application Management, Manage Service Applications and click the link for the Word Automation Services.

2. On the Word Automation Services page, in the Supported File Formats section, choose which file formats should be supported by

selecting the check box next to the format. By default, all document types are selected.

3. In the Embedded Font Support section, specify whether to disable embedded fonts. The default setting is No.

4. In the Maximum Memory Usage section, specify the percentage of available memory that should be used by the Word Automation Service. The default setting is 100.

5. In the Recycle Threshold section, specify the number of documents that should be converted by a conversion process before they are recycled. The default setting is 100.

6. In the Word 97-2003 Document Scanning section, specify whether to disable Word 97-2003 document scanning. This provides added security for Word 97-2003 documents, but it does incur some overhead cost. This feature should be disabled only if all documents loaded by the service can be trusted. The default setting is No.

7. In the Conversion Processes section, specify the number of conversion processes created on each server used by the service application. A different conversion process must be used for each conversion that is performed simultaneously. The default setting is 1.

8. In the Conversion Throughput section, set the following:

   ■ Specify the frequency (in minutes) with which groups of conversions are started. The default setting is 15.

   ■ Specify the number of conversions to start (per conversion process). The default setting is 300.

9. In the Job Monitoring section, specify the length of time (in minutes) before conversion status is monitored and, if necessary, restarted. The default setting is 5.

10. In the Maximum Conversion Attempts section, specify the maximum number of times a conversion is attempted before its status is set to Failed. The default setting is 2.

11. In the Maximum Synchronous Conversion Requests section, specify the Maximum number of synchronous conversion requests (per server). The default is 25.

12. Click OK to save the settings.

Configuring the Work Management Service

The Work Management Service aggregates tasks from across multiple systems into a single location and view. Currently the systems that the Work Management Service Application works with are Microsoft SharePoint Server 2013, Microsoft Exchange Server 2013, and Microsoft Project Server 2013. This functionality for the aggregation of tasks from within the SharePoint farm does not require additional configuration in SharePoint; it is built in to the Office stack using a provider model that will be easily extensible in the future.

Any tasks entered by the user or assigned to the user in Outlook, SharePoint, Project, or even using a mobile client will be aggregated within SharePoint Server 2013 on the user's personal My Site, providing a single location to see all tasks assigned to them in one location.

The work management service leverages SharePoint Server 2013 search functionality to aggregate SharePoint tasks in the users My Site. Tasks will be available after a full crawl of the SharePoint 2013 farm.

CHAPTER 5

Scaling Web and Service Applications

- Server Roles
- Preparing for Scaling Out to a Server Farm
- Scaling Farms with Server and Storage Groups
- Scaling Web Applications
- Scaling System Services and Service Applications

The two primary reasons for scaling out a SharePoint 2013 Server farm are to achieve high availability and to improve performance. For example, those organizations looking for high availability need at least two web servers, two application servers, and a clustered Microsoft SQL Server back end. If top performance is strictly the goal, you might have only a single four-core database server, one very fast web server, and a single application server. Whatever your goal, be aware that Microsoft SharePoint Server 2013 does not have as many limitations regarding scaling and topology choices as earlier versions. But this increased flexibility in server farm design might make it difficult for some administrators to design an appropriate physical and logical farm topology. If you are not sure how to design your specific server farm architecture, begin with a topology discussed in this chapter, and change it to meet your needs.

Remember that these topologies are not concrete rules on which to build your specific implementation; they are simply real-world suggestions about where to begin. Most medium-size and larger organizations would do well to begin with an implementation that has at least two web servers, an application server, and a clustered SQL Server back end.

> **Note**
>
> We mentioned the concept of clustering here. When using the term *clustering* in conjunction with SharePoint, we are talking about a SQL Server architecture that supports multiple SQL servers configured into a Windows Failover Cluster (WFC). This failover cluster is a combination of one or more SQL servers and two or more shared disks that will keep the SharePoint Server 2013 farm online in the event one of the servers in the cluster fails.

A cluster could also be used to provide some redundancy during patching and maintenance windows if required. The cluster appears as a single server to the network but has functionality that will provide automatic or manual failover from one node to the next in the event the current node becomes unavailable. If you are using SQL Server 2012 as your database server, you will also have the opportunity to leverage AlwaysOn Availability Groups (AAG). AAG is different from WFC, even though it uses WFC to function. AAG can also be combined with a classic WFC to provide some hardcore high availability for local and geographic failovers.

> **Note**
>
> For more information on high availability and SQL clustering using SQL Server 2008 R2, visit http://technet.microsoft.com/en-us/library/ms190202(v=sql.105).aspx.

> **Note**
>
> For more information on high availability using SQL Server 2012 and AlwaysOn Failover Clusters, visit http://technet.microsoft.com/en-us/library/ms190202.aspx.

Server Roles

Every SharePoint Server 2013 farm is made up of multiple Windows servers with each server filling a specific role within the farm. The three most common roles within the farm are the Web Server role, the Application Server role, and the Database Server role. Depending on the size and configuration of the farm, each will fall into a specific tier within the farm.

Web Server

Depending on the size and configuration of the SharePoint farm, the web server may fill several roles. At its most basic level, the role of the web server is to host web pages and web services, to direct incoming requests to the appropriate application server, and process requests from end users. In smaller SharePoint Server 2013 implementations, the web server may also host SharePoint application services normally run on application servers. In a single-server farm all three roles will be found on the sole server in the farm. In medium and large farms, multiple servers may exist as a way of providing redundancy.

Application Server

The application server hosts and manages the service features of the SharePoint farm. Application servers provide a host for all, or some, service application features. In large implementations, multiple servers can be added as application servers to the farm to provide redundancy for critical service applications. In small farms, the application and web server roles are often combined on one server. In very large implementations it may be necessary to have a farm dedicated to hosting the service applications for the SharePoint implementation.

Database Server

The database server acts as the data and configuration storage location for the farm. Databases can be hosted all on one server, or they can be deployed across multiple servers. Those instances of multiple databases can be configured to leveraged clustering and mirroring for redundancy.

Note

In dedicated services farms, the web server role is not necessary. Web servers in the remote farms contact the services farms directly.

Preparing for Scaling Out to a Server Farm

If you plan to scale out your farm, it is important to remember that the first server you run the SharePoint Products Configuration Wizard (PSCONFIG.exe) on will be the server that hosts the Central Administration web application. This server can also host other services, such as the Microsoft SharePoint Workflow Timer Service and the Microsoft SharePoint Foundation Subscription Settings Service.

In addition to server hardware planning, you should also plan your network infrastructure in advance to provide the best level of service possible. A gigabit Ethernet (Gig-E) network infrastructure should be considered the minimum size in most enterprise farm scenarios, whereas 100 Base-T network speeds are sufficient in smaller farms. Also, having multiple switches and using Network Interface Card (NIC) teaming, when possible, can add fault tolerance to your solution.

When planning for a farm, be sure to include the SQL Server installation in the planning process because it will be the foundation for your new farm. If you have database administrators (DBAs) on staff, include them in the planning from the beginning. A poorly designed and implemented SQL Server installation can easily become the bottleneck in a SharePoint products server farm.

Single-Server Farms

A single-server farm, shown in Figure 5.1, is configured with every component—including a supported SQL Server instance—installed and configured on one server. This configuration is ideal for evaluation, testing, development, isolated departmental implementations with only a small number of users (usually less than 100), and small volumes of data.

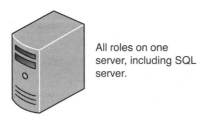

All roles on one server, including SQL server.

FIGURE 5.1
A single-server farm.

Two-Tier Farms

A two-tier farm, shown in Figure 5.2, consists of one server for hosting all SharePoint Server 2010 web and service applications, whereas another server is dedicated to hosting the SQL databases. If availability is important to your organization, a clustered or mirrored database server is recommended, which will give the database server a higher degree of availability. Any farm deployed using this architecture could possibly handle up to as many as 10,000 users, depending on the hardware, user processes, and user concurrency.

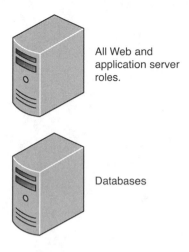
All Web and
application server
roles.

Databases

FIGURE 5.2
A two-tier farm.

Two-Tier Small Farms

With two SharePoint Server 2013 servers hosting a combination of services, both typically host the web services and have a SQL database server
at the back end. Again, SQL Server clustering or mirroring should be
leveraged for high availability at the database tier. Be aware that simply
adding another web server to the farm does not necessarily increase availability. To increase availability, you must implement load balancing using
the Microsoft Windows Server 2012 Network Load Balancing (NLB)
service or install a hardware load-balancing solution. A two-tier small
farm, shown in Figure 5.3, is not an optimal solution for load balancing
because processing is usually not evenly distributed across web servers. It
is a reasonably priced solution to start off with, and having two web
servers provides a level of fault tolerance.

Changes to the query processing component in SharePoint 2013 affect how
the components of the search service are distributed in the farm. The query
processing component has been changed so that much of the CPU and disk
load have been offloaded from SQL Server. The result is that the query
processing component will require more local resources.

> **Note**
>
> If you run the query processing component of search on your farm web
> server, you must ensure that these servers have a sufficient amount of
> resources to operate efficiently.

Web Server
Query Server

All SharePoint
Databases

Web Server
Query Server
All Other App Roles

FIGURE 5.3
A two-tier small farm.

Three-Tier Small Farms Not Optimized for Search

The standard three-tier small farm configuration, shown in Figure 5.4, consists of two web servers, one application server, and the SQL database server at the back end. This design is able to handle 10,000 to 20,000 users. The design is easily scaled by adding additional web or application servers to handle higher workloads. Load balancing the web traffic using Windows Server 2012 NLB or a third-party hardware solution allows you to take advantage of having additional web servers in the farm. The three-tier small farm will be among the most common farm architectures implemented for SharePoint Server 2013.

Three-Tier Small Farms Optimized for Search

For organizations wanting an optimized search function within its SharePoint Server 2013 implementation, the standard three-tier configuration (shown in Figure 5.5) is used, with two notable differences. The database server is configured to offload search traffic to a dedicated database at the back end, and the query and index roles are configured to run across the web and application servers. With hardware dedicated to search databases, and the query and index roles, this topology is optimized for search to work well in environments with up to 10 million items in the index.

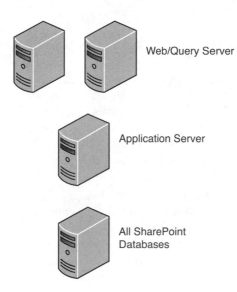

FIGURE 5.4
A three-tier small farm.

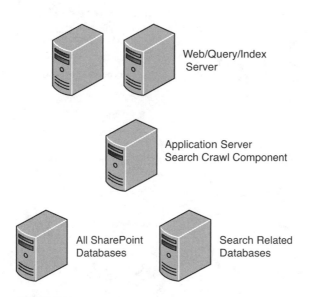

FIGURE 5.5
A three-tier small farm optimized for search.

Medium Farms

A medium farm, shown in Figure 5.6, consists of multiple web front-end servers, multiple application servers, and a dedicated SQL Server instance. Depending on the hardware and concurrency, the configuration can support up to 50,000 users and scale for search to serve approximately 40 million items. The number of users will affect the requirement for web servers. A reasonable metric is to factor 10,000 users per web server as a starting point and reduce the number of users based on how heavily the servers are utilized. If there is heavy use of client services, there will be a corresponding increase in the load on web servers.

When designing a medium-sized SharePoint Server 2013 farm, a logical starting point is to begin with all application server roles, except for search roles, on a single server. From there, based on utilization, consider adding more servers with all nonsearch roles installed, or add more servers to dedicate to specific services. For example, if performance data indicates that Excel Services is using a disproportionate amount of resources, offload this service to a dedicated server. Appropriately increase the number of database servers based on the volume of content in the environment and sizing targets for the organization. The use of monitoring software, such as Systems Center Operations Manager, can create a baseline for performance and give you insight into server farm performance.

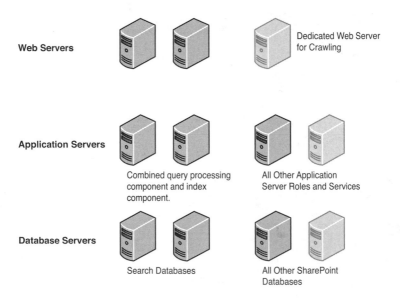

Web Servers   Dedicated Web Server for Crawling

Application Servers   Combined query processing component and index component.   All Other Application Server Roles and Services

Database Servers   Search Databases   All Other SharePoint Databases

FIGURE 5.6
A medium farm.

Large Farms

A large farm configuration, shown in Figure 5.7, consists of multiple web servers and dedicated application servers running various services, as well as multiple SQL Server instances hosting the services data through mirrored SQL Server instances, clustered SQL Server instances, AlwaysOn Availability Groups, or all three. This solution provides the high performance and resiliency necessary for large deployments. The recommended practice for scaling out a large farm is to group services or databases with similar performance characteristics onto dedicated servers and then scale out the servers as a group. Search indexes should be spread across two servers and any replicas of those indexes must run on separate physical hosts. The following topology illustrates a practical example of this concept.

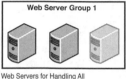
Web Server Group 1

Web Servers for Handling All
Incoming Requests

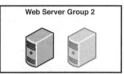
Web Server Group 2

Dedicated Web Server(s) for Crawling and
Administration

Application Servers

**Application Server
Group 1**

Query Component and
Index Servers

**Application Server
Group 2**

All Other Search Components

**Application Server
Group 3**

All Other Services Including
Central Administration

**Application Server
Group 4**

Servers for Running
Sandboxed Code

Database Servers

**Database group 1
Group 1**

Content and Configuration
Databases

**Database group 2
Group 2**

Search Databases

**Database group 1
Group 3**

All Oher SharePoint
Databases

FIGURE 5.7
A large farm.

Office Web Apps

With the release of SharePoint 2013, Office Web Apps is no longer a service or add-in component and has become a standalone product. The architecture for Office Web Apps has changed to the point that a dedicated farm is required to host the application and provide those features and functionality to SharePoint 2013.

These changes allow administrators to manage Office Web Apps farms independently of their SharePoint environments, permitting actions such as applying updates and managing scale and performance with minimal impact to the SharePoint farm(s) that the Office Web Apps farm serves.

In addition to more independent management of Office Web Apps, the new model allows for viewing and editing documents in multiple SharePoint farms, viewing files from Lync and Exchange, and integration of local file servers.

> **Note**
>
> The Office Web Apps (OWA) Server architecture does not have any sort of database requirements. Configuration information for the OWA farm is stored in a configuration file on the master server of the farm. For more information on Office Web Apps 2013, see http://technet.microsoft.com/en-us/library/jj219456.aspx.

Scaling Farms with Server and Storage Groups

The concept of Server and Storage Groups is not new, but with the introduction of the Request Management Service it becomes a much more flexible and powerful concept when implemented appropriately. Implementation of this concept is typically seen in large farm environments, not small farms.

It is recommended that when scaling out a medium or large SharePoint farm you group services, service applications, or databases that have similar performance characteristics or functions onto dedicated server resources. These dedicated servers are then scaled out as a group based on service applications, services, or databases hosted on that specific server. For example, in Figure 5.7:

- Web Server Group 1 handles all incoming requests. This means that any incoming request, whether it is from an end user, a service, or a service application, is addressed by the servers in this group.

- Web Server Group 2 provides dedicated servers for crawling content across the farm as well as the search administrative functionality for the farm.

- Application Server Group 1 hosts the query processing component and index servers that are a part of the search topology.

- Application Server Group 2 hosts the remaining components of the search service. This includes the contents and analytics processing components.

- Application Server Group 3 runs all the remaining services available in this particular farm. This would include Excel Services, Work Management Services, Access Services, and the Managed Metadata Service, to name just a few.

- Application Server Group 4 provides a location for running isolated code modules or applications.

- Database Group 1 provides the storage location for the farm content and configuration databases.

- Database Group 2 hosts the search databases.

- Database Group 3 provides the storage location for all other SharePoint databases. This may include the databases associated with the User Profile Service, Managed Metadata Service, or the Machine Translation Service.

- Server Groups are logical groupings of servers that host similar services, service applications, or databases, which are then scaled out as a group.

- Storage Groups are logical groupings of similar types of databases, which are then scaled out based on need.

The following is a practical example of how server groups may be configured in a SharePoint 2013 farm. There are many ways to break out the servers in the farm along with the services each runs and group them together logically.

> **Note**
>
> It is considered a best practice to configure the storage architecture of your storage farm so that databases of similar characteristics share the same spindle, or physical location, on the server. For example, in a SharePoint farm used primarily for collaboration, the configuration might look like the following:

1. tempdb data files and transaction logs on the fastest spindle.
2. Content database transaction log files on the second spindle.
3. Search related databases except for the Search administration on the third spindle.
4. Content database data files on spindle 4.
5. Administration databases on spindle 5.

Request Management Service

The Request Management Service is new to SharePoint 2013 and provides SharePoint and administrators the ability to better control which servers should be handling incoming requests for the farm. This is done through the use of a rules-based approach allowing SharePoint 2013 administrators the capability to determine how a given request will be handled by their SharePoint farm based on the configuration settings put in place.

The capability to manage incoming requests in this manner increases in importance as the size of the SharePoint environment grows. The larger the farm, the more important it is to be able to determine how incoming requests are addressed and handled by SharePoint. This may make it sound like Request Management is intended to replace traditional load balancing within your SharePoint farm. This is not the case; Request Management is intended to augment load balancing by providing functionality for incoming SharePoint-related requests that the load balancing solution does not clearly understand. By leveraging Request Management within the SharePoint farm, administrators gain more flexibility when dealing with some of the common issues associated with large-scale deployments (overloaded servers, poor performance, and the like).

Request Management allows administrators to determine how SharePoint will handle specific incoming requests. Some examples of these capabilities follow:

- Route incoming requests to servers based on the health score of the server. The health score of a server is a numeric value from 0 to 10, where 0 is the healthiest. This number is derived from the Policy Engine health rule, which dynamically updates the health score of the server. This score cannot be changed manually.

- Identify harmful or malicious requests, such as web robots or spiders, and deny them immediately.

- Prioritize requests by throttling lower-priority requests, such as search crawlers, in favor of higher-priority requests, such as end user requests.

- Route requests of a specific type, such as InfoPath or workflows, to a server dedicated to serving those requests.

- Simplify the troubleshooting process by isolating traffic to a specific server.

- In large-scale SharePoint 2013 farms, Request Management will become a key factor in not only scaling your farm, but better managing the performance of your SharePoint servers.

Note

The configuration of the Request Management Service is covered in more detail in Chapter 2, "Configuring Farm Operations."

Scaling Web Applications

Organizations can begin the process of expanding the scope of an installed SharePoint Server 2013 base by adding servers to the various tiers to produce the scale that is needed. As part of the installation process, it is recommended that the account used to perform the initial SharePoint Server 2013 installation be used when adding servers to the farm. Subsequent servers added to the farm need to be prepared in the same fashion as the first server. The primary installation difference is that you'll connect to an existing farm instead of creating a new farm. As you progress through the next few sections, make design notes on the nuances of each service and how those will affect your design.

A significant portion of data that is being served by SharePoint Server 2013 will be delivered from a SQL Server database. The recommended maximum ratio of web servers per SQL Server cluster is 8:1. Although you can scale out beyond this point, doing so is not recommended. However, you are not limited to eight WFE servers in a farm because you can have multiple SQL Server installations, each with a set of eight WFE servers. When you require throughput greater than is possible with eight WFE servers, you can add more SQL Server clusters as required. But don't forget: only one SQL Server cluster can host your configuration database. The SQL Server cluster that hosts the configuration database should be monitored constantly for failure.

To add more SQL Server clusters to your server farm, select a different SQL Server when creating a new content database. However, note that having more than one SQL Server cluster creates complexity in your server farm performance, disaster recovery plan, and troubleshooting efforts.

Adding a Web Server to the Farm

To scale out from a single web server that already hosts web applications, you need to install SharePoint Server 2013 on another server in the same Active Directory domain. Preferably, you should scale to a server that is on the same IP subnet and that does not host any other applications. It is also preferable to have the hardware identically configured. To add another WFE server, you must take the following steps:

1. Install SharePoint Server 2013 using the installation binaries to include any service packs or cumulative updates.

2. Run the SharePoint 2013 Products Configuration Wizard to guide you through the process of provisioning additional servers in the farm. If the SharePoint 2013 Products Configuration Wizard does not launch automatically, you can find it located at Start, All Programs, Microsoft SharePoint 2013 Products.

3. On the Welcome to SharePoint Products page, click Next.

4. A dialog box appears, shown in Figure 5.8, stating that some services might need to be restarted during configuration. Click Yes to proceed.

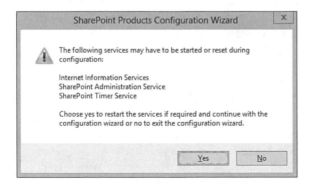

FIGURE 5.8
Click Yes to continue the configuration.

5. On the Connect to a Server Farm page, as shown in Figure 5.9, select Connect to an Existing Server Farm, and then click Next.

Remember, a server farm is a configuration database. So connecting to an existing farm means connecting to an existing configuration database.

FIGURE 5.9
Connect to an existing server farm.

6. The Specify Configuration Database Settings page allows you to specify a configuration database. You should enter the following values:

   ■ In the Database Server text box (shown in Figure 5.10), type the server name of the database server.

   ■ Click the Retrieve Database Names button to retrieve the name of the configuration databases hosted on the SQL Server instance. By default, the name of the configuration database will be SharePoint_Config.

7. As you can see in Figure 5.11, the next step is to enter a value in the farm Passphrase text box and click Next. If the passphrase is lost or misplaced, you can, as a last resort, use the SharePoint 2010 Management Shell to reset the farm passphrase.

FIGURE 5.10
Verify all information and click Next.

FIGURE 5.11
Enter your text in the Password check box, and click Next.

Note

The Windows PowerShell Set-SPPassPhrase cmdlet sets the passphrase to a new Passphrase value. If the LocalServerOnly parameter is not used, the farm encryption key is reencrypted with the new value and attempts to propagate this value to all other servers in the farm. If the LocalServerOnly parameter is used, this is updated on the local machine only, and the farm encryption key is not changed. The Passphrase value must be the same on all servers in the farm if the farm is to function correctly. So if the passphrase fails to propagate to all servers, the LocalServerOnly parameter can be used to set the remaining servers to the new Passphrase value manually.

8. The Completing the SharePoint Products Configuration Wizard page, shown in Figure 5.12, allows you to verify the configuration settings that will be applied before you click Next.

9. Confirm the settings are correct, as shown in Figure 5.12.

FIGURE 5.12
Confirm the configuration is correct, and click Next.

10. Click Next.

11. Optionally, on the Completing the SharePoint Products Configuration Wizard page, click the Advanced Settings button to specify whether Central Administration will be run from this host, as shown in Figure 5.13.

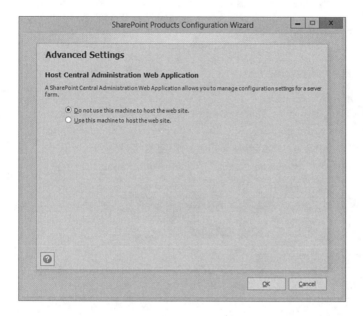

FIGURE 5.13
Do not use this machine to host the Central Administration website.

12. The SharePoint Products Configuration Wizard will proceed with configuring SharePoint according to the specifications found in the Configuration database, providing feedback during each step of the process, as shown in Figure 5.14.

13. On the Configuration Successful page, shown in Figure 5.15, click Finish.

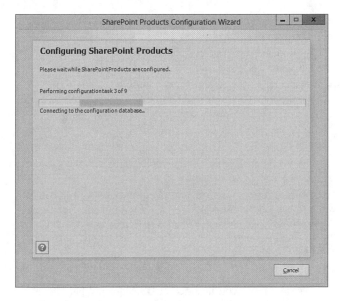

FIGURE 5.14
Configuring SharePoint Products.

FIGURE 5.15
Verify and document the information displayed at the completion of the
SharePoint Products Configuration Wizard and click Finish.

If the configuration fails, you can check the PSCDiagnostics files located in the %CommonProgramFiles%\Microsoft Shared\Web Server Extensions\15\Logs folder. If the configuration is successful, Internet Explorer will be launched, and the Central Administration website is opened. If you are prompted for credentials, you should add the Central Administration URL to your Local Intranet Zone, or alternatively your Trusted Sites list, and ensure that Internet Explorer is configured to automatically pass user credentials to sites in that list.

> **Note**
>
> If you see a proxy server error message, you need to make sure to configure your browser to bypass the proxy server for local addresses. In Internet Explorer, this setting can be configured in the Tools, Internet Options dialog box, on the Connections tab. Click LAN Settings to access the proxy server configuration settings.

After adding a server to a farm, you'll notice in IIS Manager that all SharePoint-related IIS websites are created or are in the process of being created. If all web applications in this server farm are not immediately present, wait until they have been created before continuing. If you are using host headers, your web applications are created automatically and can be used independently or added to a load-balancing solution. Remember, until you have made a DNS entry for your new server or added it to a load-balanced solution, the new server will not be used for web applications. If you did not select a public URL during the initial web application creation, you must also create an alternative access mapping for your newly created load-balanced URL. If the public URL will not change, you do not need to do the following.

Reading Servers for Load Balancing

To ready the WFE servers for load balancing, take the following steps:

1. Open Central Administration, System Settings, Configure Alternate Access Mappings in a browser.

2. Select Edit Public URLs.

3. In the Alternate Access Mapping Collection area (existing web application), choose a collection to which you want to add a URL mapping or edit a URL mapping.

4. Enter the URL, protocol, host, and port for the default zone—for example, http://portal.contoso.com:80.

5. Click Save.

Keep in mind that, by default, every web application exists on every server in the farm. If you want to serve web applications on isolated hardware, simply exclude the specific web application you do not want to serve from this server in DNS or load-balancing solutions. For example, if you have three web applications in a farm named http://portal, http://mysite and http://extranet, but you want to serve the first two from an internal set of servers and the http://extranet site from dedicated, Internet-facing hardware, your solution might look like that shown in Figure 5.16.

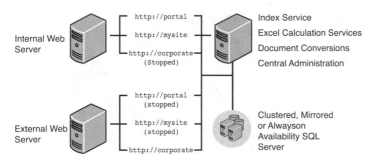

FIGURE 5.16
An example of a SharePoint farm logical configuration segregating web applications internally and externally.

In the previous example, you stop the unused web applications in IIS Manager on servers, which reduces the amount of memory used on those servers in addition to verifying IP traffic flow. When using this topology, understand that if this server is restored or if you stop, start, or restart the Windows SharePoint Services Web application service from Central Administration, all servers in the farm will start all web applications in IIS. This feature must be planned for in case there is a need to modify web applications from Central Administration.

Installing Web Parts and Custom Code

If you install additional applications, such as antivirus software or custom web parts, be sure to install them on all the necessary servers in the farm. Forgetting to implement a web.config modification on a web server, for example, can result in an inconsistent user experience in which it works for users on one web server, but not for the users on another. Here is a short list of items that are often forgotten when adding servers to a server farm:

- Custom features and solutions
- Custom apps
- Web.config modifications
- Language packs
- SharePoint-aware antivirus applications
- SSL certificates
- Third-party backup and restore software

Maintaining Internet Information Services

As a general rule, it is best to perform any SharePoint-related IIS maintenance from the Central Administration console when possible. Changes that can be made from Central Administration persist throughout the farm because they are written to the configuration database and are present on all new or replaced servers in the farm. However, there are situations that require direct IIS management, such as installing SSL certificates or implementations requiring load balancing using assigned IP addresses to accomplish IP traffic management. Using assigned IP addresses makes it easier to use hardware load balancing and to use dedicated NICs for web applications. For example, if you have two web applications in your Windows SharePoint Services farm, you can assign each web application a different IP address, with each IP address assigned to a dedicated NIC. Figure 5.17 shows the logical flow of such a setup.

> **Note**
>
> Changes made manually to IIS in the IIS Management console are not written to the configuration database and as a result must be re-created manually on each server in the farm.

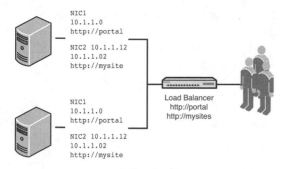

FIGURE 5.17
NICs with dedicated IP addresses allow for dedicated interfaces for normal
network communication between servers on the network.

Scaling System Services and Service Applications

The changes made to the services infrastructure in SharePoint 2010 have
been extended even further with the introduction of SharePoint 2013. The
ability of administrators to control and manage their service applications
brings with it challenges in that this ability lends itself to introducing a
level of complexity into the farm design that may be problematic. A basic
understanding of how service applications scale is mandatory before you
install a multiserver farm.

At the server level, you have SharePoint Foundation 2013 system services.
These services are called system services and service application service
instances. Both are accurate, depending on the context in which they are
used. Some system services, such as the Microsoft SharePoint Foundation
Sandboxed Code service, are not associated with a service application.
Therefore, wherever you have enabled this service is the only server where
processing will occur. To configure system services, you can browse to
Central Administration, System Settings, Manage Services on Server.

Note

In the documentation of your farm configuration, be sure to identify those
services that are service application instances and those that are not.

When a web application is first created, the groupings of service applications are specified. By default, all service applications are associated with the web application. You can modify the service applications that correspond with a particular web application at a later time. Figure 5.18 depicts the service applications that are associated with the default group.

FIGURE 5.18
Default service applications.

Figure 5.19 shows how services on the server interact with service applications.

In Figure 5.19, you can see that a system service can be directly consumed by a web application, as is the case with the Microsoft SharePoint Foundation Sandboxed Code service. However, system services are often an instance of a service application, as is the case with the User Profile service. The User Profile service is associated with the User Profile service application. The User Profile service application is associated with web applications.

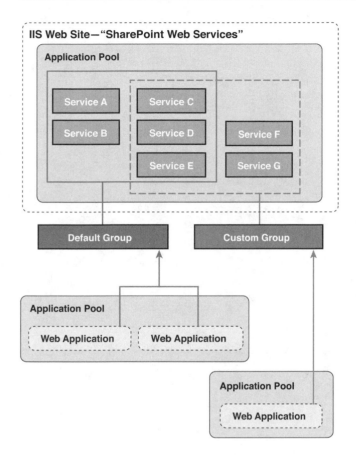

FIGURE 5.19
System services can be service application instances.

Additionally, a service application can be published, making it available across multiple server farms. However, this capability does not apply to all service applications.

Table 5.1 lists some of the services that appear on the Services on Server page in Central Administration. The chart is designed to provide additional topology guidance and recommendations for the placement of services as applicable.

Table 5.1   Services Available on the Services on Server Page

Service	Is This Service Associated with a Service Application?	Server Recommendation	Additional Information
Access Database Service2010	Yes.	Application server.	
Access Database Services	Yes.	Application server.	
App Management Service	Yes.	Application server.	
Business Data Connectivity	Yes.	Application server.	
Central Administration	No.	Application server.	This service runs the Central Administration site.
Claims to Windows Token Service	No.	Application server.	
Distributed Cache	No.	All servers by default.	Runs on all servers by default.
Document Conversions Launcher Service	No.	Application server.	Schedules and initiates the document conversions on a server.
Document Conversions Load Balancer Service	No.	Application server.	Balances document conversion requests from across the server farm. Each web application can have only one load balancer registered with it at a time.

Service	Is This Service Associated with a Service Application?	Server Recommendation	Additional Information
Excel Calculation Services	Yes.	Application server.	
Lotus Notes Connector	Yes (Search).	Application server; start this service on the index server.	This service is required to crawl content from Lotus Notes Domino servers.
Machine Translation Service	Yes.	Application server.	
Managed Metadata Web Service	Yes.	Application server.	
Microsoft SharePoint Foundation Incoming E-mail	No.	Web server or application server.	Typically, this service runs on a web server. If you need to isolate this service, you can start it on an application server.
Microsoft SharePoint Foundation Subscription Settings Service	Yes Note: This service application is deployed only by using Windows PowerShell.	Web server or application server; in hosting environments, this service is typically started on one or more application servers	Start this service if you have deployed service applications in multitenant mode or if the farm includes sites using site subscriptions. This service stores settings and configuration data for tenants in a multitenant environment. After it is started, web applications consume this service automatically
Microsoft SharePoint Foundation Web Application	No.	Web server; ensure that this service is started on all web servers in a farm. Stop this service on application servers.	This service provides web server functionality. It is started by default on web servers.

Table 5.1   Services Available on the Services on Server Page (continued)

Service	Is This Service Associated with a Service Application?	Server Recommendation	Additional Information
Microsoft SharePoint FoundationWorkflow Timer Service	No.	Web server.	This service is automatically configured to run on all web servers in a farm.
PerformancePoint Service	Yes.	Application server.	
Request Management	No.	Web server.	Manages incoming requests based on rules engine.
Search Host Controller Service	No.	Application server.	
Search Query and Site Settings Service	Yes (Search).	Application server; start this service on all query servers in a farm. However, if it becomes memory intensive, consider moving this service to a dedicated computer to free up memory for query processing.	Load balances queries across query servers. Also detects farm-level changes to the search service and puts these in the Search Admin database.
Secure Store Service	Yes.	Application server.	
SharePoint Server Search	Yes (Search).	Automatically configured to run on the appropriate computers.	This service cannot be stopped or started from the Services on Server page.

Service	Is This Service Associated with a Service Application?	Server Recommendation	Additional Information
User Profile Service	Yes.	Application server.	
User Profile Synchronization Service	Yes.	Application server.	
Visio Graphics Service	Yes.	Application server.	
Word Automation Services	Yes.	Application server.	Performs automated bulk document conversions. When actively converting, this service will fully utilize one CPU for each worker process (configured in Central Administration). If the service is started on multiple servers, a job will be shared across all the servers.
Work Management Service	Yes.	Application server.	Provides task aggregation across SharePoint, Exchange, and Project Server

---

Note

Search Service application components are deployed to servers using Windows PowerShell. This is a major change from SharePoint Server 2010, where the Search Service topology and components could be managed from the Search Administration page.

Scaling SharePoint Server 2013 Search

The most common service application that needs to be scaled out to meet user requirements is the Search Service application. There are significant changes in the Search Service in SharePoint 2013. These changes provide a much better search experience than in previous versions of SharePoint, but at a cost to administrators because the search service is much more complex and will require that administrators know Windows PowerShell.

Note

More information on changes to the Search Service application, how it is managed, configuring specific roles, how it functions, and what changes have been made can be found in Chapter 10, "Enterprise Search.

Six components are associated with the search service. These components can be configured across multiple servers within the farm to provide scalability as well as redundancy:

- Index component
- Query processing component
- Search administration component
- Crawl component
- Content processing component
- Analytics processing component

Index Component

The index component consists of index partitions and index replicas. Index partitions are portions of the search index. Each portion holds a separate part of the index and is stored on a disk within a set of files. Index replicas are contained within the index partition. There may be more than one index replica per index partition, and they will contain the same information. For each index replica you create, you must have a corresponding index partition. Index replicas can provide fault tolerance and redundancy when you create additional index replicas for each index partition and then distribute those index replicas across multiple servers.

Query Processing Component

The query processing component analyzes and processes search queries and results. Query processing has been enhanced in SharePoint Server 2013 to provide better search precision, recall, and relevance. Functionality such as query rules can be applied that may have a specific search request trigger particular settings or trigger promoted results (formerly known as Best Bets in SharePoint Server 2010).

Search Administration Component

There can be up to three search administration components for each search service application. This component is responsible for running the system processes that are essential to search.

Crawl Component

The crawl component is responsible for crawling content sources and captures not only documents within the SharePoint farm, but the metadata associated with those documents. Additional crawl components can be added to the farm to address capacity requirements, increase crawl performance, and provide high availability.

Content Processing Component

The content processing component processes crawled items and then submits those items to the index component. The content processing component functions similar to an indexing pipeline and performs operations such as linguistics processing, document parsing, and entity extraction. The component transforms the crawled items into artifacts that are included within the index component.

Analytics Processing Component

The analytics processing component analyzes all crawled items and processes that information into two main types of analyses: search analytics and usage analytics. Search analytics is the analyses that extracts links and anchor text from crawl results and stores that information in the Link database along with information about clicks on search results. Usage analytics refers to the information gathered about usage type events related to search. This could be information such as activity rankings and viewed or clicked items.

Decision Points for Scaling Out Search

Many times an administrator is tasked with improving different aspects of the overall search process. One of the goals of search in SharePoint 2013 is to return queries at subsecond latency, even in environments with 100 million documents. Microsoft has designed the search architecture in a modular fashion so that it can be transformed to accommodate performance, resilience, or both. The number of items will have an impact on farm sizing and growth. Table 5.2 depicts the numeric segmentation of items and the steps that are necessary to achieve the desired outcome.

Table 5.2 **Scaling Search Guidelines**

Number of Items	Action
Any number	For redundancy and failover, you must provision two of each search component on different servers. Search database redundancy must be set up in SQL Server.
0–10 million	All search roles can coexist on one or two servers.
40–80 million	Add one crawl server per 20 million items.
	Add one index partition per 10 million items.
	Add up to two query-processing components.
80+ million	Add one crawl server per 20 million items.
	Add one index partition per 10 million items.
	Add up to four query-processing components.
	Add one Link database per 60 million items.
	Add one analytics reporting database for each 500,000 unique items viewed each day or for every 10–20 million items.

Performance Metrics

Similarly, to improve the SharePoint 2013 Search experience, various factors have an impact on performance metrics. Table 5.3 details the key performance characteristics and how to decide when scaling of specific search components is appropriate.

Table 5.3   **Performance Metrics**

To Improve This...	Do the Following
Crawl times and results freshness	The addition of more crawl databases and content-processing components will improve results' freshness. Those crawl databases and content processing components can be distributed among their respective servers.
	Crawl health reports can be used as a tool to identify issues with crawl times or bottlenecks.
Time required for results to be returned	Adding more index replicas will help improve query latency by distributing the query load more evenly. Better suited for small topologies.
	Splitting the search index into more partitions can help reduce query latency by reducing the number of items in each index partition.
Availability of query functionality	Deploy redundant query-processing components across different application servers.
Availability of content crawling and indexing functionality	Use multiple content-processing components on redundant application servers as well as multiple crawl databases on redundant database servers.

Redundancy and Availability

Within the components of search, a number of factors provide improved performance and add fault tolerance. By monitoring the various search functions, administrators can systematically adjust certain components to achieve the desired results. Table 5.4 details which search components are redundant and how the redundancy or failover mechanism works.

Table 5.4   **Redundant Search Components**

Component	Can Be Deployed to Multiple Servers?	How Redundancy or Failover Works
Index Component	Yes	An index partition can hold up to 10 million items and represents a subset of the corpus (the collection of documents). Using a query partition can be an effective way to mirror each index partition. A general guideline is to add a query server for each index partition that is added.

Table 5.4   Redundant Search Components (continued)

Component	Can Be Deployed to Multiple Servers?	How Redundancy or Failover Works
Query processing component	Yes	Generally speaking, adding a mirrored copy of the query component and deploying it to another server should satisfy performance and redundancy requirements.
Analytics processing component	Yes	
Content processing component	Yes	
Search administration component	No	There is only one Search Administration component required in a farm.
Crawl component	Yes	Crawlers are limited to the resources that are available on any given crawl server. It is recommended that each crawler be associated with a specific crawl database.
Crawl database	Yes	For optimal performance, it is recommended that the crawl database content be stored on different physical hard disk spindles than the property database. An effective way to mitigate I/O contention is to deploy a crawl database to a separate database server. To provide redundancy, databases can be mirrored or a clustered SQL Server solution can be implemented.
Link database	No	To provide redundancy, databases can be mirrored or a clustered SQL Server solution can be implemented.
Analytics Reporting database	No	To provide redundancy, databases can be mirrored or a clustered SQL Server solution can be implemented.
Search administration database	No	Search administration resides in only one database per search service application. The only way to add redundancy is through a mirrored or clustered SQL Server implementation.

CHAPTER 6

Deploying Sites and Site Collections

- Site Creation Modes
- Site Collections and Content Databases
- Creating Site Collections
- Site Collection Security

The creation of both sites and site collections is one of the basic functions performed by SharePoint administrators and, sometimes, users. Part of the success of Microsoft SharePoint is the ease with which new sites can be provisioned, which is a major advantage over building a website from scratch. This chapter will explore the ins and outs of sites and site collections, their creation, and management.

Site Creation Modes

One critical decision that must be made by a SharePoint Server 2013 administrator in the process of planning a medium or large-scale deployment is how, and by whom, new sites will be created. Without adequate thought given to this issue, a SharePoint Server 2013 farm can quickly become unmanageable. The ease with which a new site collection can be provisioned necessitates a well thought-out governance plan to prevent an explosion of sites with no real organizational hierarchy or that are unmanageable. There are two natively supported site creation modes: administratively controlled site creation and self-service site creation. This section clarifies the differences between the two and provides some guidance in choosing a site collection creation strategy.

Determining Which Mode to Use

The decision of which site creation mode to use is dependent on many factors relating to your farm architecture and the level of a typical user's SharePoint Server education. With administratively controlled site creation, only farm administrators can create new site collections and only through Central Administration. In an environment where site collection creation must be tightly controlled, limiting this ability to farm administrators is preferred. Power users (or anyone with Full-Control or Hierarchy Manager permissions) can still create subsites directly from parent sites without needing access to Central Administration. If certain users need the capability to create site collections, possibly for informal or "throw-away" type use for temporary projects or other collaborative needs, you can enable self-service site creation. This functionality allows specified users to create their own site collections in a specified directory for these sites by using a wildcard managed path.

Before enabling Self-Service Site Creation (SSSC), you must consider the following:

1. Are your SSSC site collections going to be created in a specific web app, perhaps one for Project Team Collaboration?

2. Do you wish to use a custom form to create the request for the site collection, and if so, will a custom workflow for site creation approval be needed?

3. Will the created sites be created as a subsite or as a site collection?

4. What path will be used when the site collection is created?

5. Will a site policy be required?

> **Note**
>
> It is important to know that end users will see the option to create a new site only from their Sites page of their personal site.

One other consideration in determining how sites should be created is the handling of permissions. Site collection permissions must be specified individually, whereas subsites can inherit permissions from a parent. In a situation where many users need access to many different site collections, permissions can be difficult to manage with self-service site creation because of the need to specify permissions for each site collection individually.

Enable Self-Service Site Creation

To enable self-service site creation for a particular web application, there must be a site already created at the root of the web application. Otherwise, you will receive an error when attempting to enable self-service site creation. To enable self-service site creation, do the following:

1. Open the Central Administration website.

2. In the Application Management section, click the Manage Web Applications link.

3. On the Web Applications Management tab, select a web application by clicking it.

4. In the Security section of the management ribbon, click the Self-Service Site Creation button, as shown in Figure 6.1.

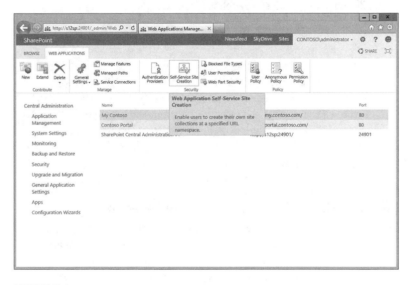

FIGURE 6.1
The Self-Service Site Creation button on the ribbon.

5. In the Self-Service Site Collection Management dialog box, select the On option to enable self-service site creation.

6. In the same dialog box, in Start a Site, do the following:

   ■ To hide the New Site option, select the first option.

   ■ Select Prompt Users to Create a Team Site Under if you want users to create a subweb under your current site collection.

NOTE: You must specify a differentiator here; the example of [%userid%] will work. Not using a differentiator will cause this feature to be ignored.

■ Select Prompt Users to Create a Site Collection Under Any Managed Path if you want for users to create site collections in other locations but on the current web app.

■ If you want to have sites created on a separate web app, select the last option, Display Custom Format, and enter the web app and location of the custom form.

Note

The custom form can be found at _layouts/15/selfservicecreate.aspx. To use your own custom form, your entry should appear as follows: http//<webapp>/_layouts/15/selfservicecreate.aspx.

---

7. Site Classification gives the users the capability to select a Site Policy.

8. Optionally, turn the Require Secondary Contact option button to On to require that a secondary contact name be supplied when users create sites using self-service site creation (see Figure 6.2). If you'll use automatic site deletion, requiring a secondary contact is recommended.

9. Click OK to save the settings.

Enabling Site Use Confirmation and Deletion

Site use confirmation and deletion provides a method of cleaning up the content database(s) by deleting sites within a web application that are unused or no longer needed. When notifications are turned on, site owners automatically receive email messages regarding sites that have been unused for a specified number of days. They can then confirm that their site collection is still in use or allow it to be deleted if automatic deletion is enabled.

Note

Outgoing email must be configured for the farm in order for notifications about sites to be sent to site contacts.

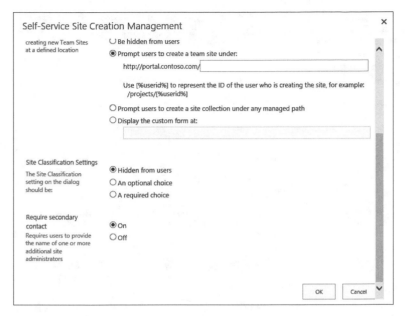

FIGURE 6.2
Self-Service Site Collection Management page used to change the settings for Self-Service Site Collections.

Enable Site Use Confirmation and Deletion

The following steps can be used to enable site use confirmation and deletion:

> **Note**
>
> Although the Confirm Site Use and Deletion link is found under the Site Collections heading, this setting is configured at the web-application level. This setting cannot be configured on a site-collection basis.

1. Open the Central Administration website.

2. On the Home page, click the Application Management heading.

3. On the Application Management page, in the Site Collections section, click the Confirm Site Use and Deletion link.

4. On the Site Use Confirmation and Deletion page, in the Web Application section, choose a web application (see Figure 6.3).

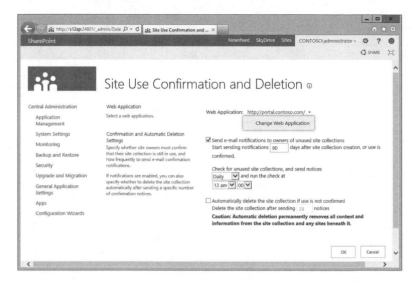

FIGURE 6.3
Choose the web application you want to configure and confirm your settings by clicking Change Web Application.

> **Note**
>
> It is important to consider using a separate web application with Site Use Confirmation and Deletion enabled when SSSC is a desired feature for your SharePoint environment.

5. In the Confirmation and Automatic Deletion Settings section (shown in Figure 6.4), select the Send Email Notifications to Owners of Unused Site Collections check box.

6. Type the number of days to wait after site creation or confirmation before sending email notifications in the text box.

7. Select the frequency and time of day to check for unused site collections and send notifications.

8. Optionally, select the Automatically Delete Site Collections if Use Is Not Confirmed check box, and in the text box type the number of notices that should be sent before deleting. Be sure to thoroughly test this functionality in your implementation before enabling it. It is possible that all site collection administrators could be notified to keep or delete a site collection.

9. Click OK to save the settings.

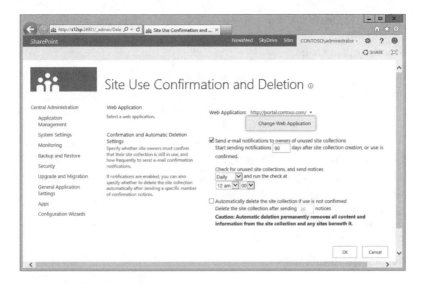

FIGURE 6.4
The Confirmation and Automatic Deletion Settings section of New Site Collection page.

Site Collections and Content Databases

As with previous versions of SharePoint, SharePoint 2013 still has its boundaries, thresholds, and supported limits. Those terms are defined by Microsoft as follows:

- **Boundaries**—Static limits that cannot be exceeded by design
- **Thresholds**—Configurable limits that can be exceeded to accommodate specific requirements
- **Supported Limits**—Configurable limits that have been set by default to a test value

When designing your SharePoint environment, it is important to take into account the previously defined terms to ensure that your SharePoint environment is built for scaling. There are three primary ways to design for scaling: the web application, Content Database, and Site Collections. In this chapter we are focusing on the capability to scale through the use of Site Collections and Content Databases.

At the time of publication, the following are limits for Site Collections and Content Databases as stated from Microsoft TechNet in Table 6.1.

Table 6.1   Limits and Boundaries for Content Databases and Site Collections

Site Collection Limits

Limit	Maximum Value	Limit Type
Site collection	750,000 (500,000 personal sites and 250,000 other sites per farm).	Supported
Website	250,000 per site collection.	Supported
MySites per farm	500,000 per farm.	Supported
Site collection size	Maximum size of the content database.	Supported
Number of device channels per publishing site collection	10.	Boundary

Content Database Limits

Limit	Maximum Value	Limit Type
Number of content databases	500 per farm.	Supported
Content database size (general usage scenarios)	200GB per content database.	Supported
Content database size (all usage scenarios)	4TB per content database.	Supported
Content database size (document archive scenario)	No explicit content database limit.	Supported
Content database items	60 million items including documents and list items.	Supported
Site collections per content database	10,000 maximum (2,500 non-personal site collections and 7,500 personal sites, or 10,000 personal sites alone).	Supported
MySites per content database	5,000 per content database.	Supported
Remote BLOB Storage (RBS) storage subsystem on Network Attached Storage (NAS)	Time to first byte of any response from the NAS cannot exceed 20 milliseconds.	Boundary

http://technet.microsoft.com/en-us/library/cc262787(v=office.15).aspx

By default, when site collections are created in SharePoint 2013, a round-robin algorithm is used to regulate the distribution of site collections across content databases. Although not immediately problematic, it does pose challenges for administrators who are deploying site collections that may become quite large.

Best Practices

Assign anticipated large site collections their own content database.

Assigning Content Databases to Site Collections

The assignment of a content database to a site collection is a five-step procedure that should be performed during off-peak hours, or when additional site collections are not being created.

Assign a Site Collection to a Content Database

Following are the five steps needed to assign a site collection to a specific content database:

1. Temporarily lock down existing content databases.

2. Create a content database to host the desired site collection.

3. Lock down the newly created content database to allow only single site collections to be created.

4. Create the new site collection.

5. Unlock the content databases that were locked in step 1 of this procedure.

Alternatively, you can use two options to assign a site collection to a content database:

1. Increase the maximum number of sites on the content database you want to target for the new site. The site will go to the content database with the largest delta between current and maximum.

2. Use PowerShell to create the sites; New-SPSite has a ContentDatabase parameter that allows the admin to specify the content database to use.

Creating Site Collections

A site collection is a grouping of sites that includes a top-level site and all subsites. Subsites are created from the top-level site through the Site

Actions menu and are generally related to the top-level site as well as each other. Subsites can inherit their security settings and navigational scheme from their parent, or they can define their own.

Configuring Host Named Site Collections

Host Named Site Collections are a novel way for "vanity URLs" to be assigned to a site collection. Host Named Site Collections also provide another mechanism besides the Alternate Access Mapping to control the URLs for SharePoint site. Using Host Named Site Collections in 2013 allows for more than one URL to be assigned to the default zone. SharePoint 2013 accomplishes this by assigning a site collection to a specified DNS entry such as http://contoso.com. In path-based site collections, up to five URLs may be used for each because of a single URL being allowed per zone. If you use Host Named Site Collections, there is no limit of five.

Typically, in most environments, site collections are created using path-based site collections. A path-based site collection is characterized by the following example: http://contoso.com/teams/prodteam1, with the site collections themselves being created under the Wildcard Managed Path/teams. In a Host Named Site Collection, the URL may resemble this: http://prodteam1.contoso.com.

Tip

Consider using Host Named Site Collections when dealing with different public URLs and when working with Secure Socket Layers and HTTPS.

Create a Host Named Site Collection Using PowerShell

To create a Host Named Site Collection using PowerShell, you need to first launch the SharePoint 2013 Management Shell from the Start menu. The following steps will enable you to create a Host Named Site Collection:

1. Type the following command:

```
New-SPSite "<URL>" -HostHeaderWebApplication "<URL
of web app> " -Name "<Title of Site>" -Description
"<Description of Site>" -OwnerAlias "<domain\user>"
-language 1033 -Template "STS#0"
```

2. Assign your additional "vanity URLs" to the site collection:

```
Set-SPSiteUrl -Identity <Normal.dot URL of the site
collection
you wish to add a URL to> -Url <https://enter your
Vanity URL here>
```

3. Verify and view that your URLs are assigned to the correct site collection:

```
Get-SPSiteURL-Identity <the original URL of the site
collection>
```

For example:

```
Get-SPSiteURL-Identity
http://portal.contoso.com/productA
```

Create a Site Collection Using PowerShell

To automate the creation of site collections, or to rapidly create additional site collections, it may be quicker to use Windows PowerShell. To use PowerShell:

1. From the Start menu, select SharePoint 2013 Management Shell.

2. At the PowerShell command prompt, type the following (press Enter after each line):

```
$template = Get-SPWebTemplate "STS#0"
```

Note

This step is assigning the Team Site Template to the $template variable. If you want to assign a different template, you will need to enter it:

```
New-SPSite -URL "<type the URL for the new site
collection>" -OwnerAlias "<domain\user>" -Template
$Template
```

Note

If you want to create a new site collection using the same template, press the up directional arrow on your keyboard to select a previously executed PowerShell command. You need to use your directional arrows to move the cursor to replace the URL and to make any changes to the Site Collection Owner.

Creating a Site Collection Using Central Administrator

The use of different site collections is important to consider in your SharePoint Information Architecture. Because SharePoint User Groups are scoped per site collection, using new site collections is an important strategy to help provide content security isolation. Also because many features are site collections, new site collections can be used to limit SharePoint user capabilities for those who may not be as familiar with SharePoint's extensive capabilities.

If you do not have the ability to create a new site collection using PowerShell, a new site collection can be created from the Central Administration website.

Create a Site Collection Using Central Administration

To create a site collection, perform the following steps:

1. Open the Central Administration website.

2. In the Application Management section, click the Create Site Collections link.

3. On the Create Site Collection page, in the Web Application section, choose the web application where the site collection should be created.

4. In the Title and Description section, type a title for the site in the Title text box and (optionally) type a description for the site in the Description text box.

5. In the Web Site Address section (shown in Figure 6.5), choose a managed path for the site, and type the URL where the site should be created.

> **Note**
>
> Only the wildcard managed paths that have already been defined will be available in the drop-down menu. See Chapter 3, "Creating Web Applications and Content Databases," for information on creating managed paths. The site's managed path is created automatically when a web application is provisioned.

6. In the Template Selection section (shown in Figure 6.6), choose a site template to use to create the top-level site in your site collection.

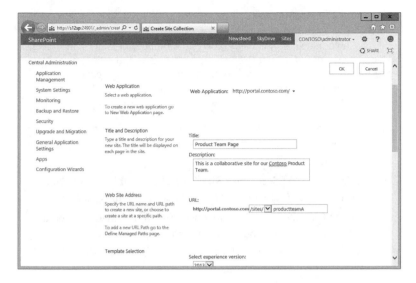

FIGURE 6.5
The Website Address section of the New Site Collection page.

FIGURE 6.6
The Template Selection section of the Create Site Collection page.

Note

The available templates will vary based on a number of factors, including which version of SharePoint Products is installed and whether any custom site templates are installed. If you have multiple language packs installed, you will also need to select a language for the site.

---

7. In the Primary Site Collection Administrator section, type the name of the user who will perform the site collection administrator duties for the site collection.

8. Optionally, in the Secondary Site Collection Administrator section, type the name of a secondary site collection administrator.

9. Click OK to create the site collection. When the site collection has been created, you will be directed to the Top-level Site Successfully Created page, where there will be a link to the newly created site collection.

Creating a Site Collection Using the Self-Service Creation

In SharePoint 2010, when an administrator enables self-service site creation (SSSC), an announcement is added to the top-level site in the site collection with a link to the self-service URL. This is not so in SharePoint 2013. Instead, in SharePoint 2013, end users create sites using a New Site link in the Sites page of the user's personal site. The default template for all sites created using the SSSC is the team site template. For SSSC to work for everyone, everyone must have the Create Site permissions at the root site collection.

Best Practice

Rather than adding everyone at the root to the Full Control, create a custom site permission and assign everyone that permission.

Create a Site Collection with Self-Service Site Collection Enabled

To create a site collection with SSSC enabled:

1. Navigate to the top-level site in the site collection and find the Sites link at the top right of the browser.

2. Click the New Site link.

3. Give your site a name.

4. Select the location at which your site will be found.

> **Note**
>
> The policies and location are specified at the web application for SSSC, only the name and location to find your site are available options.

5. Add users to the site.

6. After the site is created, you will need to browse to the Site Settings and update the user permissions.

7. Your site will now be listed in the Sites You Are Following app that is located on your Personal Site page (see Figure 6.7).

> **Note**
>
> Because there is a dependency upon the Personal sites to create a SSSC site, SSSC must be configured for the MySites web application.

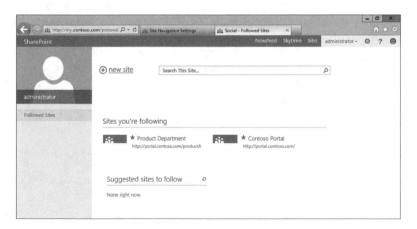

FIGURE 6.7
The Self-service site creation link located on your MySite page.

Site Collection Security

Site collection users are managed in SharePoint 2013 much the same way as they were in SharePoint 2010. Site groups are still used to manage groups of users with similar privileges. As in the previous version, security trimming prevents users from being presented with links to content they don't have access to.

There are two ways to control access to objects in SharePoint 2013:

- Permissions can be specified for a group, and then users can be given those permissions by being added to the group.

- Objects can have their own permissions collections, which can be managed independently. For example, the permissions for a list can be managed independently of the permissions for the site in which it is contained. This allows for more granular management of objects.

Configuring Site Collection Administrators and Site Owners

Site collection administrators are assigned when a site collection is created. There must always be at least one site collection administrator, and this account cannot be an Active Directory group. For reasons such as dealing with unused site confirmations and enabling administration in the event that the administrator leaves, it is always best to define at least two site collection administrators. Site collection administrators can be managed from two distinct locations: the Site Settings page of a site collection or the Application Management page in Central Administration.

Managing Site Collection Administrators from the Site Settings

To manage the Site Collection administrators from the Site Settings page, you must be a Site Collection Administrator. To manage Site Collection Administrators from the Site Settings, follow these steps:

1. Left-click the Settings menu.

2. In the Settings menu, left-click the Site Settings menu option.

3. On the Site Settings page, under the Users and Permissions section, left-click Site Collection Administrators.

4. To add a new Site Collection Administrator, type in the [domain]\[username].

   For example: **CONTOSO\jmbatchelor**

5. Click OK.

Note

To have more than one Site Collection Administrator, each administrator name must be separated by a semicolon.

Manage the Site Collection Administrators from Central Administration

As mentioned previously, you can also manage the Site Collection Administrators from Central Administration. These steps are listed next:

1. From Central Administration, left-click Application Management.

2. On the Application Management page, under the Site Collections section, left-click Change Site Collection Administrators.

3. On the Site Collection Administrators page, enter a Primary Site Collection Administrator.

4. Enter a Secondary Site Collection Administrator.

5. Click OK.

Configuring People and Groups

Groups are collections of individual users who are given the same permissions on a particular site. SharePoint Server 2013 sites are created with three basic security groups by default:

- **Owners**—Full control
- **Members**—Can contribute to existing lists and libraries
- **Visitors**—Read Only
- **Create a Custom Site Group**

To create a custom site group, follow these steps:

1. From the site where you want to create a new group, click the Settings menu and choose Site Settings.

2. In the Users and Permissions section of the Site Settings page, click the Site Permissions link.

3. On the Site Permissions page, on the management ribbon, choose Create Group.

4. On the Create Group page, in the Name and About Me Description section, type a name for the group and (optionally) a description of the purpose for the group.

5. In the Owner section, specify the group owner.

6. In the Group Settings section, specify who can view and edit group membership.

7. In the Membership Requests section, specify whether to allow requests to join or leave the group.

8. Also specify whether to autoaccept requests.

Warning

If you specify that requests should be autoaccepted, users will be automatically added to the group and granted the permissions specified for the group.

---

9. Optionally, if requests are allowed, specify an email address where requests should be sent.

10. Click Create to create the new group. The New Site Group page is shown in Figure 6.8.

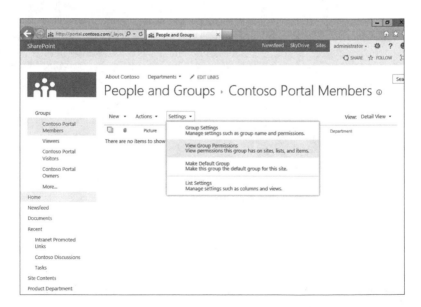

FIGURE 6.8

The View Group Permissions from the Settings menu of the People and Groups page.

View Group Permissions

Sometimes it is necessary to determine what permissions a specific group has across the entire site collection. This can be achieved in the following way:

1. From the Settings menu, choose Site Permissions.

2. Click the name of the group for which you want to view permissions.

3. Click the Settings drop-down menu and choose View Group Permissions (see Figure 6.8).

4. Review the permissions of the group for various sites in the site collection. The View Group Permissions dialog box is shown in Figure 6.9.

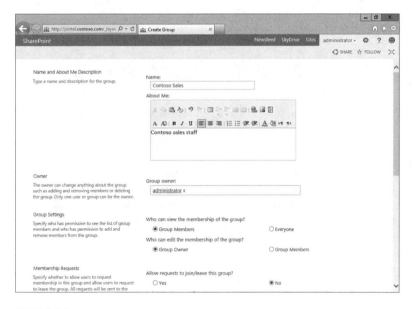

FIGURE 6.9
The new Site Group page.

Note

This page will show only the site collection root and any sites that do not inherit permissions. This could be misleading if you assume that every site the group has access to, whether permissions are inherited or not, will be listed.

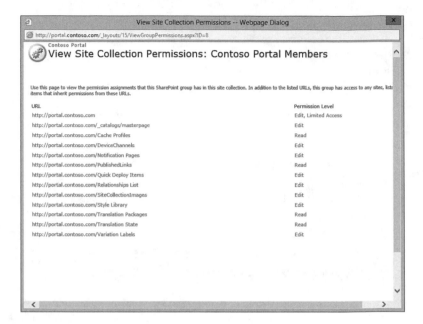

FIGURE 6.10
The View Site Collection Permissions dialog box displays a summary of the permission levels for the Site Collection.

Nest Active Directory Groups in SharePoint Groups

Although you can add users directly to almost any object, this process becomes very difficult to manage and can make it nearly impossible to manage security in a site. Use the following guidelines when granting rights, and assign permissions directly to single users only if required, such as for online presence:

1. Create an Active Directory group (when using Active Directory for authentication).

2. Create a matching permission level (if custom permission levels are required).

3. Create a matching new site group and grant it the previously created permission level.

4. Grant the new site group access to an object, such as a document, list, or web page.

Configuring Default Permission Levels

Just as site groups are a collection of users, permission levels are a collection of rights that can be assigned to groups or individual users. Permission levels should always be named the same across multiple sites, and you should never modify an existing permission level. Modifying an existing permission level can cause a document, list, or page owner to accidentally grant access to unauthorized users. Always create a new permission level, create a correlating group with the same name, and populate that group with users. Doing this assures you of an easy-to-use permission level and group environment. There are four default permission levels:

- **Full Control**—Can perform any action in the site
- **Design**—Can view, add update, delete, approve, and customize content
- **Contribute**—Can view, add, update, and delete. content
- **Read**—Can view content only

Create a Custom Permission Level

To create a custom permission level, follow these steps:

1. From the site where you want to create a new permission level, click the Settings menu and choose Site Settings.

2. In the Users and Permissions section of the Site Settings page, click the Site Permissions link.

3. On the Site Permissions page, in the Manage section of the management ribbon, click Permission Levels.

4. On the Permission Levels page, click Add a Permission Level.

Note

If you do not see the option to Add a Permission Level, you may see Manage Permission Levels on Parent Web Site. If so, this indicates that permission inheritance is turned on, and the new permission level will need to be created at the parent site.

---

5. On the Add a Permission Level page, in the Name and Description section, type a name for the permission level and (optionally) type a description.

6. In the Permissions section, select the permissions to include in the new permission level.

7. Click Create to create the new permission level.

The available permissions are enumerated in Table 6.2.

Table 6.2 **Available Permissions**

Permission	Description	Category
Manage Lists	Create and delete lists, add or remove columns in a list, and add or remove public views of a list.	List Permissions
Override List Behaviors	Discard or check in a document that is checked out to another user, and change or override settings that allow users to read/edit only their own items.	List Permissions
Add Items	Add items to lists, add documents to document libraries, and add web discussion comments.	List Permissions
Edit Items	Edit items in lists, edit documents in document libraries, edit web discussion comments in documents, and customize web part pages in document libraries.	List Permissions
Delete Items	Delete items from a list, documents from a document library, and web discussion comments in documents.	List Permissions
View Items	View items in lists, documents in document libraries, and web discussion comments.	List Permissions
Approve Items	Approve a minor version of a list item or document.	List Permissions
Open Items	View the source of documents with server-side file handlers.	List Permissions
View Versions	View past versions of a list item or document.	List Permissions
Delete Versions	Delete past versions of a list item or document.	List Permissions
Create Alerts	Create email alerts.	List Permissions
View Application Pages	View forms, views, and application pages; enumerate lists.	List Permissions

Permission	Description	Category
Manage Permissions	Create and change permission levels on the website, and assign permissions to users and groups.	Site Permissions
View Web Analytics Data	View reports on website usage.	Site Permissions
Create Subsites	Create subsites such as team sites.	Site Permissions
Manage Web Site	Grants the capability to perform all administration tasks for the website as well as manage content and permissions.	Site Permissions
Add and Customize Pages	Add, change, or delete HTML pages or web part pages, and edit the website using a Windows SharePoint Services–compatible editor.	Site Permissions
Apply Themes and Borders	Apply a theme or borders to the entire website.	Site Permissions
Apply Style Sheets	Apply a style sheet. (Cascading Style Sheets, or .CSS, file) to the website.	Site Permissions
Create Groups	Create a group of users that can be used anywhere within the site collection.	Site Permissions
Browse Directories	Enumerate files and folders in a website using SharePoint Designer and Web DAV interfaces.	Site Permissions
Use Self-Service Site Creation	Create a website using Self-Service Site Creation.	Site Permissions
View Pages	View pages in a website.	Site Permissions
Enumerate Permissions	Enumerate permissions on the website, list, folder, document, or list item.	Site Permissions
Browse User Information	View information about users of the website.	Site Permissions
Manage Alerts	Manage alerts for all users of the website.	Site Permissions
Use Remote Interfaces	Use Simple Object Access Protocol (SOAP), Web DAV, the Client Object Model, or SharePoint Designer interfaces to access the website.	Site Permissions

Table 6.2　**Available Permissions (continued)**

Permission	Description	Category
Use Client Integration Features	Use features that launch client applications; without this permission, users will have to work on documents locally and upload their changes.	Site Permissions
Open	Allow users to open a website, list, or folder to access items inside that container.	Site Permissions
Edit Personal User Information	Allow a user to change his or her own user information, such as adding a picture.	Site Permissions
Manage Personal Views	Create, change, and delete personal views of lists.	Personal Permissions
Add/Remove Personal Web Parts	Add or remove private web parts on a web part page.	Personal Permissions
Update Personal Web Parts	Update web parts to display personalized information.	Personal Permissions

Add a User to a Site

Follow these steps to add a user to a site:

1. From the Settings menu, click Site Settings.

2. Select People and Groups from the Users and Permissions section.

3. From the People and Groups page, individual users can be added to the site or new groups can be created. To add a user to a site group or assign permissions to the user directly, click the New drop-down menu and choose Add Users.

4. Type the usernames, group names, or email addresses of users to be added.

5. Choose a group to add the user to, or choose the permissions to assign directly.

6. Click OK.

Modify User Properties and Permissions

Follow these steps to modify user properties and permissions:

1. From the Settings menu, choose Site Settings.

2. Select Site Permissions from the Users and Permissions section.

3. Select the check box next to the user you want to edit permissions for.

4. In the Modify section of the management ribbon, click Edit User Permissions. Figure 6.11 shows the Edit Permissions window.

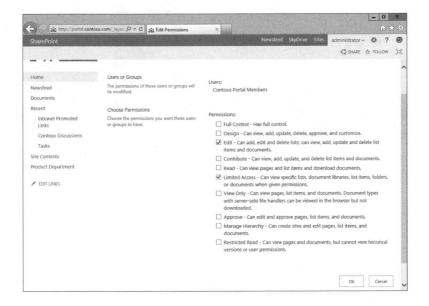

FIGURE 6.11
The Edit Permissions page for a user.

5. Modify the permissions of the user.

6. Click OK to save the changes.

Configuring List and Library Security Settings

Lists and libraries, like sites, have permissions that can be inherited from the parent site or explicitly defined. When a new list or library is created, it inherits the permission settings of its parent site by default.

Break the Permission Inheritance of a List

Use the following steps to break the permission inheritance of a list:

1. From the list where you want to break security, click the List tab in the List Tools section of the management ribbon.

2. In the Settings section of the ribbon, click List Permissions.

3. On the List Permissions page, in the Inheritance section of the ribbon, click Stop Inheriting Permissions, as demonstrated in Figure 6.12.

FIGURE 6.12

The Stop Inheriting Permissions option on a list allows you to create unique security needs for a list separate from the site the list is contained within.

Check Permissions

Use the following steps to check permissions:

1. From the list where you want to break security, click the List tab in the List Tools section of the management ribbon.

2. In the Settings section of the ribbon, click List Permissions.

3. In the Check section of the ribbon, click Check Permissions.

4. In the Check Permissions dialog box, type the name of a user or group to check permissions for.

5. Click Check Now to check permissions for the specified user or group.

6. Review the permissions for the specified user or group. The Check Permissions dialog box is shown in Figure 6.13.

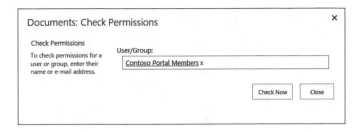

FIGURE 6.13
The Check Permissions dialog box.

CHAPTER 7

Deploying Business Intelligence Technologies

- Business Intelligence Components
- Business Intelligence Considerations
- Business Intelligence Setup
- Excel Services
- PowerPivot for SharePoint Server 2013

The business intelligence (BI) features inside of SharePoint Server 2013 have vastly improved over those available in SharePoint 2010. SharePoint Server 2013 now provides the ability for architects and administrators to "right-size" their business intelligence environment while also extending BI capabilities across multiple farms. Because BI is such a large topic of its own, this chapter focuses on the configuration and setup of two core components in the SharePoint Server 2013 BI Feature Set: Excel Services and PowerPivot for SharePoint 2013.

Business Intelligence Components

The components and architecture of SharePoint Server 2013 are broken into two categories: BI tools and BI Services. Business Intelligence in SharePoint Server 2013 makes better use of Excel Services as a way to lower the administrative burden and allow for more granular architectural decisions. For instance, Power View for SharePoint 2013 no longer depends on PowerPivot workbooks but uses Excel Services to support

Power View for SharePoint. The BI tools that are a part of SharePoint
Server 2013 are as follows:

- Power View for SharePoint
- SQL Server 2012 Reporting Services for SharePoint
- PowerPivot for SharePoint
- Excel Services
- PerformancePoint Services
- SQL Server Analysis Services (can be external to SharePoint
  Server Farm)
- Visio Services

If you are considering the deployment of BI into your SharePoint 2013
farm, it is important that you read Chapter 4, "Creating and Configuring
Service Applications," for the configuration of the service applications.
To support BI, you must have properly configured the following service
applications:

- Excel Services
- PerformancePoint Services
- Visio Services

Business Intelligence Considerations

SharePoint 2010 brought about the capability for more flexible farm architectures, allowing services to be federated and consumed across the enterprise. Unfortunately, BI in SharePoint was not provided this same luxury,
and thus required all the services to be local to the deployed farm. Another
challenge often faced in SharePoint 2010 was PowerPivot. The PowerPivot
for SharePoint setup and configuration have been greatly improved in
SharePoint Server 2013. Administrators are no longer required to deploy
PowerPivot for SharePoint in order to allow users the ability to work with
a PowerPivot workbook. This functionality is now configurable out of the
box with Excel Services.

Another improvement worth noting in SharePoint Server 2013 is the capability to work with SQL Server Analysis Services. Analysis Services is no
longer required to be a direct component of SharePoint Server 2013 farm.

> **Note**
>
> SQL Server Analysis Services is now shareable between multiple SharePoint Farms. It is important to consider more than one server for SSAS in environments where BI is considered mission critical.

Business Intelligence Requirements

Business Intelligence features in SharePoint Server 2013 have many dependencies. Table 7.1 shows the dependencies BI for SharePoint Server 2013 Requirements.

Table 7.1   **BI for SharePoint 2013 Requirements**

Business Intelligence Component	Configuration Requirements
PowerPivot for SharePoint 2013	Instance of SQL Server 2012 SP1 CTP3 Analysis Services in deployment mode.
	Excel Services must be configured and Analysis Services registered in the Excel Services configuration.
	Secure Store Service and the unattended service account.
Excel Services	Analysis Server in SharePoint Mode.
	Secure Store Service must be configured (data refresh scenarios).
	Kerberos constrained delegation if user delegate credentials are needed.
PerformancePoint Services	ADOMD.net V11.
	Secure Store Service must be configured (data refresh scenarios).
	Kerberos constrained delegation if user delegate credentials are needed.
Visio Services	Secure Store Service must be configured (data refresh scenarios).
	Kerberos constrained delegation if user delegate credentials are needed.

> **Note**
>
> All Analysis Services Servers must be at least SQL 2012 SP1 CTP3.

Business Intelligence Setup

Business Intelligence is a considerably deep topic, and because of this it is important to understand the needs of your organization and users prior to deploying the involved technologies. The following sections cover major areas of consideration in your SharePoint environment.

Business Intelligence Features

SharePoint Server 2013 can be configured for different levels of business intelligence. Each level beyond the out-of-the-box capabilities of SharePoint provides additional features. These additional features require further installation and configurations depending on your level of SharePoint BI configuration.

Table 7.2 highlights the different types and levels of BI features that can be chosen for installation and configuration.

Table 7.2 **SharePoint BI Feature Levels**

Level	Features	Install or Configure
SharePoint Only	Native Excel Services Features	Excel Services and other services included with SharePoint Server 2013.
SharePoint with Analysis Services in SharePoint Mode	Basic Business Intelligence Features	Install Analysis Services in SharePoint mode. Register AnalysisServices Server in Excel Services.
SharePoint with Reporting Services in SharePoint Mode	Power View Schedule Data refresh	Install Reporting Services in SharePoint mode. Install Reporting Services add-in for SharePoint.
All PowerPivot Features	PowerPivot Gallery PowerPivot Management Dashboard BISM link file content type	Deploy PowerPivot for SharePoint 2013 add-in.

http://msdn.microsoft.com/en-us/library/96ce12ba-0ce1-40dd-94a3-0c7fcd7f9010

Farm Service Applications

Two service applications are needed for advanced business intelligence configurations in SharePoint Server 2013: the Secure Store Service Application and the SQL Server Analysis Services. Note that the SQL Server Analysis Services application is not out of the box.

Secure Store Service Application

Many times users need to access data that exists outside of the SharePoint environment. This most always occurs in BI scenarios. Because of the need for external data access, service applications for SharePoint provide two ways for users to access this external data. The first option is for users to access data using Integrated Windows Authentication; that is, using Constrained Kerberos delegation. The second and more easily configured option (refer to Chapter 4) is the Secure Store Service.

> **Note**
>
> Secure Store is required if PowerPivot workbooks will be using a scheduled data refresh.

The Secure Store Service acts as a broker between the user and the location where external data exists; this is done through impersonation. The Secure Store uses impersonation for BI services so that SharePoint users can use the BI features within SharePoint and its unattended service account or by specifying a target application.

> **Note**
>
> Visio and Excel are examples of client-side applications that are associated with BI tools. Although these tools can publish directly to SharePoint, they cannot use the Secure Store Service application to authenticate for data sources.

SQL Server Analysis Services

SQL Server Analysis Services (SSAS) is important in your SharePoint Server 2013 architecture and planning, as well as an essential requirement for the more advanced BI SharePoint capabilities. SQL Server Analysis

Services provides a service running in the background for Excel Services to load, query, and refresh PowerPivot Data Models.

Best Practice

Install the SSAS services on a dedicated server if there will be numerous BI activities.

Excel Services

Excel Services, a service application in SharePoint Server 2013, is used to publish Excel 2013 workbooks so that users across the organization may access them inside a web browser. When a user publishes workbooks, he or she is publishing them to a SharePoint document library. The power of Excel Service is its capability to connect to external data sources. Excel Services is available only in the Enterprise edition of SharePoint Server 2013. Excel Services uses SSAS as a PowerPivot server.

Note

Workbooks cannot be edited in the browser by users.

Excel Services Components and Features

Excel Services is composed of the following components:

- Excel Web Access web part
- Excel Calculation Services
- Excel Web Services
- SQL Server 2012 Analysis Services server in PowerPivot mode

Note

For more on the configuration of Excel Services, refer to Chapter 4.

Table 7.3 outlines the available Excel Services features.

Table 7.3 **Available Excel Services**

	SharePoint Server Only	**SharePoint Server with Excel Web App**	**SharePoint Server with Excel Web App (Office Web Apps Server View Mode)**
Excel Web Access Web Part	X	X	
Refresh Data Connections	X	X	
View and interact with Power View Reports	X	X	
View and interact with PowerPivot data models	X	X	
Refresh PowerPivot data models	X	X	
Refresh data by using the Excel Services unattended service account	X	X	
Refresh data by using Secure Store and Windows Credentials	X	X	X
Refresh data by using Effective User Name Connections	X	X	
Kerberos Delegation	X	X	

Provided by Microsoft TechNet (http://technet.microsoft.com/en-us/library/ ee4244405)

As you can see, many capabilities are provided out of the box. However, the following capabilities are not included in Excel Services out of the box and will require configuring SQL Server Analysis Services as well as PowerPivot for SharePoint 2013.

- Accessing the workbook as a data source outside of the farm
- Scheduled Data Refresh
- PowerPivot Gallery
- Management Dashboard
- Business Intelligence Center

Configuring SQL Server Analysis Services

In SharePoint Server 2013, Excel Services must be configured to use SQL Server Analysis Services (SSAS) in order for data models to be processed. This configuration is ultimately about the user experience, allowing users to work with workbooks in the browser. Without the Analysis Services, Excel Services will not be able to load, query, or refresh the data models that are being used by the user requested workbooks.

For Excel Services to load, query, or refresh data models, register the SQL Server Analysis Services server in the Excel Services configuration.

> **Note**
>
> Because the SQL Server Analysis Services server can be located outside of the immediate SharePoint farm, the only requirement is that the SSAS server be in the same Active Directory forest as the SharePoint farm that will be connecting to it.

Associate an SSAS Server to the SharePoint Farm

To associate an SSAS server to the SharePoint farm, follow these steps:

1. Go to Central Administration.
2. Click Application Management.
3. Under the Service Applications section, select Manage Service Applications.
4. Click Excel Services Application (see Figure 7.1).
5. Click Data Model Settings (see Figure 7.2).
6. On the Data Model Settings page, click Add Server (see Figure 7.3).
7. Type in the SQL Server Analysis Services server (see Figure 7.4), and click OK.

Try to upload a sample workbook to validate that your configuration is correct. Then, using your web browser, open the sample workbook. Finally, to ensure that Excel Services is running correctly and caching the date correctly, click one of the slicers to alter the data being displayed.

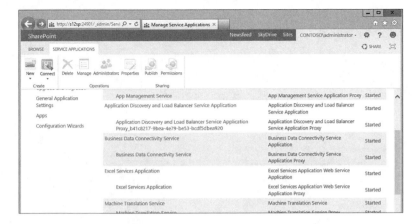

FIGURE 7.1
The list of service applications on this web application as shown in SharePoint Central Administration.

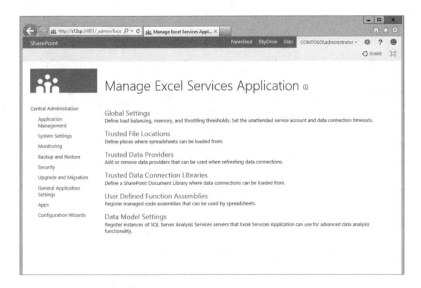

FIGURE 7.2
The Manage Excel Services Application page used to change the Excel Services Application setting from within SharePoint Central Administration.

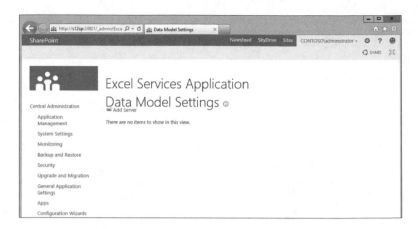

FIGURE 7.3
The Data Model Settings page that allows for additional servers containing data sources to be added to the configuration.

FIGURE 7.4
The Add Server page allows you to type in the name of the SQL Server Analysis Services server that will be used by Excel Services.

PowerPivot for SharePoint Server 2013 is greatly improved by providing core functionality out of the box. Features beyond the out-of-the-box capabilities require that back-end services be running so that PowerPivot can access data across SharePoint farms. The installation of PowerPivot for SharePoint will be required if you need to use workbooks as data sources, schedule data refreshes, or want use of the PowerPivot Management Dashboard. SQL Server Analysis Services is vital to PowerPivot for SharePoint because Excel Services uses SSAS as a PowerPivot Server.

Note

Many times workbooks will contain analytical data from environments that use PowerPivot for Excel. If that data needs to be accessed through the browser and from other servers, you must have PowerPivot for SharePoint.

Installing PowerPivot for SharePoint

Microsoft provides the spPowerPivot.msi file, a Windows Installer package for the SQL Server 2012 SP1 Feature Pack. This file's purpose is to allow the extension of the SharePoint servers so that they can add PowerPivot for SharePoint capabilities and features such as the PowerPivot Gallery and Schedule Data Refresh. The .msi file is also responsible for the deployment of SSAS client libraries and the PowerPivot for SharePoint 2013 Configuration tool and placing copies of the installation files needed for PowerPivot onto the SharePoint servers, PowerShell scripts, and the SharePoint .wsp solution packages.

The installation of PowerPivot for SharePoint Server 2013 must meet the following minimum requirements:

- PowerPivot must be installed on a Microsoft SharePoint Server 2013 farm member.

- On a SharePoint Server 2013 farm member, PowerPivot must be installed using spPowerPivot.msi.

- You must install SQL Server Analysis Services server in PowerPivot mode.

- The user installing PowerPivot for SharePoint must have Local Administrator Access to the server it is being installed on.

- The user installing PowerPivot for SharePoint must be a member of the SharePoint Farm Administrators group.

Executing the spPowerPivot.msi File

As mentioned previously, the spPowerPivot.msi file is essential when configuring PowerPivot for SharePoint. When the .msi file is executed, it installs the following .wsp files:

- PowerPivotFarmSolution.wsp
- PowerPivotFarm14Solution.wsp
- PowerPivotWebApplicationSolution.wsp

Notice that two of the three .wsp files are farm solution scoped and one is web application scoped. These .wsp solution packages are installed in C:\Program Files\Microsoft SWL Server\110\Tools\PowerPivotTools\ SPAddinConfiguration\Resources.

Note

The spPowerPivot.msi file does not deploy PowerPivot to the SharePoint farm, and the .msi file will need to be set up on all WFEs and Application Servers.

Install PowerPivot Using spPowerPoint.msi

Use the following steps to install PowerPivot for SharePoint:

1. Download the spPowerPivot.msi file from Microsoft.

2. Double-click the spPowerPivot.msi file after it launches (see Figure 7.5), and click Next.

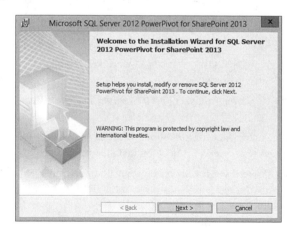

FIGURE 7.5
The spPowerPivot.msi installation launch screen.

3. Accept the terms in the license agreement, and click Next.

4. Select the features that you want to install (see Figure 7.6), and click Next.

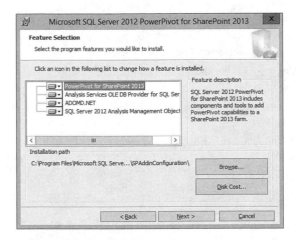

FIGURE 7.6
The feature selection dialog box that allows you to select which features to be
installed on this SharePoint server.

5. After the features have been installed, the screen shown in
   Figure 7.7 appears.

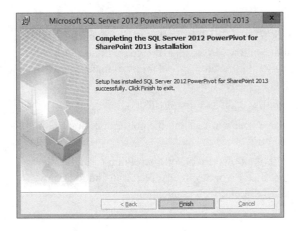

FIGURE 7.7
The final splash screen acknowledging a successful installation of SQL Server
2012 PowerPivot for SharePoint 2013.

Install PowerPivot Using PowerShell

Using PowerShell to install the spPowerPivot.msi file provides more flexibility if you are scripting your farm installs and configurations.

To install, open the SharePoint PowerShell command prompts using elevated permissions and type the following:

```
Msiexec.exe /I SPPowerPivot.msi
```

To install while also producing a log with verbose logging, use the following PowerShell command:

```
Msiexec.exe /i SpPowerPivot.msi /L*v
c:\test\install_log.txt
```

When scripted installs and configurations are needed, the install should be run in "quiet" mode. A "quiet" installation prevents installation dialogs or prompts and warnings from being displayed during the install process. To perform a quiet installation, use the following steps:

Using elevated permissions, open the command prompt.

Type the following command:

```
Msiexec.exe /I spPowerPivot.msi /q
```

Configuring PowerPivot for SharePoint Service Application

After you have installed the spPowerPivot.msi file, you will need to start the PowerPivot Configuration tool. You can find this tool under your installed applications on your SharePoint Server.

The configuration of PowerPivot has two major steps:

1. The first step validates your settings and the configuration of your farm to support PowerPivot.

2. The second step with the PowerPivot for SharePoint Configuration tool is to create the PowerPivot Service Application and to deploy the solutions to your farm and web application.

If you do not have a service application already created for PowerPivot for SharePoint, the Configuration tool will create one for you. To complete the configuration process, you will need to create Target Application ID for the Secure Store service and the unattended service account for the data refresh.

> **Note**
>
> Refer to Chapter 4 for configuration of service accounts for more on the unattended service account.

After you have created the Target Application for the Secure Store Unattended Service Account, you will need to enter those parameters inside of the PowerPivot Configuration tool, as shown next.

The following configurations are available inside of PowerPivot and may be configured using the Configuration tool.

If you want to script the creation and use scripting to replicate your PowerPivot for SharePoint configurations, the Configuration tool builds and also allows for you to copy the script for reuse.

Table 7.4 describes the values that are used to configure the server.

TABLE 7.4 **PowerPivot for SharePoint Configuration Settings Available in the PowerPivot Configuration Tool**

Page	Input Value	Source	Description
Configure or Repair PowerPivot for SharePoint	Default Account	Current user	The default account is a domain Windows user account used to provision shared services in the farm. It is used to provision the following: ■ PowerPivot service application ■ Secure Store Service ■ Excel Services ■ The web application pool identity ■ The site collection administrator ■ The PowerPivot unattended data refresh account By default, it uses the domain account of the current user. It is recommended that you replace the default value unless you are configuring a server for evaluation and non-production purposes. You can change service identities later, using Central Administration. Optionally, in the PowerPivot Configuration tool, specify dedicated accounts for the following: ■ Web application, using the Create Default Web Application page (assuming that the tool is creating a web application for the farm). ■ PowerPivot unattended data refresh account, using the Create Unattended Account for Data Refresh page in this tool.

Page	Input Value	Source	Description
	Database Server	Local PowerPivot named instance, if available	If a database engine instance is installed as a PowerPivot named instance, the tool populates the database server field with this instance name. If you did not install the database engine, this field is empty.
			Database Server is a required parameter. It can be any version or edition of SQL Server that is supported for SharePoint farms.
	Passphrase	User input	If you are creating a new farm, the passphrase you enter is used as the passphrase for the farm. If you are adding PowerPivot for SharePoint to an existing farm, type the existing farm passphrase.
	SharePoint Central Administration port	Default, if needed	If the farm is not configured, the tool provides options to create the farm, including creating an HTTP endpoint to Central Administration. It picks a randomly generated port number that is not in use.
	PowerPivot for Excel Services ([ServerName]\PowerPivot)	User input	The PowerPivot server is required for Excel Services to Enable the core PowerPivot capabilities. The server name you type on this page is also added to the list on the Configure PowerPivot Servers page.
Configure New Farm Database Server	Farm Account PassPhrase SharePoint Central Administration port	Default, if needed	The settings default to what you entered on the main page.

TABLE 7.4   PowerPivot for SharePoint Configuration Settings Available in the PowerPivot Configuration Tool (continued)

Page	Input Value	Source	Description
Create PowerPivot Service Application	Service Application Name	Default	PowerPivot Service Application Name. The default name is Default PowerPivot Service Application. You can substitute a different value in the tool.
	Database Server	Default	The database server to host the PowerPivot service application database. The default server name is the same database server used for the farm. You can substitute a different value than the default server name.
	Database Name	Default	The name of the database to create for the PowerPivot Service Application Database. The default database name is based on the service application name, followed by a GUID to ensure a unique name. You can substitute a different value in the tool.
Create Default Web Application	Web Application Name	Default, if needed	If no web applications exist, the tool creates one. The web application is configured for classic mode authentication and listens on port 80. The maximum file upload size is set to 2047, the maximum allowed by SharePoint. The larger file upload size is to accommodate the large PowerPivot files that will be uploaded to the server.

Page	Input Value	Source	Description
	URL	Default, if needed	The tool creates a URL based on the server name, using the same filenaming conventions as SharePoint.
	Application Pool	Default, if needed	The tool creates a default application pool in IIS.
	Application Pool Account and Password	Default, if needed	The application pool account is based on the default account, but you can override it in the tool.
	Database Server	Default, if needed	The default database instance is preselected to store the application content database, but you can specify a different SQL Server instance in the tool.
	Database Name	Default, if needed	The name of the application database. The database name is based on the filenaming conventions of SharePoint, but you can choose a different name.
Deploy Web Application Solution	URL	Default, if needed	The Default URL is from the default web application.
	Maximum File Size (in MB)	Default, if needed	Default setting is 2047. SharePoint document libraries also have a maximum size, and the PowerPivot setting should not exceed the document library setting.

TABLE 7.4   PowerPivot for SharePoint Configuration Settings Available in the PowerPivot Configuration Tool (continued)

Page	Input Value	Source	Description
Create Site Collection	Site Administrator	Default, if needed	The tool uses the default account. You can override it in the Create Site Collection page.
	Contact E-mail	Default, if needed	If Microsoft Outlook is configured on the server, the tool will use the email address of the current user. Otherwise, a placeholder value is used.
	Site URL	Default, if needed	The tool creates the site URL, using the same URL naming conventions as SharePoint.
	Site Title	Default, if needed	
Activate PowerPivot Feature in a Site Collection	Site URL		URL of the site collection for which you are activating PowerPivot features.
	Enable premium feature for this site		Enable the SharePoint site feature PremiumSite.
Create Secure Store Service Application	Service Application Name	Default, if needed	Type the name for the Secure Store service application.
	Database Server	User input	Type the name of the database server to use for the Secure Store service application.

Page	Input Value	Source	Description
Create Secure Store Service Application Proxy	Service Application Name	Default, if needed	Type the name for the Secure Store service application you typed in the previous page.
	Service Application Proxy	Default, if needed	Type the name for the Secure Store service application proxy. The name will appear in the default connection group that associates applications with SharePoint content web applications.
Update Secure Store Service Master Key	Service Application Proxy	Default, if needed	Type the name of the Secure Store service application proxy you typed in the previous page.
	Passphrase	User input	The master key used for data encryption. By default, the passphrase used to generate the key is the same passphrase that is used to provision new servers in the farm. You can replace the default passphrase with a unique passphrase.
Create Unattended Account for DataRefreshID	Target Application	Default, if needed	Create a target application to store credentials for unattended PowerPivot data refresh. The application ID can be descriptive text.
	Friendly Name for Target Application	Default, if needed	
	Unattended Account User Name and Password	Default, if needed	Type credentials of a Windows user account that is used by the target application to run unattended data refresh. For more information, see Configure Excel Services data refresh by using the unattended service account in SharePoint Server 2013 (http://technet.microsoft.com/en-us/library/hh525344(office.15).aspx).

TABLE 7.4 PowerPivot for SharePoint Configuration Settings Available in the PowerPivot Configuration Tool (continued)

Page	Input Value	Source	Description
Create Excel Services Service Application	Site URL	Default, if needed	Type the site URL of the site collection associated with the target application. To associate with additional site collections, use SharePoint Central administration.
	Service Application Name	Default, if needed	Type a service application name. A service application database with the same name is created on the SharePoint farm's database server.
Configure PowerPivot Servers	Service Application Name	Default, if needed	Service application name you typed on the previous page.
	PowerPivot Server Name	List of Registered PowerPivot Servers.	The server name typed on the main page is automatically added to this page.
Register PowerPivot Addin as Excel Services Usage Tracker	Service Application Name		Service application name you typed on the previous page.

found at http://msdn.microsoft.com/en-us/library/96ce12ba-0ce1-40dd-94a3-0c7fcd7f9010.

Deploy PowerPivot

To deploy PowerPivot for SharePoint, follow these steps:

1. Run the PowerPivot for SharePoint 2013 Configuration Wizard (see Figure 7.8).

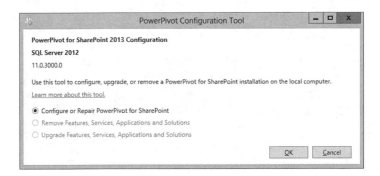

FIGURE 7.8

The beginning screen of the PowerPivot Configuration tool allowing PowerPivot for SharePoint to be installed, features removed, or features upgraded.

2. Check for any yellow highlighted tasks.

   In Figure 7.9, note that beside the Secure Store there is a yellow caution sign. This yellow caution sign indicates that the Secure Store Service has not been properly configured and that PowerPivot for SharePoint will not be configured correctly so that it may access external data sources. Resolve any errors, and then from within the PowerPivot for SharePoint Server 2013 Configuration Wizard, click the Validate button.

3. After you have validated all configuration steps, the image shown in Figure 7.10 appears.

4. When the Run button is displayed (see Figure 7.11), click Run.

   The Activity Progress Dialog Box appears (see Figure 7.12).

   When the PowerPivot Configuration tool completes successfully, the image shown in Figure 7.13 appears.

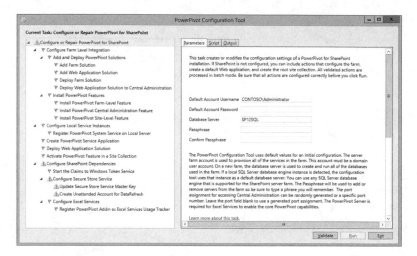

FIGURE 7.9
The PowerPivot Configuration tool validation of setup shows errors in the
Configure SharePoint Dependencies Section.

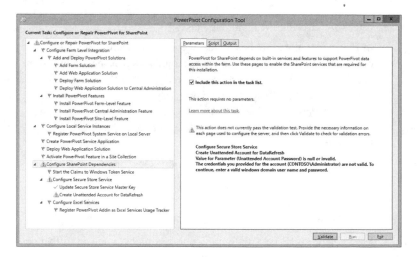

FIGURE 7.10
When all tasks for PowerPivot configuration are completed, the validation dialog
box indicates that validation succeeded.

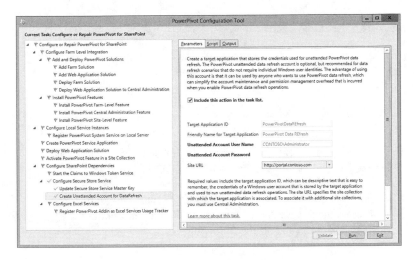

FIGURE 7.11
After the validation of tasks occurs, the Run button is enabled. When you click it, the deployment and configuration of the PowerPivot for SharePoint Service Application begin.

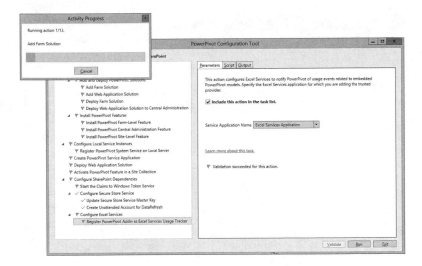

FIGURE 7.12
The Activity Progress dialog box appears after you click Run.

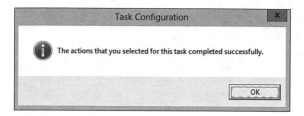

FIGURE 7.13
The Task Configuration dialog box appears when all of the actions have been completed that were specified in the Configuration tool.

5. To ensure that the PowerPivot for SharePoint Configuration tool created the service application, go to SharePoint Central Administration and do the following:

- Click Application Management.

- On the Application Management page, under the Service Applications section, select Manage Service Applications.

- Scroll to find the PowerPivot Service Application.

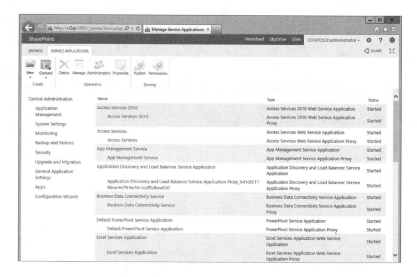

FIGURE 7.14
The PowerPivot Service Application will appear in the list of services on the Manage Service Applications page inside of SharePoint Central Administration.

> **Note**
> If you did not change the default settings inside of the Configuration tool, the name of the service application will be Default PowerPivot Service Application, as seen in Figure 7.15.

6. Configure the PowerPivot Service Application Settings and ensure the Service Application is working.

7. Click the PowerPivot Service Application. You should see a screen similar to Figure 7.15.

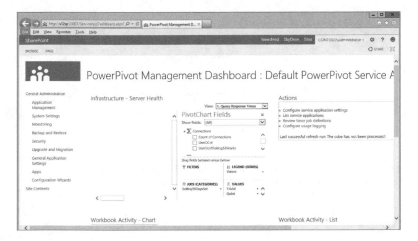

FIGURE 7.15
After clicking the PowerPivot Service Application in Central Administration, you will be directed to the PowerPivot Management Dashboard.

Administer the SharePoint Service Application

After PowerPivot is successfully deployed, the PowerPivot Management Dashboard is created. This dashboard is designed to provide intelligence about the use of business intelligence in your SharePoint Server 2013 environment.

The PowerPivot Dashboard is also used to ensure that PowerPivot is configured properly for your organization. Upon the creation and setup of PowerPivot for SharePoint, update and review each of the actions in the Actions section of the PowerPivot Management Dashboard:

1. In the Actions section on the PowerPivot Management Dashboard, click Configure Service Application Settings. You are redirected to the PowerPivot Settings page for additional service application configurations (see Figure 7.16).

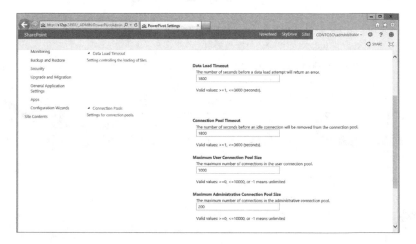

FIGURE 7.16
A few of the configurable settings for the PowerPivot for SharePoint Service Application that the PowerPivot Configuration tool deployed.

> **Note**
>
> Configuration changes on the PowerPivot Settings page are made only to the web application that this PowerPivot Service Application is provisioned to.

2. In the Actions section on the PowerPivot Management Dashboard, click List Service Applications to be redirected to the Manage Service Applications page in Central Administration.

3. In the Actions section on the PowerPivot Management Dashboard, select Review Timer Job Definitions to set the schedule type and web application for the timer job, as seen in Figure 7.17.

> **Note**
>
> Timer jobs can be scheduled to run weekly, daily, minutes and can be scheduled to start at a specific time.

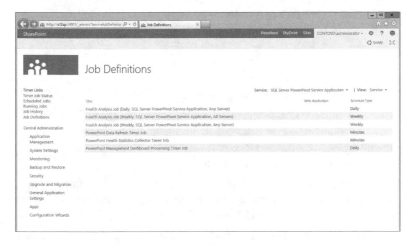

FIGURE 7.17
The job definitions lists are the timer job definitions as defined for the SQL
Server PowerPivot Service Application. Notice the schedule types available.

4. In the Actions section on the PowerPivot Management Dashboard,
   click Configure Usage Logging to be redirected to the Configure
   Usage and Health Data Collection page in Central Administration, as
   seen in Figure 7.18.

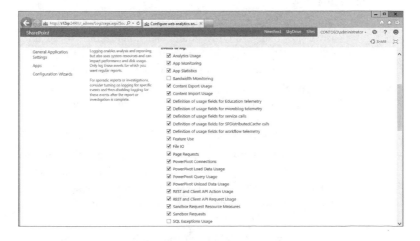

FIGURE 7.18
The usage and logging settings as defined in Central Administration.

Note

PowerPivot is already enabled for event logging.

Configure the PowerPivot Settings Page

Depending on the load and dependency needs of BI in the organization, it may be important to alter the default settings from the previous step 1. Remember, these configuration changes are for the PowerPivot Service Application for the assigned web application.

The following settings can be configured in the PowerPivot Settings page. This information can be found in more detail at http://msdn.microsoft.com/en-us/library/b2e5693e-4af3-453f-83f3-07481ab1ac6a.

▪ **Data Load Timeout**—Increase or decrease the value to change how long the PowerPivot service waits for a response from the SQL Server Analysis Services (PowerPivot) instance to which it forwarded a load data request. Because very large datasets take time to move over the wire, you must allow sufficient time for the PowerPivot service instance to retrieve the Excel workbook and move the PowerPivot data to an Analysis Services instance for query processing. Because PowerPivot data can be unusually large, the default value is 30 minutes.

▪ **Connection Pools**

  ▪ **Connection Pool Timeout**—Increase or decrease the value to change how many minutes an idle data connection will remain open. The default value is 30 minutes. During this period, the PowerPivot service will reuse an idle data connection for read-only requests from the same SharePoint user for the same PowerPivot data. If no further requests are received for that data during the period specified, the connection is removed from the pool. Valid values are from 1 to 3600 seconds.

  ▪ **Maximum User Connection Pool Size**—Increase or decrease the value to change the maximum number of idle connections the PowerPivot service will create in individual connection pools for each SharePoint user, PowerPivot dataset, and version combinations.

    The default value is 1000 idle connections. Valid values are −1 (unlimited), 0 (disables user connection pooling), or 1 to 10000.

These connection pools enable the service to more efficiently support ongoing connections to the same read-only data by the same user. If you disable connection pooling, every connection will be created anew.

- **Maximum Administrative Connection Pool Size**—Increase or decrease the value to change the maximum number of idle connections the PowerPivot service will create in individual connection pools for each SharePoint user, PowerPivot dataset, and version combinations. The default value is 1000 idle connections. Valid values are [ms]1 (unlimited), 0 (disables user connection pooling), or 1 to 10000. These connection pools enable the service to more efficiently support ongoing connections to the same read-only data by the same user. If you disable connection pooling, every connection will be created anew.

- **Data Refresh**

  - **Business Hours**—This allows you to specify a range of hours that define a business day. Data refresh schedules can run after the close of a business day to pick up transactional data that was generated during normal business hours.

  - **PowerPivot Unattended Data Refresh Account**—Specify a predefined Secure Store Service target application that stores a predefined account for running PowerPivot data refresh jobs. Be sure to specify the target application name and not the ID. The target application for unattended data refresh is created automatically if you used the New Server option in SQL Server Setup to install PowerPivot for SharePoint. Otherwise, you must create the target application manually.

  - **Refresh Jobs to Run in Parallel**—Specifies how many jobs (refresh Timer Jobs) can run in parallel.

  - **Maximum Processing History Length**—The maximum number of days of processing history that may be kept.

  - **Disable Data Refresh Due to Consecutive Failures**—If the data refresh job fails the specified number of instances, data refresh will be disabled.

  - **Disable Data Refresh for Inactive Workbooks**—Specifies the number of data refresh cycles to check for workbook inactivity.

- **Disk Cache**

  - **Keep Inactive Database in Memory (in hours)**—Specifies the number of hours to keep an inactive PowerPivot database in memory to service new requests. The default is 48 hours.

  - **Keep Inactive Database in Cache (in hours)**—Specifies the number of hours after which an inactive PowerPivot database is deleted from the cache. This must be greater than the Keep Inactive Database in Memory setting.

  - **Health Rule Settings**—For more information on Health Rule Settings, see http://msdn.microsoft.com/en-us/library/a01e63e6-97dc-43e5-ad12-ae6580afc606.

  - **Load to Connection Ratio (default is 20%)**—This health rule is triggered if the number of load events is high relative to the number of connection events, signaling that the server might be unloading databases too quickly or that cache reduction settings are too aggressive.

    This configuration setting corresponds to the following rule definition on the Review Problems and Solutions page: PowerPivot: The ratio of load events to connections is too high.

  - **Data Collection Interval (default is 4 hours)**—You can specify the data collection period used for calculating the numbers used for triggering health rules. Although the system is monitored constantly, the thresholds used to trigger health rule warnings are calculated using data that was generated over a predefined interval. The default interval is 4 hours. The server retrieves system and usage data collected over the previous 4 hours to evaluate the load-to-collection ratio.

  - **Check for Updates to PowerPivot Management Data.xlsx file (default is 5 days)**—The PowerPivot Management Dashboard.xlsx file is a data source used by reports in PowerPivot Management Dashboard. In a default server configuration, the .xlsx file is refreshed daily, using usage data collected by SharePoint and the PowerPivot System Service. In the event that the file is not updated, a health rule reports it as a problem. By default, the rule is triggered if the timestamp of the file has not changed for 5 days.

■ **Usage Data Collection**

  ■ **Query Reporting Interval**—Specifies an interval of time for
    reporting query statistics. Query statistics are reported as a
    single event to minimize server-to-server communication.

  ■ **Usage Data History**—Specifies how long to keep a historical
    record of usage data. Usage information appears in the
    PowerPivot Management Dashboard. The reports will be less
    effective if you specify too low a value for usage data history.

  ■ **Response Threshold—This** is determined by the following
    values. Each upper limit is needed in order to specify where
    one category stops and another begins. These categories and
    limits are used to establish a baseline for performance meas-
    ures to monitor trends. These measures and the ability to
    analyze them will appear on the PowerPivot Management
    Dashboard.

  ■ **Trivial Response Upper Limit**—The upper limit for complet-
    ing a trivial request, such as server-to-server communications
    that establish a user connection to PowerPivot data. Trivial
    requests are excluded from report data.

  ■ **Quick Response Upper Limit**—The upper limit (in millisec-
    onds) used to set the threshold for completing requests
    quickly; quick requests might include querying a small data
    set.

  ■ **Expected Response Upper Limit**—An upper limit (in
    milliseconds) that sets the threshold for completing a query in
    an expected amount of time. Most queries should fall within
    this category.

  ■ **Long Response Upper Limit**—This is an upper limit
    (in milliseconds) that sets the threshold for completing a long
    running request. Few requests should fall into this category.

PART II

CONFIGURING

IN THIS PART

CHAPTER 8

Configuring Enterprise Content Types and Metadata

- Understanding Enterprise Content Management
- Configuring Managed Metadata Services
- Understanding Managed Taxonomies, Folksonomies, and Term Sets
- Understanding Enterprise Content Types
- Consuming Metadata

Today's information economy is now imposing significant technical and compliance requirements on organizations for the management of enterprise content. Enterprise Content Management (ECM) is the discipline for managing documents and metadata often into petabytes and now even exabytes. Large organizations can no longer ignore the requirements necessary for managing these mountains of documents and retrieving them in a meaningful manner. With SharePoint, the solution is to leverage managed taxonomies via enterprise content types and enterprise metadata. The purpose of this chapter is to help you understand enterprise content types and metadata and how to implement them in Microsoft SharePoint Server 2013.

Understanding Enterprise Content Management

Enterprise content types and metadata are the backbone of data classification, retention, retrieval, and consumption. To remain competitive, organizations can no longer afford to ignore their information assets. The enterprise must now be committed to understanding its intellectual property and establishing the capability to make strategic or tactical decisions by leveraging its intellectual property. For an organization to more efficiently consume the data that it owns, it is now a requirement to establish a taxonomy structure for the classification and organization of this information. An enterprise taxonomy is the result of applying information classification methodologies and techniques for hierarchically structuring an organization's information.

Furthermore, organizations are allowing for the classification of content created by users, who tag information with freely chosen keywords, and for the cooperation among groups of users to create such classifications. This community-based contributed metadata is known as *folksonomy*.

Many organizations still utilize traditional information retention and classification techniques. These techniques are very limited and consist of four basic approaches to file retention, as outlined in Table 8.1.

TABLE 8.1   **File Retention Types**

Retention Type	Definition
Structured	Files and other data organized into folders; databases; and offline tapes, disks, or physical files in many locations.
Unstructured	Files stored in user profile spaces, detached drives, USB thumb drives, email .pst files, tapes in personal file cabinets, physical files in personal cabinets, and so forth in many disparate locations.
File share	Network or local file storage locations bound by domain constraints, which are usually established for physical locations in larger corporations. There could be an innumerable amount of file shares for a large corporation. Files shares can be either structured or unstructured, and they are often used to store data that would not need the functionality of SharePoint to maintain.
SharePoint	A central location without domain constraints, either structured or unstructured, that provides the capability to add custom searchable metadata and tagging, which compliments data and becomes part of the artifact.

Each approach has its advantages and disadvantages.

Structured retention follows the basics of taxonomy by classification—files, databases, other offline storage media, and physical files are organized into folders or libraries with meaningful references. The caveat is that structured retention doesn't take into account the potential need for multiple classifications and associations. Files can be assigned to only one physical location. To overcome this, organizations have resorted to using referential pointers or placeholders. These symbolic links are placed in alternative file locations that are pertinent. However, removal of the files, databases, or original physical media and files can result in the residual effect of bad references not being removed.

Unstructured retention follows the basics of a stack of unfiled papers in the inbox on your desk. Essentially, it's just a stack of data placed in a single location for easy access. Often, a heavy reliance on naming conventions is used to provide some aspect of taxonomy. The limitation here is that only so much data can be captured in the names of files, databases, and folders.

File shares can take on aspects of either structured or unstructured retention. The deviation is that file shares tend to be accessed by multiple people; therefore, consistent and formal organization is the key to creating effective file shares. Using this approach, files are often organized into multiple shares, using the shares themselves as one form of classification and then using the file structure as a second classification. File shares also provide a sense of security and help prevent inadvertent loss of data due to failures on individual machines. Security boundaries in the form of Access Control Lists (ACLs) are used to manage the permissions for reading and writing to these file shares.

SharePoint incorporates all the aspects of file shares, with several added bonuses. With file shares, the limitation on access is based on physical access constraints. A user requires direct network access or virtual private network (VPN) access to use the files in a share. With SharePoint, that is no longer a constraint. File access is based intrinsically on the rights and permissions of the authenticated user and is constrained only by the capability to connect to the SharePoint Server 2013 site itself. In addition to this, SharePoint has enabled the expanded classification of data. Data repositories are organized into types of information at a high level, but cross-classification or links can be created to other pieces of information artifacts. This directly correlates to the way relational data is managed and structured in enterprise databases.

SharePoint Server 2013 allows for the expanded use of term sets that are managed at the service-application level. The result is that you have the capability to define universally applicable managed term fields that can be used as attributes to augment navigation; to search, sort, and filter; and for policy and workflow operations. These syndicated metadata lists or classifications can then be applied to any of the aforementioned.

Configuring Managed Metadata Services

Managed Metadata Services, also known as *term stores*, allows for the organization of terms, lists, and classifications to be leveraged across multiple SharePoint web applications or site collections. Managed Metadata Services can be published to, or subscribed to, from another SharePoint farm or multiple SharePoint farms. Managed Metadata Services are accessible through Central Administration, Application Management, Manage Service Applications, and the Managed Metadata Service.

As a best practice, the Managed Metadata Services Content Type Syndication Hub should be created as its own site collection and can exist in any web application. Multiple Content Type Syndication Hubs can be used to serve up different subsets of content types, allowing for a great degree of applied customization so that they fit the needs of any organization. Only one syndication hub can be enabled per site collection. In addition to providing the Content Type Syndication Hub, each Managed Metadata Services Application provides a dedicated term store. The term store is capable of servicing one or many term set groups, and each group is able to host one or many term sets.

Creating the Content Type Syndication Hub Site Collection

The Content Type Syndication Hub is used to manage the content types to be published via the Managed Metadata Service. Site collections within other web applications subscribe to the central repositories for managed metadata and content types published by the Managed Metadata Service application. There is a one-to-one relationship between a Managed Metadata Service application and a Content Type Syndication Hub. Organizations can establish as many Content Type Syndication Hubs and Managed Metadata Service applications as needed to meet data management policies and requirements. (See Figure 8.1.)

Managed paths can be created to correlate the management policies of an organization. If an organization has no need for multiple Content Type Syndication Hubs, using an explicit inclusion path to host the Content Type Syndication Hub is acceptable. If an organization has a requirement to employ multiple Content Type Syndication Hubs, it would be more appropriate to use a wildcard-inclusion managed path.

Data-retention policies and document templates are prime examples of why an organization might implement multiple Content Type Syndication Hubs. There are many regulatory reasons why organizations might have different data management policies that apply to independent bodies in the organization. The human resources department might need to retain application, resume, and employee records data for seven years; the Sarbanes-Oxley Act (in the USA) requires that financial data be retained for specific durations; and for liability reasons, the retention of patent and contracts data might need to extend for upwards of 20 years.

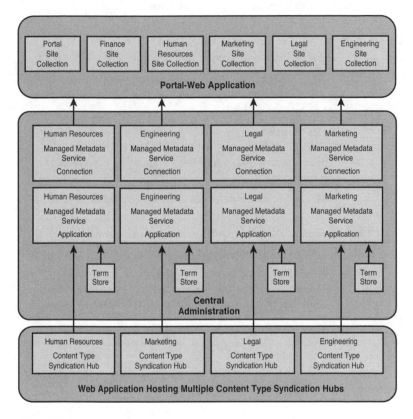

FIGURE 8.1
Example of multiple Content Type Syndication Hubs and Managed Metadata Service applications.

Human resources or benefits administrators might have a significant number of specialized document templates to handle the specialized and sometimes sensitive work that they handle. Setting up independent Content Type Syndication Hubs can provide the capability to incorporate specialized document-retention policies, autoexpiration policies that provide significant space reduction without the excessive work of manual purging, and customized and secured document types and templates. These are examples of why you might create multiple Content Type Syndication Hubs.

To begin creating this pairing of service application to Content Type Syndication Hub, you should create a site collection in the Content Type Syndication Hub Web application previously created.

Create a Metadata Services Site Collection

Perform the following steps to create the Managed Metadata Services site collection:

1. Open Central Administration, click Application Management, and select Create Site Collections.

2. Select the web application by clicking the web application drop-down arrow and selecting the Change Web Application menu item. Choose the appropriate web application from the list of available web applications.

3. Type the title and description for the Managed Metadata Services site.

4. Type the name of the primary site collection administrator.

5. Click OK to create the site collection.

Figure 8.2 shows an example of a top-level, data management policy configuration applied to the Content Type Syndication Hubs.

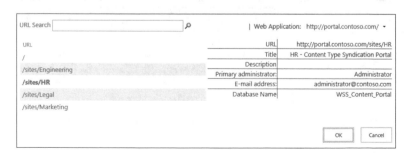

FIGURE 8.2
Example of a complex Content Type Syndication Hub taxonomy.

Activating the Content Type Syndication Hub

Before the new site collection will function as the management engine for content types, you need to activate the site collection feature for the Content Type Syndication Hub.

> **Note**
>
> The feature should be activated automatically during service application creation. However, it is always wise to verify that this feature has been activated.

To do this, open the site collection in a new window and go to the Site Settings page. Within the Site Collection Administration section of the Site Settings page, click the Site Collection Features link. On the Features page, click Active to activate the Content Type Syndication Hub feature, as shown in Figure 8.3.

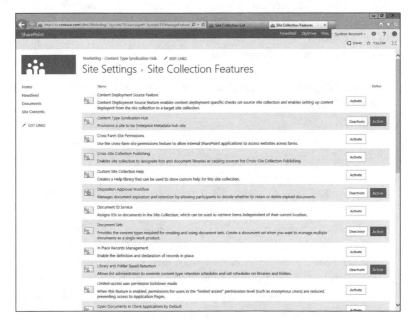

FIGURE 8.3
Activating the Content Type Syndication Hub on a site collection.

> **Note**
>
> Activate the Content Type Syndication Hub within the newly created site collection before trying to link it to the service application for Managed Metadata Services. The Managed Metadata Services Application can be created before attaching it to a Content Type Syndication Hub.

Creating the Managed Metadata Service Application

To enable the Content Type Syndication Hub so that the content type data it contains can be consumed by other sites within SharePoint, you need to provision the Managed Metadata Service application and link it to the Content Type Syndication Hub. The Managed Metadata Service application can be accessed through Central Administration, Application Management, Manage Services Application.

The Managed Metadata Service application functions as the publisher for term stores and, optionally, content types created within the Content Type Syndication Hub. Additionally, Managed Metadata Connections consume the data being published from the Managed Metadata Service application. Both the Content Type Syndication Hub's data and the term stores' data are published by the service application.

Create a Managed Metadata Service Application

Perform the following steps to create a Managed Metadata Service application:

1. Open Central Administration, select Application Management, and click Manage Service Applications.

2. Click the New button on the far left side of the ribbon, and select Managed Metadata Service. The Create New Managed Metadata Service dialog box appears.

3. Fill in the appropriate name. It is a good practice to intelligently name the Content Type Syndication Hub that will be linked to this Managed Metadata Service. Generally, this is done by filling in the name, title, and description of the Content Type Hub site collection.

4. Fill in the database information. Always name the database to reflect the metadata being stored within this service.

5. Select or create an application pool to handle the publishing of content types and metadata to the Managed Metadata Connections. Specify an appropriate user to obtain the necessary IIS service isolation.

> **Note**
>
> Application pools isolate the memory space that a specific service uses; therefore, you might consider evaluating the available memory on the web front-end servers before configuring these services in isolated application pools.

6. Type the URL for the site collection that contains the Content Type Syndication Hub that is to be published by this Managed Metadata Service application, as shown in Figure 8.4.

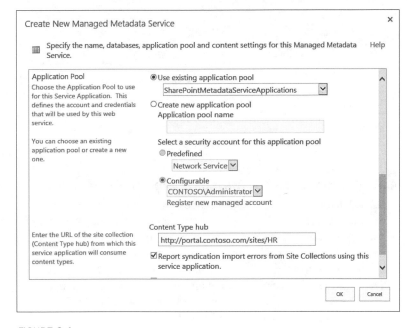

FIGURE 8.4
Managed Metadata Service application pool settings with an optional hub link configuration.

The completed creation of Managed Metadata Service applications should look like Figure 8.5 with respect to the site collections created and displayed in Figure 8.2. Each service application functions as a publisher of the metadata and content types contained within each Content Type Syndication Hub site collection. The Content Type Syndication Hub link in each Managed Metadata Service Application is what ties the site collection's Content Type Syndication Hub to the service application.

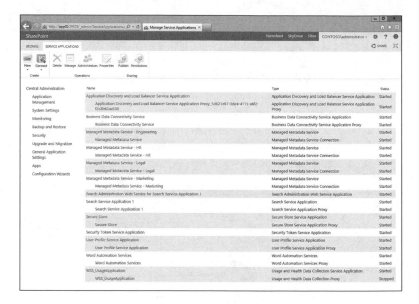

FIGURE 8.5
List of Managed Metadata Service applications.

Modifying the Managed Metadata Service Connection

Along with the Managed Metadata Service application, SharePoint 2013 utilizes the Managed Metadata Service Connection to provide the conduit for web applications to subscribe to both content types consumed from the Content Type Syndication Hub and also the term sets stored within its term store. The connection can be set as the default service application to handle both managed keywords as well as column-specific term sets. Figure 8.6 shows the management dialog box for the Managed Metadata Service Connection where these settings can be configured.

Manage a Metadata Service Connection

Perform the following steps to manage these connections:

1. Open Central Administration, select Application Management, and click Manage Service Applications.

2. Click the row to the right of the Managed Metadata Service Connection name that you want to edit.

3. Select Properties from the management ribbon.

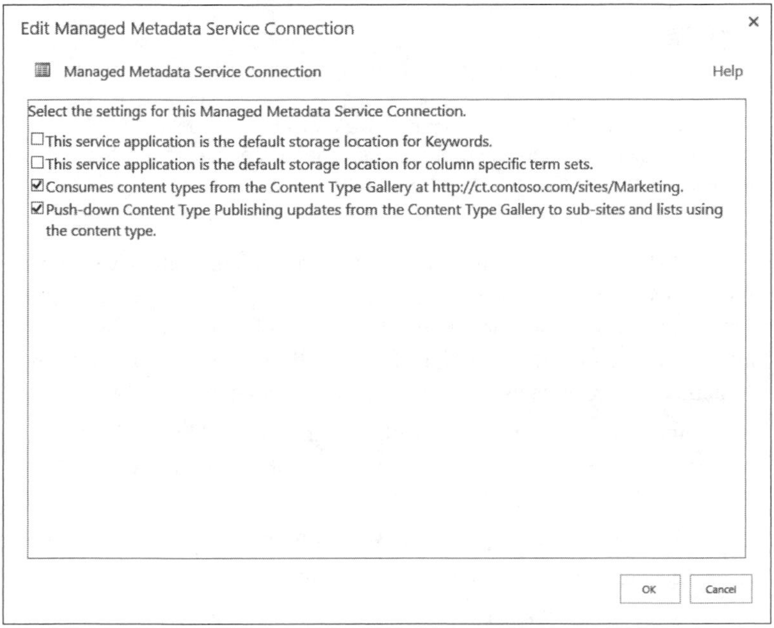

Edit Managed Metadata Service Connection   ×

Managed Metadata Service Connection   Help

Select the settings for this Managed Metadata Service Connection.

☐ This service application is the default storage location for Keywords.

☐ This service application is the default storage location for column specific term sets.

☑ Consumes content types from the Content Type Gallery at http://ct.contoso.com/sites/Marketing.

☑ Push-down Content Type Publishing updates from the Content Type Gallery to sub-sites and lists using the content type.

OK   Cancel

FIGURE 8.6
Editing the Managed Metadata Service Connection.

Associating Managed Metadata Service Applications

Web applications can be directly associated with any and all available Managed Metadata Service Connections. Alternatively, each metadata service application can be added to the default service connection associations' application proxy group.

Note

During the initial Managed Metadata Service configuration, you have the option of adding it to the default proxy group by selecting the check box that referenced the default service connections list (also known as the default proxy group).

The list of default service connections can be changed from Central Administration, Application Management, Configure Service Application Associations. If you select the default link, you are presented with the dialog box to modify the selected default associations.

Warning

Be sure to exercise caution when changing associations! If you remove the association a web application had to a service application that was in use, you are affecting all functionality in the given web application. For example, if columns depended on the associated service application, those columns will cease to function properly.

Figure 8.7 shows the associations enabled for a web application. Custom connection selections can be made for each web application. You can use the associations wholesale or create a custom set of associations by specifying a custom group of connections from the drop-down menu. There are two methods that can be used to get to the associations:

- You can manage service connections through the Manage Web Applications section of Central Administration. To accomplish this, do the following:

  1. Select a web application by clicking it.

  2. Select Service Connections from the ribbon.

- You can access the Configure Service Application Associations section through the Application Management page on the Service Applications section of Central Administration:

  1. Select Configure Service Application Associations from the Service Applications section.

  2. Select the application in which to manage the associations by clicking its name under the heading Web Application/Service Application.

The Configure Service Application Associations dialog box is displayed as shown in Figure 8.7.

Publishing the Managed Metadata Service Application

The Managed Metadata Service application must be published before the metadata can be consumed by interfarm web applications. It is not required that the service application be consumed from a web application within the same farm. Figure 8.8 displays the publishing dialog box used to extend this capability.

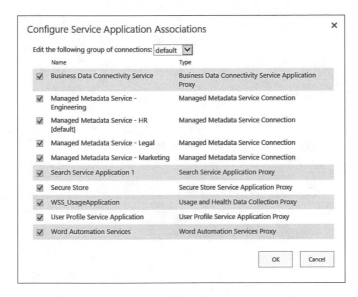

FIGURE 8.7
The Configure Service Application Associations dialog box.

Publish the Managed Metadata Service Application

To publish the service applications for interfarm consumption, perform the following steps:

1. Open Central Administration, select Web Applications, and select Manage Service Applications.

2. Select a web application by clicking its row in the white space to the right of the application name.

3. Click Publish on the ribbon.

4. Enable the capability for metadata services for interfarm consumption by selecting the Publish This Service Application to Other Farms check box (see Figure 8.8).

A trust relationship needs to be established with the remote farm. You can use the wizard to do this, or you can specify the web application pool identity from the consuming web application in the Service Application Permissions page. Note the difference between the Administrators and Permissions groups on the management ribbon. Administrators administer the service application, and the Permissions section defines accounts that can consume the service application.

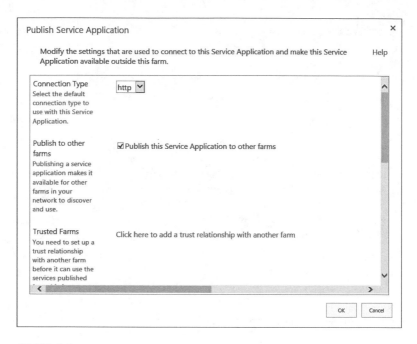

FIGURE 8.8
The Publish Service Application dialog box.

The remote farm uses a unique published URL similar to that shown in the following code sample to establish communication with the service application:

```
urn:schemas-microsoft-com:sharepoint:service:
4b81a879045044e88bdc42a48ee9f60d#authority=urn:
uuid:5d621e873de44115a8f2f2c3b62aa500&authority=
https://app01:32844/Topology/topology.svc
```

Starting the Managed Metadata Web Service

After configuring the Managed Metadata Service application, you must define what physical server will service the application within the farm. Creating the Managed Metadata Service application makes the service application available throughout the farm, but you must next define where the processing will occur. If you do not perform this last step, the content types, managed keywords, and term sets will not be available to any web applications within the farm.

Note

To start these services, browse to Central Administration, System Settings, Manage Services on Server. The Services on Server page will be displayed where you can perform the following:

1. Select the server that you will be managing from the Servers drop-down menu at the top of the page.

2. Find the Managed Metadata Web Service reference, and click the Start link on the rightmost side of that page.

Configuring Administrators for Management Metadata Services

Administrators of the Managed Metadata Service can be specified, as shown in Figure 8.9, by clicking the area to the right of the Managed Metadata Service application name and then selecting Administrators from the ribbon. By default, users added as administrators for Management Metadata Services will have limited access to Central Administration. Farm administrators already have rights to manage all service applications.

FIGURE 8.9
Adding administrators for Managed Metadata Services.

Understanding Managed Taxonomies, Folksonomies, and Term Sets

Managed taxonomies are collections of term sets, managed content types, and keywords that are provided through the Managed Metadata Services. Global taxonomies can employ the community for modification and maintenance of the terms within the term store. The result of this process is known as folksonomies because of the community involvement in the management of terms.

Term sets are used within taxonomies to organize the terms into meaningful categories. Term sets are maintained as members of groups within the term store. These groups allow for isolated security settings for each term group, and therefore provide for the flexible assignment of maintenance tasks and contributing parties.

Enterprise Metadata: The Term Store

The term store is the central repository for the hierarchical representation of terms that can be used through syndication to classify data stored within SharePoint Server 2013. The subscription of terms can be used for data classification, retention, retrieval, and consumption. The term store provides a vehicle for the management of these terms and their hierarchical structure, groups, and relationships.

Corporate taxonomies are often not maintained as a global policy but rather by the community haphazardly tagging content with whatever terms they can think of at the time. This approach provides a degree of separation and a potentially high degree of gaps in search results. To provide for more succinct management of terms and still provide for community involvement, the term store incorporates a mix of managed taxonomy and contributed folksonomy to the definition of the term sets.

Managed Metadata Roles

SharePoint 2013 has four distinct roles for managed metadata. These roles are defined specifically for the interaction with the term store. The purpose of role-based abstraction is to facilitate the granular permission sets that can exist in both taxonomy policy use as well as creation. Roles are the distinct barriers in the permission policy and provide the framework for security.

The benefit is the capability for corporate user communities to participate in both the consumption of these terms and in the creation and refinement of the term sets. Who better to know which categorical specifics are needed to organize the mountains of data than the corporate community itself? This logic parallels that of the contributor and consumer roles that have been in place for other content within SharePoint.

Table 8.2 identifies the specific roles available for the term store and the actions that each group of users can perform.

TABLE 8.2   **Managed Metadata Roles and Capabilities**

Role	Capabilities
Contributor	Create, rename, copy, reuse, move, and delete term sets.
	Modify a term set's properties.
	Create, rename, copy, reuse, merge, deprecate, move, and delete terms.
	Modify a term's properties.
Group Manager	Perform all actions available to the contributor role.
	Import term sets.
	Assign users to or remove users from the contributor role.
	Modify the term set's properties.
Term Store Administrator	Perform all actions available to the group manager role.
	Create and delete term groups.
	Assign users to or remove users from the group manager role.
	Modify the term store properties.
Farm Administrator	Create a new term store.
	Connect to an existing term store.
	Assign users to or remove users from the term store administrator role.

Assigning Term Store Administrators

You also have the flexibility of defining different administrators for each term store. Similar to the permissions associated with content owners or Content Type Syndication Hub site owners, Term Store Administrators (as shown in Figure 8.10) can create new term set groups, assign users to the group manager role, and import metadata terms. Users who have been assigned to the group manager role are able to add terms to the term store.

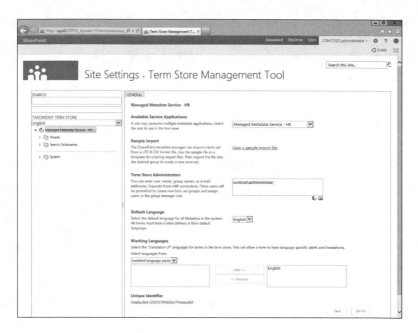

FIGURE 8.10
Assigning term store administrators.

Using the Term Store Management Tool

SharePoint 2013 includes the Term Store Management Tool. This tool is used to manage terms and term sets. You should become familiar with a few basic processes that should become second nature while working in the term store.

Creating Metadata Groups

Term sets, also referred to as metadata groups, are organized into groups that define a hierarchy and serve as a permissions handler for the term sets that are contained within them. A folksonomy depends on the contributions of an organization's general community to keep it up-to-date. By using groups, you can compartmentalize the assignment of rights and allow a greater degree of flexibility to the contributing agents.

Create a New Term Set Group

To create a new term set group, do the following:

1. Open Central Administration, select Application Management, and click Manage Service Applications.

2. Click the Managed Metadata Service link in the Service Applications list.

3. Highlight the Managed Metadata Service Name on the leftmost navigation pane of the Term Store Management Tool.

4. Select New Group from the drop-down menu. The cursor focuses automatically on the new unnamed group so that you can then type the new group's name.

> **Tip**
>
> If you do not see the drop-down arrow when selecting an object, be sure the Central Administration URL is included in your Local Intranet sites.

To delete a term set group, highlight the group name and select Delete Group from the drop-down menu. This is a permanent action, so use caution when deleting term store groups. All term sets and the included hierarchy will also be deleted.

Creating Managed Term Sets

Term sets are child elements under the term set groups. There can be one or many term sets assigned to a term set group.

Create a Managed Term Set

To create a managed term set, do the following:

1. Highlight the group name.

2. Select New Term Set from the drop-down menu.

3. To modify the term set properties, click the term set and modify the properties on the rightmost panel.

4. Define the stakeholders. Stakeholders are people who should be notified that changes are going to be made to a term set.

5. The submission policy can be used to prevent a term set from being edited, with the exception of term sets that are managed by the term store administrator role.

Note

The person defined as the term set contact does not have modification permissions. However, if a contact is specified for a term set, site users can make suggestions about the term set and the defined contact will be notified via email about the suggestion. If you do not want to use the feedback feature, leave this field blank.

Creating Managed Terms

Terms can be either the direct child of the top-level term set identifier or another term. The entire term's contextual hierarchy describes the meaning of the term. In the following example, the term Red, by itself, means nothing; however, when the term is put into context, the meaning becomes clearer. Figure 8.11 shows an example of a contextual hierarchy that self-describes the term Red.

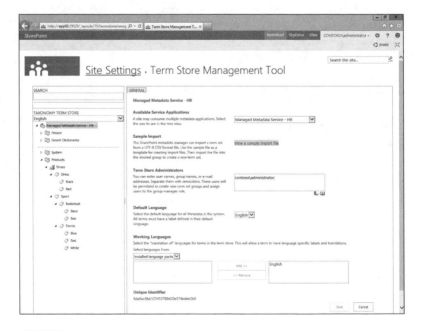

FIGURE 8.11
A term's contextual hierarchy.

As you can see in Figure 8.11, the term Red can have very different meanings!

To create a new term from the user interface, do the following:

1. Highlight the term set or term that will be the parent, and select Create Term from the drop-down menu.
2. Press Enter, or click anywhere on the screen.

After you type text for the term's label, the Term Store Management tool automatically begins to create another term as a sibling to the one just created. This automated action is intended to allow for the rapid creation of terms at the same level. If you do not need to create the next new term, you can click any other term, term set, group, or property area to remove the partially created term.

Note

A term can be disabled within tagging tools. This capability can be useful if a term is being modified, is no longer needed, or is used only temporarily.

Arranging Managed Terms or Term Sets into a Hierarchy

Taxonomy is more than a way of organizing terms to classify and tag data. One of the most important aspects of managed terms with respect to taxonomy is the capability to arrange them into a cascading hierarchy. This arrangement provides a self-describing term set with which to associate navigation, search, sort and filter, policy, and workflow operations. The following options are available for arranging your hierarchy:

- To copy a term or term set, highlight the term or term set name and select the Copy Term [<Set>] from the drop-down menu. The term or term set is duplicated at the same level as its source. The name of the new term or term set is prepended with Copy of.

- To copy a term with all its child terms, highlight the term and select Pin Term with Children from the drop-down menu. This duplicates all child terms to the new term. Remember to rename the new term copy after duplication.

- To search and verify that terms are not being duplicated, you can use the Reuse Term or Term Set functionality.

- To merge terms, highlight the term and select Merge Term from the drop-down menu. Doing this removes the term that is being merged, and all content that has been tagged with this term still references the legacy term. To account for this, the term being merged is added to the other labels of the destination term.

> **Warning**
>
> After terms are merged, the other label cannot be deleted.

■ To deprecate a term, highlight the term and select Deprecate Term from the drop-down menu. Doing this discontinues the use of the term and removes it from availability for tagging. This procedure does not remove all references to the term, and the term can still be used for search and backward compatibility.

■ To move a term or term set, highlight the term or term set and select Move Term [<Set>] from the drop-down menu. Select the new parent for the term or term set for the term being moved, or select the new group for the term set being moved.

> **Note**
>
> A term cannot be moved under the seventh-level terms in a term set. Only seven levels are allowed in the term set hierarchy.

Defining Term Synonyms

The capability to refer to a term by another name provides the contributors the ability to tag content with terms comfortable to them. It gives you the ability to provide a grouping within the synonyms for navigation, search, sort and filter, policy, and workflow operations.

Define Term Synonyms

Term synonyms can be defined by doing the following:

1. Select the term to modify, and open its properties.

2. Locate the Other Labels area of the properties, and enter synonyms for the term.

3. Save the term by clicking the Save button at the bottom of the dialog box.

> **Note**
>
> Only one label can be entered per line. Press Enter to add a new line.

Defining Terms in Multiple Languages

The capability to associate a term to more than one language requires that the appropriate language packs be installed for both Windows Server OS and for SharePoint Server 2013. After the required language packs have been installed, you are given the ability to manage terms consistently across multiple languages where users have chosen to use other available system languages.

Associate a Term to More Than One Language

To associate a term to more than one language, perform the following steps:

1. Select the term to modify, and open its properties.

2. Locate the Language drop-down and choose the desired language; then enter the desired Default Label for the chosen language.

3. Save the term by clicking the Save button at the bottom of the dialog box.

Custom Properties

Custom properties are additional details that can be stored about a term. These properties can be shared across pinned instances of the same term across the term store or can be local to a single instance. These properties can be used to extend the details available about a term.

Create a Custom Property for a Term

To create a custom property for a term, perform the following steps:

1. Select the term to modify, and open its properties.

2. Select the Custom Properties tab.

3. Select Add for either shared properties or local properties as desired.

4. Specify the desired Property Name and an appropriate Value.

5. Save the custom property by clicking the Save button at the bottom of the dialog box.

Managing Keywords

Keywords are independent terms that have no hierarchical precedence. As a result, they are wholly independent of any term set and have no parents or child terms. They are meant to remain independent and can be added or maintained only by the term store administrator:

- To create a new keyword, highlight Keywords and select New Keyword from the drop-down menu.
- To delete a keyword, highlight the keyword and select Delete Keyword from the drop-down menu.

Converting Managed Keywords into Managed Terms

You can convert managed keywords into managed terms by moving them from the keywords set into a term set. Doing this removes the term from the keywords set and allows it to subsequently have child terms assigned to it. The term automatically inherits the permissions of the term set that it is assigned to.

To move the keyword into a term set, do the following:

1. Highlight the keyword.

2. Select Move Keyword from the drop-down menu.

3. Select the new parent for the term for the keyword being moved.

Importing Managed Term Sets

Although terms sets can be created by using the Term Store Management tool via the user interface, a large and complex hierarchy is very time consuming to create. For mature taxonomies, you should use the importing functionality.

The term store allows for only seven levels of hierarchy within a taxonomy set. Specific column information about an import file is located in Table 8.3, and an example is shown in the code block that follows the table.

TABLE 8.3   **Import Term Set File Format***

Column	Additional Information
Term Set Name	The term set name.
Term Set Description	The term set description.
LICD	The locale identifier that represents the language of the term set. For example, 1033–English.

Column	Additional Information
Available for Tagging	Set to TRUE to allow users to use the term. Set to FALSE to prevent users from using the term.
Term Description	An optional description for the term.
Level 1–7 Terms	The seven columns of the term hierarchy. You must provide a value for all levels down to the level of the term that you are representing.

The term set import file format is a .csv file that contains only 12 columns. Name and Description columns can be encapsulated in quotes, as shown in the code sample that follows.

The sample shown next is an example of a term set import file. Although there is no data represented down to the seventh level of abstraction, be aware that the commas are required to notate the hierarchy. All parent levels are required for proper classification within the term set. The LCID is the language code that the term set is written in. The Available for Tagging Boolean field designates whether the term is available for discovery during tagging for navigation, search, sort and filter, policy, and workflow operations.

> **Tip**
>
> In the main Managed Metadata Services management page is a link to view a sample import file. If you are new to taxonomies, this is a great place to begin your import file creation.

```
"Term Set Name","Term Set
Description","LCID","Available for
Tagging","TermDescription","Level 1 Term","Level
2 Term","Level 3
Term","Level 4 erm","Level 5 Term","Level 6
Term","Level 7
Term""Sites","Locations where the organization has
offices",,TRUE,,,,,,,,"Locations",,1033,TRUE,,
"North
America",,,,,,"Locations",,1033,TRUE,,"North
America","Washington",,,,,"Locations",,1033,TRUE,
,"North
America","Washington","Redmond",,,,"Locations",
,1033,TRUE,,"North
```

```
America","Washington","Seattle",,,,"Locations",
,1033,TRUE,,"North
America","Washington","Tacoma",,,,"Locations",,
1033,TRUE,,"North
America","Massachusetts",,,,,"Locations",,1033,
TRUE,,"North
America","Massachusetts","Boston",,,,"Locations
",,1033,
TRUE,,"North
America","Massachusetts","Cambridge",,,,
"Locations",,1033,TRUE,,
"Europe","England","London",,,,"Locations",,
1033,TRUE,,"Europe",
"Germany","Berlin",,,,"Locations",,1033,TRUE,,
"Europe","Austria","Vienna",,,,
```

Understanding Enterprise Content Types

Content types allow you to separate the declaration of list metadata from the list itself so that you can reuse the same metadata in multiple columns. List metadata is the collection of fields associated with each column in the list. Content types consist of site columns, which in turn are bound to fields.

To understand content types in the context of document management, you might find it helpful to think of each document as an item in a list in which the list columns map to document properties. This is a fundamental concept—that document properties map directly to site column definitions. SharePoint Server 2013 uses the site column definitions to create document properties, to copy data to and from documents as they move into and out of SharePoint document libraries, to associate information management policies and templates with documents, and to manage the state of workflow instances that might be associated with a given document. This capability to capture workflow state extends the scope of content types to include document behavior as well as static properties.

Creating Content Types

Content types are site-collection scoped. In this chapter, we are referring to the Content Type Syndication Hub site collection.

Create a New Enterprise Content Type

To create a new enterprise content type, complete the following steps:

1. Browse to the Content Type Syndication Hub—for example, http://portal.contoso.com/hr/.

2. From Site Actions, select Site Settings.

3. Select Site Content Types in the Galleries grouping.

4. Click Create. You should now see the New Site Content Type page as shown in Figure 8.12.

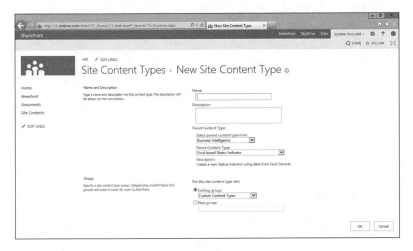

FIGURE 8.12
Creating a new site content type.

5. Type a name and description for the new content type into the appropriate fields.

6. Choose an existing content type as the parent by selecting it from the Select Parent Content Type From drop-down list. To locate the parent type and then filter the list by group, use the Parent Content Type drop-down menu. Every content type is derived either from the base system content type or from one of its child types. This built-in inheritance mechanism enables one content type to extend its functionality by incorporating all the columns declared in its parent.

Note

If you'll use the content type in a document library, the Document content type must be in the prior lineage. Otherwise, you will not be able to use the content type in a library. For example, if you are inheriting from the HR content type for a policy template, HR must be inherited from Document.

---

7. To make it easier for users to find your new content type, select an existing group or type the name of a new group that best describes how your content type is to be used.

8. Click OK to return to the Site Content Type summary page.

Note

After the content type has been created, you can add the columns that best describe the metadata you want to use in your documents. Use the Add from Existing Site Columns link to select from the existing site columns, or create a new column if the existing columns do not meet your needs.

Managing Content Type Dependencies

Content types can be based on other content types. When changes are made to a parent content type, those changes are not reflected automatically in child content types that derive from it unless those changes are explicitly pushed down to the derived content types. Pushing down the changes from a parent content type to its child types means that the schema associated with each child is overwritten with the new schema defined in the parent. You can prevent this overwriting by marking the child content type as sealed. Sealed content types are not affected by push-down operations.

Mark Content Type as Sealed

To mark content type as sealed, perform the following steps:

1. Open the Site Content Type page from Galleries within Site Settings.

2. Select the content type by clicking its name.

3. Click the Advanced Settings link.

4. From the Site Content Type Advanced Settings page, select the Yes option button in the Read Only section.

5. Click OK to save the changes.

Consuming Metadata

Metadata is of little use unless it can be consumed by SharePoint Server 2013 at the site-collection level. The most useful taxonomy would be without merit if not for the columns, navigation, search, sort and filter, policy, and workflow operations that make up the consumption of its data. Managed metadata as consumed by document libraries and lists is the embodiment of a successful taxonomy policy.

The majority of consumption centers around site columns because these provide the basis for filtering and navigation. Tagging is also pertinent to the consumption of metadata. Search, workflow, and policy operations are consumers of the columnar and tag information.

Working with Site Columns

SharePoint Server 2013 ships with a default collection of predefined site columns. These site columns are organized into groups that map loosely to the way each column is typically used. To see the available site columns, browse to the Site Columns gallery, which is found under Site Actions, Site Settings, Site Columns in the Galleries grouping.

From the Site Columns gallery, you can view or edit the definition of existing columns or create new columns for the site you are currently viewing. The name of the column appears as a hyperlink under the Site Column heading. If a column name does not appear as a hyperlink, it means that the column is declared in a parent site of the site you are viewing. To modify column definitions declared within a parent site, you must first go to the parent site and then to its Site Columns gallery. To modify an existing column definition, click its hyperlink.

> **Note**
>
> Columns created in the Site Columns gallery are available only within the current site and subsites.

From the New Site Column page, you can specify the name, data type, and group affiliation for the new column. Although every column belongs to a group, the groups are used only to organize the columns. You can change the group affiliation at any time. In practice, you often need to use columns from many groups when creating a new content type. Although the New Site Column page contains a Description text box that can hold informative text about how a given field should be used, the built-in site columns do not make use of this property. It is good practice, however, to include a brief description when creating new site columns to make it easier to match a given column to its intended use.

> **Tip**
>
> When choosing an existing site column, you should be aware that this list includes both sealed and unsealed columns that have been added by various features that have been enabled on your site. Using sealed site columns might cause problems with your content type declarations because they cannot be removed through the user interface after they have been added to a content type. This problem is exacerbated when modifying an existing content type from which other content types have been derived. Table 8.4 lists some of the sealed columns that are added by the publishing feature. Use caution when adding them to custom content types.

TABLE 8.4   **Sealed Site Columns Added by the Publishing Feature**

Column Name	Column Group
Article Date	Publishing Columns
Browser Title	Publishing Columns
Contact	Publishing Columns
Contact E-mail Address	Publishing Columns
Contact Name	Publishing Columns
Contact Picture	Publishing Columns
Hide from Internet Search Engines	Publishing Columns
Hide Physical URLs from Search	Publishing Columns
Meta Description	Publishing Columns
Meta Keywords	Publishing Columns
Scheduling Start Date	Publishing Columns
Scheduling End Date	Publishing Columns
Sitemap Change Frequency	Publishing Columns
Sitemap Priority	Publishing Columns
Target Audiences	Publishing Columns
Byline	Page Layout Columns
Catalog-Item URL	Page Layout Columns
Image Caption	Page Layout Columns
Page Content	Page Layout Columns
Page Icon	Page Layout Columns

Column Name	Column Group
Page Image	Page Layout Columns
Rollup Image	Page Layout Columns
Summary Links	Page Layout Columns
Summary Links 2	Page Layout Columns

Creating Managed Metadata Site Columns

In addition to having a collection of predefined site columns, custom site columns can be added to augment the tagging of list and document data. Custom columns can be added to any list within SharePoint. A custom site column can be enabled to consume managed metadata.

Create a Custom Managed Data

Perform the following steps to begin creating a custom managed metadata site column:

1. Open the list or document library to which you want to add the column.

2. Click the Library tab under Library Tools.

3. Click the Library Settings button on the far right on the management ribbon, as shown in Figure 8.13.

4. Under the Columns section, click Create Column.

FIGURE 8.13
A document's Library tab on the management ribbon.

5. The Create Column page opens, as shown in Figure 8.14.

6. Type the Column name.

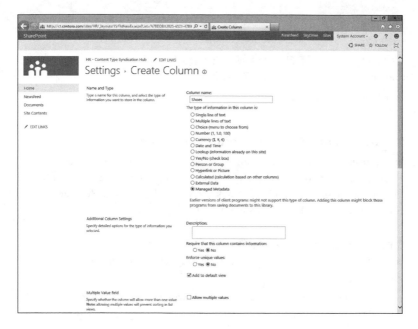

FIGURE 8.14
Creating the Managed Metadata site column.

7. Select the Managed Metadata option from the type of information list. This enables the managed term list selection area.

8. Configure the additional properties, including Description, Require That This Column Contains Information, Enforce Unique Data, and Add to Default View.

9. Make sure to select the Allow Multiple Values check box if you need to allow multiple value inputs in the metadata field.

10. Select the appropriate Display value. The Display value can be either the term label or the entire term hierarchical path.

11. Select a managed term set, as shown in Figure 8.15. The search field is provided to aid in this process by filtering the term sets listed by the search entry parameter, as shown in Figure 8.16. Only one term set can be selected. You can also edit a new term set in the term store management tool.

12. You can also type a default value for the column. The choice list is populated with the data retrieved from the term set.

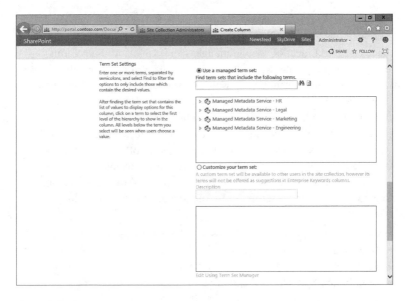

FIGURE 8.15
Using a managed term set.

FIGURE 8.16
Filtered managed term set list for the selection of a term set.

It is important to understand the significance of selecting the managed term sets in the Managed Metadata column. The use of a managed term set provides a central location where changes can be made to the column selection or tagging data. Regardless of which list or document library uses the column for classification purposes, all data across the entire site will be synchronized. This is the fundamental change in global taxonomy policies that the term store has empowered within SharePoint Server 2013. Data isn't isolated within a single site collection; therefore, it does not need to be duplicated to exist symbiotically in another site collection or web application. Data changes automatically flow across all consumer sites with minimal administrative effort. The only step you need to take to use this data is to select it for consumption by the Managed Metadata column, as shown in Figure 8.15.

To make this selection of data even easier, the capability to search the available term stores for the correct term reference filters out all the unmatched term sets, and it minimizes the potential for improper term set selection. Figure 8.16 shows a filtered term set result where Red was entered in the search field. Red matches both the Shoes term set and the Locations term set, although "Locations" is a partial word match.

> **Note**
>
> Search filtering returns even partial label matches.

Managed Metadata and Document Management

Gathering document metadata is an important part of an effective document management solution. However, most users focus on the document content and not the metadata. Consequently, important metadata is often captured inconsistently or not at all. The document upload process in SharePoint helps avoid this problem by enabling users to enter metadata during file upload. Likewise, it can also enforce entering metadata within an Office Application, such as Microsoft Word.

The columns are displayed during the file upload into the document library, as shown in Figure 8.17. Required fields are highlighted with a red asterisk.

Depending on the column settings, either one value or many values can be selected to tag the document. Figure 8.18 is the dialog box displayed while selecting term labels to tag the document with.

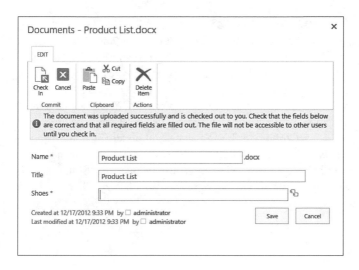

FIGURE 8.17
Document upload properties.

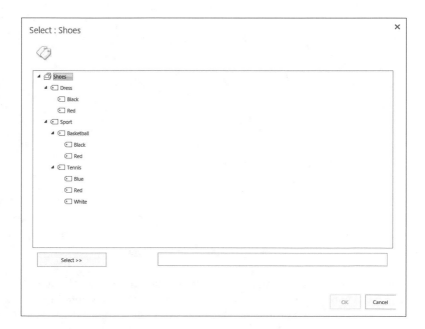

FIGURE 8.18
Term Label Selection dialog box during file upload.

Metadata Navigation Settings

Metadata navigation can be enabled on any list in SharePoint. This provides linking to managed terms that are being referenced in Managed Metadata columns within the list. By default, content types and folders are available for a list. A Managed Metadata column must be enabled on a list for the metadata to be used as a navigational hierarchy. You can configure metadata navigation by browsing to Document or List, Library or List Tools, Library or List, Library or List Settings, and under General Settings selecting Metadata Navigation Settings to display the page as shown in Figure 8.19. The Configure Key Filters area also enables the list to be filtered in views by the metadata noted in the Available Key Filter Fields area.

FIGURE 8.19
The page for configuring metadata navigation and key filters.

Managed keywords are consumed from all metadata connections that are subscribed to by the site collection. As Figure 8.20 shows, keywords are automatically suggested based on input. The label must match the data in a term store or an error will be presented.

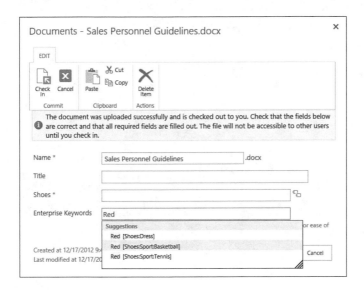

FIGURE 8.20

Tagging with managed terms.

CHAPTER 9

Configuring Document Management

- Managing Documents in SharePoint 2013
- Document IDs and Sets
- List and Library Relationships
- Document Version Control
- Workflows
- Inbound Email
- Offline Support
- The Document Center
- In-Place Records Management
- The Records Center
- eDiscovery

Document management is one of the most important processes in any organization. As document workspaces grow while organizations shift to paperless processing, the mountains of electronic copies begin to grow exponentially. Beyond dealing with the documents themselves, organizations also face a shift in the way they handle documents. Document versions, workflows, libraries, unique IDs, document sets, collaboration spaces, and offline availability must be considered when developing the document management policies for an organization. The purpose of this chapter is to provide you with an understanding of how Microsoft SharePoint Server 2013 provides the resources and tools to efficiently and effectively manage documents.

Managing Documents in SharePoint 2013

SharePoint Server 2013 provides a robust feature set for collaboration with improvements in document management. These features include document sets and document IDs, as well as additional functionality to improve the content types and columns features.

Organizations planning to implement SharePoint 2013 need to consider these features and evaluate how they will enhance either existing or newly formulated collaboration models. SharePoint document management, managed metadata, and other features center on the intrinsic methodologies of collaboration and community contribution.

Document Management

Your organization might already have a document management plan. This plan might simply be a definition of document types, and it could be as involved as the entire process life cycle for managing document control and change management. Document management is the evolution of planning and design that encompasses the document life cycle for an organization. Ideally, the design and development of a document management plan is a management function.

This chapter focuses on how SharePoint 2013 can be used to implement a document management plan. The following are some key factors that should be included in a well-rounded document management plan:

- **Participant roles description**—Identifies key participants for the document management processes and what their responsibilities will be. This description breaks down the specific roles and defines the relationships with other roles within the plan.

- **Catalog of document types**—An exhaustive list of categories that the organization must maintain, and the specific policies and requirements that govern each type of data.

- **Document organizational taxonomy**—An organized and logical schema for organizing, tagging, and otherwise identifying the documents that will be maintained within the document management plan. The more detailed and expanded this taxonomy is, the greater the degree is of cross-referencing capabilities available for tag-based identification. The fine line here is that the taxonomy should not be too complex or cumbersome to use.

- **Document movement plan**—Describes the policies and procedures for how documents should be transitioned between servers, people, storage media, and so forth.

▪ **Workflow plan**—Outlines the major steps necessary in a document life cycle and the relationships these steps have to their participant roles. This plan establishes the flow of data from end to end and encapsulates any change-management procedures.

Document management can mean different things to different people. These subtle differences are directly related to how people understand its use. In general, document management is the process of applying organizational policies and rules to how documents are created; where and how they are stored; how long they are retained; and, ultimately, when and how they are destroyed.

The first fundamental step an organization needs to take before it can begin creating lists and libraries to store its documents is to understand how these documents will be created and managed. The lists and libraries are then built around these defining factors.

For example, a document library that will be used by the legal department needs to have standard templates for various legal documents. These templates can be depositions, contracts, disclosure and noncompetition agreements, and so on. The templates should be stored as content types within the library for ease of creation and also tagging. Documents that need to be kept should be sent to the retention library to be held for the specific length of time for the content type.

These specific document-management requirements determine how an organization approaches document management. Several attributes make up the framework of this document-management approach:

▪ Content types

▪ Metadata columns

▪ Lookup columns

▪ Records Center Send To link

▪ Information management policy

Document Collaboration

There is often a great deal of confusion between document management and document collaboration. Document collaboration is the process of two or more people creating, editing, tagging, and interacting with the document and also communicating about it.

A document might not require any collaboration simply because a single person performs all tasks related to its creation and editing. Collaboration typically exists on a document when that document is either being created or revised and needs the input of two or more people. Document management might also be required as part of that collaboration, but sometimes there is no need for management, just collaboration. After the document is created, it can be processed through a workflow plan so that additional work can be done on it. At some point within the document life cycle, the document can be switched from a collaboration document to a managed document.

You should always consider the overhead of having document-management features turned on by default because these features can require additional resource investment in disk space for version and auditing information. If business needs and logic require these specific document-management capabilities, the resource requirements for disk space and performance should be analyzed.

Document Libraries

Document libraries are the primary container for storing and managing documents. They include all the elements required to enable collaboration and document management across documents that are stored within them. A document library can also be saved as a template so that other document libraries can be defined using the same predefined information—including content types, rights management policies, versioning requirements, workflows, and more—rather than just having a blank library. This method of organization reduces the amount of configuring that needs to be done to establish a new document library.

All the previous functionality from SharePoint 2010 has been included:

- Major and minor versioning
- Required checkout
- Content types
- Information management policies
- Built-in workflows
- Incoming e-mail support
- Document IDs
- Document sets
- Metadata navigation
- Relational lists
- Multiple check-in
- Content organizer; rule-based submission

New features that have been added in SharePoint 2013 include the following:

- **SkyDrive Pro**—SkyDrive Pro assists users by making it easier to work with documents offline. SkyDrive Pro allows users to sync files across multiple devices while enforcing SharePoint's document management capabilities for metadata, workflow, and compliance.

- **eDiscovery**—Provides organizations with the ability to research and manage records that are required for litigation and compliance reporting. eDiscovery uses SharePoint's search capabilities to locate records throughout SharePoint and provide the functionality to hold and freeze records and manage discovery efforts by case files.

Note

Although sites that were created using the Document Workspace site template will continue to work in SharePoint 2013, sites using this template are no longer supported. The capability to perform document collaboration is now included in the Team Site site template.

Settings for document libraries can be changed by browsing to the Library tab, Library Settings in the Settings section, which displays the Library Settings administration page as shown in Figure 9.1.

Library permissions can be accessed by browsing to the Library tab, Library Permissions in the Settings section. Figure 9.2 shows that a library, by default, inherits permissions from its parent. However, this behavior can be disabled and independent permissions established instead. These unique permissions on the library or items control access and security trimming, which as a result control the capability to see the library or content within it. A person who does not have read access to the library cannot see the library because of the security trimming related to the user's view. The library will also not be displayed in any of the user's search results.

Note

Many tasks related to configuring and managing document libraries are left to the end user, not the SharePoint administrator.

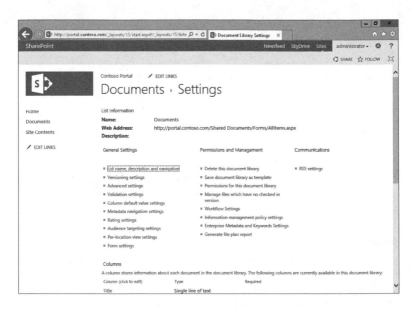

FIGURE 9.1
Document library settings.

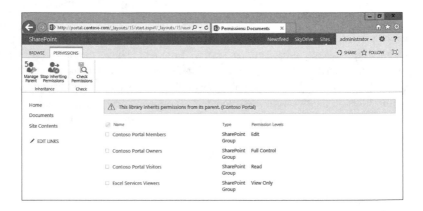

FIGURE 9.2
Document library Permission tools tab.

Document IDs and Sets

Two new features within SharePoint 2013 are the use of document IDs and document sets. These two features are important tools for document management. Document IDs provide a unique identifier for each document within a site collection. Document sets enable documents to be grouped into a version-capable or distributable group. A version-capable or distributable group can be packaged (through the use of a .zip file) and distributed in its entirety. Previous versions of SharePoint provided document control at an individual document level only—that is, groups of documents folders were the only option.

Document IDs

Another new feature in SharePoint 2013 provides you with the capability to assign unique document IDs to an item. Following is a list of the key elements of a document ID:

- Unique metadata tagging
- Site-collection scoped
- Activated through a site collection feature
- Defined logical naming structure
- Consumed by enterprise components, lists, and libraries as well as the Records Center, Document Center, search, and workflow.

The Document ID Service must be enabled before document IDs can be assigned to any documents within a site collection.

Enable the Site Collection for the Document ID Service

To enable the Site Collection feature for the Document ID Service, perform the following steps:

1. Browse to Settings, Site Settings, Site Collection Features under Site Collection Administration.

2. Click the Activate button in the Document ID Service section, as shown in Figure 9.3.

FIGURE 9.3
Activate the Document ID Service site collection feature.

> **Note**
>
> You can also enable document IDs on a site collection within Windows PowerShell using the following command:
>
> ```
> enable-spfeature -id [idcharacters] -url [site collection URL]
> ```

After the Site Collection feature has been enabled, you can configure the naming convention that will be used within the site collection, as shown in Figure 9.4. The naming convention entered prefixes all document IDs with the characters you specify in this screen. A timer job is enabled that automatically processes the new document ID to implement it across your site collection. You can also reset all document IDs in the site collection to begin with the entered characters.

FIGURE 9.4
Document ID Settings page.

The Document ID field is not automatically enabled in a view, but it can be selected from Create View by completing the following steps:

1. Access the Library tab, Create View to create a custom view.

2. Enter a name for the custom view.

3. Select the Document ID check box, as shown in Figure 9.5.

As documents are created, unique IDs will be associated with each and, as shown in Figure 9.6, the Document ID field is a value that can be used in columns and in search.

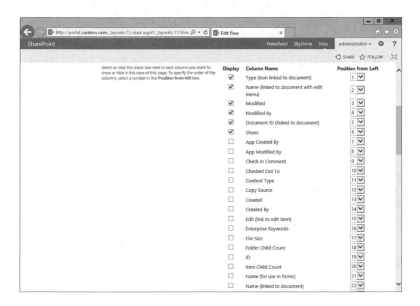

FIGURE 9.5
Select the Document ID check box in Create View.

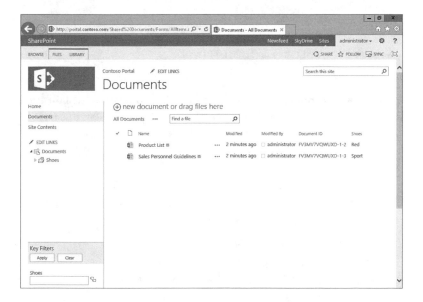

FIGURE 9.6
A custom document view that includes the Document ID field.

Managing Document Sets

A document set is a content type that allows you to group documents that can then be managed as a set. The management of this set of documents can be based on a workflow or metadata, thus making the document set a perfect container within a document library for grouping key documents. Newly introduced in SharePoint Server 2013 is the capability for search to index content within document sets. In addition, document sets can also use folders for better managing content.

Activate Document Sets Within a Site Collection

To enable document sets within a document library, you need to verify that the Document Sets site collection feature has been activated:

1. Click Settings, Site Settings.

2. Under Site Collection Administration, select Site Collection Features.

3. Click the Activate button in the Document Sets section if it is not already activated, as shown in Figure 9.7.

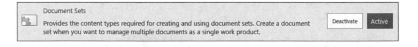

FIGURE 9.7
Activate the Document Sets site collection feature.

Enable Management of Content Types Within a Document Library

After the site collection feature has been activated, you can start to enable document sets within a document library. To do this, you need to allow for the management of content types on the document library by completing the following steps:

1. Navigate to the document library by clicking its title.

2. When you're in the document library, select Library on the management ribbon for the document library.

3. Select Library Settings in the Settings section.

4. Under General Settings, select Advanced Settings.

5. Ensure that the Content Types section shows the Yes option is selected for Allow Management of Content Types, as shown in Figure 9.8.

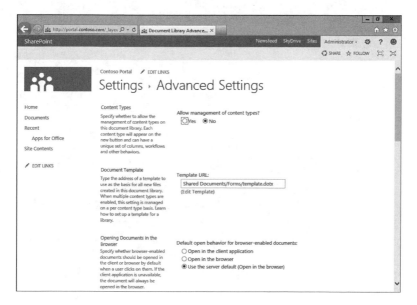

FIGURE 9.8
Allow Management of Content Types option in the Content Types section.

After you have enabled the management of content types within the document library, a Document Sets content type can be added to the document library. This allows document sets to be created from the New Document menu on the Document Library management ribbon.

Add Document Sets to the Document Library

To add a Document Sets content type to the available New Document menu options, complete the following steps:

1. Navigate to the document library by clicking its title.

2. When you're in the document library, select Library on the management ribbon for the document library.

3. Select Library Settings in the Settings section.

4. Scroll down to the Content Types section, and select Add from Existing Site Content Types, as shown in Figure 9.9.

> **Note**
>
> The Document Set content type will not be available here until the Document Sets site collection feature is activated.

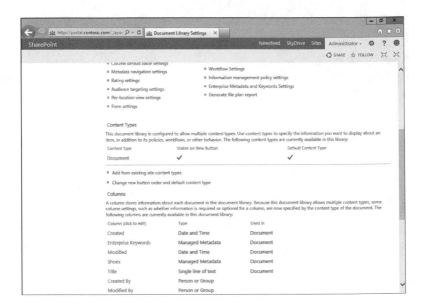

FIGURE 9.9
Add document sets from existing site content types.

5. On the Add Content Types page, select Document Set from the Available Site Content Types list.

6. Click Add and then click OK to save your changes.

Note

You can change the default document type and menu display order using the Change New Button Order and Default Content Type link in the Content Types section of the document libraries settings page.

List and Library Relationships

SharePoint 2013 provides you with the capability to link multiple libraries or lists with common information. To manage these relationships, SharePoint offers two options to enforce this relationship behavior and provides an added measure of data integrity: one prevents referenced data from being removed from another list without the references being removed first, and the other option provides you with the capability to cascade that removal. Figure 9.10 shows the two options for restricting the action on deletes to one of the following:

- **Restrict Delete**—If an attempt is made to delete an item from the list that is being referenced for a lookup column, SharePoint displays an error message informing the user that the row cannot be deleted because it is being referenced in another list.

- **Cascade Delete**—If an attempt is made to delete an item from a list that is being referenced for a lookup column, SharePoint deletes that row from the list, as well as rows that reference it from any other list that used that value in a lookup column, as shown in Figure 9.10.

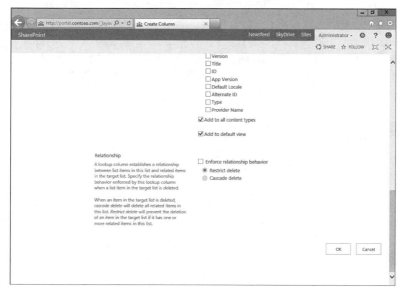

FIGURE 9.10
Enforcing relationship behavior on a lookup field.

Check In/Check Out

SharePoint provides the capability to handle the Check Out for Edit option within its document libraries. To properly maintain document history and version integrity, it is important for users to check out documents before they edit them.

SharePoint provides several unique features as part of the Check Out functionality. These features provide for single-user locking, restricted visibility to those with the ability to check out a document, and an offline sandbox that retains the working copy on the user's computer while the user is editing the document and until it is checked back in. The Check In feature provides the capability to check in a document with comments, which provides the user the means to note what was changed within the document.

Administrators frequently encounter the situation where a document is checked out by an individual who is not available to check the document back in or who just forgot to check the file back in. SharePoint provides the capability to take ownership of an already checked-out file and either undo the check-out or perform a check-in of the document. However, the other person's changes will not be saved, and that user will need to incorporate them at a later date.

SharePoint 2013 provides the capability to check in or check out multiple documents at the same time. By selecting the check box next to the desired items, a user can check in or check out all the selected items at the same time, as shown in Figure 9.11.

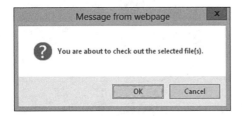

FIGURE 9.11
Check in or check out multiple documents at the same time.

Content Types

Document libraries store documents based on properties set up within the library's document type source template. Content types are a collection of settings, metadata, workflows, and policies that define the source template. There can be more than one source template document type set up for a document library. Document types can have a content type associated with them that provides consistent data management and workflow rules across multiple documents, libraries, and sites.

In SharePoint 2013, content types can be created at many levels in the farm, from enterprisewide content types to site-level content types.

List and libraries can make use of content types by enabling them in the settings for the list or library.

Enable Content Type Management

To enable content type management on a list, as shown in Figure 9.12, perform the following steps:

1. Navigate to the document library by clicking its title.

2. In the document library, browse to Library on the management ribbon for the document library.

3. Select Library Settings in the Settings section.

4. Under General Settings, select Advanced Settings.

5. In the Content Types section, under Allow Management of Content Types, select Yes.

6. Click OK to apply changes.

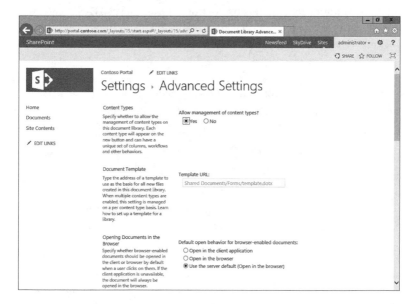

FIGURE 9.12
Allow Management of Content Types section.

The default content type and the order in which the content types appear in the new document drop-down list are configurable from the list settings.

> **Note**
>
> Any document type can be uploaded into any document library regardless of the configured content types. Content types dictate only types available in the new document selection list.

Each content type can have its own configuration settings, such as a unique file template, file type, workflow settings, document information panel (DIP), information management policy, and column metadata values. These content type settings can be inherited from enterprise content types, and metadata can be leveraged from the managed metadata services. More information on enterprise content types and metadata can be found in Chapter 8, "Configuring Enterprise Content Types and Metadata," which covers enterprise content types and managed metadata.

Document Version Control

Document libraries support version control at several levels. By default, versioning is not enabled but is enabled in the document library settings. Versions are complete copies of the document, not deltas.

Enabling Versioning

To enable versioning, perform the following steps:

1. Navigate to the document library by clicking its title.
2. In the document library, select Library on the management ribbon for the document library.
3. Select Library Settings in the Settings section.
4. Under General Settings, select Versioning Settings.
5. Select the versioning options required, as shown in Figure 9.13, under Document Version History.

Depending on the process flow and business requirements put in force by the document management plan within an organization, document versioning requirements might be succinctly different. Some document management plans might require approval for inclusion within the library. Retention policies might require the pruning of older versions and the removal of drafts or minor revisions upon the publication of a major version.

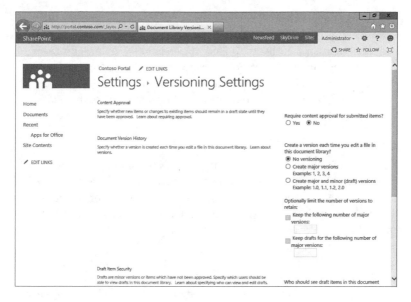

FIGURE 9.13
Document Version History settings.

Content Approval

You can designate that a document or document set be approved before the version becomes available for consumption. This requirement might include changes to existing documents as well as the addition of new items. This can be used in conjunction with an approval workflow to streamline the approval process.

Major Versioning

All versions are considered to be "published" versions when major versioning is enabled in a document library. The option is provided to the user during check-in to identify which version the file or document set should be marked with. Only whole-number versions are created and retained.

Major and Minor Versioning

Minor versions that are marked with the fractional number in the second octet are considered drafts. This option is designed to support the publishing model in which draft versions or working copies are used until a point in time when publishing will change the major version number. Major versions are marked as "published" in the versions list. When a document is checked in, users can choose to mark it as one of the following version types: Existing Minor, New Minor, or New Major. Users can also elect to keep the document checked out, with the exception of checking it in as Major version, because there could be a workflow attached to the Major version publishing.

Version Pruning

The choice of either versioning structure allows for limiting the number of versions retained by the document library. These limits can be established at both the Major and Minor version levels. Pruning works on the first-in, first-out basis, with older versions being pruned. If a major version is removed, all minor versions related to that major version are also removed. Version pruning is a significant planning issue that affects the content database sizes, quotas, and disaster recovery. Because each version is a complete copy of the document, not a delta, decisions regarding pruning can significantly affect the infrastructure requirements, the length of retention, and the ability to recover.

Draft Item Security

Drafts are minor versions or items that have not been approved. The Draft Item Security feature specifies which users should be able to view drafts in the document library. There are three options that can be set in the Versioning settings for the document library, as shown in Figure 9.14:

- Any User Who Can Read Items
- Only Users Who Can Edit Items
- Only Users Who Can Approve Items (and the Author of the Item)

Note

As an administrator, you need to understand that without pruning turned on, large numbers of document versions can be created, which can greatly increase the size of the SQL database.

If you are using large file sizes (greater than 200MB) and do not want to keep those items stored in the SQL Server database, you can use Remote Binary Large Object (BLOB) Storage (RBS) outside of SQL on a file system.

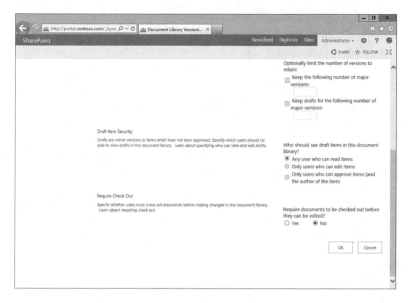

FIGURE 9.14
Draft Item Security and Require Check Out sections.

Workflows

SharePoint provides several default workflows that can be used for controlling actions that happen to the document at a specific point in its life cycle. These default workflows include the following:

- **Approval**—Routes a document for approval. Users with the correct permissions can approve or reject the document, reassign the approval task, or request changes to the document.

- **Collect Feedback**—Routes a document for review. Reviewers can provide feedback, which is compiled and sent to the document owner when the workflow is completed.

- **Collect Signatures**—Gathers signatures needed to complete an Office document.

- **Disposition Approval**—Manages document expiration and retention by allowing participants to decide whether to retain or delete expired documents.

- **Three-State Workflow**—Can be activated at the site-collection level to provide a workflow for tracking the status of items.

Many organizations have needs that extend beyond the capabilities of the default workflows. The default workflows are not sufficient for the complete business solution models of some organizations; for that reason, the following additional tools are available that can be used to create much more complex workflow designs:

- **SharePoint Designer**—Designed for the power user, it provides the capability to create multistep workflows that have many more options than the default workflows.

- **Visual Studio**—Used by developers to create complex business logic workflows, such as state machine workflows.

Many third-party companies have also developed custom workflow tools to make the end user's life as easy as possible. These tools provide for the designing and deploying of workflows without the need for a developer.

Assigning Workflow Settings

Workflow settings can be assigned to a document library or list by enabling them in the settings for the list or library. To enable a workflow on a list or library, follow these steps:

1. Navigate to the document library by clicking its title.

2. In the document library, select Library on the management ribbon for the document library.

3. Select Library Settings in the Settings section.

4. Under Permissions and Management, select Workflow Settings.

5. Select the versioning options required, as shown in Figure 9.13, under Document Version History.

Custom workflow templates created through either SharePoint Designer, Microsoft Visual Studio, or a third-party tool will be available after they have been added to the site collection. Workflows are assigned by reference to the available workflow templates.

Inbound Email

Enabling inbound email support in a document library provides the benefit of integrating SharePoint with email. Email is the most common method of document collaboration used today. Perhaps the simplest and least intrusive way to introduce SharePoint sites to existing users is to email–enable a document library and then add the address to an existing distribution list being used by a team. After this is done, all documents sent by team members are copied into the site for future reference and searching.

When you enable a document library for incoming email, you need to ensure that the name you choose for the list email address is unique in your SharePoint farm because only one address can be used with a specific name—for example, listName@contoso.com or listName@serverName.contoso.com.

Mail-Enabling a Document Library or List

To mail-enable a document library or list, complete the following steps:

1. Navigate to the document library by clicking its title.

2. In the document library, select Library on the management ribbon for the document library.

3. Select Library Settings from the Settings section.

4. Under Communications, select Incoming Email Settings.

5. Configure the incoming email settings for the document library.

> **Note**
>
> Inbound email must be enabled from Central Administration to be able to enable inbound email in the library or list. Email settings can be configured in Central Administration, Systems Settings, as shown in Figure 9.15.

Grouping Submissions

Submissions can be grouped by the subject line of the email or by the sender. These options can help to preserve the original context of the file, even if you choose not to archive the original email message. If Yes is selected for the Overwrite Files with the Same Name option, a random number is appended to the filename of any new documents with the same names that are emailed to the library, as shown in Figure 9.16.

FIGURE 9.15
Email and Text Messages options in the System Settings area in Central Administration.

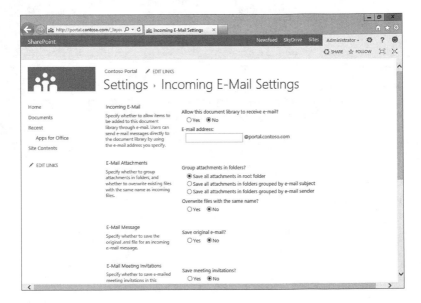

FIGURE 9.16
Email Attachments section.

Allowing Contributions from Outside the Organization

Mail-enabled libraries are an excellent way to allow users from outside the organization who do not have access to the SharePoint site to submit files for review internally. To support this feature, you must enable the Archive All Email Regardless of Sender option. This is enabled in the Email Security section of the document library incoming email settings by selecting the Accept Email Messages from Any Sender option, as shown in Figure 9.17.

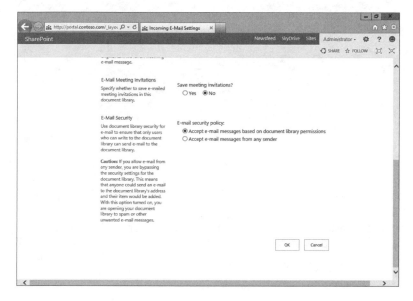

FIGURE 9.17
Options for accepting email from outside the organization.

The Document Center

The Document Center template, shown in Figure 9.18, is a tailored site template that has many of the document management settings enabled by default. It's a convenient mechanism for organizations to create a central repository for documents that have been finalized or are considered important enough to centrally manage.

The Document Center template should not be confused with the Records Center template, which is discussed later in this chapter. The records center is there to deal with official files within the business, such as compliance requirements. The document center, however, is aimed at creating a document repository. The document center is also a template that can accommodate editing of documents as well as uploading them, but these functions are controlled through permissions for key content managers.

FIGURE 9.18
Document Center example.

After it is created, the document center has several functions turned on by default:

- Versioning: major and minor
- Metadata navigational settings
- Drop-off library (content organizer)
- Document ID Search web part
- Document break-down web parts (highest rated, newest, and modified by me)
- Upload Document button

Documents can be added to the document center in several ways. These include the following:

- By using the Upload a Document button
- By using the Send to Other Location function
- Via part of a workflow using the officialfile.asmx web service
- By creating a new document directly in a library in the document center

SharePoint 2013 includes the capability to use the Send To function in combination with the content organizer feature, which allows the same automated routing mechanism to be used that's available in the Records Center template.

Enabling the Content Organizer

To enable the content organizer feature, complete these steps:

1. Click Settings, Site Settings.

2. Under Site Actions, select Manage Site Features.

3. Click the Activate button in the Content Organizer section if it is not already activated, as shown in Figure 9.19.

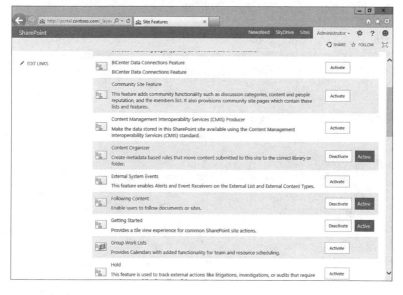

FIGURE 9.19
Content Organizer feature activation.

For example, a document library for a legal site is used for creating and updating legal documents, petitions, motions, and contracts. When a new document becomes a final version, it is sent to the document center to be stored in the correct library. In the document center are several libraries for storing these documents, and they are structured based on the regions and case number that the document is created for.

Content Organizer and Send To Functionality

The content organizer feature must first be enabled in the site where the documents are being sent to. After the content organizer site feature is enabled, a new document library, Drop Off Library, will be available in the document center. This library acts as a routing mechanism for incoming documents. It uses content organizer rules to match the content type and metadata with the correct document library and thereby routes them to their respective storage libraries. In the example we used earlier, the legal documents are sent to the drop-off library. The Send To function does not remove the original document from the source library; instead, it creates a full copy of the document in the drop-off library. The document was created using the various legal document content types. These content types have several metadata required fields, such as client name, case number, and region.

In the document center, a content organizer rule is created that defines the content type match and the condition of the match that determines which document library the document is routed to after it arrives in the drop-off library.

Creating Content Organizer Rules

To create content organizer rules, complete the following steps:

1. Click Settings, Site Settings.

2. Under Site Administration, select Content Organizer Rules.

3. Click the Add New Item link. The dialog box shown in Figure 9.20 will be displayed.

When specifying a submission content type to be used, you must ensure that the type also exists at the target location library in the document center. (See Figure 9.21.) In the earlier example, the enterprise content types for various legal documents must also be assigned to the target location library in the document center.

Multiple conditions can be added to the content organizer rule as well, such as region=north and Report Status=Final. To add more conditions, click the Add Another Condition link, as shown in Figure 9.22.

On the site collaboration space where the actual documents are located, create a Custom Send To Destination link. This is done via the Advanced settings in the Library Settings menu accessed via the Library tab on the management ribbon.

FIGURE 9.20
Content Organizer Rules: New Rules page, with the Rule Name, Rule Status and Priority, and Submission's Content Type sections.

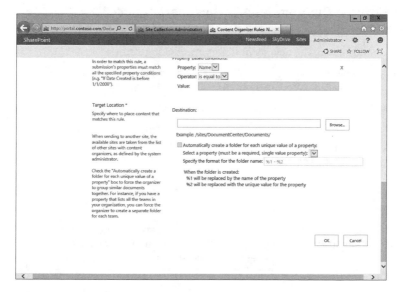

FIGURE 9.21
Content Organizer Rules page, Target Location section.

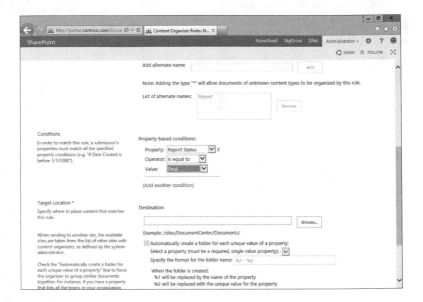

FIGURE 9.22
Content Organizer Rules page, Conditions section.

Creating a Custom Send To Destination Link

Follow these steps to create the Custom Send To Destination link:

1. Navigate to the document library by clicking its title.

2. In the document library, select the Library tab on the management ribbon for the document library.

3. Select Library Settings in the Settings section.

4. Under General Settings, select Advanced Settings.

5. Configure the Custom Send To Destination for the document library, as shown in Figure 9.23.

Note

Only one custom Send To destination can be created per document library, although using workflow can aid in the creation of multiple Send To locations based on business logic and status of the document.

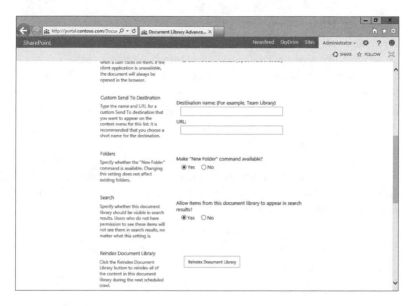

FIGURE 9.23
Custom Send To Destination section.

When creating the custom Send To location, you should ensure that you specify the drop-off library as the final destination because it is the only library that has the content organizer associated with it. The URL should be something similar to the following:

http://portal.contoso.com/DocumentCenter/DropOffLibrary.

When a document is now uploaded or sent to the drop-off library, it will be routed correctly. A timer job definition is created for each web application for processing the content organizer rules.

> **Note**
>
> By default, the Content Organizer Processing timer job is set to Daily, so if you want the documents to be moved quicker from the drop-off library, change the timings for the definition rule in Central Administration.

After the timer job has successfully run, documents will be routed to the correct library location in the order specified by the active priority that was defined in the content organizer rules.

Metadata Navigation and Filtering

More and more, documents are stored in sites like the document center. The result is that when people need to find information, their search center results or views return far too many items for them to efficiently find what they need.

To counter this trend, SharePoint 2013 includes a configuration option in the document library called Metadata Navigation Settings. These settings allow for the creation of custom metadata and for tag-based query web parts to be placed on the Quick Launch toolbar. This allows the user to quickly sort and filter for documents based on attributes defined on the Metadata Navigation Settings page. To configure the Metadata Navigation Settings, complete the following steps:

1. Navigate to the document library by clicking its title.

2. In the document library, select the Library tab on the management ribbon for the document library.

3. Select Library Settings from the Settings section.

4. Under General Settings, select Metadata Navigation Settings.

5. Configure the metadata navigation settings for the document library, as shown in Figure 9.24.

FIGURE 9.24
The Configure Navigation Hierarchies section for a document library.

After these settings are configured, the new query web parts appear below the site navigation area and can be used to filter and sort for content in the document library. When using filter and sort, all documents in the library are returned that match the filter, even if the documents were in folders or document sets. All items matching the sort criteria are returned, as shown in Figure 9.25.

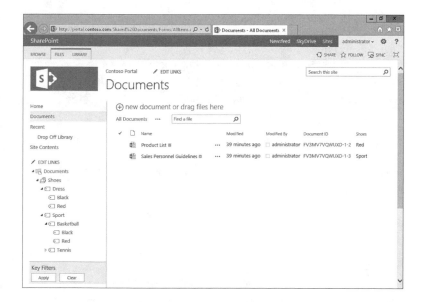

FIGURE 9.25
The documents with attributes specified in the Metadata Navigation Settings area.

Records Management

Organizations have the responsibility to handle the maintenance of permanent records. Physical records, while limited, were easy documents for retrieval, but limitations such as losing original records could become quite costly.

Microsoft SharePoint Server 2013 provides the capabilities to capture and maintain records while adhering to complex levels of records management policies. Records Management within SharePoint Server 2013 provides information that is readily usable to entire organizations. As records are processed in SharePoint, SharePoint provides capabilities such as in-place records management and the Records Center to manage these data artifacts. When combined with other features such as search and metadata tagging, SharePoint provides managed yet secure access for record classification and retrieval.

Managing Information Management Policies

Information management policies are a set of rules applied to document libraries and content types. These policies enable administrators to control how document information is retained, audited, and disposed of. The task of defining and managing these policies typically is performed by a compliance officer, records manager, or other content specialist. There are three ways that information management policies are defined:

- On a document library, including folders
- On a content type
- At the site-collection level

Furthermore, four key areas can be defined for a policy:

- Retention
- Auditing
- Barcodes
- Labels

Document libraries always enforce policies that are defined on the specific content types included within the library. However, additional policies can be defined at the library level, which then affect all content types within the library, including folders.

Configuring Source of Retention Settings

One of the primary settings that can be configured at the document library level is the source of retention. This setting configures where a library receives its retention schedule from. There are only two options: Content Types and Library and Folders. To change the Source of Retention settings for a document library, perform the following steps:

1. Navigate to the document library by clicking its title.

2. After you have accessed the document library, select Library Tools, Library on the ribbon for the document library.

3. Select Library Settings from the Settings section.

4. Under Permissions and Management, select Information Management Policy Settings.

5. On the Library-Based Retention Schedule page, click the Change Source link.

6. Select either Content Types or Library and Folders, as shown in Figure 9.26.

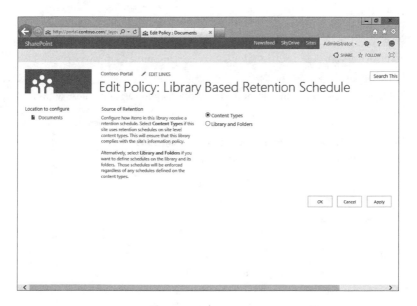

FIGURE 9.26
Source of Retention.

SharePoint Server 2013 provides the functionality of enterprise content types; therefore, it makes more sense to maintain control of policies via content types. This approach allows you to have centralized control of both the templates and metadata defined on the content type and a centralized policy mechanism regarding how to manage documents of the associated type.

One reason to establish retention policies for the document library, however, might be that you want to enforce a standard approach to document retention in the library itself, regardless of the content types it contains. This policy might establish a rule for all documents older than 90 days within the library, which can be automatically moved to an external data source while a link is left in place.

An information management policy on a content type must be defined within the properties of the content type. If the content type is an enterprise content type, policies must be defined in the Content Type Store site. Permission-level requirements for defining policies are also a possible reason why users who are only site administrators might choose to enable and create policies at the library level rather than the content-type level.

Retention

Retention involves defining what to do with an item when a particular stage is reached, and it is usually triggered by a defined action of some sort. SharePoint Server 2013 allows for retention policies for records and nonrecords.

Table 9.1 lists these configuration event options and the applicable actions for each.

TABLE 9.1 **Retention Policy Configuration Options**

Configuration Option	Acceptable Values Definitions
Event	By time period
	Created
	Modified
	Set by a custom formula installed on the server
Action	Move to Recycle Bin
	Permanently delete
	Transfer to another location (which works with farm Send To locations)
	Start a workflow (which can also use custom-developed workflows)
	Skip to next stage
	Delete previous drafts
	Delete all previous versions
Recurrence	Available only for certain actions (such as delete previous drafts)
	Defined by a period of time

SharePoint Server 2013 allows you to have more than one retention policy action defined for a specific event, as shown in Figure 9.27.

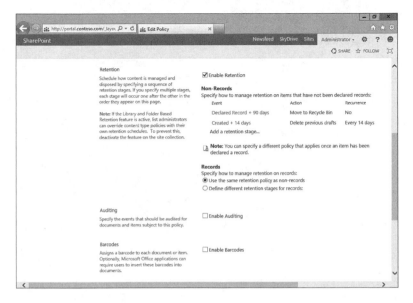

FIGURE 9.27
Retention policies for nonrecords.

Declaring Records

Contributors can be provided with the permissions to convert a document into a record by declaring it a record. The capability to do so is controlled by the site collection administrator via records declaration policies. To manage these policies, perform the following tasks:

1. Click Setting, Site Settings.

2. Under Site Collection Administration, select Record Declaration Settings.

3. Select the appropriate level of actions that can be performed by contributors and administrators within the site collection, as shown in Figure 9.28.

Typically, after a document has been declared as a record, it has reached a stage in its life cycle where it has a legal, compliance, or business process requirement. Records have two possible options when being configured:

1. Use the same retention policy as the nonrecords.

2. Define a different set of retention requirements after it becomes a record.

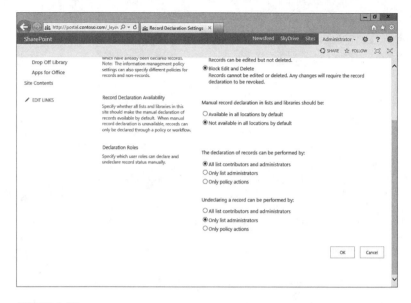

FIGURE 9.28
All list contributors and administrators have the ability to declare records in this library or list.

After a document becomes a record, it can be sent automatically as part of a workflow to the official corporate records center to become part of the audit and compliance requirements of the business. The declaration of the document as a record can require that the document be sent to the document center, as in the case of a final version of a company's employee benefits policy, which when completed must be available to all employees in the organization through the document center.

The determination of what becomes a record is subject to the discretion of the organization's legal counsel or records manager and the processes defined within data and records management policies.

Auditing

When auditing is enabled, it addresses and logs information related to the following actions, and that information can then be viewed as part of an audit trial policy (as shown in Figure 9.29):

1. Open or download documents, view items in lists, or view item properties.

2. Edit items.

3. Check out or check in items.

4. Move or copy items to another location in the site.

5. Delete or restore items.

FIGURE 9.29
Settings for auditing policy information.

Users can query SharePoint to assemble reports of audit event information as needed.

Document Bar Codes

Document bar codes are similar to document labels, but instead of text, they represent a unique identifier rendered in a machine-readable format. To view the generated bar code, click the View Properties command on the document drop-down list.

Document Labels

The document label feature is designed to assist in organizing documents for systematic storage and retrieval. Document labels are text labels that SharePoint can generate automatically based on a content type's metadata. Document labels can be printed and attached to a physical copy of the document or inserted as graphics into the file. Changes to a document label can be prevented after the label is attached to a document, as shown in Figure 9.30.

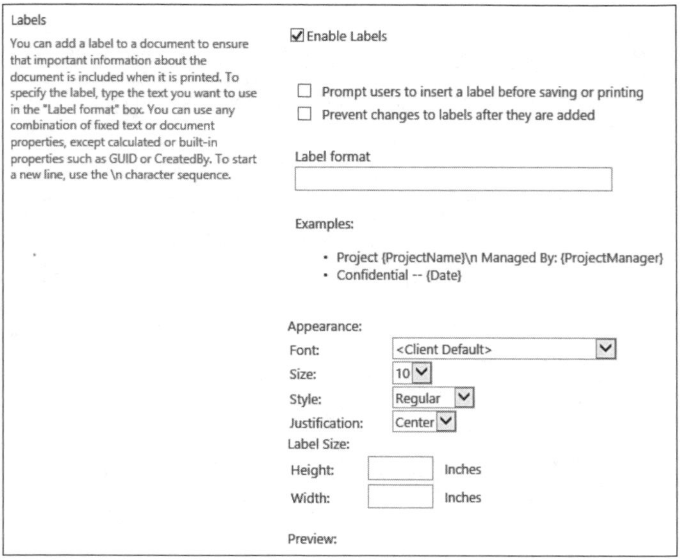

Labels

You can add a label to a document to ensure that important information about the document is included when it is printed. To specify the label, type the text you want to use in the "Label format" box. You can use any combination of fixed text or document properties, except calculated or built-in properties such as GUID or CreatedBy. To start a new line, use the \n character sequence.

☑ Enable Labels

☐ Prompt users to insert a label before saving or printing
☐ Prevent changes to labels after they are added

Label format

[   ]

Examples:

- Project {ProjectName}\n Managed By: {ProjectManager}
- Confidential -- {Date}

Appearance:
Font: [<Client Default>   ▼]
Size: [10 ▼]
Style: [Regular ▼]
Justification: [Center ▼]
Label Size:
Height: [   ] Inches
Width: [   ] Inches

Preview:

FIGURE 9.30
Document labels policy settings.

After an Information Management policy has been applied, you can view details for the policy by looking at the compliance details for a document that used the content type affected by the policy or that exists in a library that has had a policy applied to it. To view the compliance information, click the Compliance Details by selecting the document's Open menu and the second Open menu again, as shown in Figure 9.31.

In-Place Records Management

SharePoint Server 2013 allows for in-place records management and provides functions to allow users to declare records within lists and libraries and extending control and responsibility for records management beyond the SharePoint Server 2013 Records Center.

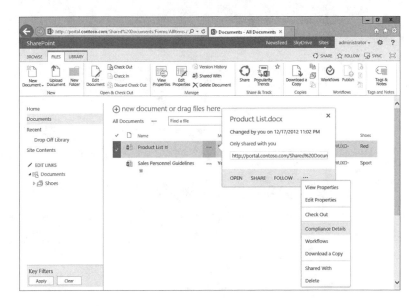

FIGURE 9.31
Example of navigating to a document's Compliance Details.

Enabling In-Place Records Management

Enabling In-Place Records management requires the activation of the corresponding Site Collection feature. To activate this Site Collection feature, perform the following steps:

1. Click Site Actions, Site Settings.

2. Under Site Collection Administration, click Site Collection Features.

3. Activate the In-Place Records Management feature if it is not already active, as shown in Figure 9.32.

Configure Record Declaration Within a List and Library

Official record declaration is governed by either a policy or a workflow that invokes the declaration. You can, however, allow records declaration at the list or library level. The following two choices are available when enabling this option, as shown in Figure 9.33:

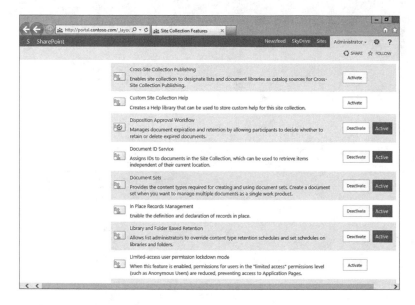

FIGURE 9.32
In Place Records Management feature for site collections.

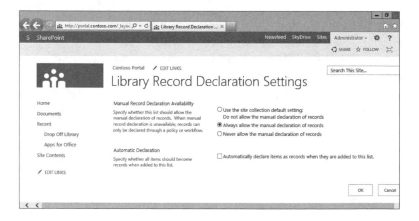

FIGURE 9.33
Library Record Declaration Settings page.

Users must then be allowed to declare records within the desired library. To allow for Manual Record Declaration with a library, perform the following steps:

1. Navigate to the document library by clicking its title.

2. After you access the document library, select Library Tools, Library on the management ribbon for the document library.

3. Select Library Settings in the Settings section.

4. Under Permissions and Management, click Library Record Declaration Settings.

5. Select Always Allow the Manual Declaration of Records, and then click OK.

A new option named Declare Record is available in the Documents tab on the management ribbon under Library Tools, as shown in Figure 9.34. Select the document that you want to declare, and then click the Declare Record button.

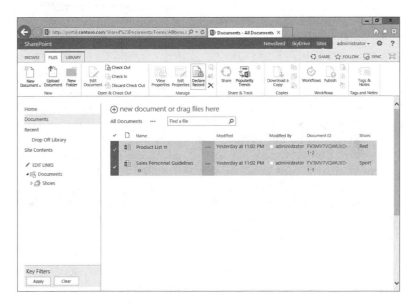

FIGURE 9.34
Option to manually declare a record.

Configure Automatic Declaration

Some lists or libraries need to have all documents become records, and although the list or library might exist in a standard collaboration site, it holds formal records. To initiate this process, go back to the Record

Declaration setting in the library and choose Automatically Declare Items as Records When They Are Added to This List, as shown in Figure 9.33.

> **Note**
>
> For any existing items in the library, you need to check them out and then check them in for the lock to be put into place. For all new items, the process is automatic as you are requested to check the document in.

The Records Center

SharePoint Server 2013 also provides the Records Center as a possible central repository for managing organization records. So how does an organization choose whether to deploy an enterprise Records Center, leverage In-Place Records Management, or both? An organization should first look to its processes to answer these questions in conjunction with the classifications of records such as contracts, project deliverables, and corporate communication.

To successfully deploy the Records Center, you must use management of the capabilities previously discussed including the Content Organizer, Metadata Navigation and Filtering, and Information Management Policies. Security is also a key consideration; considerations for using a dedication site collection or web application should be carefully planned. A special group, called Records Center Web Service Submitters, is created in the Records Center site. This group allows you to define the other application pool IDs, which allow them to submit items using the officialfile.asmx web service. When users or workflows submit items to the Records Center, the Web application's application pool, rather than the user, has the job of communicating and submitting the records.

After you create the records center site, a configuration page is available from the Site Actions menu that outlines the steps required to configure the site and get it up and running. The primary steps, which are shown in Figure 9.35, are as follows:

1. Create the required content types.
2. Create the record libraries.
3. Create content organizer rules.
4. Design the site welcome page.

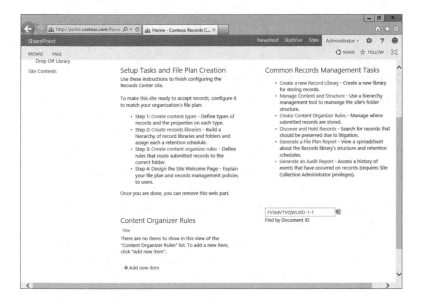

FIGURE 9.35
Records Center Management page.

Even though enterprise content types are configured in the farm, they still need to be subscribed to within the records center site collection before they can be added to the organizer rules.

As you did with other sites, such as the Document Center, you create document libraries with the specific information management policies assigned to them. After these document libraries are created, configure the content organizer rules to define which content types get routed to which library. You can customize the welcome page, and you can change web parts just as you can with any other site.

After the primary configuration steps are completed, the next step is to define how information will get routed to the records center. There are several methods you can use to make this happen:

- By using the Send To function (which uses the officialfile.asmx web service)

- Through an automated workflow (which uses the officialfile.asmx web service)

- As part of email journaling (which is configured with Microsoft Exchange Server)

■ By manually submitting a record (which requires users to manually denote records)

Configuring the Farm Send To Option

The Send To function can be defined from either of two locations: from the advanced properties in a document library or from the Farm option in SharePoint Central Administration.

To configure the farm Send To locations, perform the following steps:

1. Open Central Administration, General Application Settings, External Service Connections, Configure Send To Connections.

2. Select the web application from the drop-down list for which the Send To location will show up.

3. You can also choose to allow the sites in the web application to send items outside the site subscription, perhaps to another farm where a global records management system is in place.

4. Make sure to specify a friendly name in the Display Name field. This is the name that users see when they select the document in the library. Naming conventions are important, especially if multiple Send To locations are available to the user in both farmwide and locally configured locations.

5. Specify the Send To URL. To create the connection, you must specify the URL of the records center site, including the web service file name, officialfile.asmx.—for example, http://server/site url/_vti_bin/officialfile.asmx.

6. You can also choose to allow users to manually submit files to the records center using the Send To feature on the document menu.

> **Note**
>
> If the planned approach for official files is to have the process automated by a workflow only, you need to clear the Allow Manual Submission from the Send To menu check box.

7. Choose what to do with the item being sent to the records center. There are three options: Copy, Move, and Move and Leave a Link.

8. Click OK to create the Send To connection.

Configuring the Content Organizer Rules and Permissions

To automatically route documents to the correct library, you configure routing rules that are based on content types and metadata values. The same process applies when creating libraries as well as those for the document center. To create a content organizer rule, do the following:

After the rule is created, grant submission rights to the application pool ID that will be used by the sending process, as shown in Figure 9.36. To grant submission, rights, perform the following steps:

1. Click Settings, Site Settings.

2. Under Users and Permissions, click People and Groups.

3. Click the Groups header in the left navigation pane.

4. Select the Record Center Web Service Submitters group from the list.

5. Grant permission by adding the application pool ID to the group. Click the New button to add the application pool ID.

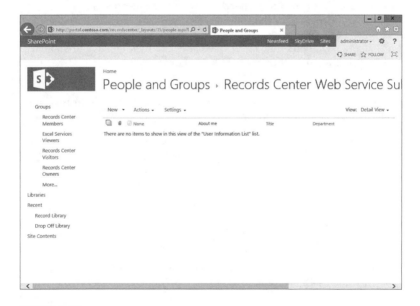

FIGURE 9.36
Records Center Web Service Submitters page.

Now that the content organizer rule and required libraries are in place, the new library is ready to accept records submitted by users. The Allow

Manual Submission setting must be enabled on the document library itself before the record center content organizer rule will be able to process documents submitted with the Send To feature. The Send To feature can be configured for the site collection or for an individual document library.

To enable Manual Submission on the site collection for all document libraries other than those that have custom record declaration settings, perform the following steps:

1. Click Site Actions, Site Settings.

2. Under Site Collection Administration, click Record Declaration Settings.

3. In the Record Declaration Availability area, select Available in All Locations by Default to enable the Send To menu item to be available in all document libraries.

Note

Not all document libraries will need to allow for manual submission of records to the records center. Before enabling this at the site collection, you should ensure that the records management policy is adapted for this setting and content organizer rules have been put in place to support document libraries as they are created.

To enable Manual Submission on the document library, which turns on the Send To menu item in the document drop-down menu, perform the following steps:

1. Navigate to the document library by clicking its title.

2. In the document library, select Library Tools, Library in the management ribbon for the document library.

3. Select Settings, Library Settings.

4. Under Permissions and Management, select Record Declaration settings.

5. Configure Manual Record Declaration Availability to Always Allow the Manual Declaration of Records.

The records center content organizer rule can be verified by sending a document that has been created with a matching type from a document library.

Perform the following steps to use the Send To functionality, as shown in Figure 9.37:

1. Inside a document library, click a check box to select a document

2. Click the Files tab on the ribbon, and select the Send To option within the Copies grouping.

3. Select the Records Center name that you configured in the farm's Send To settings.

4. The record will be sent to the drop-off library in the Records Center.

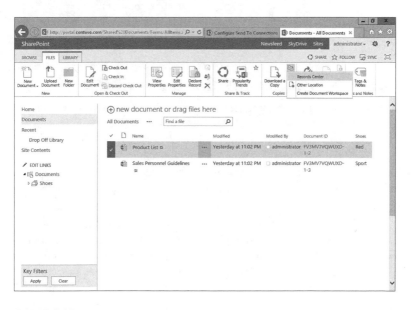

FIGURE 9.37
Manual submission of a document to the records center.

After the record has been submitted, an Operation Completed Successfully screen is displayed, as shown in Figure 9.38, unless additional metadata is required in the destination library in addition to the metadata already stored in the content type itself.

FIGURE 9.38
Submission to records center completed successfully.

eDiscovery in SharePoint Server 2013

SharePoint Server 2013 introduces a new eDiscovery capability available to legal and records professionals for the discovery of electronic content. The eDiscovery capability allows for discovery of electronic content across the SharePoint 2013 farm environment and Exchange Server 2013. The Exchange Server 2013 configuration also supports the capability to search across Lync archives if configured to archive in Exchange Server 2013.

At the heart of these capabilities is the eDiscovery Center, which provides a centralized site within SharePoint from which to discover, freeze, and export content within SharePoint. These features also provide the capability to perform SharePoint In-Place holds to take snapshots of SharePoint Sites to preserve them, allowing users to continue on with daily functions without compromising the preservation of documents and site content.

eDiscovery preserves content at the site and site collection levels. A requirement for the eDiscovery functionality to work is that a search service application has been previously provisioned prior to utilizing eDiscovery. To put a hold on a site or a site collection, you must create a Discovery Case in the eDiscovery Center by performing these tasks:

1. Navigate to the eDiscovery Center.

2. Select Create New Case.

3. Provide a Title, Description, and URL Name for the eDiscovery case and click Create. This creates the Case set.

4. Click New Item under Identify and Hold to build a new eDiscovery Set.

5. Provide an eDiscovery Set name (see Figure 9.39).

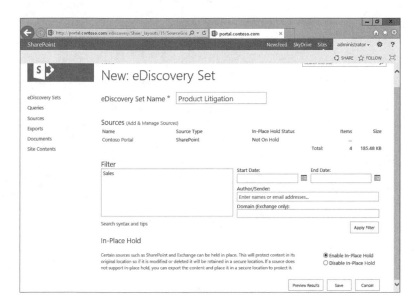

FIGURE 9.39
Example of a new eDiscovery Set being applied.

6. Add a Source by clicking Add & Manage Sources and providing the URL to the desired SharePoint site.

7. Specify any Filters, relevant Start and End Dates, and the name or email address of authors, and then click Apply Filter.

8. You can choose to Preview Results and choose SharePoint to reveal SharePoint specific results. Optionally, choose to Enable In-Place Hold and click Save to put the hold into effect.

To minimize the impacts of holds on storage requirements, the eDiscovery hold process is designed to minimize effects on storage space utilization by only making copies of content that have been modified or deleted. Otherwise, eDiscovery ensures that the original data that's on hold has been preserved. Users may continue to use the site as normal. If an item were to be modified or deleted, eDiscovery copies the item to a Preservation Hold Library in the site where the content exists. Only users with web application permission or site collection administration permission have the ability to see any content within this library.

CHAPTER 10

Enterprise Search

- Design Considerations
- Deploying the First Server in the Farm
- Scaling Search to Multiple Servers

When configuring the Search Service Application, SharePoint professionals who have deployed and maintained FAST for SharePoint 2010 will be familiar with much of the architecture and administrative tasks detailed in this chapter. However, if you are familiar only with SharePoint Server 2013 and SharePoint Server 2010 search architecture, you'll want to take a close look at the verbiage and terminology throughout the configuration scripts and management user interfaces. Many components in SharePoint Server 2013 are very different than in SharePoint Server 2010 but have the same or a similar name. An example is that the Query Server in SharePoint Server 2010 was responsible for answering user queries. Likewise, an Index Server in SharePoint Server 2010 was responsible for indexing, including content processing. In SharePoint Server 2013, there is a component named Query Processing Component, and it does *not* retrieve a results list from the index based upon user queries. Its role is applying filter rules and logic and then retrieving results from the Indexing Component. The Indexing Component actually retrieves the results list from the index. This example shows why you'll want to pay close attention to scripts, user interface options, and figures within this chapter.

Design Considerations

Before creating your target farm architecture diagram, you'll need to understand your requirements and use cases. Common requirements are the total number of items, types of documents, required document handlers and iFilters, query response time, and incremental update time. Common use cases are small intranets, large enterprise search, and search for public websites. It's also important to understand your design options before committing to a search farm topology. There are limitations in both complexity and scale; balancing limitations with requirements demands an understanding of search components, databases, topologies, and hardware.

Search Components and Databases

In SharePoint Server 2013, search components are also known as services, both Windows server services and web services, which reside on one or more servers in the SharePoint Server 2013 farm. All search components (services) are managed by the Search Host Controller service. The Search Host Controller service is enabled when starting the "[el]find[el]search service", either from Central Administration or Windows PowerShell. You do not directly start or stop Search Services; however, you modify the search topology and apply the configuration. The services will be started and stopped as needed by timer jobs on each individual server. If services that you believe should be running are not, check that the Search Host Controller service is running and that the SharePoint Timer service is started.

Search Components

Search components communicate with other search components and with search databases. The following search components are available in SharePoint Server 2013:

- **Crawl Component**—This component retrieves metadata and crawls actual content. It sends the metadata along with the full text to the content processing component. Content sources can be file shares, websites and SharePoint applications. Many other sources are available by using third-party connectors. The Crawl component is also responsible for invoking connectors and protocol handlers to connect to other third-party content sources. There can be multiple Crawl Components per Service Application, up to the number of servers in the SharePoint Server 2013 farm.

- **Content Processing Component**—This component is responsible for transforming crawled items and sending the text to the Indexing component. Content such as links, anchor text, and URLs are sent to the Analytics Processing component. Example operations are document parsing, word breaking, language detection, and entity extraction.

- **Analytics Processing Component**—This component analyzes crawled items and both tracks and reports on usage patterns. These results are both sent to the Content Processing component for inclusion in the index along with being available for custom reports. You can optimize your search configuration based on analytics reporting and gain insight into what your users are seeking. The types of analysis performed are the following:

  - Link and Anchor Text Analytics
  - Click Distance Calculation
  - Search Clicks Analysis
  - Social Tags and Distance
  - Deep Links
  - Search Reports
  - Usage Counts
  - Recommendations
  - Activity Ranking
  - Custom Events

- **Index Component**—This component is very different than in SharePoint Server 2010. The Index Component receives content from the content processor component and writes out relevant data to the search index. Unlike in SharePoint Server 2010, the Index Component also responds to incoming queries and sends/receives data to/from the Query Processing Component. The Index component also physically moves around indexed content when you modify the search topology. The Index architecture supports multiple partitions and replicas. A partition is a logical portion of the entire index. A replica is a copy of a partition on a separate server for the purpose of high availability.

- **Query Processing Component**—This component is responsible for optimizing queries for precision and relevance and also processes any Query rules created in Search Service Application administration.

- **Search Administration Component**—This component manages the search topology and modifications to search components.

> **Note**
>
> An easy way to remember the difference in the Host Controller service and Search Administration service is as follows: Host Controller manages services on a specific server; Search Administration service is responsible for the entire farm.

Search Databases

Search databases should handle at least 10 IOPS (Input/Ouput per second) per each required DPS (document per second). There are at least four databases per Search service application:

- Crawl database records and stores data for every crawled item. Examples of information stored in the crawl database are item name, URL, last crawl time, and last update type (add, update, delete).

- Link database stores unprocessed data, such as URL links within pages and documents, from the content processor component. The Analytics processing component analyzes data in the Link database.

- Analytics Reporting database stores the output of usage analysis and is used for generating search reports.

- Search Administration database stores search farm settings for the topology and location of all search components. The Search Administration database also stores content sources, crawl rules, query rules, managed properties, crawl schedules, and analytics settings.

Hardware Requirements

Hardware requirements vary widely depending on the complexity of your configuration and number of items crawled. However, the following list is a good starting point for determining your hardware needs:

Table 10.1   **Recommended Hardware Requirements for SharePoint Server Search 2013**

Index Component	16GB minimum	
Analytics Processing Component	8GB minimum	
Crawl Component	8GB minimum	64 bit, 4 cores minimum, 8 recommended
Content Processing Component	8GB minimum	
Query Processing Component	8GB minimum	
Search Administration Component	8GB minimum	

SQL Search databases require 2,000 IOPS at a minimum, with many implementations requiring upwards of 7,000 IOPS. To be sure, reference TechNet for the latest recommendations. Thorough testing should be performed before production deployment to validate your hardware and database design. Many factors, such as virtual hosts and storage, aren't always considered yet can have a large impact on search performance.

Software Limits

SharePoint Server 2013 search is very robust, but you should be aware that limitations exist. For small implementations these limits will most likely not apply, but for larger server farms or those crawling external content, the following table is a good starting guide for limitations:

Table 10.2   **Software Boundaries for SharePoint Server 2013 Search**

Limit	Maximum Value
Search service applications	20 per farm
Crawl databases	5 crawl databases per search service application
Crawl components	2 per search service application
Index components	60 per search service application
Index partitions	20 per search service application
Index replicas	3 per index partition
Indexed items	100 million per search service application; 10 million per index partition
Crawl log entries	100 million per search application
Link database	2 per search service application

Table 10.2   Software Boundaries for SharePoint Server 2013 Search (continued)

Limit	Maximum Value
Query processing components	1 per server computer
Content processing components	1 per server computer
Scope rules	100 scope rules per scope; 600 total per search service application
Display groups	25 per site
Alerts	100,000 per search application
Content sources	50 per search service application
Start addresses	100 per content source
Concurrent crawls	20 per search application
Crawled properties	500,000 per search application
Crawl impact rule	No limit
Crawl rules	No limit
Managed properties	50,000 per search service application
Values per managed property	100
Indexed managed property size	512KB per searchable/queryable managed property
Managed property mappings	100 per managed property
Retrievable managed property size	16KB per managed property
Sortable and refinable	16KB per managed property managed property size
URL removals	100 removals per operation
Authoritative pages	1 top-level and minimal second- and third-level pages per search service application
Keywords	200 per site collection
Metadata properties recognized	10,000 per item crawled
Analytics processing components	6 per search service application
Analytics reporting database	4 per search service application

Limit	Maximum Value
Maximum eDiscovery KeywordQuery text length	16KB
Maximum KeywordQuery text length	4KB
Maximum length of eDiscovery KeywordQuery text at Search service application level	20KB
Maximum length of KeywordQuery text at Search service application level	20KB
Maximum size of documents pulled down by crawler	64MB (3MB for Excel documents)
Navigable results from search	100,000 per query request per search service application
Number of entries in a custom entity extraction dictionary	1 million
Number of entries in a custom search dictionary	5,000 terms per tenant
Number of entries in a thesaurus	1 million
Ranking models	1,000 per tenant
Results removal	No limit
Term size	300 characters
Unique terms in the index	2^31 (>2 billion terms)
Unique contexts used for ranking	15 unique contexts per rank model
User defined full text indexes	10

Designing a Search Topology

When designing a search topology there are two primary factors to consider: high availability and performance. A proven design method for most implementations is first designing to your availability requirements. Doing so often provides more than sufficient hardware for performance. It's smart to have at least two service machine instances for every search component to enable fault tolerance.

After you have requirements for your search deployment, you should review Microsoft TechNet at http://technet.microsoft.com/en-us/sharepoint/fp142366 for updated search scenarios and associated sample topologies. For this chapter, three sample scenarios are shown: Small Farm with 10 million items, Medium Farm with 40 million items, and Large Farm with 100 million items.

Small Search Farms

For most small organizations that will be crawling only SharePoint content and a small quantity of web and file share content, a small search topology will be sufficient. Using the minimum hardware requirements listed in Table 10.1, Figure 10.1 shows a small server farm that will support up to 10 million items. Keep in mind that the depicted small server farm is also serving publishing and collaboration traffic for SharePoint Server 2013. If either of those functions requires an intense amount of CPU and memory, the following search topology would be insufficient.

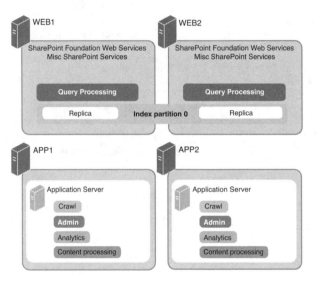

FIGURE 10.1
Small search farm topology for 10 million items.

The small search farm topology in Figure 10.1 is only for small implementations that have limited web and collaboration traffic and fewer than 10 million items. If traffic is more than a few requests per second, you should strongly consider adding two additional web servers to the server farm.

If you'll have fewer than 10 million items and also have significant web and collaboration traffic, you should consider a topology similar to Figure 10.2.

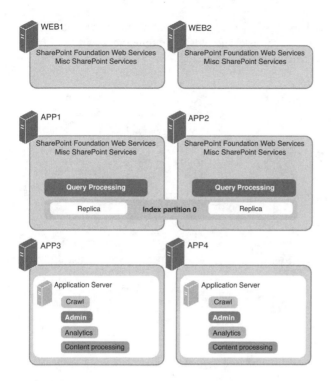

FIGURE 10.2
Small search topology with added web and collaboration capacity.

Medium Search Farms

If you'll have more than 10 million items in your index, you'll want to begin with a medium farm topology, as shown in Figure 10.3. Medium search farms are often crawling content sources other than just SharePoint Server 2013. When crawling sources such as file shares, the 10-million-item limit is easily reached in many organizations. Medium search farms with redundant components are also beneficial for crawling Line of Business systems that host valuable business content. There is a substantial increase in required hardware from a small search farm and a large search farm. First, as shown in Figure 10.3, six physical servers are being used to host 12 virtual machines. This design accommodates a highly available solution, so you could remove 50% of the servers if your service level agreement (SLA) doesn't justify the cost. Second, there are two index partitions to create two subsets of the index. Multiple Index partitions for large data sets are actually faster than a single, very large partition.

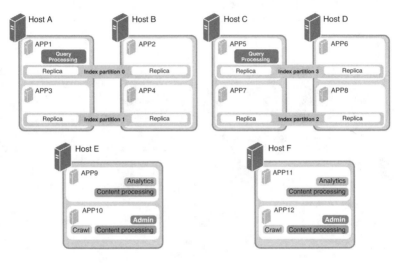

FIGURE 10.3
A medium search server farm can host up to 40 million items in indexes.

Large Server Farms
If you need more than 40 million items, a large server farm is your next option. A larger server farm can host up to 100 million items but will take another significant increase in hardware usage. As shown in Figure 10.4, large server farms will take substantial engineering, testing, and maintenance efforts. Many factors go into a well-running large search server farm, such as virtual hosts, network, Storage Area Networks, Ethernet, firewalls, and more.

Deploying the First Search Server in the Farm

Unless you used the Farm Configuration Wizard, you'll need to first create the search service application before creating a multiserver search topology. If you used the Configuration Wizard, you can skip to the "Scaling Search to Multiple Servers" section.

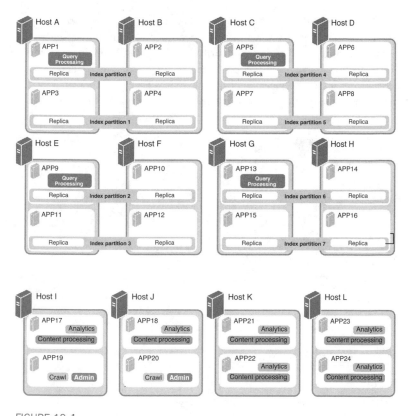

FIGURE 10.4
A large server farm can index up to 80 million items.

Creating the Search Service Application

Like all service applications, a search service application is created from the Manage Service Applications page, which can be accessed from the Service Applications section of the Application Management page of Central Administration. From the New menu, click Search Service Application, as shown in Figure 10.5.

The service application creation dialog begins with asking for a Service Application name and Managed Account, as shown in Figure 10.6. The Service Application name is entirely up to you, but a simple and recognizable name is recommended. If you'll use a managed account that does not yet exist, know that any configuration on the Create Service Application page will be lost when you select the Register New Managed Account link. This account must be a managed service account, and it will be the same for all search services in the farm. Like other managed service accounts, it can be changed from the Configure Service Accounts page under the General Security section of the Security page in Central Administration. Depending on your security requirements, you may use a dedicated account for Search Services. Unless you are in a highly secured environment, you'll likely share an account for all search accounts except the crawl account.

FIGURE 10.5
Option to create a new search service application.

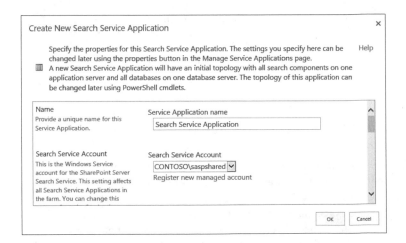

FIGURE 10.6
You must name the Service Application and define a managed service account.

Next, you must decide if you'll use an existing application pool for the Search Administration Service component (Search Admin Web Service) or if you'll create a new one. If you are configuring anything but a small search farm topology, you should create a dedicated Application Pool. However, register a new managed account only if your security policy mandates it. Multiple accounts only complicate the management of your Search farm architecture.

Last, you must decide if you'll use an existing Application Pool for the Search Query and Site Settings Service. Like the Search Admin Web Service, create a unique managed account only if your security policy mandates it. Unlike SharePoint Server 2010, however, you can share the application pool between the Search Admin Web Service and Search Query and Site Settings Service. Unless you are short on server resources, you should create a dedicated Application Pool for each Search Service.

> **Note**
>
> The initial topology with your new search service application will have all components on one application server and all databases on one database server. This topology can be changed later using Windows PowerShell, but it cannot be changed from the user interface.

After completing the required information on the New Search Service Application page, click OK at the bottom, and the appropriate databases and web services will be created and configured.

If you will have search administrators who are not farm administrators, you need to give them permission to manage the search service application. From the Manage Service Applications page, highlight your new search service and click the Administrators button in the management ribbon to open the page shown in Figure 10.7.

You can add individual accounts or Active Directory groups on this page. For the Search Service, Full Control is the only permission option. Individuals added here will be granted access to Central Administration but will have links only to pages to manage this service.

Examining the Search Administration Page

From the Manage Service Applications page shown in Figure 10.5, highlight your new search service and click the Manage button in the management ribbon to open the Search Administration page. This page presents dashboards for System Status, Crawl History, and displays Search

Application Topology. This design of including dashboards continues throughout many of the search management pages.

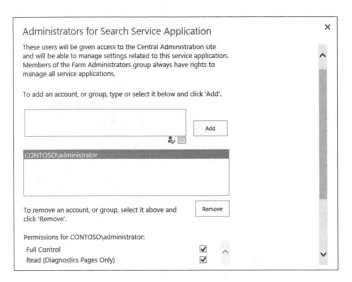

FIGURE 10.7
Configure search service administrators.

The Quick Launch area has links to search management pages organized as Diagnostics, Crawling, and Queries and Results, as shown in Figure 10.8. The Search Application Topology dashboard in the lower portion of the page is not shown in Figure 10.8 and is discussed later in this chapter.

Several configuration links in the System Status dashboard are presented as links that open dialog boxes or as toggles:

- The Default Content Access Account sets or changes the account used for authentication by the crawler for this search application.

- The Contact Email Address applies to all search applications on this farm.

- The Proxy Server configuration is a farmwide setting and takes you to farmwide Search Settings.

- The Search Alerts Status can be toggled, and it should be disabled when resetting the index so that users do not receive alerts on saved searches as existing content is recrawled.

- The Query Logging option can be toggled as needed. Query logging is necessary for all query reports.

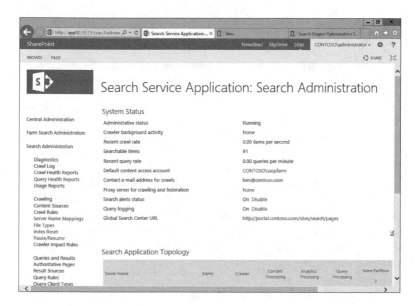

FIGURE 10.8
Search Administration page.

- The Global Search Center URL should be completed before you give users access to web applications associated with this Service Application. Generally, it's a good idea to have precreated this search center before creating the Search Service Application.

Scaling Search to Multiple Servers

The changes to the server architecture in SharePoint Server 2013 are a significant management learning curve. Very little remains the same from SharePoint Server 2010, except the basic Service Application creation process. However, the new architecture is very flexible and scales well beyond the capability in SharePoint Server 2010. The primary reasons you'll scale to multiple search servers are performance and availability. Often, creating a highly available topology will meet the performance requirements of small to medium environments.

> **Note**
>
> Although it's not addressed directly in this chapter, keep in mind that you must have high availability on SQL Server as well. Every search database should have some level of SQL fault tolerance, such as Always on Availability groups or Mirroring.

If you are limited by memory on the server hosting the content processing component, perhaps adding 8GB of RAM would resolve the bottleneck. This is less expensive than adding another server to the farm. However, if the bottleneck were server I/O, then adding additional RAM would likely not help. Use common sense and increase existing server capacity before adding additional servers to the farm. This will ease administration and reduce overall solution complexity. Table 10.3 shows the metrics that should be monitored and used to determine if additional search servers or hardware are required.

Table 10.3   Monitoring Metrics for Performance

Metric	Action
Full Crawl Time	Additional crawl databases and content processing components.
Query Result Time	To reduce query latency, you should add index replicas. To improve query throughput, you could also create additional search partitions.
Query Processing Availability	Add additional Query processing components.
Content Crawling, Processing, and Indexing Availability	Multiple crawl databases and multiple content processing components.

> **Note**
>
> Don't place the primary and secondary servers for a Search component on the same Virtual Machine Host. For example, if you placed Index Replica A on APP1, and Index Replica B on App2, yet APP1 and App2 were hosted on the same VM host, you'll have lost both servers that process that Search function should the VM host fail.

Guidelines for Scaling Search Components

Always check Microsoft TechNet for the latest guidelines because they can and do change over time. The following table lists scaling guidelines at the time of publishing:

- **Administration Component**—Always have two in every farm for high availability.

- **Index Partition**—Add one index partition for every 10 million items.

- **Index Component**—Two components for each index partition.

- **Query Processing Component**—Two query processing components will service up to 80 million items. Four query processing components are required for more than 80 million items.

- **Content Processing Component**—Two content processing components up to 10 million items, four content processing components up to 40 million items, and six content processing components for solutions up to 100 million items.

- **Analytics Processing Component**—Two analytics processing components up to 40 million items, and six analytics processing components for solutions up to 100 million items.

- **Crawlers**—Two crawlers should be sufficient for all search solutions up to 100 million items.

- **Crawl database**—Add one crawl database per 20 million items. This is the minimum recommendation, and additional crawl databases may further increase performance.

- **Link database**—Add one link database per 60 million items.

- **Analytics Reporting Database**—Add one analytics reporting database for every 10 million items or when views exceed 500K per day.

Cloning an Existing Topology

After you have created the Search Service application, the initial topology of a new Search Service application will have all components on one application server and all databases on one database server. The Search Application Topology can be seen on the Search Administration page, but unlike SharePoint Server 2010, the topology cannot be changed from the user interface.

> **Tip**
>
> You can use the export-spenterprisesearchtopology cmdlet to dump the topology to an XML file. You can edit that XML file and then use import-spenterprisesearchtopology cmdlet to update. Some administrators find this easier than PowerShell scripts.

Now, all changes must be made in Windows PowerShell. Figure 10.9 is an example of the topology view in Search Administration immediately after creation.

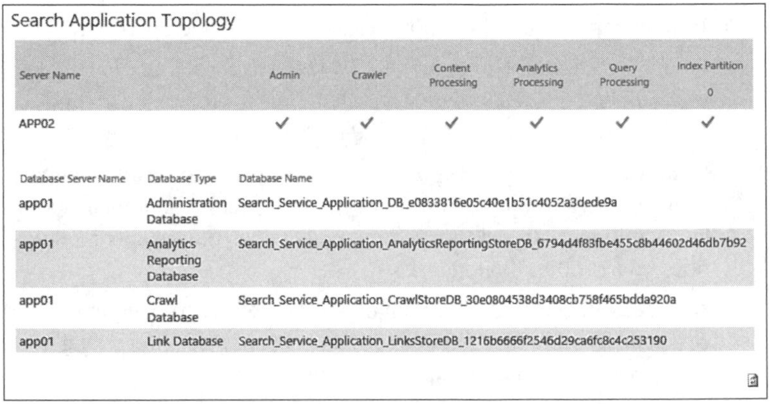

Search Application Topology

Server Name	Admin	Crawler	Content Processing	Analytics Processing	Query Processing	Index Partition 0
APP02	✓	✓	✓	✓	✓	✓

Database Server Name	Database Type	Database Name
app01	Administration Database	Search_Service_Application_DB_e0833816e05c40e1b51c4052a3dede9a
app01	Analytics Reporting Database	Search_Service_Application_AnalyticsReportingStoreDB_6794d4f83fbe455c8b44602d46db7b92
app01	Crawl Database	Search_Service_Application_CrawlStoreDB_30e0804538d3408cb758f465bdda920a
app01	Link Database	Search_Service_Application_LinksStoreDB_1216b6666f2546d29ca6fc8c4c253190

FIGURE 10.9
Search Application Topology page.

As shown in Figure 10.9, all services are on the server app02 and all databases are on app01. In the following examples, three additional servers will be added to the search topology: APP02, FE01, and FE02. Figure 10.10 shows the current search farm topology and where search components (services) are located immediately after service application creation.

The first method for changing your search topology and adding servers to the search topology is by cloning the existing single server topology and modifying. This example moves the Query Processing Component and Indexing Component to both FE01 and FE02. To clone and modify an existing topology, the following steps must be followed:

1. Create an Identity variable for every target search server in the farm. In this example, it would look like this:

```
$hosta = Get-SPEnterpriseSearchServiceInstance -Identity
"app02"
$hostB = Get-SPEnterpriseSearchServiceInstance -
Identity "fe01"
$hostC = Get-SPEnterpriseSearchServiceInstance -
Identity "fe02"
```

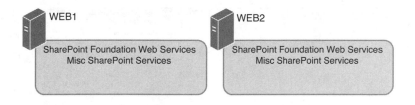

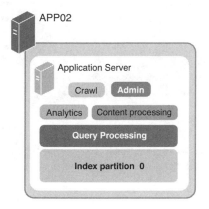

FIGURE 10.10
All search components are on APP02 before modification.

2. Start the Search service instance on all target servers, as shown in
   the following scripts:

```
Start-SPEnterpriseSearchServiceInstance -Identity
$hostA
Start-SPEnterpriseSearchServiceInstance -Identity
$hostB
Start-SPEnterpriseSearchServiceInstance -Identity
$hostC
```

3. Verify the Search Host Controller service is started in Task Manager
   on all target servers, as shown in Figure 10.11, along with the Search
   Crawler service.

4. Retrieve the Search Service Application GUID and assign a variable;
   this example assigns the variable $SSA to the Search Service
   Application:

```
$SSA = Get-SPEnterpriseSearchServiceApplication
```

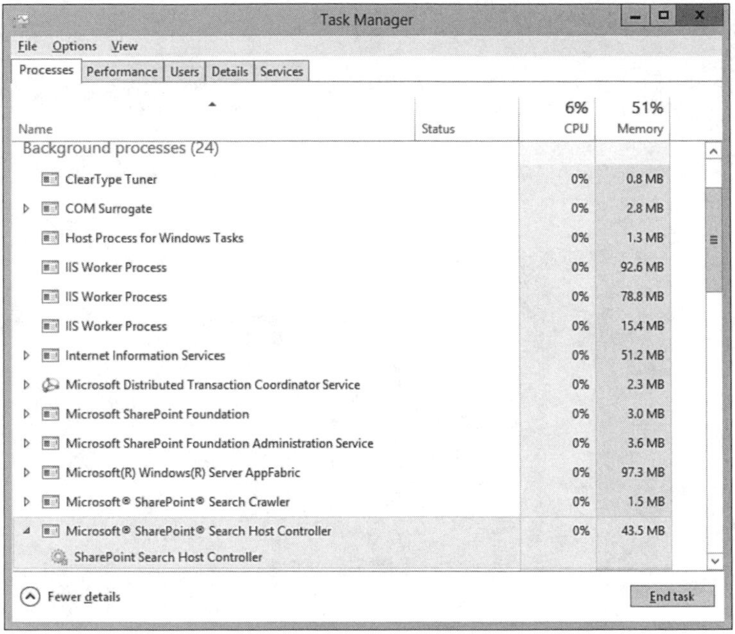

FIGURE 10.11
Verify the Search Host Controller has been started.

5. Get the Search Topology ID associated with $SSA and assign a variable. This example uses $active:

```
$active = Get-SPEnterpriseSearchTopology -Active -
SearchApplication $SSA
```

6. Clone the topology as the active topology. This example uses $cloneTOP as the new topology variable:

```
$cloneTOP = New-SPEnterpriseSearchTopology -
SearchApplication $ssa -Clone -SearchTopology $active
```

7. Remove servers as necessary. This example removes the Query Processing Component and Indexing Component from APP02.

8. Get the component GUID by executing the following command:

```
Get-SPEnterpriseSearchComponent -SearchTopology
$cloneTOP
```

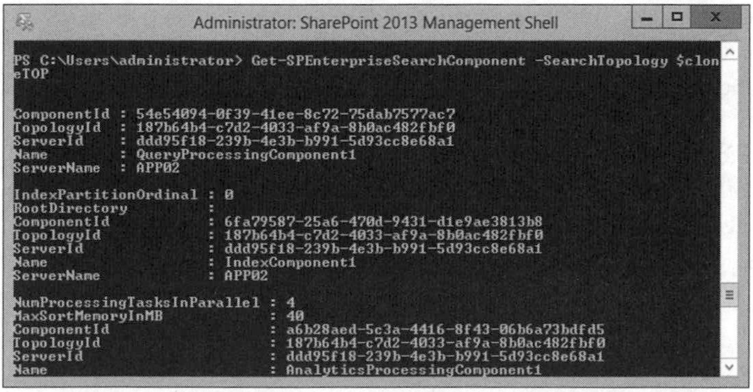

FIGURE 10.12
GUIDs for Search Components.

9. As shown in Figure 10.12, the GUIDs for APP02 for both the Query Processing Component and Indexing Component are displayed. Next, run the following commands to remove those components:

```
Remove-SPEnterpriseSearchComponent -identity 6fa79587-
25a6-470d-9431-d1e9ae3813b8 -
searchtopology $clonetop
Remove-SPEnterpriseSearchComponent -identity 54e54094-
0f39-41ee-8c72-75dab7577ac7 -
searchtopology $clonetop
```

10. If you run the following command again, you'll see the components have been removed from APP02:

```
$SSA = Get-SPEnterpriseSearchServiceApplication
```

11. Add search components as required. This example adds the Query Processing Component and Indexing Component to both FE01 and FE02:

```
New-SPEnterpriseSearchQueryProcessingComponent -
SearchTopology $cloneTOP -SearchServiceInstance
$hostB
New-SPEnterpriseSearchIndexComponent -SearchTopology
$cloneTOP -SearchServiceInstance $hostB -
IndexPartition 0
New-SPEnterpriseSearchQueryProcessingComponent -
SearchTopology $cloneTOP -SearchServiceInstance
$hostC
```

```
New-SPEnterpriseSearchIndexComponent -SearchTopology
$cloneTOP -SearchServiceInstance $hostC -
IndexPartition 0
```

12. After you have the topology exactly how you want it to be, you need to apply, also referred to as *activating*, the topology with the following command:

```
Set-SPEnterpriseSearchTopology -Identity $cloneTOP
```

Depending on the complexity of your design and speed of your servers, this command may take several minutes or over an hour. If you modify a very large server farm, this command could take several hours to complete. The amount of time is greatly dependent upon whether you moved or added index replicas. If you added index partitions and have content in the existing partition, you need to run an additional command before activating the new topology:

```
$ssa.PauseForIndexRepartitioning()
```

The Search Service application is paused during index repartitioning and cannot crawl or index content. Also, users will not be able to run queries. You will not be able to access the Windows PowerShell console where the activation command runs. Also, the Search Administration page in Central Administration does not show that the Search service application has been paused for index repartitioning, so command-line monitoring is required. You will probably want to restart the Host Controller service on the servers hosting index components to correct the document count and free up memory used during repartitioning.

During the topology application, the Server Application Topology screen will display "Please note that a different topology is currently being activated," as shown in Figure 10.13.

After this command has completed, your farm topology should look like Figure 10.14 in Search Administration.

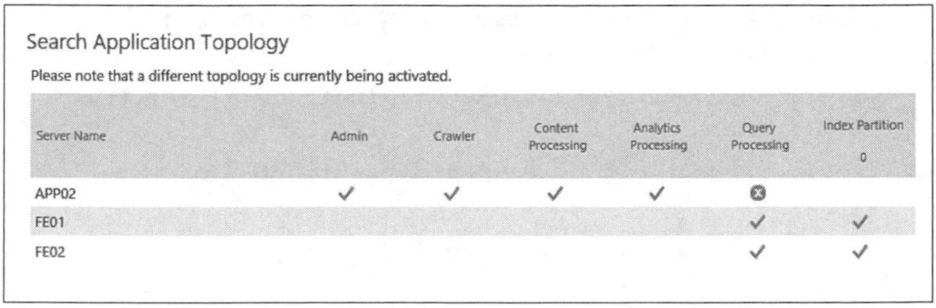

Search Application Topology

Please note that a different topology is currently being activated.

Server Name	Admin	Crawler	Content Processing	Analytics Processing	Query Processing	Index Partition 0
APP02	✓	✓	✓	✓	✗	
FE01					✓	✓
FE02					✓	✓

FIGURE 10.13
Example of an incomplete topology activation.

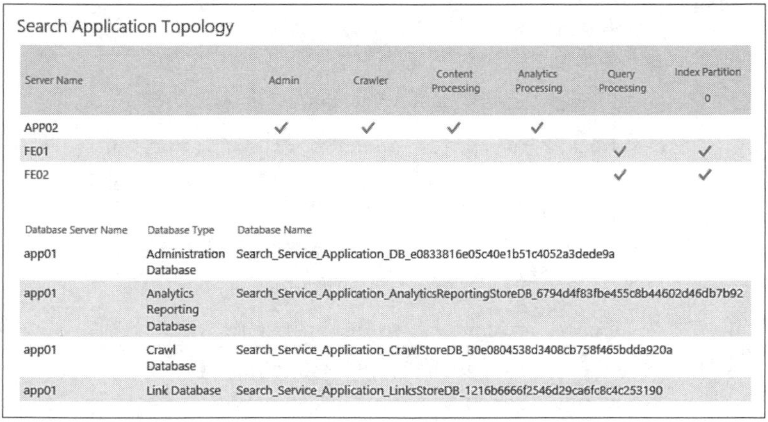

Search Application Topology

Server Name	Admin	Crawler	Content Processing	Analytics Processing	Query Processing	Index Partition 0
APP02	✓	✓	✓	✓		
FE01					✓	✓
FE02					✓	✓

Database Server Name	Database Type	Database Name
app01	Administration Database	Search_Service_Application_DB_e0833816e05c40e1b51c4052a3dede9a
app01	Analytics Reporting Database	Search_Service_Application_AnalyticsReportingStoreDB_6794d4f83fbe455c8b44602d46db7b92
app01	Crawl Database	Search_Service_Application_CrawlStoreDB_30e0804538d3408cb758f465bdda920a
app01	Link Database	Search_Service_Application_LinksStoreDB_1216b6666f2546d29ca6fc8c4c253190

FIGURE 10.14
Service components have been moved to FE01 and FE02.

Creating a New Topology

If this is a brand-new farm or a farm with very few items in the index, it's likely easier to create a new farm topology and activate that topology than to modify an existing topology. Using the same topology example that was used in cloning an existing topology, the follow steps enable you to create a new topology with the same outcome:

1. Assign a variable to all target servers and start the service instance on those servers with the following commands:

```
$hostA = Get-SPEnterpriseSearchServiceInstance -
Identity "app02"
$hostB = Get-SPEnterpriseSearchServiceInstance -
Identity "fe01"
```

```
$hostC = Get-SPEnterpriseSearchServiceInstance -
Identity "fe02"
Start-SPEnterpriseSearchServiceInstance -Identity
$hostA
Start-SPEnterpriseSearchServiceInstance -Identity
$hostB
Start-SPEnterpriseSearchServiceInstance -Identity
$hostC
```

Tip

You can check the status of services instances from Windows PowerShell using the Get-SPEnterpriseSearchServiceInstance -Identity $hostA command.

---

2. Assign a variable to the Search Service Application:

   ```
   $ssa = Get-SPEnterpriseSearchServiceApplication
   ```

3. Create a new topology and assign a variable:

   ```
   $newTopology = New-SPEnterpriseSearchTopology -
   SearchApplication $ssa
   ```

4. Create all necessary components on server farm members:

   ```
   New-SPEnterpriseSearchAdminComponent -SearchTopology
   $newTopology -SearchServiceInstance
   $hostA
   New-SPEnterpriseSearchCrawlComponent -SearchTopology
   $newTopology -SearchServiceInstance $hostA
   New-SPEnterpriseSearchContentProcessingComponent -
   SearchTopology $newTopology -
   SearchServiceInstance $hostA
   New-SPEnterpriseSearchAnalyticsProcessingComponent -
   SearchTopology $newTopology -
   SearchServiceInstance $hostA
   New-SPEnterpriseSearchQueryProcessingComponent -
   SearchTopology $newTopology -
   SearchServiceInstance $hostB
   New-SPEnterpriseSearchIndexComponent -SearchTopology
   $newTopology -SearchServiceInstance $hostB -
   IndexPartition 0
   New-SPEnterpriseSearchCrawlComponent -SearchTopology
   $newTopology -SearchServiceInstance $hostB
   ```

5. Apply the new topology:

```
Set-SPEnterpriseSearchTopology -Identity $newtopology
```

Farmwide Search Settings

Although most configurations are unique to the search service instance, the farmwide settings are followed by all crawlers. Some settings that are identified as farm settings are just default settings that can be overwritten by local services settings. The settings page shown in Figure 10.15 can be accessed from the Central Administration page by clicking General Application Settings and then clicking Farm Search Administration under the Search section.

Farm Search Administration

Farm-Level Search Settings

Proxy server for crawling and federation	None
Time-out (seconds)	60, 60
Ignore SSL warnings	No

Search Service Applications

Name

Search Service Application

FIGURE 10.15
Farmwide Search Settings page.

Because the crawler for websites is essentially a browser, the proxy settings are the same as for Internet Explorer with the exception of an option that directs federated queries to use the same settings.

The default connection timeouts of 60 seconds are for connection to content sources and for waiting for request acknowledgments.

The Boolean Ignore SSL Warnings choice controls whether the browser will treat sites as legitimate even if their certificate names do not exactly match. If this setting is not selected, a site with a faulty certificate will not be crawled.

Managing Crawler Impact Rules

Crawler impact rules are an optional mechanism to control the rate at which the crawler indexes a source. The crawler impact rule site-configuration settings are for a particular crawler target regardless of which search service, content source, or crawler instance is addressing the target. The Crawler Impact Rules management page can be accessed from the Search Service Application Administration page by clicking Crawler Impact Rules, under the Search section. It can also be opened from any search service Search Administration, but the configurations are always farmwide. On this page, click Add Rule to open the Add Crawler Impact Rule page, shown in Figure 10.16, or select an existing rule to edit.

FIGURE 10.16
Add Crawler Impact Rule page.

Valid crawler impact rules do not define the protocol (http://, https://, or file://) because the rule applies without regard to the connector used in the crawl or the content source containing the target. Here are some examples:

- Site name: 'www.contoso.com'
- All inclusive: '*'
- Partial: '*.contoso.com'
- Machine name: 'WEB01'

If you want to limit the number of simultaneous requests, you can change the default of 8 to any number, but the recommendation is not to exceed 256. A useful example is when you must first build the index. You can create a rule for 8 and throttle the requests to 1.

You can also configure the crawler to request one document at a time and send the requests to the queue. There is a large difference between one simultaneous request and a 1-second delay. Rarely will you need to set the delay greater than 1 second.

Note

Reducing the crawl rate can extend the crawl time so much that the crawl does not complete before it's time to start again. However, it can also prevent overloading a slow host, which results in a faster crawl rate because the source remains responsive.

Configuring the Search Service Application

There isn't room in this book to cover all facets of SharePoint Server 2013 Search administration. In fact, several books are dedicated to the topic. This section covers the basics you'll need to know for any SharePoint Server 2013 search installation.

Managing File Types

For each search service application, you can instruct the crawler as to what type of files should be crawled by using the Manage File Types page shown in Figure 10.17. The crawler requests only the file types that appear on the Manage File Types screen from content sources.

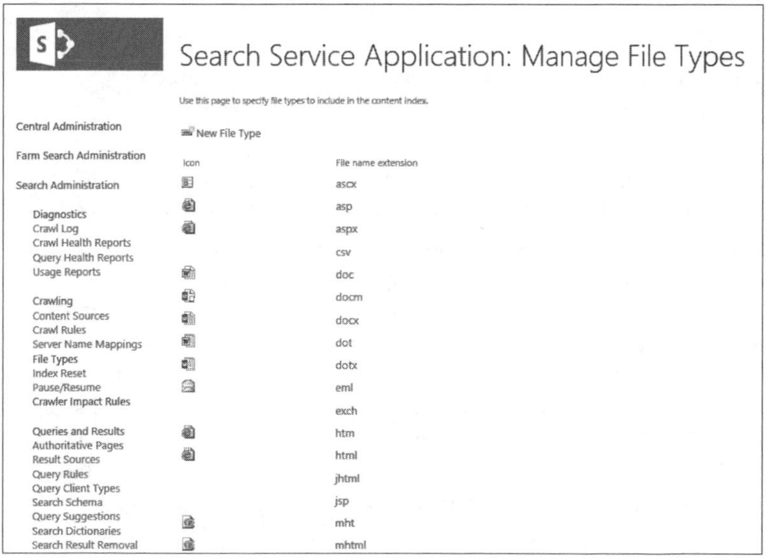

FIGURE 10.17
Manage File Types page.

To add a new file type, follow these steps:

1. Click the File Types link in the Quick Launch area of the Search Service Management page, as shown in Figure 10.17 to open the Manage File Types page.

2. Click the New File Type link. The Add File Type page appears, as shown in Figure 10.18.

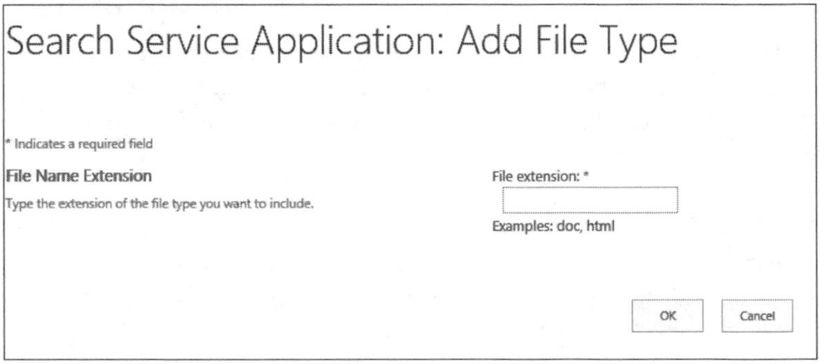

Search Service Application: Add File Type

* Indicates a required field

File Name Extension

Type the extension of the file type you want to include.

File extension: *

Examples: doc, html

[OK]   [Cancel]

FIGURE 10.18
Add File Type page.

3. Enter the file's extension in the File Extension input box.

4. Click OK.

At this point, the crawler processes all files with this extension. SharePoint 2013 uses both the new Format Handlers and the old iFilters for document processing. However, if you do not have either one installed on your server or servers for a file type, only the properties of the files can be crawled. Because iFilters are used by various search engines, they are installed on the operating system and configured for the search product. SharePoint does not provide an interface to indicate which iFilters have been installed on your servers or a tool for installing iFilters. You must follow the setup instructions from the iFilter's manufacturer to install and use the iFilter. These instructions should also include configuring the icon for the file type. You must also rely on your deployment documentation to inform you whether the correct iFilter for that file type has already been installed.

> **Note**
>
> SharePoint Server 2013 includes native support for crawling PDF files. You must define the File Type, but a document handler or iFilter is not required, and you cannot replace the native format handler.

To remove a file type for a search service application, click Delete on the context menu of the file type listing on the Manage File Types page, as shown in Figure 10.19.

FIGURE 10.19
Delete the filename extension listing.

Creating and Managing Content Sources

Creating content sources is the first administrative task in building an aggregated search and indexing topology. This work is accomplished inside the Search Service interface. To manage content sources, open the administration page for your search service and click the New Content Source link in the Quick Launch area, as shown in Figure 10.20.

FIGURE 10.20
The New Content Source link.

Essentially, a content source is a collection of start addresses that are accessed with the same type of connector and collectively managed. A start address is the URL location where the crawler starts the process. The crawl settings define the depth and potentially the width for the crawl process. The content source types include the following:

- SharePoint sites
- Websites
- File shares
- Exchange public folders
- Line of business data
- Custom repositories defined by custom connectors

The crawl setting terminology varies so that the settings that appear are appropriate for the selected content source type. To create a new content source, click the New Content Source link to open the Add Content Source page and then follow these steps:

1. Enter a name for the content source.

2. Select the content source type.

3. Enter the start address or addresses. All of them must match the content source type.

4. Select the crawl settings.

5. Select the crawl schedule or schedules.

6. Select the High or Normal priority for the content source processing.

7. Optionally, select Start Full Crawl of This Content Source.

8. Click OK.

Last, you can quickly edit content sources, including starting crawls, by hovering the mouse over a content source and clicking the arrow, as shown in Figure 10.21.

Configuring Crawl Rules

Crawl rules allow you to configure include/exclude rules, specific security contexts for crawling that are different from the default content access account, and the actual path to which you want the rule to apply.

Crawl rules are global to the search service and are relative to the target site, not a content source. For example, you can have two content sources: one each for http://WSS01/sites/IT and http://WSS01/sites/HR. Both can be covered by one crawl rule with a path of http://WSS01. Likewise, you can also specify a crawl rule for a subset of a content source, such as http://WSS01/sites/legal, if http://WSS01/ was the listing in the content source.

FIGURE 10.21
Hover over a content source and select the arrow to edit or start a crawl.

To manage existing crawl rules or create new ones, click the Crawl Rules link in the Quick Launch in Search Administration, which opens the Manage Crawl Rules page. If your search service has several crawl rules defined, use the Test button to locate any existing rules that might impact crawls of the site where you intend to create a new rule.

To create a new crawl rule, select New Crawl Rule link. The new crawl rule page is shown in Figure 10.22.

> **Note**
>
> Crawl rules are applied in the order listed on the Manage Crawl Rules page.

Crawl Rule Paths
Enter a URL path in the Path input box in the following form:

- Web application: http://www.contoso.com
- Web application path: http://www.contoso.com/path
- All inclusive: http://*
- Scheme independent: *://www.contoso.com

Path	Path: *
Type the path affected by this rule.	`*://*.contoso.com`
	Examples: http://hostname/*; http://*.*; *://hostname/*
	☐ Use regular expression syntax for matching this rule
Crawl Configuration	◉ Exclude all items in this path
Select whether items in the path are excluded from or included in the content index.	☐ Exclude complex URLs (URLs that contain question marks - ?)
	○ Include all items in this path
	☐ Follow links on the URL without crawling the URL itself
	☐ Crawl complex URLs (URLs that contain a question mark - ?)
	☐ Crawl SharePoint content as http pages
Specify Authentication	◉ Use the default content access account (CONTOSO\saspservice)
Use the default content access account to access items in the path.	○ Specify a different content access account
	○ Specify client certificate
	○ Specify form credentials
	○ Use cookie for crawling
	○ Anonymous access

FIGURE 10.22
New Crawl Rule page.

Crawl rule paths can also include regular expressions (REGEX) and be case sensitive if required.

Exclude/Include Options

You can also set the crawl information to exclude all items in the path or to include all items in the path. If you select Include All Items in This Path, you also have the following options:

- **Follow Links on the URL Without Crawling the URL Itself**— This is useful when the starting point of a crawl is a menu.

- **Crawl Complex URLs**—If you want to crawl content where there is content beyond a '?', select this option. Complex URLs are common with SharePoint and also often point to information contained in databases.

- **Crawl SharePoint Content as HTTP Pages**—If you want the crawler to ignore SharePoint content, such as security and versions, you can select this. It is often desirable to crawl external SharePoint Server content as HTTP pages when the audience is the Internet. This prevents accidental surfacing of private information regarding security and minor versions, among other things.

Crawl Rule Authentication

You can specify unique authentication via a crawl rule. The indexer uses the default content access account unless you create a crawl rule to change this behavior. Simply enter the username and password to access the resource. You can also restrict basic authentication. The unique account specified here is not included in managed accounts, and the password must be manually changed. Changing this account triggered a full crawl in the previous version.

You can specify a client certificate to access a content source. This certificate must first exist in the index server's Personal Certificate Store for the local computer before it will show up in the selection list.

> **Note**
>
> For Information Rights Management (IRM) files stored in SharePoint, the crawler will be able to index the files. However, for IRM files in other storage, the certificate for the crawler account must have read permission on the files.

Crawl rules also support Forms-Based authentication (FBA) and cookie-based authentication. Crawler rules do not support FBA with complex authentication pages that change content without refreshing the page or require entries or selection based on content appearing on the page.

> **Note**
>
> Be careful setting these one-off content source passwords of unmanaged accounts using crawl rules. Remember that this password must be manually changed whenever the account's password changes. This should be a documented process in your search-and-indexing maintenance plan, as well as in your disaster recovery plan.

Removing Search Results

If content will be crawled by your search engine that should not be presented in search results, you need to immediately remove it from search results.

> **Note**
>
> Removing content from content source will initiate a "deletion" crawl for that content, but the content will continue to appear in search results until removed from the index.

Remember that search results are derived from the index, so removal of the content itself is not sufficient. The information must be removed from the index.

To remove content from search results, open the Remove URLs from Search Results page by clicking the Search Result Removal link in the Queries and Results group of the Quick Launch area of the Search Administration page. It is important to remember that these settings exist only in this specific Service Application and wouldn't be available in other search service applications.

Enter the URLs of the content to be removed in the URLs, one per line, and click Remove Now. The security descriptor for the item is NULLED out so that it cannot be security trimmed and therefore is not returned in search results. In addition, crawl rules will be created to prevent the content from being indexed in subsequent crawls, which will remove it from the index.

Note

Sometimes only the permissions were wrong on content that was crawled. If the error has been corrected on the content but it has not been re-crawled, search results might still expose inappropriate information to users even if they cannot access the complete documents. In this case, remove the content from the index using the search results removal tool and delete the crawl rule after the permissions have been corrected. Because changes to permissions trigger a recrawl even on file share content in SharePoint Server 2013, the next incremental crawl will update the index.

Configuring and Reading Health Reports

Each search service application in SharePoint Server 2013 provides reports for both query and crawl processing that will be useful in monitoring performance; identifying potential bottlenecks; and projecting the need for additional resources, including components. We will cover an overview of these reports.

Note

For more information, see http://technet.microsoft.com/en-us/library/jj219611(v=office.15).aspx.

Health reports contain information only after a full crawl has completed because analytics is now part of search functionality. Also, analytics processing continues after crawling has completed, so some reports will exhibit a lag time during heavy resource usage.

Users do not need to be either a farm or search administrator to view these reports. A user who has Read permissions for the search service application can view the application status page, the health reports, and the crawl log.

The reports are accessed from the Diagnostics section of the Quick Launch on the Search Service Application page. The various reports are opened by tabs across the page, as shown in Figure 10.23. The filter options change for some reports.

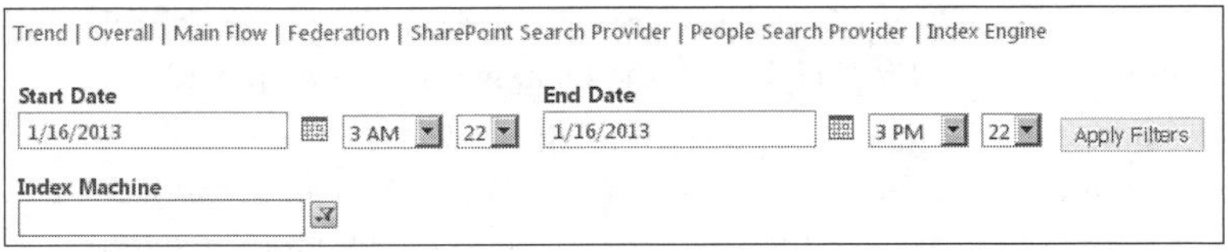

Trend | Overall | Main Flow | Federation | SharePoint Search Provider | People Search Provider | Index Engine

Start Date   **End Date**

1/16/2013   [▦] 3 AM ▼ 22 ▼   1/16/2013   [▦] 3 PM ▼ 22 ▼   Apply Filters

Index Machine

[   ] [✓]

FIGURE 10.23
Top of Health Reports page.

Overview of Query Health Reports

The Query Latency Trend report shows the query latency in milliseconds by percentile across all results pages using the Search Service Application. This report also shows the query rate, the crawl rate, and the partial update rate for analytics during the same time period.

The Overall Query Latency report shows the number of queries per minute with an overlay of latency in milliseconds broken down into the following areas:

- **Server Rendering**—The time it took the server to render the results page

- **Object Model**—The time taken by communications between the web server and the back-end process

- **Back-End**—Time taken to transform the query, retrieve results from the index, process the results, and return them to the object model

The Main Flow report shows the latency in milliseconds for the query pipeline processes, such as rule condition matching, query transformation, routing, result mixing, layout selection, logging, and so on. The Federation Query Latency report gives the query latency in milliseconds for all result source types. This report becomes more useful when filtered for a specific federated provider.

The SharePoint Search Provider report provides the latency for all queries processed by the local SharePoint search provider, including keyword parsing, linguistics, security trimming for recommendations, construction of the security token, index lookup, result type processing, custom security trimming, and summary generation. This report includes an overlay of the query rate during the time period to show the impact of the number of queries on the latency.

The People Search Provider report provides the same type report as the SharePoint Search Provider but for the local people search provider.

The Index Engine report uses data from all result pages to show the query latency for specific index engine selected in the filter. This report includes an overlay of the average time during a given minute it took the index engine to return results. Lookups with no results are not included.

> **Note**
>
> If the Federation Query Latency report indicates that a specific provider's latency is slowing the results page load time, you may choose to configure the appropriate web part to load asynchronously so that the rest of the page loads while waiting for the results in that web part. Users' perceptions of query latency are how long it takes for the results page to load.

Overview of Crawl Health Reports

The Crawl Rate report gives a summary and graph of the number of items crawled per minute, including total number of items, items changed and recrawled, items not changed and not crawled, items crawled because security changed on them, items deleted from index because they were deleted from the content source, crawl retries, and crawl errors.

The Crawl Latency report gives a summary and graph either in total or by server of the amount of time in milliseconds that each content item is in the following pipeline subsystems—Crawler, protocol handler, repository, and SQL.

The Crawl Queue report shows the number of items to be crawled. The *Links to* process queue contains URLs that to be crawled to determine items to crawl. The Transactions queued is the number of URLs that have been crawled and are ready for processing by the crawl pipeline.

The Crawl Freshness report shows the time between the time the document was changed and the time it was indexed.

The Content Processing Activity report gives the amount of time spent in various components of the pipeline—Linguistics, Parsing, Document Summary Generation, and Indexing. It can be reported by content source, server, component, and activity.

The CPU/Memory Load report presents the CPU utilization (percentage) used and the Memory utilization (MB) as well as the system overview for the MSSDmn, MSSearch, NodeRunner, and Timer.

The Continuous Crawl report gives (within an overlay of discovery time in minutes) the time in milliseconds that these processes took—Time in Links Table, Time in Queue Table, Crawler Time, Protocol Handler Time, Repository Time, Content Pipeline Time, and SQL Time.

Monitoring Crawl Logs

The crawl log provides information on the results of crawls, including whether content was successfully added to the index, was excluded by a crawl rule, or if there were processing errors. It also contains information such as the time of the last successful crawl and any crawl rules that were applied.

Frequent review of crawl logs not only reveals issues that the crawler is encountering, but also highlights potential problems for users within the farm. The crawler account has full read rights given via application policy. If that account cannot access content, you can rest assured that users cannot either or that the crawler is attempting to use the wrong protocol for the content. The error messages usually expose the reasons for the error.

Crawl logs will also provide quick insight into which portions of your farm are growing and which are stagnant.

Crawl Log Views

The crawl log is accessed from the Diagnostics section of the Quick Launch on the Search Service Application page. Six views of the log information are arranged as tabs across the top of the page.

The Content Source view gives a quick summary of items crawled per content source, not per crawl. This is the current status of items within the content source showing successes, warnings, errors, top-level errors, and deleted items. It also gives some performance data on the duration of the last crawl compared to averages for the past 24 hours, past 7 days, and past 30 days. This information is evidence of changes in size of content for the content source but not individual addresses.

The Host Name view summarizes items per host, even if crawled by different protocol handlers showing successes, warnings, errors, deleted items, top-level errors, and the total number of crawled items.

The Crawl History view provides a summary of crawl transactions completed during a crawl organized by content source. The type of crawl is specified as follows:

- **F: Full**—Can be scheduled or manually initiated. All items are crawled.

- **I: Incremental**—Can be scheduled or manually initiated. Only items that have changed since the last crawl are crawled.

- **D: Delete**—Is only initiated by removal of start addresses from a content source. This crawl removes items from the index before a full or incremental crawl starts.

- **C: Continuous**—Essentially an incremental crawl that runs very frequently.

This view also shows performance data. Be careful with the numbers on this view. The number of transactions in a crawl can be greater than the number of items in a content source because there could be multiple crawl transactions per item.

The Error Breakdown view is useful in troubleshooting because it summarizes errors by content source or host name.

The Databases view provides a document count per crawl database for this search application.

The URL view is a search tool in the MSSCrawlURLReport table in the crawl database(s). You may search by content source, URL, or host name and filter the results on the Status, Message, Start Time, and End Time fields.

Some columns are common across several views of the crawl log:

- **Successes**—Items were successfully crawled and indexed.

- **Warnings**—Items may not have been successfully crawled and indexed.

- **Errors**—Items were not successfully crawled, and index information may be incorrect.

- **Top Level Errors**—Errors at the top level of a crawl, including start addresses, virtual servers, and content databases. Although appearing as a separate count, they are also included in the Errors column as well. A single error here could indicate that an entire web application or database was not indexed.

- **Deletes**—Items that were removed from the index because they are no longer in the content being crawled or as a result of a delete crawl.

- **Not Modified**—Items still exist but were not changed since the last crawl.

- **Security Update**—Items crawled because the security settings had changed.

- **Security Error**—Items where the security update caused an error.

The last three columns appear only in the Crawl History view.

Analyzing Usage Reports

Although Health Reports and Crawl Logs help determine how the system is performing, Usage Reports give information on whether it is providing a useful service to users. This information is useful to search professionals and to site collection administrators as well, so it is available to both. For site collection administrators, the search reports are found under Site Settings, Site Collection Administration, Popularity and Search Reports, and are filtered for the site collection activities.

For the search service application, Usage Reports are accessed from the Diagnostics section of the Quick Launch on the Search Service Application page.

Whereas Health Reports and Crawl Logs are displayed in web pages, Usage Reports are Excel spreadsheets generated by the analytics processing component. They can be opened on the server if Office Web Applications is installed, or they can be periodically saved to a trusted location for Excel services.

Note

Information contained in these reports is not security trimmed for the user viewing them and could expose data not available to all users.

There are five reports; four have different time periods available:

■ The Number of Queries report shows the number of search queries performed, identifying search query volume trends and times of high and low search activity. If there are times where query volume is so high that crawling impacts response time, adjusting crawl schedules may be appropriate.

■ The Top Queries reports give the most popular search queries either by day (current month) or by month (last 12 months). This information can expose the need to present some information to users without the need for a user-initiated search.

■ The Abandoned Queries report provides popular queries by day or month that received low click-through, which generally indicates that the search results did not meet the users' needs. Because user dissatisfaction at the inability to locate content lowers search usage, steps should be taken to improve the findability of content. This may involve using query rules to improve results or exploration of improving tagging with metadata.

■ The No Result Queries reports reveal popular queries by day or month that returned no results. These queries are worse than abandoned queries. Efforts should be taken to see if content exists that should have been located by the query and, if so, query rules should be created or adjusted to improve the query's results. Adding metadata to the content can also improve findability.

■ The Query Rule Usage reports are available by day and by month. They show how often query rules trigger, how many dictionary terms they use, and how often users click their promoted results. They indicate how useful your query rules and promoted results are to users.

Configuring Search Relevance Settings

Search results relevance settings can be managed through the authoritative pages in the search service. The relationship of individual documents or content items to authoritative pages is defined in terms of click distance. Click distance is not based on URL depth. If all other ranking elements are equal, the more clicks that are required to traverse from the authoritative page to the content item, the less relevant that item is for a given query. Placing a link to an object on an authoritative page elevates that object in search results, with no regard to the actual location of the object.

Your farm will have some locations that contain official, approved content for your organization. These locations are the URLs you should enter into the Authoritative Web Pages input boxes, which are shown in Figure 10.24.

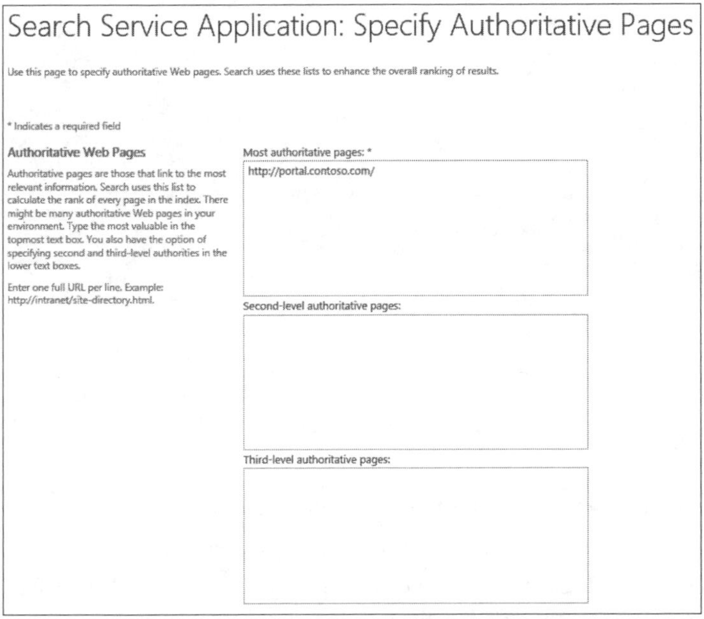

Search Service Application: Specify Authoritative Pages

Use this page to specify authoritative Web pages. Search uses these lists to enhance the overall ranking of results.

* Indicates a required field

Authoritative Web Pages

Authoritative pages are those that link to the most relevant information. Search uses this list to calculate the rank of every page in the index. There might be many authoritative Web pages in your environment. Type the most valuable in the topmost text box. You also have the option of specifying second and third-level authorities in the lower text boxes.

Enter one full URL per line. Example: http://intranet/site-directory.html.

Most authoritative pages: *

http://portal.contoso.com/

Second-level authoritative pages:

Third-level authoritative pages:

FIGURE 10.24
The Authoritative Web Pages input boxes.

You can achieve levels of granularity by entering primary, secondary, and tertiary URLs, thereby formulating an overall hierarchical relevance topology for your search application. URLs within the same input box are grouped equally, meaning that there is no hierarchical order implied by the URL list. In addition, wildcards, such as http:foo/*, are not accepted in these boxes.

You can also insert file shares as authoritative page sources. Use the file:// protocol scheme when defining file systems. For example, file://fileserver1/archive specifies the archive file share as an authoritative location.

You can also set some sites to be the lowest on the relevance scale by placing their URLs in the Sites to Demote input box, which is shown in

Figure 10.25. You should consider the resource implications of recalculating the ranking of your indexes immediately rather than recalculating them during normal schedules.

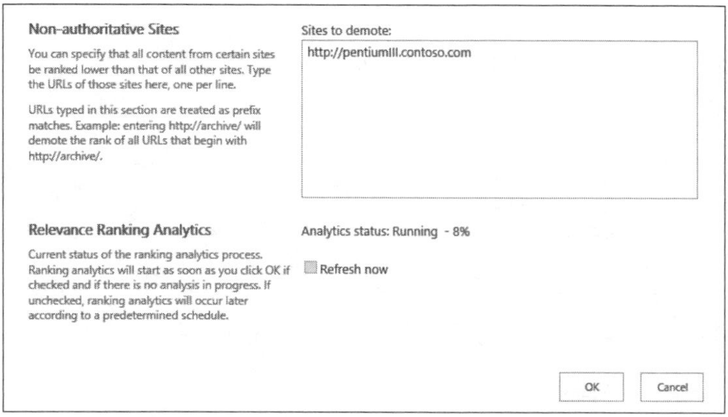

FIGURE 10.25
The Non-authoritative Sites input boxes.

To set relevance settings, perform the following steps:

1. Open the Administration page for your search service.

2. In the Quick Launch area, click the Specify Authoritative Pages link under the Queries and Results heading.

3. Input the URLs in the appropriate boxes as required to configure relevance settings for your environment.

4. Select the Refresh Now check box if you want to have the relevance settings recomputed immediately.

5. Click OK.

Adding a Server Name Mapping

There might be situations where content needs to be crawled using an address other than one of the Alternate Access Mapping URLs defined for user access to SharePoint content. Create server name mappings to override how URLs are shown in search results, and correct the name displayed to users. The Server Name Mapping management page is accessed by clicking Server Name Mapping in the Crawling section of the Search Service Management page of the Quick Launch navigation area. Click the

New Mapping link to open the Add Server Name Mapping page shown in
Figure 10.26.

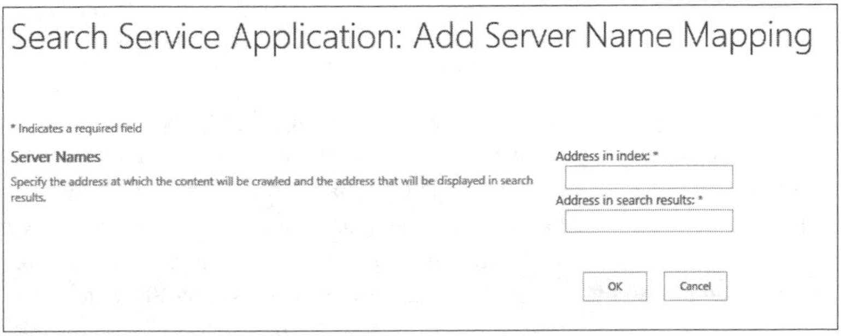

Search Service Application: Add Server Name Mapping

* Indicates a required field

Server Names

Specify the address at which the content will be crawled and the address that will be displayed in search
results.

Address in index: *

[   ]

Address in search results: *

[   ]

[OK]   [Cancel]

FIGURE 10.26
Add Server Name Mapping page.

Instances where this might be required include the following:

■ The need to crawl content using HTTP when users will access it
using HTTPS.

■ It is necessary to crawl with Windows authentication when the
normal authentication method is not supported for the crawler, such
as smart-card authentication.

Search Schema

Although a search query across the full text of a document might be useful,
the power of an enterprise search query comes from its capability to query
attributes or properties of objects, whether it can crawl the actual content
or not. The Search schema contains two types of properties:

■ Crawled properties are automatically extracted from crawled content,
and the metadata field is added to the search schema. The text values
of crawled properties that are included in the index are treated the
same as text content unless they are mapped to a managed property.

■ Managed properties are created to group common properties with
dissimilar names under standardized names and expose this grouping
to search tools. Users can perform specific queries over managed
properties.

Crawled properties can be columns on a list or document library, metadata
for a content type, or properties within the properties of a document

created in a Microsoft Office application. If your users use custom names in these scenarios, mapping crawled properties to a managed property will be more difficult than if they used existing properties or columns. Dete mining which custom properties should be grouped into a managed property is frequently a time-consuming research job, particularly if there is no naming convention established.

The value in mapping crawled properties to managed properties is that it groups metadata into usable units. The metadata (crawled properties) are grouped into a logical, single unit (managed properties). Multiple crawled properties can be mapped to a single managed property, or a single crawled property can be mapped to multiple managed properties. Managed properties can then be used to create search scopes and enable your users to focus their search to a limited portion of the corpus. Managed properties can also be included in the Advanced Search web part interface to narrow a query to specific properties and in the Refinement web part for focusing on specific search results. We discuss these uses later in this chapter.

Note

Grouping crawled properties into managed properties is essential for many search functionalities. For example, suppose you have three document types: document type A, which lists the author in the Author metadata field; document type B, which lists the author in the Creator metadata field; and document type C, which lists the author in the Originator metadata field. In this scenario, you have (essentially) the same metadata for three document types residing in three metadata fields. When these documents are crawled, each metadata field is entered into the property store as separate crawled properties. However, you can group these three crawled properties into a single managed property so that you can use them as a single unit when querying for author names across these three document types.

To administer metadata properties, navigate to the Metadata Property Mappings page shown in Figure 10.27 by clicking the Metadata Properties link under the Queries and Results heading of the Search Service Application page.

Use this page to create and modify managed properties and map crawled properties to managed properties. Changes to properties of existing content take effect after the next full crawl, but they are applied to new content during incremental crawls.

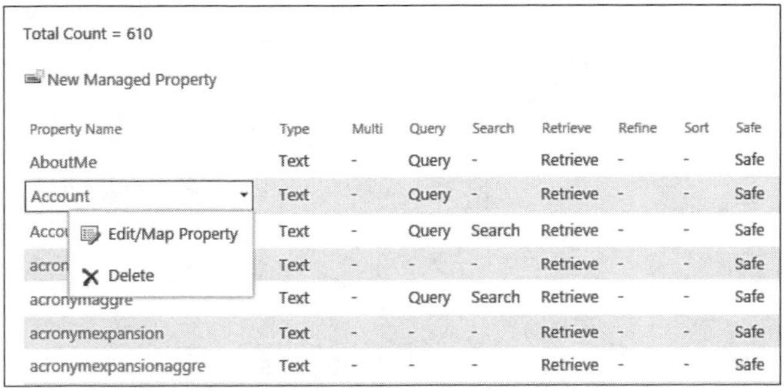

Property Name	Type	Multi	Query	Search	Retrieve	Refine	Sort	Safe
AboutMe	Text	-	Query	-	Retrieve	-	-	Safe
Account	Text	-	Query	-	Retrieve	-	-	Safe
Acco[Edit/Map Property]	Text	-	Query	Search	Retrieve	-	-	Safe
acron[Delete]	Text	-	-	-	Retrieve	-	-	Safe
acronymaggre	Text	-	Query	Search	Retrieve	-	-	Safe
acronymexpansion	Text	-	-	-	Retrieve	-	-	Safe
acronymexpansionaggre	Text	-	-	-	Retrieve	-	-	Safe

Total Count = 610

New Managed Property

FIGURE 10.27
Metadata Property Mappings page.

On this page, several properties of each managed property are displayed, including a linked name and linked crawled properties mapped to the managed property. If you need to configure a new managed property, click the New Managed Property link to open the property page shown in Figure 10.27.

> **Note**
>
> To learn more about managing the search schema, see http://technet.microsoft.com/en-us/library/jj219630(v=office.15).

Configuring Result Sources

Search scopes are no longer available in SharePoint Server 2013. In their place are *result sources*. Result sources can be created at the Service Application, Site Collection, or Site levels. However, this section is scoped to creating result sources within the Service Application.

With the notable exception that search scopes could be added to a drop-down list in a search web part, result sources are much more powerful. Result sources can be scoped to sites, lists, and libraries, but now also to federated sources that are OpenSearch 1.1 compliant and Microsoft Exchange Server. To create a new result source, do the following:

1. From the Query and Results group in Search Service Application administration, select the Result Sources link, as shown in Figure 10.28.

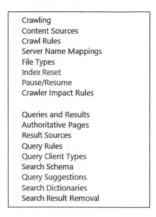

FIGURE 10.28
Select the Result Sources link in the Queries and Results Group to Add or Edit Result Sources.

2. From the Manage Results Sources page, you can create a new one or edit properties, as shown in Figure 10.29.

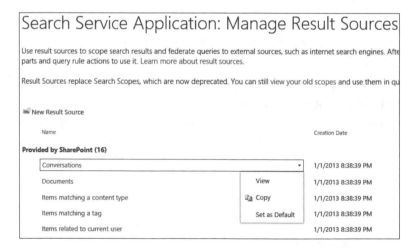

FIGURE 10.29
Hover over a result source and right-click to see the available options.

3. Select New Result Source.

4. Enter the desired Result Source Name, Description, and protocol.

5. Select whether this will be SharePoint content or People Search results.

6. Optionally, you can use the Query Transform option for advanced custom queries.

7. Select Basic or Default Authentication.

For creating the equivalent of a SharePoint Server 2010 Search scope, you'll want to use the Query Builder. Upon opening the Query builder, as shown in Figure 10.30, note the Property filter drop-down list.

FIGURE 10.30
The Property filter allows you to scope search queries to managed properties.

Last, if you want to use a property that is custom, you'll want to select Show All Managed Properties and reopen the property filter list.

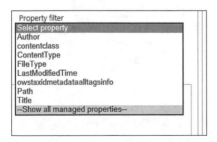

FIGURE 10.31
To see custom managed properties, select Show All Managed Properties in the drop-down menu.

Search Diagnostics and Monitoring

The health reports discussed previously can reveal that problems or bottlenecks exist in the various pipeline processes or in communications between the various components of SharePoint 2013 search. Diagnosing the reasons behind these issues or bottlenecks may require several tools.

For those familiar with FAST Search for SharePoint 2010, the command-line tools used for examining processes, and the centralized logging provided, note that those are missing from SharePoint 2013. However, the good news is that an extensive array of tools exists for monitoring operations and diagnosing search issues.

Because of space limitations, we will assume knowledge of basic Windows tools. This section only includes special sections or reports from those tools.

The Event Viewer from the server operating system will have a collection of events collected from numerous search sources displayed under Applications and Services Logs, Microsoft, Office Server, Search, Operational. Search components will also appear in the normal Windows logs.

Task Manager can provide some quick information regarding processes and their statuses and performance. In Figure 10.32, mssearch.exe is the crawler with the filtering daemon (Mssdmn.exe) that parses Microsoft Office documents.

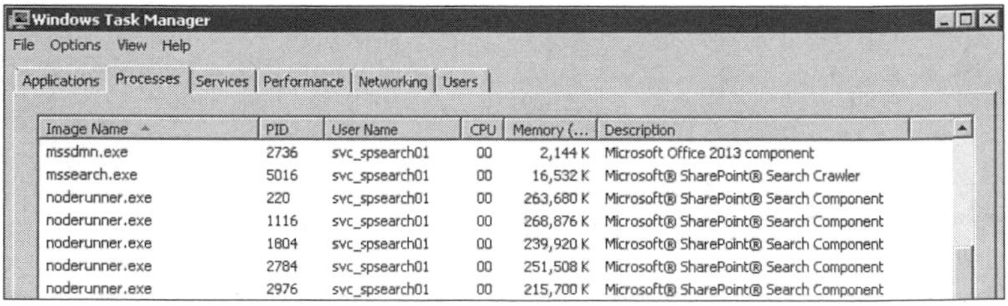

FIGURE 10.32
Task Manager displaying search components.

The other search components are running under the new integrated FS4SP and FSIS functionality as instances of noderunner.exe, although Task Manager does not indicate the individual components.

Resource Monitor (resmon.exe) can be launched from the Performance tab of Task Manager and provides the capability to select processes with more detailed information on resource consumption. In Figure 10.33 the noderunner processes are still not identified by component. However, low memory seems to be the bottleneck that is probably causing much of the disk thrashing. Only Search components were selected for this real-time capture.

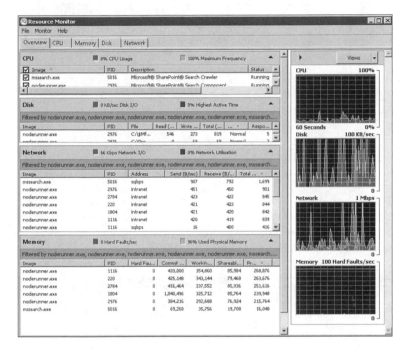

FIGURE 10.33
Resource Monitor view of process and resource utilization.

Process Explorer and Process Monitor are two free Microsoft tools that can be downloaded and will give the details of which component's noderunner is executing. These tools are free-standing executables that do not require an installation process.

Process Explorer shows a list of the currently active processes, including the names of their owning accounts. Hovering over a process gives complete information including for the noderunner.exe the location of the tracelogs for the application, as shown in Figure 10.34.

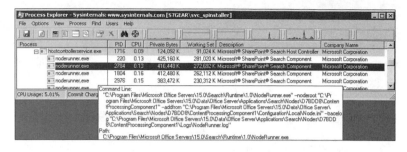

FIGURE 10.34
Process Explorer detailed view of a noderunner.exe process.

> **Note**
>
> For more information, see http://technet.microsoft.com/en-us/
> sysinternals/bb896653.aspx.

Process Monitor shows real-time file system, Registry, and process/thread activity. It displays session IDs and usernames, reliable process information, and full thread stacks for each operation and can log simultaneously to a file. In Figure 10.35, a filter limits the processes displayed.

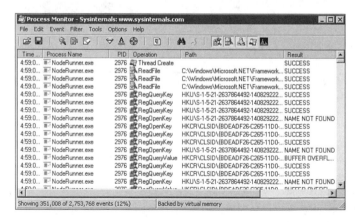

FIGURE 10.35
Filtered view of search processes in Process Monitor.

A portion of a Process Monitor XML log file identifies IndexComponent1 as the component is being executed by one instance of noderunner.exe:

```
<Owner>S7GEAR\svc_spsearch01</Owner>
<ProcessName>NodeRunner.exe</ProcessName>
<ImagePath>C:\Program Files\Microsoft Office
Servers\15.0\Search\Runtime\1.0\NodeRunner.exe</Image
Path>
<CommandLine>&quot;C:\Program Files\Microsoft Office
Servers\15.0\Search\Runtime\1.0\NodeRunner.exe&quot;
--noderoot &quot;C:\Program Files\Microsoft Office
Servers\15.0\Data\Office
Server\Applications\Search\Nodes\D7BDD8\
IndexComponent1
```

Note

For more information, see http://technet.microsoft.com/en-us/
sysinternals/bb896645.aspx.

Windows Management Instrumentation (WMI) provides many classes to monitor the SharePoint 2013 environment. For each manageable resource, there is a corresponding WMI class.

Information about search processes can be accessed with the following PowerShell cmdlet:

```
Get-WmiObject Win32_Process -Filter "Name like
'noderunner.exe'
OR Name like 'mssearch.exe' OR Name like
'mssdmn.exe'"
¦ Select-object
ProcessId,CommandLine,CreationDate,WorkingSetSize ¦
fl ¦ more
```

A partial example of the results is shown in Figure 10.36.

Note

For more information, see http://technet.microsoft.com/library/
ee198925.aspx.

FIGURE 10.36
Results of filtered Get-WMIObject cmdlet.

Other Microsoft Monitoring Tools

If you use Microsoft System Center Operation Manager, the Monitoring Pack for SharePoint Server 2013 monitors and provides alerts for automatic notification of events indicating service outages, performance degradation, and health monitoring, including 50 monitors for SharePoint Server Search.

> **Note**
>
> For more information, see http://www.microsoft.com/en-us/download/details.aspx?id=35590.

Using the Performance Monitor tool (perfmon.exe) included with the server operating system, monitor collection sets can be manually built to collect or view performance information from all members of your farm using the same counters that SCOM uses in its monitoring pack.

> **Note**
>
> For more information, see http://technet.microsoft.com/en-us/library/cc749115.aspx.

> **Note**
>
> For more information, see http://go.microsoft.com/fwlink/p/?LinkID=199580.

SQL Server Reporting Services can be used to create, deploy, and manage ready-to-use reports for your organization or to extend and customize reporting functionality.

> **Note**
>
> For more information, see http://go.microsoft.com/fwlink/p/?LinkId=253387.

Configuring Usage and Health Data Collection

Only a member of farm administrators can make changes to Usage and Health Data Collection. From the home page of Central Administration, click Monitoring and in the Reporting section of the Monitoring page, click Configure Usage and Health Data Collection.

Enable Usage Data Collection must be checked (enabled) before data is collected from any component. On this page, the only search component of interest is Analytics Usage.

Health Data Collection and Log Collection (including the schedules) can be managed from this page as well as the log and database configurations. These configurations can also be managed with PowerShell.

> **Note**
>
> For more information, see http://technet.microsoft.com/en-us/library/ee663480.aspx.

Diagnostic Logging

Diagnostic logging can also be configured by clicking Configure Diagnostic Logging in the Reporting section of the Monitoring page of Central Administration.

There are 25 categories of events that may be configured on this page. For SharePoint Enterprise Search the category name is SharePoint Server Search, not Search. The entire category can be enabled collectively, or the 25 activities listed under that category can be managed independently.

Because diagnostic logging incurs extra overhead on the servers, extensive logging should only be enabled when troubleshooting. By default, the logs are placed in the ULS logs directory, but this location can be changed on this page.

Viewing Diagnostic Logs

To retrieve specific log entries, PowerShell is your friend as long as the account being used has securityadmin role on the SQL server instance and dbo on databases to be accessed and is a farm admin. From the SharePoint 2012 Management Shell, the following cmdlet extracted a number of entries:

```
Get-SPLogEvent | Where-Object {$_.Category -eq "Crawler:Content
Plugin"} Format-List
```

An example of one of the entries is:

```
Timestamp     : 1/4/2013 2:35:29 PM
Continuation : False
Process       : mssearch.exe (0x02C8)
ThreadID      : 272
Area          : SharePoint Server Search
Category      : Crawler:Content Plugin
EventID       : ajqe0
Level         : High
Message       : CSSFeedersManager statistics
Continuous Crawl group: #items in
              plugin 0; #items in batches ready to
submit: 0; # submitted = 0
Correlation  : 00000000-0000-0000-0000-000000000000
Context       : {}
```

This cmdlet can also be piped to a new UI for viewing the ULS logs. The cmdlet

```
Get-SPLogEvent | Out-GridView
```

launches the view shown in Figure 10.37.

This view can be sorted by clicking the column header and is filtered by entering properties in the search box. Raw, sorted, or filtered data can be exported to a spreadsheet.

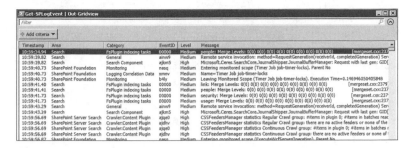

FIGURE 10.37
Out-Gridview UI present ULS logs in readable and manageable format.

> **Note**
>
> For more information, see http://technet.microsoft.com/en-us/library/
> ff463595.

Search Component Diagnostic Logs

Each Search component running under noderunner.exe keeps a separate log
file at C:\Program Files\Microsoft Office Servers\15.0\Data\Office Server\
Applications\Search\Nodes\ <SearchServiceApplication>\<component>\
Logs folder. These logs expose more detailed operational information
unique to that component that may be useful in troubleshooting.

Configuring SharePoint Health Analyzer Alerts

SharePoint 2013 includes a SharePoint Health Analyzer tool that can be
used to check for potential configuration, performance, and usage problems by running predefined health rules against servers in the farm.

On the Monitoring page in Central Administration, click Review Rule
Definitions under Health Analyzer. The only default search rule is named
Search. One or more crawl databases may have fragmented indices.

Your developers can help you create additional rules if needed.

> **Note**
>
> For more information, see http://technet.microsoft.com/en-us/library/
> ee663484.aspx.

Examining Search Component Status

Some of the functionality of FS4SP command-line tools has been replaced with PowerShell Cmdlets. The primary one for checking the status of the search components is Get-SPEnterpriseSearchStatus.

This cmdlet always requires a parameter identifying the search application, so it is easier to establish that as a variable:

```
$SSA = Get-SPEnterpriseSearchServiceApplication <Service
Application Name>
```

To record information about the search service application components, use this command:

```
$SSA > <path>\ssa.txt
```

Complete information about the application topology will be presented as:

```
Name                   : Search Service Application
Id                     : 1617eea3-567e-408b-a8db-
e318043d4bba
ServiceName            :
SearchQueryAndSiteSettingsService
CrawlTopologies        :
CrawlStores            : {SP2013_Search_CrawlStore}
ActiveTopology         : TopologyId: 8f2e48cb-eed6-
4b0b-82c1-32148cb5ac98,
                         CreationDate: 11/26/2012
1:19:00 PM, State: Active,
                         Components:
         ContentProcessingComponent
[ContentProcessingComponent1,
         344e4edb-3e00-490b-a8d1-039c58e9d15f]
                         part of 8f2e48cb-eed6-
4b0b-82c1-32148cb5ac98 on V15APP1,
         AdminComponent[AdminComponent1,
                         7bc5fbed-9332-4b8e-
b913-1b3daf691742] part of
                         8f2e48cb-eed6-4b0b-82c1-
32148cb5ac98 on V15APP1,

QueryProcessingComponent[QueryProcessingComponent1,
                         610efb74-c53e-40e0-9524-
```

```
439357822494] part of
                              8f2e48cb-eed6-4b0b-
82c1-32148cb5ac98 on V15APP1,

    CrawlComponent[CrawlComponent0,
                              0c9bd00e-4228-40b8-
acff-83c5f7dd9bbf] part of
                              8f2e48cb-eed6-4b0b-
82c1-32148cb5ac98 on V15APP1,

    IndexComponent[IndexComponent1,
                              8b7ed2da-ba91-4eca-
8604-948b831c0d5a] part of
                              8f2e48cb-eed6-4b0b-
82c1-32148cb5ac98 on V15APP1,

AnalyticsProcessingComponent
[AnalyticsProcessingComponent1,
                              04832da0-de5a-437e-9040-
c1cb6a58aa22] part of
                              8f2e48cb-eed6-4b0b-
82c1-32148cb5ac98 on V15APP1
SearchAdminDatabase    : SearchAdminDatabase
Name=SP2013_Search
Status                 : Online
DefaultSearchProvider  : SharepointSearch
Properties             :
{Microsoft.Office.Server.Utilities.SPPartitionOptions}
```

Those results will provide the information to identify individual components. For the state of each component, type the following:

```
Get-SPEnterpriseSearchStatus –SearchApplication $SSA
```

This command will return the following information:

```
Name
         State     Description
----

         -----     -----------
IndexComponent1
Active
```

```
Cell:IndexComponent1-SPf0fc8f20be95I.0.0          Active
Partition:0                                       Active
AdminComponent1                                   Active
QueryProcessingComponent1                         Active
ContentProcessingComponent1                       Active
AnalyticsProcessingComponent1                     Active
AdminComponent2                                   Active
CrawlComponent0                                   Active
```

Detailed information on individual components can be obtained with other parameters. For instance, Figure 10.38 displays the results of a detailed health report on IndexComponent1. (Health reports cannot be piped to a text file.)

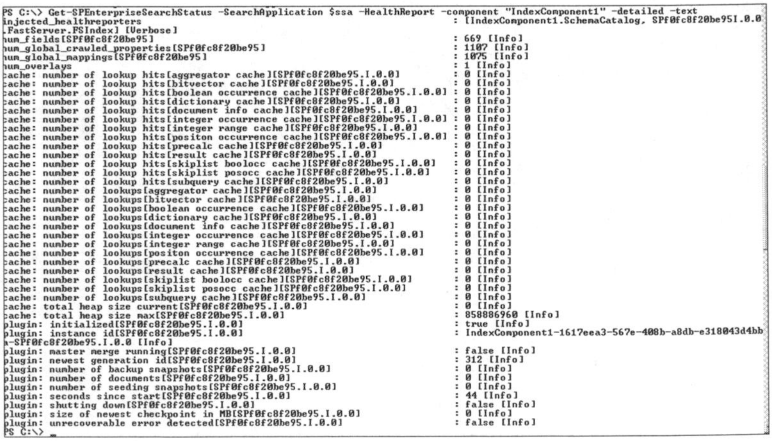

```
PS C:\> Get-SPEnterpriseSearchStatus -SearchApplication $ssa -HealthReport -component "IndexComponent1" -detailed -text
injected_healthreporters                                          : [IndexComponent1.SchemaCatalog, SPf0fc8f20be95I.0.0
.FastServer.FSIndex] [Verbose]
num_fields[SPf0fc8f20be95]                                        : 669 [Info]
num_global_crawled_properties[SPf0fc8f20be95]                     : 1107 [Info]
num_global_mappings[SPf0fc8f20be95]                               : 1075 [Info]
num_overlays                                                      : 1 [Info]
cache: number of lookup hits[aggregator cache][SPf0fc8f20be95.I.0.0] : 0 [Info]
cache: number of lookup hits[bitvector cache][SPf0fc8f20be95.I.0.0] : 0 [Info]
cache: number of lookup hits[boolean occurrence cache][SPf0fc8f20be95.I.0.0] : 0 [Info]
cache: number of lookup hits[dictionary cache][SPf0fc8f20be95.I.0.0] : 0 [Info]
cache: number of lookup hits[document info cache][SPf0fc8f20be95.I.0.0] : 0 [Info]
cache: number of lookup hits[integer occurrence cache][SPf0fc8f20be95.I.0.0] : 0 [Info]
cache: number of lookup hits[integer range cache][SPf0fc8f20be95.I.0.0] : 0 [Info]
cache: number of lookup hits[positon occurrence cache][SPf0fc8f20be95.I.0.0] : 0 [Info]
cache: number of lookup hits[precalc cache][SPf0fc8f20be95.I.0.0] : 0 [Info]
cache: number of lookup hits[result cache][SPf0fc8f20be95.I.0.0]  : 0 [Info]
cache: number of lookup hits[skiplist boolocc cache][SPf0fc8f20be95.I.0.0] : 0 [Info]
cache: number of lookup hits[skiplist posocc cache][SPf0fc8f20be95.I.0.0] : 0 [Info]
cache: number of lookup hits[subquery cache][SPf0fc8f20be95.I.0.0] : 0 [Info]
cache: number of lookups[aggregator cache][SPf0fc8f20be95.I.0.0]  : 0 [Info]
cache: number of lookups[bitvector cache][SPf0fc8f20be95.I.0.0]   : 0 [Info]
cache: number of lookups[boolean occurrence cache][SPf0fc8f20be95.I.0.0] : 0 [Info]
cache: number of lookups[dictionary cache][SPf0fc8f20be95.I.0.0]  : 0 [Info]
cache: number of lookups[document info cache][SPf0fc8f20be95.I.0.0] : 0 [Info]
cache: number of lookups[integer occurrence cache][SPf0fc8f20be95.I.0.0] : 0 [Info]
cache: number of lookups[integer range cache][SPf0fc8f20be95.I.0.0] : 0 [Info]
cache: number of lookups[positon occurrence cache][SPf0fc8f20be95.I.0.0] : 0 [Info]
cache: number of lookups[precalc cache][SPf0fc8f20be95.I.0.0]     : 0 [Info]
cache: number of lookups[result cache][SPf0fc8f20be95.I.0.0]      : 0 [Info]
cache: number of lookups[skiplist boolocc cache][SPf0fc8f20be95.I.0.0] : 0 [Info]
cache: number of lookups[skiplist posocc cache][SPf0fc8f20be95.I.0.0] : 0 [Info]
cache: number of lookups[subquery cache][SPf0fc8f20be95.I.0.0]    : 0 [Info]
cache: total heap size current[SPf0fc8f20be95.I.0.0]              : 0 [Info]
cache: total heap size max[SPf0fc8f20be95.I.0.0]                  : 858886960 [Info]
plugin: initialized[SPf0fc8f20be95.I.0.0]                         : true [Info]
plugin: instance id[SPf0fc8f20be95.I.0.0]                         : IndexComponent1-1617eea3-567e-408b-a8db-e318043d4bb
a-SPf0fc8f20be95.I.0.0 [Info]
plugin: master merge running[SPf0fc8f20be95.I.0.0]                : false [Info]
plugin: newest generation id[SPf0fc8f20be95.I.0.0]                : 312 [Info]
plugin: number of backup snapshots[SPf0fc8f20be95.I.0.0]          : 0 [Info]
plugin: number of documents[SPf0fc8f20be95.I.0.0]                 : 0 [Info]
plugin: number of seeding snapshots[SPf0fc8f20be95.I.0.0]         : 0 [Info]
plugin: seconds since start[SPf0fc8f20be95.I.0.0]                 : 44 [Info]
plugin: shutting down[SPf0fc8f20be95.I.0.0]                       : false [Info]
plugin: size of newest checkpoint in MB[SPf0fc8f20be95.I.0.0]     : 0 [Info]
plugin: unrecoverable error detected[SPf0fc8f20be95.I.0.0]        : false [Info]
PS C:\> _
```

FIGURE 10.38
Health Report on an idle Index Component.

> **Note**
>
> For more information on using Get-SPEnterpriseSearchStatus, see http://technet.microsoft.com/en-us/library/jj219672.aspx.

> **Note**
>
> For a complete list of PowerShell cmdlets specifically for SharePoint Search, see http://technet.microsoft.com/en-us/library/ee906563.aspx.

CHAPTER 11

Web Content Management

- Understanding the Publishing Infrastructure
- Managing Master Pages
- Managing Page Layouts
- Managing SharePoint Designer 2013 Access
- Configuring Composed Looks
- Understanding Large Page Libraries
- Managing Navigation

SharePoint Server 2013 is an extensible web content management platform. Many administrators notice that SharePoint Server 2013 lacks a fully functioning portal out of the box. Due to SharePoint's extensibility, there is no way to deliver a portal that will fit the requirements of every enterprise.

To build a unique portal that will meet the needs of their organization, administrators must activate the Publishing Infrastructure feature set included in SharePoint Server 2013. This chapter discusses the core features most administrators will use when building and managing an enterprise portal.

Understanding the Publishing Infrastructure

The publishing infrastructure of SharePoint Server 2013 contains many features and a wide range of functionality. The major elements of this infrastructure are master pages, page layouts, and content types. Before we continue with the details of the publishing infrastructure, here is an overview of the major components:

- **Master pages**—Microsoft Office SharePoint Server 2013 uses ASP.NET master pages to define the look and feel of the common page elements used in a site. The use of master pages reduces a site's design and development overhead by imparting changes made within a single file to the entire site. Master pages commonly include headers, footers, and navigation controls. SharePoint Server 2013 master pages also contain the ribbon user interface.

- **Page layouts**—Page layouts are another key component of the SharePoint Server 2013 publishing infrastructure. Page layouts reference a SharePoint Server 2013 master page and control how the content is presented to the user. Page layouts depend on content types to provide instruction as to what information should be surfaced in the page layout. Page layouts are stored in the Master Page Gallery and can, like master pages, be applied throughout a site.

- **SharePoint Designer 2013**—SharePoint Server 2013 now allows for designers to use a number of web design tools. SharePoint Designer is a tool that was previously used by administrators and designers for customizing the design of master pages and page layouts in sites. SharePoint Designer 2013 no longer supports an integrated design view; however, users are still allowed to work with site source code. SharePoint Designer 2013 is a free program; therefore, limiting access to this tool is critical to maintaining control of the content and layout of a SharePoint Server 2013 site. With SharePoint Server 2013, you have the capability to limit or completely block access to SharePoint Designer 2013 through both Central Administration and the Site Settings menu.

> **Note**
>
> Although the Design view for visually modifying site content has been removed with SharePoint Designer 2013, users can still modify site source code for master pages and page layouts.

- **Composed Looks**—SharePoint Server 2013 has brought about significant change with regard to customizing site appearance. These changes make working with SharePoint Server 2013 appearance easier for the end user. As with many aspects of SharePoint Server

2013, the amount of latitude given to the end user to customize a site's color scheme and fonts depends on the level of control that is allocated to the user.

■ **Navigation**—Navigation settings provide site administrators with the capability to manage a site's Global Navigation shown at the top of the page and Current Navigation shown on the left side of the page.

■ **Image Renditions**—SharePoint Server 2013 provides improvements for the optimization of images by providing the ability to manage multiple image sizes tailored for various device platforms and bandwidth scenarios. This topic is covered in more detail in Chapter 10, "Enterprise Search."

■ **Device Channels**—Device channels give SharePoint the capability to define the look and feel for a site on a specific device, such as a tablet or a Windows phone. A specific device channel is assigned an individual master page defining the look and feel for that specific target device or devices. This topic is covered in more detail in Chapter 10.

■ **Cross-Site Publishing**—Allows content managers and administrators to store content in document libraries or lists enabled for cross-site publishing and publish across multiple site collections via the Search Index and Content Search Web Parts.

■ **Catalogue-enabled libraries and lists**—When activated, the Cross-Site Publishing feature gives administrators the capability to promote a list or library to a catalog. In doing so, that list or library is published, and the content within is available to other publishing site collections.

Enabling the Publishing Infrastructure

Many SharePoint Server 2013 site templates do not have the Publishing Infrastructure enabled. To determine whether a site has the Publishing Infrastructure enabled, open the Settings menu. If you do not see the Design Manager option, as shown in Figure 11.1, you most likely do not have the Publishing Infrastructure enabled.

To enable the Publishing Infrastructure, you must first activate the feature at the site-collection level and also for any site within the collection where it is required.

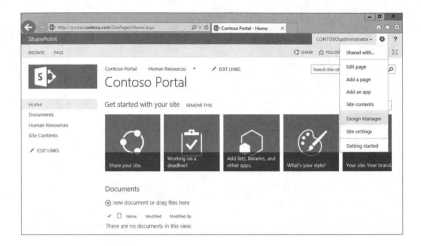

FIGURE 11.1
A Publishing Infrastructure Settings menu.

Enable the Publishing Infrastructure for the Top-Level Site

To enable the Publishing Infrastructure for the top-level site, perform the following steps:

1. From the Settings menu, open Site Settings and select Site Collection Features in the Site Collection Administration grouping.

2. Click the Activate button to the right of the SharePoint Server Publishing Infrastructure feature, as seen in Figure 11.2.

3. From the Setting menu, open Site Settings and select Manage Site Features in the Site Actions grouping.

4. Click the Activate button for the SharePoint Server Publishing feature, as seen in Figure 11.3.

Managing Master Pages

After enabling the publishing infrastructure, you can add and remove master pages and select the availability of those master pages within your sites. In SharePoint Server 2013, you now have the flexibility of branding application master pages without modifying the files on the web server.

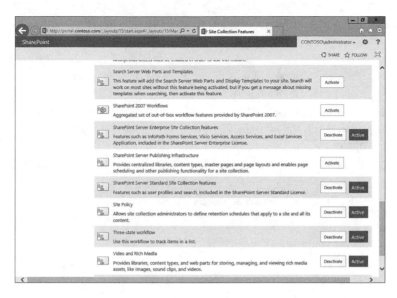

FIGURE 11.2
Click Activate to enable the feature.

FIGURE 11.3
Click Activate to enable the feature.

Enable Application Master Pages to Use the Site Master Page

To enable application master pages to use the site master page, do the following:

1. Browse to Central Administration, Application Management, Manage Web Applications.

2. Select the web application you want to modify, and then select General Settings from the Web Applications tab on the management ribbon.

3. Scroll down until you see the Master Page Setting for Application _Layouts Pages option, as shown in Figure 11.4.

4. Select Yes to reference site master pages.

FIGURE 11.4
Select Yes to have application pages reference site master pages.

Master pages are applied in the Site Settings area. There are two options for master pages: Site Master Page and System Master Page. The Site Master Page is used by all publishing pages, such as those in the /Pages/ library. If you configured the _layout pages to use site master pages, those pages will adhere to this setting.

The System Master Page is the second option that you can configure. This master page is used for all forms and view pages throughout the site—essentially, all pages except those in publishing libraries inherit the system master page.

Change the Site or System Master Page

To change the site or system master page, perform the following steps:

1. From the Settings menu, open Site Settings and select Master Page in the Look and Feel grouping.

2. In the drop-down menu for either the Site Master Page section or the System Master Page section, select a master page, as shown in Figure 11.5.

FIGURE 11.5
Change the master page via the drop-down menu.

3. If desired, you can reset all subsites to inherit this master page.

4. Click OK.

> **Tip**
>
> Subsites can inherit the system master page without activating the publishing infrastructure on those subsites. This reduces the page size and the complexity of managing those subsites.

You can also upload custom master pages that are created by your developers or designers. This allows for greater delegation of administration than with a nonpublishing site collection. Without the publishing infrastructure enabled, a site collection administrator cannot change or upload master pages without SharePoint Designer 2013. To upload a custom master page for use, do the following:

1. From the Settings menu, open Site Settings and select Master Pages and Page Layouts in the Web Designer Galleries grouping to get to the page shown in Figure 11.6.

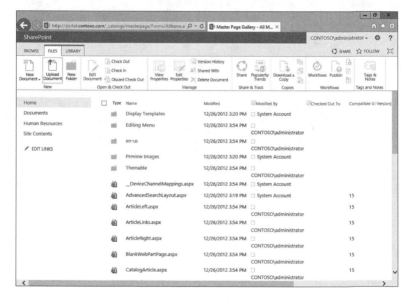

FIGURE 11.6
Select Upload Document to upload your custom master page.

2. Select the Files tab from the management ribbon.

3. Select Upload Document.

4. Browse and select your custom master page.

5. Click OK.

Before master pages will work for nonadministrative users, they must first be published and approved in the Master Page and Page Layout Gallery. To publish a master page, Select Publish a Major Version, as shown in Figure 11.7.

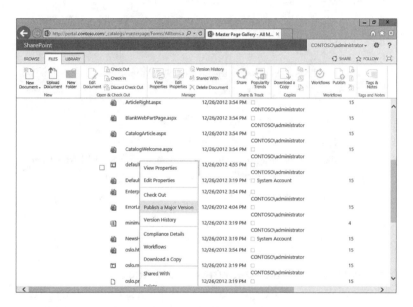

FIGURE 11.7
Select Publish a Major Version to make the master page available.

Managing Page Layouts

Page layouts are the component of SharePoint Server 2013 that define the look and feel, as well as the placement, of your content in a site. These pages define content zones, including the placement of web part zones and field controls; they can also contain web parts. The content type and associated page layout control the information collected for the page. This content type also defines what type of content, such as text or images, needs to be collected for the field. This collected information is stored in a list and is displayed on the page, according to the page layout.

Upload a New Page Layout

To upload a new page layout, do the following:

1. From the Settings menu, open Site Settings and select Master Pages and Page Layouts in the Web Designer Galleries grouping.

2. Select Files tab on the management ribbon.

3. Select Upload Document.

4. Browse and select your custom master page.

5. Select Publish a Major Version in the page layout drop-down menu.

6. Click OK.

You can also control which page layouts are available to end users in a publishing site.

Limit the Page Layouts Available to Users

To limit the page layouts available to users, follow these steps:

1. From the Settings menu, open Site Settings and select Master Pages and Site Templates from the Look and Feel grouping.

2. Highlight the allowed page layouts and click Add, as shown in Figure 11.8.

3. Click OK.

Managing SharePoint Designer 2013 Access

By utilizing SharePoint Designer 2013, users can create and modify page layouts and master pages. Although the design view within SharePoint Designer is no longer available, users still have the ability to create and modify workflows and business solutions to modify the source of site content. Given that SharePoint Designer 2013 is such a powerful tool, untrained users can easily break site operability if access is not managed. To prevent SharePoint Designer 2013 editing of master pages and page layouts, you can disable SharePoint Designer 2013 access. A farm administrator can limit the use of SharePoint Designer 2013 in a web application, and site collection administrators can limit the use of SharePoint Designer 2013 in a site collection, assuming it is allowed for the web application it is contained in.

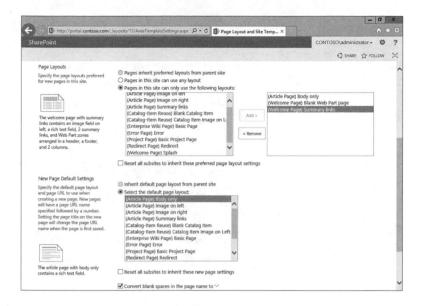

FIGURE 11.8
Click Add or double-click to allow specific page layouts.

Limit SharePoint Designer 2013 Access for a Web Application

To limit SharePoint Designer 2013 access for a web application, do the following:

1. Browse to Central Administration, Application Management, Manage Web Applications.

2. Select the web application you want to modify.

3. From the General Settings drop-down menu, on the Web Applications tab, select SharePoint Designer.

4. Deselect the type of access you want to deny in SharePoint Designer 2013, as shown in Figure 11.9.

5. Click OK.

Only SharePoint Designer 2013 features that are enabled for the web application are available to manipulate in Site Collection Administration.

FIGURE 11.9
Deselect options you do not want to have in your site.

Limit SharePoint Designer 2013 Functionality Within a Site Collection

To limit SharePoint Designer 2013 functionality within a site collection, do the following:

1. From the Settings menu, open Site Settings.

2. In the Site Collection Administration grouping, select SharePoint Designer Settings.

3. Select or deselect SharePoint Designer 2013 settings, as shown in Figure 11.10.

4. Click OK.

Table 11.1 shows the restrictions and their corresponding results when modifying SharePoint Designer 2013 settings in Site Collection Administration.

FIGURE 11.10
Deselect settings to make them unavailable.

Table 11.1   **SharePoint Designer 2013 Setting Restriction Descriptions**

Setting	Result for Headings
Enable SharePoint Designer	Gives either all access or no access to the site from SharePoint Designer 2013.
Enable Detaching Pages from the Site Definition	Allows or disallows editing a page with content on it in SharePoint Designer 2013 to customize it.
Enable Customizing Master Pages and Page Layouts	Allows or disallows editing and customizing master pages and page layouts in SharePoint Designer 2013.
Enable Managing of the Web Site URL Structure	Allows or disallows editing and managing the URL structure of a site from SharePoint Designer 2013.

Configuring Composed Looks

With SharePoint Server 2013, the ability to customize the appearance of sites has undergone significant changes with the introduction of Composed Looks. The changes to SharePoint Server 2013 have made it easier for site administrators to customize the color scheme and fonts used within the site. To browse the predefined designs and change the appearance for a site, browse to Settings, Site Settings, and Change the Look in the Look and Feel grouping. You'll be presented with a page similar to Figure 11.11.

FIGURE 11.11
You can easily change the appearance in SharePoint Server 2013.

Using the Large Pages Library

SharePoint Server 2013 includes the capability to use folders in publishing site libraries, which is the /Pages/ library. With the capability to use folders, you can organize the pages created for your site instead of having them all in a single library. With this enhancement comes the capability to structure pages for a site in a nested folder structure.

Creating a nested folder structure allows designers to logically connect the global navigation and current navigation menus. When new pages are created and a site has been configured to use autonavigation, the new page is added to the root of the pages library and is automatically added to the Global Navigation and Current Navigation menus. If new pages are not added to the root of the pages library, the autonavigation setting will not work. To resolve this, you will need to explicitly add each item to the Global Navigation and Current Navigation Menus.

Managing Navigation

When you activate the publishing infrastructure for a site, the navigational options are greatly enhanced. You can assign an audience to both headings and links using Active Directory groups through the Title and URL text boxes, as shown in Figure 11.12.

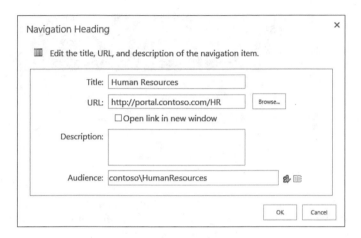

FIGURE 11.12
Use the Audience text box to select the Active Directory group to target a navigational item.

You can also granularly control headings and links.

Add an Item to the Navigation Menu

To add an item to the Navigation menu, perform the following steps:

1. Browse to Settings, Site Settings.

2. In the Look and Feel grouping, click Navigation.

3. For the Global Navigation section, also referred to as the Top Link Bar, select whether to display the same navigation items as the parent site. If you are in the top-level site settings, this option will be grayed out.

4. Select whether to display subsites in the current navigation. The current navigation is also referred to as the Quick Launch area, as shown in Figure 11.13.

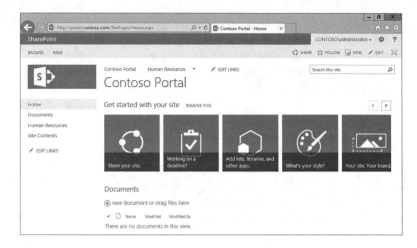

FIGURE 11.13
Current navigation including Human Resources.

5. For both global and current navigation, set the maximum number of dynamic items to show. Use caution when raising this setting beyond the default of 20. Always test the navigation with a load testing tool when you increase this number.

6. Decide whether to sort pages manually or automatically.

7. You can edit, add, or delete headings and links. Headings are displayed on the navigation page, and links appear as fly-outs under the heading. In Figure 11.14, the Payroll link and the Recruiting link are displayed under the Human Resources heading.

Tip

If you do not see your headings and links in the Global Navigation area, verify they were created under Global Navigation and not under Current Navigation. This is a common mistake made by both new and seasoned administrators.

---

8. Decide whether to make the Show Ribbon and Hide Ribbon commands available.

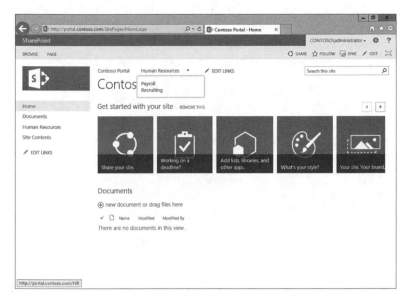

FIGURE 11.14
The selection of links in the Global Navigation under the Human Resources heading.

CHAPTER 12

Branding in SharePoint 2013

- Branding Levels
- Composed Looks
- Design Manager
- Image Renditions
- Managed Metadata Navigation
- Minimal Download Strategy (MDS)

The newly introduced features relating to the design and branding of the SharePoint 2013 platform provide site administrators and web developers with many more options to customize the look and feel of their SharePoint 2013 environment than ever before. The introduction of Composed Looks takes out-of-the-box branding to the next level, and the Design Manager functionality of Publishing sites allows for a more systematic and industry-standard method of implementing a full branding solution. Fully scoped branding solutions continue to be supported and provide a deep level of customization that many enterprise collaboration environments require.

Branding Levels

This chapter is intended to provide a high-level introduction into the branding capabilities and supporting components that are available within the SharePoint 2013 platform. It contains a breakdown of the multiple levels of branding available as well as a discussion of the tools that support these levels. The following section details the levels of branding and the scenarios to which these levels apply.

Basic Site Branding

The most basic way to customize or brand your SharePoint 2013 environment is by editing your site pages. This can be done using the Page Editor in SharePoint Designer 2013 or through the use of Composed Looks built in to SharePoint 2013. Editing pages in SharePoint 2013, using the Page Editor, functions identically to how it worked within SharePoint 2010. Pages are edited through the browser, thus providing fewer branding capabilities than are available when using SharePoint Designer to change the look and feel.

Editing the page with SharePoint Designer 2013 (SPD 2013) has become much more difficult than with previous versions of SharePoint. With SPD 2013, Microsoft has removed the Design view from the application and now requires that any modifications to web parts or components within a page be edited strictly in the Code view window. Although the removal of the Design view functionality can be seen as a degradation of functionality for SPD 2013, it was removed from the application because it was an older technology. The Design view was incapable of properly displaying many of the updated web technologies such as HTML5 and CSS3. In place of Design view within SPD 2013, Microsoft recommends using the newly introduced Design Manager functionality to create custom master pages to support the look and feel of your SharePoint 2013 sites. The Design Manager is discussed in detail later in this chapter.

Mid-Level Branding

A mid-level branding effort is a situation that requires a more involved branding scenario than can be achieved through the use of Composed Looks. Design Manager, introduced in SharePoint 2013, can help create branding solutions that require a greater level of customization and a more structured deployment scenario.

Full-Scoped Branding

A full-scoped branding effort is required when it becomes necessary to provide a custom look and feel to a site, yet limitations exist with Design Manager that can't be overcome or when Design Manager is unavailable, such as with SharePoint Foundation 2013 and with many out-of-the-box site templates. The Design Manager functionality is available only within a site that has the Publishing Feature enabled. In many internal enterprise environments, out-of-the-box collaborative sites do not have the Publishing feature activated, causing the Design Manager's sandboxed design solution to be unavailable.

It is worth noting that the activation of the Publishing Feature within a site will subsequently disable the use of the Minimal Download Strategy (MDS), which is a new feature introduced with SharePoint 2013. The concepts of the Minimal Download Strategy are discussed later in this chapter.

In these scenarios, enterprise branding of the SharePoint sites will include the development of a full solution package that is deployed within the environment. These solutions will usually rely on feature stapling and attaching to web event receivers within the SharePoint Object Model. This will apply the branding seamlessly during the creation of new sites within the environment. The topic of creating a full-scoped branding solution is an advanced and involved topic that will not be covered within this book. These solutions, however, are standard SharePoint WSP solution packages that often require full trust and are deployed to the environment through the use of PowerShell and/or Central Administration for deployment.

SharePoint Online

Office 365's SharePoint Online sites offer a limited set of branding functionality as compared to an on-premise installation of SharePoint 2013. The tenant-based nature of the O365 environments takes itself away from the use of full-scoped solution deployment as a branding option. Instead, designers and developers within O365 will need to rely more on the Design Manager functionality to brand any public-facing Publishing-based sites in O365. The sandboxed solutions created as a result of the Design Manager implementation are compatible with the O365 environment and should be utilized in this approach.

Composed Looks

Composed Looks are available within SharePoint Foundation 2013 and SharePoint Server 2013. Much like the Theme functionality of SharePoint 2010, Composed Looks are intended to be created through the browser and provide power users with the capability to change aspects of the look and feel of their site. To some degree, Composed Looks are the evolution of SharePoint 2010 Themes in that they allow site administrators to create a collection of basic site look-and-feel characteristics, such as font schemes, color palettes, custom master pages, and custom background images, and then apply this collection of design artifacts to a SharePoint site. Composed looks are scoped to the Site Collection level, which allows for any site within the Site Collection to apply the Composed Look, as shown in Figure 12.1:

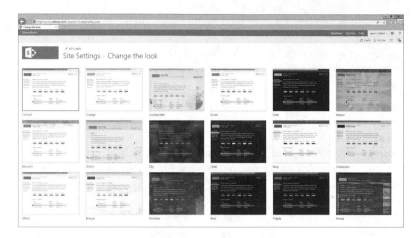

FIGURE 12.1
Composed Looks for a Site Collection.

1. To create and apply a new Composed Look, navigate to the Site Settings page.
2. Click Settings, Change the Look.
3. Select Composed Look preview.
4. Change selections for the Look.
5. Click Try It Out.
6. Review the preview look and then click Yes, Keep It to apply the look to the current site.

Custom Composed Looks

Custom Composed Looks can be defined within the Site Collection and will allow your organization to create any number of branding combinations and provide these combinations to all sites within the Site Collection. A Composed Look is a collection of four attributes: a master page, a background image, a Font Scheme selection, and a Theme selection. The individual Composed Looks definitions are defined within the Composed Looks Gallery, as shown in Figure 12.2, where the site collection and custom definitions can be defined using the following process:

1. On the Site Settings page, click the Composed Looks link under the Web Designer Galleries section.
2. Click new item to create a new Composed Look, as shown in Figure 12.3.

FIGURE 12.2
Composed Looks Gallery page.

FIGURE 12.3
New Composed Look form.

3. In the New Item dialog box, enter data for each of the required fields. The Display Order for the item defines what order the Composed Look will display within the selection page.

4. Click Save to complete the creation of the definition.

Custom Master Pages

With the use of Composed Looks, site administrators have the ability to define a custom master page to be included within their definition. Although technically, any master page can be added to a site collection and used as part of a Composed Look, the lack of the Design view in

SharePoint Designer 2013 will make it difficult for some organizations to easily create custom master pages. In these situations, special care should be taken to ensure that the master pages that are created outside of the current environment do not include additional functionality that might not be available due to local environment limitations. One example of this situation could be where a master page is created with the Design Manager, which is available only when the Publishing feature is activated, and then ported to a different site to be used within a Composed Look. Certain publishing-specific functionality might not be available.

Custom Font Schemes and Themes

Custom Font Schemes and Themes selections can be developed to further the custom look and feel of your site branding. The font schemes and theme selections are XML definitions of the specific fonts or colors that are defined with that selection. Custom font schemes and themes can be created offline as .spfont and .spcolor files, respectively, and then uploaded to the Themes gallery where they will be available for selection within the Composed Looks customization page. The following steps detail the process for adding custom Font Schemes and Themes to the list of available selections part of the Composed Looks customization:

1. Navigate to the Site Settings page.
2. Click the Themes link within the Web Designer Galleries section.
3. Click the New Document link, and then upload the .spfont or .spcolor file to the Theme gallery, as shown in Figure 12.4.

Design Manager

The SharePoint Design Manager makes it easier than ever to style and publish websites. Design Manager provides the capability to integrate a higher level of branding functionality into a site than is possible with Composed Looks. The Design Manager is new to SharePoint 2013 and allows site collection administrators to implement the branding of a site using more traditional web development processes by uploading design files from other web development tools, such as straight HTML. Under the cover, SharePoint will take the uploaded HTML and process it into a corresponding master page. As updates are made to the HTML page, SharePoint keeps both files in sync within the master page gallery. The sync process between the original HTML definition and the SharePoint generated master page requires that all modifications be made within the HTML file and not within the master page. SharePoint will manage the conversion of the HTML with the master page.

FIGURE 12.4
Site Collection Theme Gallery.

> **Note**
>
> The uploading of design files using Design Manager is typically done within a development environment. Because of that, it's best practice to create a folder for the design package to assist in keeping all the necessary files for the individual design together.

The creation of a branding solution with the Design Manager is an iterative process where the original HTML is modified to include design artifacts that SharePoint will include with the associated master page. These artifacts are Snippets, and they contain specific code definitions that encapsulate specific SharePoint functionality which, after the addition of the Snippet into the raw HTML page, will be parsed by SharePoint and included within the master page. It is necessary for the user to publish the HTML file once before Snippets can be added to the page.

Using the Design Manager requires that you proceed through a series of steps that take you through the process of applying a custom branding design to a SharePoint site. When first navigating to the Design Manager, along the left side of the page, the individual steps are provided. The following sections detail the procedures to take at each step of the process.

1. Welcome

The Welcome Page of the Design Manager provides links to start the branding design process within your site. It provides a link to import a design package or pick a preinstalled look. Importing a design package allows the user to start with a WSP-based design package that can be applied to a site. The WSP should contain the necessary design artifacts, such as HTML pages, CSS files, script artifacts, and so on, that are required to apply the basic design to the site. From this imported package, you may be able to further enhance your design by modifying the files imported. The imported WSP package will be activated as a Sandboxed Solution within the site, and actions on this solution, such as deactivating or removing, are performed the same as any standard Sandboxed Solution. By selecting the Pick a Preinstalled Look option on the Welcome page, as shown in Figure 12.5, the site will navigate to the Composed Looks selection page to allow for the design to be selected. The following procedure details the process for importing a design package.

FIGURE 12.5
Design Manager Welcome page.

Import a Complete Design Package

To import a complete design package, perform the following steps:

1. Start the Design Manager. (For example, on the Settings menu choose Design Manager.)

2. Within the Welcome page, select the Import a Complete Design Package link.

3. Click the Browse button next to the Package Name text field.

4. In the File dialog box, select the solution package to upload, and click OK.

5. After SharePoint processes the upload, the Solutions Gallery of the site is displayed and the uploaded package is visible and activated.

Note

A design solution package cannot be deactivated while in use.

2. Manage Device Channels

The SharePoint Design Manager also includes the capability to target the look and feel of your site through Device Channels. A Device Channel allows the designer to identify individual channels for which to format the content, such as all mobile devices, or specific devices such as a Windows Phone. With each Device Channel, an individual master page is assigned for the channel and each of the channels is tagged with a priority. As devices access the site, the listing of channels as shown in Figure 12.6 is traversed, and the first matching channel is used to serve the site content.

FIGURE 12.6
Design Manager Device Channels.

Create a Channel

To create a channel, perform the following steps:

1. Start Design Manager. (For example, on the Settings menu, choose Design Manager.)

2. In the numbered list, select Manage Device Channels.

3. On the Design Manager: Manage Device Channels page, choose Create a Channel, as shown in Figure 12.7.

4. On the Device Channels–New Item page, in the Name text box, enter a name for the device channel.

5. In the Alias text box, enter an alias for the device channel. The alias must be alphanumeric characters and may not contain spaces. You will use the alias to refer to the device channel in code and in other contexts.

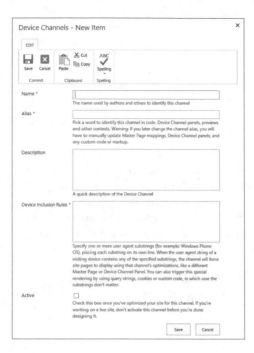

FIGURE 12.7
New Device Channel dialog box.

6. In the Description text box, enter a brief description of the devices or browsers that the channel will capture.

7. In the Device Inclusion Rules text box, enter the user agent substrings for the channel. A request for a webpage will use this channel if any of the strings that you provide match the user agent string of the request.

8. If you are ready to make the channel available to render pages, select the Active check box.

9. Click Save.

Change a Device Channel

To change a Device Channel, perform the following steps:

1. Start Design Manager. (For example, on the Settings menu, choose Design Manager.)

2. In the numbered list, select Manage Device Channels.

3. On the Design Manager: Manage Device Channels page, choose Edit or reorder existing channels, shown in Figure 12.6.

4. In the Device Channels list, select the device channel that you want to change, and then, on the Items tab, choose Edit Item.

5. To change the name of the device channel, enter a new name in the Name text box.

6. To change the alias of the device channel, enter a new alias in the Alias text box.

Note

If you change a device channel's alias, you must manually change the alias in other places where it is used. For example, you must manually change the alias in custom code or markup, and you must manually change the mappings between the device channel and master pages.

---

7. To change the description of the device channel, enter a new description in the Description text box.

8. To change the device inclusion rules, edit the strings in the Device Inclusion Rules text box.

9. To make the device channel active, select the Active check box. To make the channel inactive, clear the Active check box.

10. Click Save.

Note

SharePoint provides a Default Device Channel for the site to use. By default, all traffic coming into the site will be processed through this channel. When assigning priorities to Device Channels, the Default Channel should always have the lowest priority because it will essentially act as a "catch-all" for site traffic that doesn't match a custom Device Channel. Since the Default Channel handles any unmatched content, it is required to ensure that all content is handled by the site, and as a result, the Default Channel cannot be modified or deleted from the site.

Delete a Device Channel

To delete a Device Channel, perform the following steps:

1. Start Design Manager. (For example, on the Settings menu, choose Design Manager.)

2. In the numbered list, select Manage Device Channels.

3. On the Design Manager: Manage Device Channels page, choose Edit or reorder existing channels.

4. In the Device Channels list, select the device channel that you want to delete.

5. On the Items tab, choose Delete Item.

6. Click OK.

Note

The Default Channel cannot be deleted.

Change the Order of the Device Channels

To change the order of the Device Channels, perform the following steps:

1. Start Design Manager. (For example, on the Settings menu, choose Design Manager.)

2. In the numbered list, select Manage Device Channels.

3. On the Design Manager: Manage Device Channels page, choose Edit or reorder existing channels.

4. On the Items tab, choose Reorder Channels.

5. On the Device Channel Reordering page, choose the channel whose order you want to change, and then select Move Up or Move Down.

6. After the channels are ordered the way that you want them, click OK.

3. Upload Design Files

For SharePoint to parse the design files and produce the corresponding master pages and page layouts, it is necessary to upload the design files to the Master Page Gallery of the site. Like any other document library, the Master Page Gallery provides the options to upload single files or multiple files. To upload the design files to the Master Page Gallery, navigate to the document library and upload the single design files, upload multiple files, or bulk upload the files using File Explorer.

Tip

To keep the design files organized, create a folder within the Master Page Gallery to contain all the design files relating to the individual design.

One great enhancement of SharePoint 2013 is the capability to connect the Master Page Gallery document library as a mounted drive from a client computer. This allows for a seamless integration between a third-party web development tool such as Microsoft Expression Web or Adobe Dreamweaver and the upload process to get the design files within SharePoint. To support the direct mapping of the drives to the Master Page Gallery, the front-end servers within the environment must have WebDAV enabled and IIS configured to allow for the connection.

Note

Although the use of Design Manager is supported within a production environment, it is best practice to develop all solutions within a development environment; then, after the proper deployment testing and validation occurs, deploy the solution into a production environment. Under this scenario, enabling WebDAV for drive mapping is not necessary or recommended in a production environment.

---

4. Edit Master Pages

The Edit Master Pages section of the Design Manager provides the capability to add HTML files to be converted to master pages and the capability to create a minimal master page to use as a baseline for the site design. Although the title of the step within the Design Manager indicates that master pages will be edited, no actual editing occurs within the browser on the site.

Each SharePoint 2013-based master page within the Master Page Gallery will have an associated HTML file that has been converted into the master page. The edits to the master pages are the result of edits applied to the associated HTML files, either through an upload of a new version of an existing master page or through the direct editing of an HTML file within a third-party tool that contains a mapped drive to the Master Page Gallery. After SharePoint detects a new version of the HTML baseline file, the page conversion process is triggered, and the results of the conversion are displayed within the master page listing within Design Manager, as shown in Figure 12.8. Selecting the Conversion Successful link for a master page results in navigating to the page preview, where the master page will be displayed as a preview of the current site. From the Page Preview page, the Snippets link in the top-right navigation menu takes you to the page where Snippets can be created and added to the baseline HTML file. Additionally, it is possible to create a new minimal master page, which will produce the minimal master page HTML file that then immediately has a corresponding master page associated with it. The following sections detail the procedure for creating new master pages and uploading existing ones.

FIGURE 12.8
Design Manager Edit Master Pages page.

Edit an Existing Master Page

To edit an existing master page, perform the following steps:

1. Select the Edit Master Pages link within the Design Manager.

2. View a listing of the available HTML master pages, and note the Conversion Status.

3. Select the Conversion Successful link for the master page HTML file. This navigates to the Page Previewer page.

4. Select the Change Preview Page drop down.

5. Choose Select Page and then enter a URL of a page within the site to preview, or select the General Page Layout to view a generic look of the page.

6. Select the Snippets in the top-right navigation menu. The Snippets editor, as shown in Figure 12.10, enables you to construct dynamic content for the HTML master page that you add into the main HTML file. The Snippets are then parsed appropriately during the conversion process.

7. Construct a Snippet and copy the contents from the editor window.

8. Paste the snippet code into the HTML master page.

9. Re-upload the master page or save the master HTML page within the web development tool that is mapped to the Master Page Gallery. This will trigger the conversion of the page automatically when the upload is complete.

10. Visit the Preview page, as shown in Figure 12.9, to view any errors or to view the imported look.

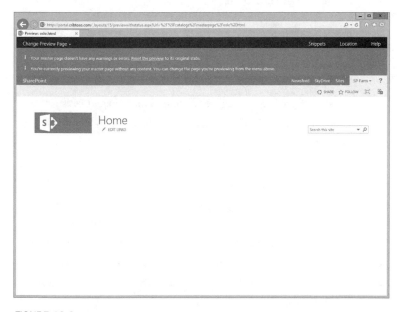

FIGURE 12.9
Master Page Design Preview page.

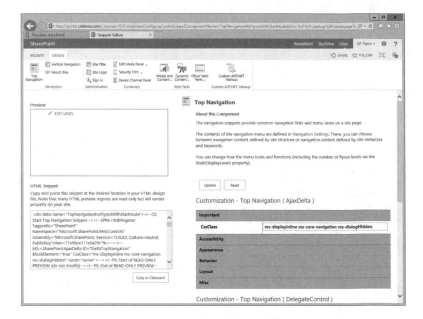

FIGURE 12.10
Design Manager Snippet Editor page.

Create a Minimal Master Page

To create a minimal master page, perform the following steps:

1. Select the Minimal Master Page link.

2. Enter a name for the new master page and then select OK.

   This creates a new HTML master page, which is then automatically converted to a SharePoint master page.

3. Edit the master page as defined in the previous section.

Publish a Master Page in Design Manager

To publish a master page in Design Manager, perform the following steps:

1. Navigate to the Edit Master Pages page of the Design Manager.

2. Click the ellipse (…) of the master page that requires publishing.

3. Within the pop-out menu of the master page file, click the ellipse to view the file options.

4. Select the Publish a Major Version menu item.

5. Enter comments into the publishing dialog; then click OK.

6. Verify that the file was published by inspecting the Approval Status of the file.

Publish a Master Page in the Master Page Gallery

To publish a Master Page in the Master Page Gallery, perform the following steps:

1. In the Settings drop-down, select Site settings.

2. Within the Web Designer Galleries group, select the Master Pages and Page Layouts link.

3. In the Master Page Gallery List, select the HTML master page to be published.

4. Select the Publish a Major Version from the item's drop-down menu, or in the page ribbon, select Files, Workflows, Publish button to publish the file.

5. Edit Display Templates

The Display Templates defined within the Design Manager are a listing of Search-related controls and web parts. These display template definitions can be customized to enhance the look, feel, and behavior of search items within the page. The modification of the HTML within these controls is managed identically to the process defined for updating the master pages within the site design. To edit the controls, modify the HTML instance of the template from the Edit Display Template page, as shown in Figure 12.11, and the associated control within the system will be updated accordingly.

Tip

To create a new instance of a Display Template, it is recommended that you locate a template that is similar to the new template to be created and then copy the original and modify the HTML to suit your needs.

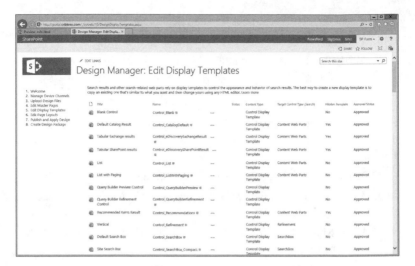

FIGURE 12.11
Design Manager Edit Display Templates page.

6. Edit Pages Layouts

Page Layout creation and modification within the Design Manager is almost identical to the creation process of master pages in that the Page Layouts start as HTML that is then parsed to produce an associated ASPX Page Layout page.

To create a new Page Layout within the Design Manager, as shown in Figure 12.1, select the Create New Page Layout link, enter the name of the Page Layout within the dialog box, and then click OK. The new Page Layout HTML file is created, and the conversion process executes to build the ASPX version of the page. At this point, editing the contents of the Page Layout is similar to the edit process for a master page in that the HTML file is edited or has Snippets added to it, and the SharePoint page conversion process updates the associated ASPX page.

7. Publish and Apply Design

The Publish and Apply Design page provides instructions to ensure that all the aspects of your design solution are ready to be included within the deployment solution. It is essential for all the files relating to the design, such as CSS, JavaScript, images, and so on, be checked in and published before they are included in the solution package that is generated. Additionally, the Publish and Apply Design page provides a link to the Site Master Page Settings page. On this page, the site administrator has the capability to select different master pages for the various device channels, as shown in Figure 12.13. If all master pages within the design are fully published, they will be available within the master page selection drop-downs. Additionally, the Site Master Page Settings page will allow for a custom Theme and a custom Alternate CSS to be configured.

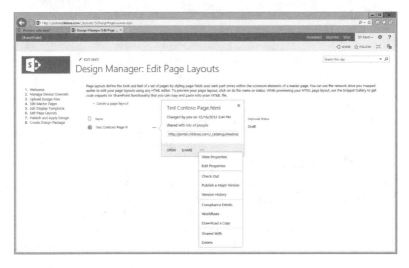

FIGURE 12.12
Design Manager Edit Page Layouts page.

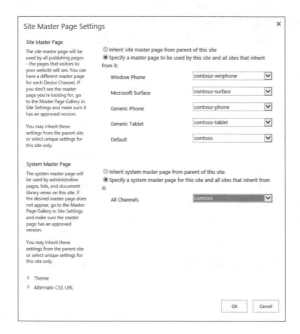

FIGURE 12.13
Site Master Page Device Channel Assignments.

8. Create the Design Package

The use of Design Manager within your branding process is only part of a branding solution. As is best practice with any solution development process, the development should always be performed within a development environment and then deployed to a production environment. The use of Design Manager is no exception to this rule. After the branding solution is complete and all pages are fully published, the solution can be exported to a design package that can then be deployed to another site, SharePoint Farm, or O365. The WSP that is generated with the Design Manager, as shown in Figure 12.14, is a sandboxed solution after it is created, deployed, and activated in the local Solutions Gallery. The WSP itself will contain the published version of all files relating to the design of the current site. This will include but is not limited to all HTML, Master Pages, Page Layouts, CSS, JavaScript, images, and the features necessary to activate the branding within the site.

FIGURE 12.14
Design Manager Create Design Package page.

Create the Design Package

To create the design package, perform the following steps:

1. Start Design Manager. (For example, on the Settings menu, choose Design Manager.)

2. In the numbered list, select Create Design Package.

3. In the Design Name field, enter the desired name for the solution package.

4. If desired, mark the check box next to the Include Search Configuration in this package.

5. Select the Create button to build the design package.

Image Renditions

One of the many major improvements to the SharePoint 2013 user experience is the move to better support mobile devices. Image renditions are one of the improvements in the capabilities of SharePoint 2013 that can help to improve the optimization of images. Performance enhancement is achieved by SharePoint managing multiple versions of an image of varying sizes and only serving the appropriate image based on the device and scenario. This allows an end user working through a mobile phone to not require a large, high-fidelity image to be downloaded; therefore, it consumes less bandwidth. Adhering to web development best practices, the use of Image Renditions also allows for the same code base to be used for all devices, while the image that is rendered matches the definition for the device. Image Renditions allow an original large-scaled image with many smaller-scaled variants to be used within the SharePoint site.

Dynamically generating image renditions of various sizes on-the-fly is a process-intensive and unnecessary scenario. SharePoint circumvents this issue by storing multiple instances of the original as variants within the database to provide for a one-time conversion at image upload time and then serve the appropriate variant at runtime. SharePoint is able to manage the storage and quick retrieval of the images with the use of SQL Blob caching. For image renditions to work, Blob caching must be configured for the web application within the web.config.

The available Image Renditions for a site can be found in Site Settings, Look and Feel, Image Renditions. The renditions are defined per site collection, and there is a select set of default renditions. You can add new renditions by selecting the Add New Item link on the Image Renditions page and then completing the fields within the Image Rendition dialog. New renditions require a name, height, and width to be created. Multiple image and video file types are supported for Image Renditions. The following table lists the supported image and video file types.

Supported File Types

Image Renditions are supported on multiple image and video file types. Table 12.1 contains a listing of the file types supported with Image Renditions.

Table 12.1   **Image Renditions Supported File Types**

Type	Supported File Types
Images	gif, jpg, jpeg, jpe, jfif, bmp, dib, png, tif, tiff, ico, wdp, hdp
Videos	wmv, wma, avi, mpg, mp3, mp4, asf, ogg, ogv, oga, webm

Modifying and Using Renditions

Utilizing the Image Rendition, as shown in Figure 12.15, within the content is performed within the page as attributes for an image. The follow procedure details the steps required to edit the renditions that are implemented for select images.

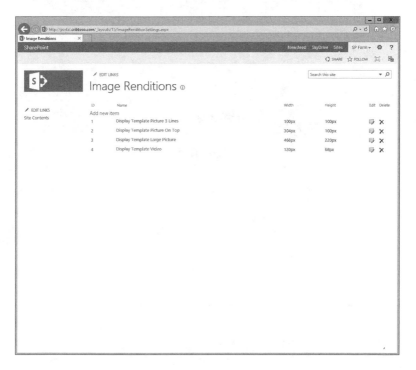

FIGURE 12.15
Image Rendition Definitions for a Site Collection.

Edit an Image Rendition for a Site Collection
To edit an image rendition for a Site Collection, perform the following steps:

1. Navigate to the Site Collection's Site Settings.
2. Select Look and Feel, Image Renditions.
3. Select the Edit link for an individual rendition.
4. Update the appropriate values and click Save.

Edit a Rendition for an Individual Image
To edit a rendition for an individual image, perform the following steps, as shown in Figure 12.16:

FIGURE 12.16
Editing Image Rendition for an individual image.

1. Navigate to an image library within the site.
2. Hover over an image in the library and select the ellipse (...) button.
3. Select Edit Renditions.
4. In the Rendition page, as shown in Figure 12.17, select Click to change for the image.
5. Drag the Crop tool to select the area of the image to display. The crop tool will maintain the aspect ratio defined for the image rendition.

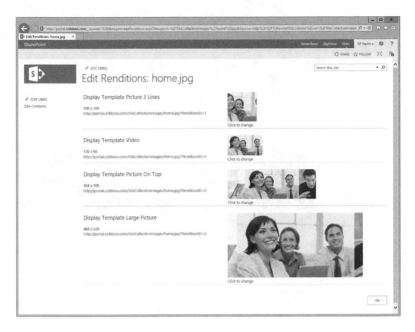

FIGURE 12.17
Edit Renditions for image.

Optimize Images Within a Page

To optimize images within a page, perform the following steps:

1. Insert an image on a page.

2. In the Image tab of the ribbon, select the Pick Rendition button, as shown in Figure 12.18.

3. Select the rendition to use for that image.

Versioning

Image renditions are versioned apart from the version of the actual image files. If a rendition of an image is modified uniquely from the Site Collection default rendition, a property is stored within the property bag of the modified image file with the specifications of the new rendition size.

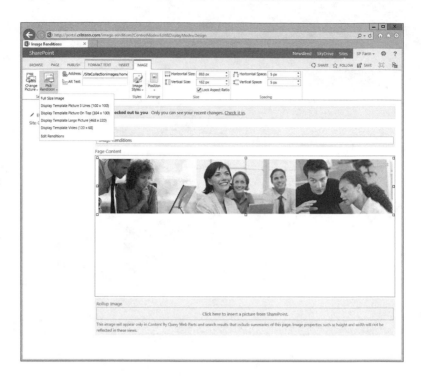

FIGURE 12.18
Customize the Rendition used by an image within a page.

Managed Metadata Navigation

Managed Metadata Navigation within SharePoint 2013 is another exciting
new feature of the platform in that it provides an easily manageable definition of navigation elements that can be utilized across Site Collections. In
SharePoint 2010, the only solution to providing consistent cross-site
collection navigation was to either manually sync the navigation elements
or develop a custom solution which used a single point of reference for
menu items. The Managed Metadata Navigation functionality now
provides this capability by binding the navigation menu items to a term set
within the Managed Metadata Service, which can be accessible by multiple
web applications and, in turn, multiple site collections.

The configuration and management of the Managed Metadata Navigation
is detailed further in Chapter 8, "Configuring Enterprise Content Types and

Metadata," and will not be covered here. However, it is important to understand the existence and capabilities of the Manager Metadata Navigation to allow for proper planning and architecting of the branding solution.

Minimal Download Strategy

The Minimal Download Strategy (MDS) functionality of SharePoint 2013 improves the rendering performance of pages when browsing content that has large areas of the page that do not change often. Many times, with internal enterprise collaboration environments, the main chrome of the page is static and defined within the master page for the site. This area often remains consistent, whereas the content areas of the pages will change much more frequently. In SharePoint 2010, navigating between these pages would trigger the entire page to be redrawn. In SharePoint 2013, using the Minimal Download Strategy functionality, only the areas of the page that change frequently are redrawn.

SharePoint 2013 determines the area of the page that requires a re-rendering through the use of the Download Manager. The Download Manager manages the implementation of MDS by interfacing between the server and the client. The Download manager understands which controls will remain static, such as images, and which controls are dynamic, such as the Quick Launch. During each page load, the Download Manager can determine the areas and controls of the page to re-render, thus minimizing the download time by using cached instances of the static controls.

Enabling and Disabling MDS

Enabling and disabling the MDS can be performed on a per-site basis by modifying the SPWeb.EnableMinimalDownload property and setting its value to False. Though the EnableMinimalDownload property can be modified directly using PowerShell against the SharePoint SPWeb object, it is preferred to enable or disable MDS on a site by activating or deactivating the Minimal Download Strategy (Id: 87294C72-F260-42f3-A41B-981A2FFCE37A) Site-scoped feature, as shown in Figure 12.19. This feature essentially toggles the value of the EnableMinimalDownload property, and any site template within SharePoint 2013 that requires the use of MDS has this feature activated along with the site template.

FIGURE 12.19
Minimal Download Strategy Site-Scoped feature.

Note

The Minimal Download Strategy is not compatible with publishing site collections or collaboration sites that have the Publishing features activated. Often, when navigating to a site that has Publishing activated, and the page is performing a render, then re-render of the page immediately, it is a result of having MDS activated onsite with Publishing activated.

CHAPTER 13

Configuring the Social Experience

- Social Architecture
- User Profile Service
- Enabling Social Features for Users and Groups
- Configuring My Sites

SharePoint 2013 has added a great deal of capability to the Social Experience. This increased capability adds the much needed flexibility so that administrators and their organizations can right-size their social experience by limiting features and privacy settings or by even easily providing open access to everything social.

Social Architecture

The social architecture in SharePoint 2013 provides organizations the ability to scale with the growth and adoption of SharePoint as a social platform. The social architecture is made up of the following:

- Web applications.
- Site Collections (My Site Host with explicit managed path and Personal Sites as a wildcard managed path).
- Content Database—Feed posts, sites, documents, following, personal storage space.
- Profile Database—People and tag following, user profile properties.
- Social Database—Social tags.

- Services.

- Managed Metadata Service application.

- Search Service application.

- User Profile Service application.

- SkyDrive Pro—In an on-premise environment, the limits you place on your My Site quota and how much SkyDrive Pro is used can impact feeds.

User Profile Service

The User Profile Service in Microsoft SharePoint Server 2013 is a shared service that provides a central location to create and manage various features and capabilities related to information about users in the farm. The features and capabilities managed by the User Profile Service are as follows:

- User profile properties

- Audiences

- Profile synchronization

- Settings specific to My Site

The information contained within a user profile is used as the basis for all social and personal functions. Administration of user profiles within Microsoft SharePoint Server 2013 can be delegated to a service application administrator rather than to the farm administrator.

Note

For detailed information about the User Profile Service, see http://technet.microsoft.com/en-us/library/ee662538.aspx.

Creation and Maintenance Tasks in the User Profile Service

Before performing any of the creation or maintenance steps within the User Profile Service, make sure the My Site Host site collection was created from the My Site host template. Also, an individual must be a service administrator to perform these steps.

Create a User Profile Service Application

To create a User Profile Service application, do the following:

1. Browse to Central Administration, Application Management, Manage Service Applications. The Manage Service Application page appears, as shown in Figure 13.1.

FIGURE 13.1

Manage Service Application page showing a partial list of the service applications that can be managed from this page.

2. On the management ribbon, in the Create group, click New. The list of service applications appears, as shown in Figure 13.2.

3. Click User Profile Service Application. The Create New User Profile Service Application dialog box appears, as shown in Figure 13.3.

4. In the Create New User Profile Service Application dialog box enter a unique name in the Name text box.

5. A service application requires the use of an application pool. This pool identifies the account and credentials that will be used by this service. In the Application Pool section, do the following:

   ▪ Select the Use Existing Application Pool option, and choose an existing application pool from the drop-down list. Or select the Create New Application Pool option to create a new one.

   ▪ For the Select a Security Account for This Application Pool option, select the Predefined option and choose an existing predefined security account from the drop-down list. Or select the Configurable option, and choose an existing managed account from the drop-down list.

FIGURE 13.2
The Service Applications list on the New menu.

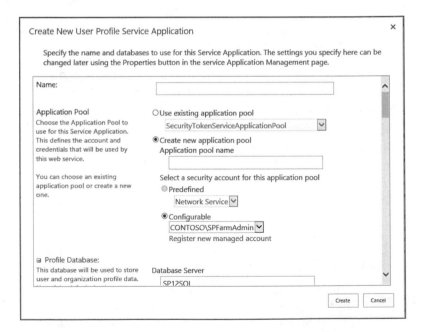

FIGURE 13.3
Create New User Profile Service Application dialog box showing the options available when creating a new User Profile Service.

You can register a new managed account by clicking the Register New Managed Account link, which displays the Register Managed Account dialog box.

6. The profile database is used to retain the user and organization profile information. In the Profile Database section, do the following:

   ■ In the Database Server text box, enter the name of the database server on which the profile database will be located.

   ■ In the Database Name text box, enter the name of the database that will be created in the server you specified in the preceding step.

   ■ Select the Windows Authentication (Recommended) option as the authentication method for the database when you want to use Integrated Windows Authentication. Or select the SQL Authentication option, and enter the relevant credentials in the Account and Password text boxes that will be used to connect to the database.

   If you want to specify a failover server (used in database mirroring) for the profile database, enter the server name in the Failover Database Server text box in the Failover Server section. Unless you have pre-created the databases, you'll likely complete this section at a later time.

7. The profile synchronization database is used to retain configuration and staging information for synchronization of profile information from external sources. In the Synchronization Database section, do the following:

   ■ Enter the name of the database server in the Database Server text box. This is the server where the synchronization database will be located.

   ■ Enter the name of the database in the Database Name text box. This will be the name of the database that will be created in the server specified in the preceding bullet point.

   ■ Select the Windows Authentication (Recommended) option as the authentication method for the database when you want to use Integrated Windows Authentication. Or select the SQL Authentication option, and enter the relevant credentials in the Account and Password text boxes that will be used to connect to the database.

8. If you want to specify a failover server (used in database mirroring) for the synchronization database, enter the server name in the Failover Database Server text box in the Failover Server section. Unless you have pre-created databases, you'll want to do this at a later time.

9. The social tagging database is used to store social tags and notes created by users. In the Social Tagging Database section, do the following:

   ■ In the Database Server text box, enter the name of the server on which the social tagging database will be located.

   ■ In the Database Name text box, enter the name of the database that will be created in the server specified in the preceding step.

   ■ Select the Windows Authentication (Recommended) option as the authentication method for the database when you want to use Integrated Windows Authentication. Or select the SQL Authentication option, and enter the relevant credentials in the Account and Password text boxes that will be used to connect to the database.

10. If you want to specify a failover server (used in database mirroring) for the social tagging database, enter the server name in the Failover Database Server text box in the Failover Server section. Unless you have pre-created databases, you'll want to do this at a later time.

11. From the drop-down list in the Profile Synchronization Instance section, select the machine in the farm on which you would like to run the Profile Synchronization service.

12. In the text box in the My Site Host section, enter the URL of the site collection where you would like to provision the My Site host.

Note

Make sure the site collection you have provisioned is based on the My Site Host template.

---

13. In the My Site Managed Path section, enter the managed path where all the personal sites will be created. This, combined with the My Site Host URL, will form the URLs for My Sites—for example,

http://<My Site Host Web Application Path>/<My Site Managed Path>/<Site Naming Format> will be the URL for the personal site for a user.

Three formats are available to name new My Sites:

- Username (does not resolve conflicts)—For example, http://<My Site Host Web Application Path>/ <My Site Managed Path>/username.

- Username (resolves conflicts by using domain_username)— For example, http://<My Site Host Web Application Path>/<My Site Managed Path>/username or .../domain_username.

- Domain and username (will not have conflicts)—For example, http://<My Site Host Web Application Path>/ <My Site Managed Path>/domain_username.

14. Select Yes or No from the drop-down list in the Default Proxy Group section if you want the proxy of this service to be part of the default proxy on this farm.

15. Click Create. You can also click Cancel to cancel out of the operation.

Edit a User Profile Service Application

To edit a User Profile Service application, do the following:

1. Browse to Central Administration, Application Management, Manage Service Applications. The Manage Service Application page appears.

2. Scroll down, and in the Type column, click the User Profile Service Application link to select the row. (See Figure 13.4.)

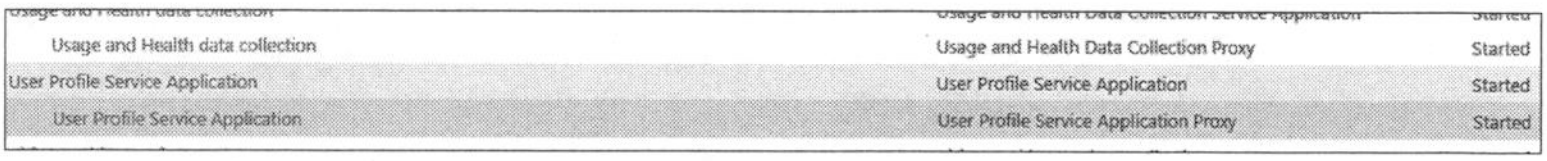

Usage and Health data collection	Usage and Health Data Collection	Started
Usage and Health data collection	Usage and Health Data Collection Proxy	Started
User Profile Service Application	User Profile Service Application	Started
User Profile Service Application	User Profile Service Application Proxy	Started

FIGURE 13.4
User Profile Service Application link indicating that it has started.

3. On the management ribbon, click Properties. The Edit User Profile Service Application dialog box appears.

4. Modify the relevant information.

5. Click OK to save the changes, or click Cancel to cancel out of the operation.

Delete a User Profile Service Application

To delete a User Profile Service application, do the following:

1. Browse to Central Administration, Application Management, Manage Service Applications. The Manage Service Application page appears.

2. Scroll down, and in the Type column, click the User Profile Service Application link to select the row.

3. On the management ribbon, click Delete. The Delete Service Application dialog box appears, as shown in Figure 13.5.

FIGURE 13.5
Delete Service Application dialog box.

4. In the Delete Service Application dialog box, confirm that you selected the correct service.

5. Select the Delete Data Associated with the Service Applications check box if you want to delete all the data associated with the selected service. Leave it unselected if you do not.

6. Click OK to delete the service application, or click Cancel to cancel out of the operation.

Service Administration

Administration of the User Profile Service can be done by the farm administrator or by someone the farm administrator delegates the appropriate permissions to. This service application administrator can administer only the services that she has been given the permission for. This delegation capability allows the farm administrator to assign others the administrative responsibilities for specific services, thereby freeing up the farm administrator's time to focus on standard farm administration tasks.

Delegate the Administration of a User Profile Service

To delegate the administration of a User Profile Service from within Central Administration, do the following:

1. Browse to Central Administration, Application Management, Manage Service Applications. The Manage Service Application page appears.

2. Scroll down, and in the Type column, click the User Profile Service Application link to select the row.

3. On the management ribbon, click Administrators. The Administrators for User Profile Service Application dialog box appears, as shown in Figure 13.6.

4. In the provided fields, enter the group or account and click the Add button to add them to the list.

5. Make sure any newly added account is highlighted in the list.

6. In the Permissions for Account list, select the Full Control check box.

7. Click OK.

Note

Delegating service administration privileges can also be done via Windows PowerShell by using the Get-SPServiceApplication, Get-SPServiceApplicationSecurity, New-SPClaimsPrincipal, Grant-SPObjectSecurity, and Set-SPServiceApplicationSecurity cmdlets. Details of the relevant script can be found at http://technet.microsoft.com/en-us/library/ee721057(v=office.15).aspx.

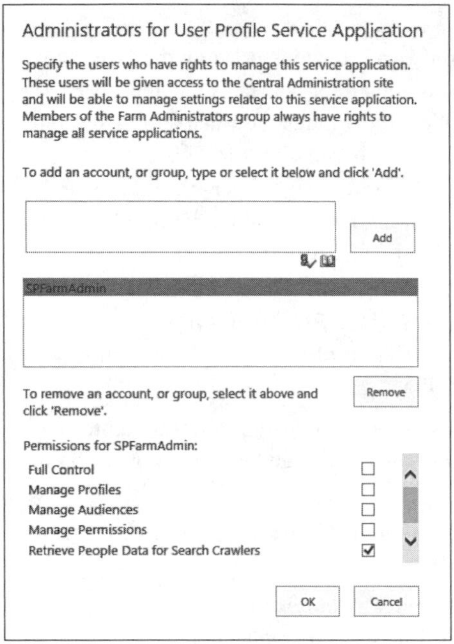

Administrators for User Profile Service Application

Specify the users who have rights to manage this service application.
These users will be given access to the Central Administration site
and will be able to manage settings related to this service application.
Members of the Farm Administrators group always have rights to
manage all service applications.

To add an account, or group, type or select it below and click 'Add'.

	Add

SPFarmAdmin

To remove an account, or group, select it above and
click 'Remove'. | Remove |

Permissions for SPFarmAdmin:

Full Control	☐
Manage Profiles	☐
Manage Audiences	☐
Manage Permissions	☐
Retrieve People Data for Search Crawlers	☑

OK	Cancel

FIGURE 13.6
Administrators for User Profile Service Application dialog box.

Profile Property Administration

The Manage Profile Service page of the User Profile Service application is
the central page to manage all currently available properties; you also
create new user profile properties there. Custom profile properties can be
created to complement the out-of-the-box user profile properties to retain
additional information related to personal or business attributes. For
example, custom profile properties can be used to help associate users with
additional business information based on those properties, thereby allowing
for the creation of specific audiences. Having this additional information
facilitates the organization of users from multiple business perspectives.

Note

Detailed information about user profile properties is available at
http://msdn.micro.com/en-us/library/cc262327.aspx.

Create a New User Profile Property

To create a new user profile property, do the following:

1. Browse to Central Administration, Application Management, Manage Service Applications. The Manage Service Application page appears.

2. Scroll down, and in the Type column, click the User Profile Service Application link to select the row.

3. On the management ribbon, click Manage. The Manage Profile Service: User Profile Service Application page appears, as shown in Figure 13.7.

FIGURE 13.7
User Profile Service Application page with all the administrative options available.

4. Within the Manage Profile Service page, in the People section, click Manage User Properties. The Manage User Properties page appears, as shown in Figure 13.8.

5. At the top of the properties list, click New Property. The Add User Profile Property page appears, as shown in Figure 13.9.

6. In the Property Settings section, do the following:

   ■ Enter the internal name of the property in the Name text box.

   ■ Enter the display name of the property in the Display Name text box.

   ■ Select the data type of the property from the Type drop-down list. Note that clicking the Edit Languages button allows you to designate alternative display names in different languages for properties.

- Enter the maximum amount of characters allowed for this property in the Length text box.

- Selecting the Configure a Term Set to Be Used for This Property check box allows you to associate this profile property with a managed metadata term set and select a term set from the drop-down list that appears.

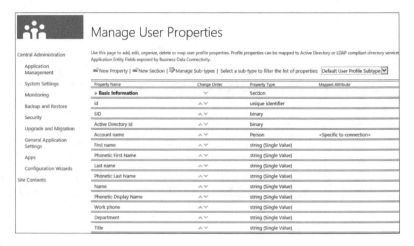

FIGURE 13.8
Manage User Properties page.

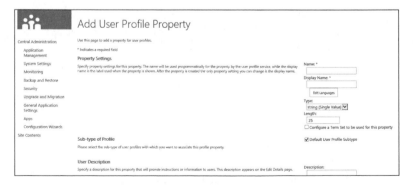

FIGURE 13.9
Add User Profile Property page.

7. Select the Default User Profile Subtype check box in the Sub-Type of Profile section to associate the default user profile subtype with this property.

8. Enter the description of the property in the Description text box in the User Description section. Note that clicking the Edit Languages button allows you to designate alternative descriptions in different languages for properties.

9. In the Policy Settings section, do the following:

    ▪ Select one of the following options from the Policy Setting drop-down list: Required, Optional, or Disabled.

    ▪ Select one of the following options from the Default Privacy Setting drop-down list: Only Me or Everyone.

    ▪ Select the User Can Override check box to allow the user to override these settings.

10. The Edit Settings section allows you to designate whether the user can change the values for this property in this user profile. Choose one of the following options:

    ▪ Allow Users to Edit Values for This Property, to allow users to change the value.

    ▪ Do Not Allow Users to Edit Values for This Property, to deny users the capability to change the value.

Note

When adding a Profile Property that is intended for editing by the user, *do not* set Policy Setting to Required while leaving the Edit Settings option selected to Do Not Allow Users to Edit Values for This Property.

---

11. The check boxes in the Display Settings section allow you to designate the property to do any of the following:

    ▪ Show in the Profile Properties section of the user's profile page.

    ▪ Show on the Edit Details page.

    ▪ Show updates to the property in newsfeeds.

12. The settings in the Search Settings section associate different behaviors with the property, depending on the searches executed:

    ▪ Select the Alias check box to designate the property as aliased.

- Select the Indexed check box to designate the property as indexed. Note that even if you check this box and if the visibility is set to Only Me, it will not be indexed.

13. In the Property Mapping for Synchronization section, click Remove to delete or change an existing mapping.

14. The settings in the Add New Mapping section allow you to set up mappings for the property when synchronizing user profile data. To correctly use the following settings, profile synchronization must be configured:

   - Specify the Source Data Connection by selecting it from the drop-down list.

   - Specify the Attribute by selecting it from the drop-down list.

   - Specify the Direction by selecting it from the drop-down list.

15. Click OK to create the property, or click Cancel to cancel the operation.

Edit an Existing User Profile Property

To edit an existing user profile property, do the following:

1. On the Manage Profile Service page, scroll down the list of properties to find the one you want to edit.

2. Hover the cursor over the desired property, click the down arrow to display the context menu, and select Edit. (See Figure 13.10.)

3. The Edit User Profile Property page appears. Modify the information desired, and then click OK to save the change or Cancel to cancel the operation.

Delete an Existing User Profile Property

To delete an existing user profile property, do the following:

1. From the Manage Profile Service page, scroll down the list of properties to find the one you want to delete.

2. Hover the cursor over the desired property, click the down arrow to display the context menu, and select Delete.

3. A confirmation dialog box appears. Click OK to delete the property or click Cancel to cancel the operation.

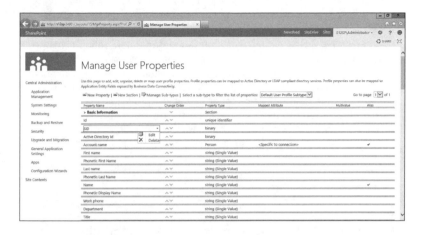

FIGURE 13.10
Profile Property context menu showing the options to either edit or delete the
Profile Property.

Profile Synchronization

Profile synchronization allows you to bring together user and group information between the external data stores and the user profile store in
SharePoint Server 2013. Profile synchronization within SharePoint Server
2013 facilitates the bulk import of information from that external store into
SharePoint Server 2013. It also facilitates the export of information modified within SharePoint Server 2013 back to the external store. Profile
synchronization facilitates maintaining the consistency of the user profile
within SharePoint Server 2013 with multiple external data sources. The
external sources supported by SharePoint Server 2013 are Active Directory
Domain Services (AD DS) 2003 SP2 and AD DS 2008, Business
Connectivity Services (BCS), Novell eDirectory v. 8.7.3 LDAP, Sun Java
System Directory Server version 5.2, and IBM Tivoli version 5.2.

> **Note**
>
> Only Active Directory Domain Services allows for the synchronization of
> groups. Full and incremental synchronization is provided by all these serv-
> ices with the exception of Novell eDirectory—it does not support incre-
> mental synchronization.

Note

SharePoint 2013 User Profile Synchronization has a new option aimed to reduce import and synchronization times—Active Directory Direct Import. This option now allows for an import to occur against an Active Directory forest that contains several domains. Although only one connection per domain is permitted, the Direct Import capability produces significant time savings when compared to the previous approach in SharePoint 2010. Additionally, the direct import allows for LDAP filters to be used. Most importantly—make sure that Active Directory is your authoritative source for identify information.

Note

For more on the Active Directory Import, see this TechNet article: http://technet.microsoft.com/en-us/library/jj219646.aspx.

Create a New Profile Synchronization Connection

To create a new profile synchronization connection, do the following:

1. Browse to Central Administration, Application Management, Manage Service Applications. The Manage Service Application page appears.

2. Scroll down, and in the Type column, click the User Profile Service Application link to select the row.

3. On the management ribbon, click Manage. The Manage Profile Service: User Profile Service Application page appears.

4. In the Synchronization section, click the Configure Synchronization Connections link. The Synchronization Connections page appears. (See Figure 13.11.)

5. At the top of the page, click the Create New Connection link. The Add New Synchronization Connection page appears, as shown in Figure 13.12.

6. Enter a name for the connection in the Connection Name text box.

7. Select the type of the connection from the drop-down list.

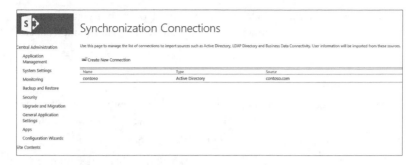

FIGURE 13.11
Synchronization Connections page showing the Create New Connection button.

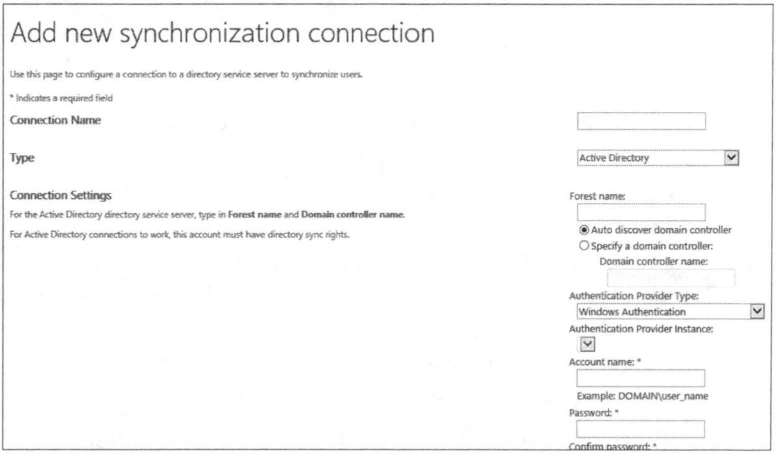

FIGURE 13.12
Add New Synchronization Connection menu showing the Connection Name and options for a new connection.

8. In the Connection Settings section, do the following:

   ■ In the Forest Name text box, enter the name of the forest that you want to connect to.

   ■ Select either the Auto Discover Domain Controller option or the Specify a Domain Controller option. If the latter is selected, enter the name of the domain controller into the

Domain Controller Name text box. However, if you specify a Domain Controller and it is offline for any reason, the connection will fail.

■ Select the Authentication Provider Type from the drop-down list.

■ Enter the account credentials of the account to connect to the domain controller in the Account Name and Password fields.

■ Enter the desired port in the Port text box.

9. In the Containers section, click the Populate Containers button to display the directory service containers in the list, and then select the desired containers. You can also click the Select All button to select all the containers.

10. Click OK to execute the operation, or click Cancel to cancel the operation.

Edit an Existing Profile Synchronization Connection's Connection Filters

To edit an existing profile synchronization connection's connection filters, do the following:

1. Browse to Central Administration, Application Management, Manage Service Applications. The Manage Service Application page appears.

2. Scroll down, and in the Type column, click the User Profile Service Application link to select the row.

3. On the management ribbon, click Manage. The Manage Profile Service: User Profile Service Application page appears.

4. In the Synchronization section, click the Configure Synchronization Connections link. The Synchronization Connections page appears.

5. Hover the cursor over the relevant connection and click the down arrow to expose its context menu (as shown in Figure 13.13).

6. Select Edit Connection Filters. The Edit Connection Filters page appears (as shown in Figure 13.14).

7. In the Exclusion Filters for Users section, in the Attribute drop-down list, select the user profile property for which you want to apply a filter, configure the filter parameters (Operator and Filter) for that property, and then click the Add button.

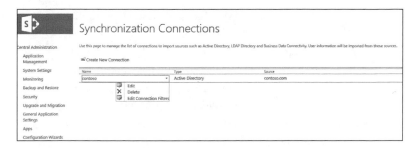

FIGURE 13.13
Connection Context menu showing the Edit, Delete, and Edit Connection Filters options.

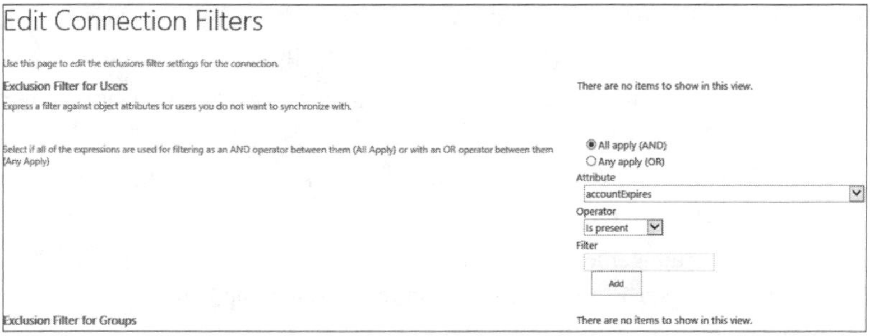

Edit Connection Filters

Use this page to edit the exclusions filter settings for the connection.

Exclusion Filter for Users

Express a filter against object attributes for users you do not want to synchronize with.

Select if all of the expressions are used for filtering as an AND operator between them (All Apply) or with an OR operator between them (Any Apply)

There are no items to show in this view.

- ● All apply (AND)
- ○ Any apply (OR)

Attribute
accountExpires

Operator
Is present

Filter

Add

Exclusion Filter for Groups

There are no items to show in this view.

FIGURE 13.14
Edit Connections Filters page showing the exclusion filter options for users and groups.

8. In the Exclusion Filter for Groups section, in the Attribute drop-down list, select the group profile property for which you want to apply a filter, configure the filter parameters (Operator and Filter) for that property, and then click the Add button.

9. Click OK to execute the operation, or click Cancel to cancel the operation.

Delete an Existing Profile Synchronization Connection

To delete an existing profile synchronization connection, do the following:

1. Browse to Central Administration, Application Management, Manage Service Applications. The Manage Service Application page appears.

2. Scroll down, and in the Type column, click the User Profile Service Application link to select the row.

3. On the management ribbon, click Manage. The Manage Profile Service: User Profile Service Application page appears.

4. In the Synchronization section, click the Configure Synchronization Connections link. The Synchronization Connections page appears.

5. Hover the cursor over the relevant connection, click the down arrow to expose its context menu, and select Delete.

Map Profile Properties

The Mapping Profile Properties section allows you to assign mappings between the profile properties and the directory source properties. To map profile properties, follow these steps:

1. Browse to Central Administration, Application Management, Manage Service Applications. The Manage Service Application page appears.

2. Scroll down, and in the Type column, click the User Profile Service Application link to select the row.

3. On the management ribbon, click Manage. The Manage Profile Service: User Profile Service Application page appears.

4. In the People section, click the Manage User Properties link. The Manage User Properties page appears. (See Figure 13.15.)

Manage User Properties

Use this page to add, edit, organize, delete or map user profile properties. Profile properties can be mapped to Active Directory or LDAP compliant directory services. Profile properties can also be mapped to Application Entity Fields exposed by Business Data Connectivity.

New Property | New Section | Manage Sub-types | Select a sub-type to filter the list of properties: Default User Profile Subtype ▾   Go to page 1 ▾ of 1

Property Name	Change Order	Property Type	Mapped Attribute	Multivalue	Alias
> **Basic Information**	⌄	Section			
Id	∧∨	unique identifier			
SID	∧∨	binary	objectSid		
Active Directory Id	∧∨	binary			
Account name	∧∨	Person	<Specific to connection>		✔
First name	∧∨	string (Single Value)	givenName		
Phonetic First Name	∧∨	string (Single Value)	msDS-PhoneticFirstName		
Last name	∧∨	string (Single Value)	sn		

FIGURE 13.15
Manage User Properties page showing the toolbar menu options of New Property, New Section, and Manage Sub-types.

5. Hover the cursor over the property you want to map, click the down arrow to display the menu, and click Edit. The Edit User Profile Property page appears. (See Figure 13.16.)

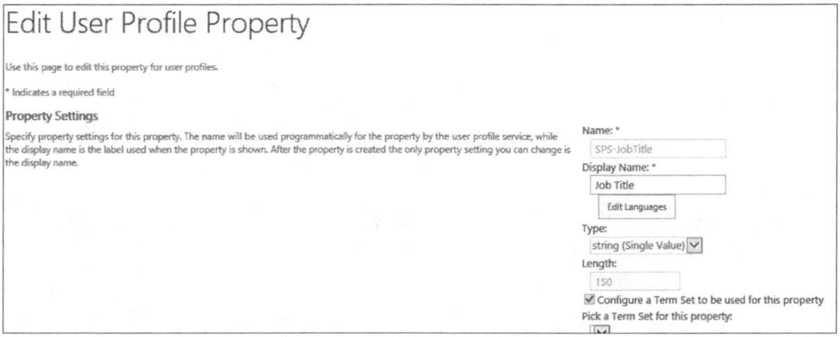

FIGURE 13.16
Edit User Profile Property page showing the property settings for a user profile edit.

6. In the Add New Mapping section, select the Source Data Connection from the drop-down list, select the Attribute from the drop-down list, and then select the Direction of the mapping (Import or Export).

7. Click OK to save the mapping, or click Cancel to cancel the operation.

Configure Synchronization Settings

The Configure Synchronization Settings page (shown in Figure 13.17) allows you to manage the settings for profile synchronization of users and groups.

To configure the synchronization settings, complete the following steps:

1. Browse to Central Administration, Application Management, Manage Service Applications. The Manage Service Application page appears.

2. Scroll down, and in the Type column, click the User Profile Service Application link to select the row.

3. On the management ribbon, click Manage. The Manage Profile Service: User Profile Service Application page appears.

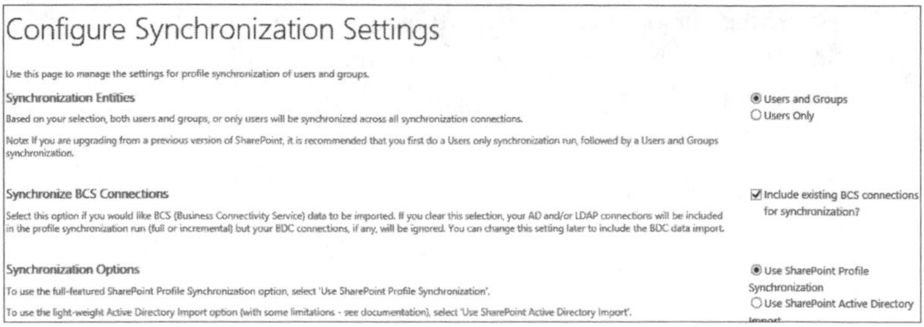

FIGURE 13.17
Configure Synchronization Settings page showing the options for Synchronization Entities, BCS Connections, and Synchronization Options.

4. In the Synchronization section, click the Configure Synchronization Settings link. The Configure Synchronization Settings page appears.

5. In the Synchronization Entities section, select the Users and Groups option to synchronize users and groups across all connections, or select the Users Only option to synchronize just users.

6. In the Synchronize BCS Connections section, select the Include Existing BCS Connections For Synchronization? check box to import your Business Connectivity Service (BCS) data during synchronization. Clear this check box if you do not want to include your BCS data during synchronization.

7. In the External Identity Manager section, select the Enable External Identity Manager option to use an external entity management system for profile synchronization. Select the Use SharePoint Profile Synchronization option to use SharePoint profile synchronization.

Enabling Social Features for Users and Groups

One of the many capabilities a farm administrator controls is who has access to the social features within SharePoint Server 2013. These social features allow a user to bring into play the additional collaborative aspects of social networking within SharePoint Server 2013. The social features of the User Profile Service in SharePoint Server 2013 consist of the following:

■ My Sites are site collections that consist of a majority of social features in SharePoint 2013. Technically, a My Site is a site collection, and all rules governing site collections apply.

- Profile Pages are publicly accessible pages that are provided as a part of the My Site Host Collection. They are usually filled with details about interests, other social connections, activity feeds, and your personal photo.

- People and Expertise Searching provides the capability to search for people based on skills or other criteria.

- Organizational charts provide users the capability to navigate the organization's hierarchy.

- Social tagging provides the user the capability to tag any object in SharePoint—not just a document. This allows for the user to follow items of interest while aggregating this information in a single location.

- Audiences groups are groups of similar users with consistent memberships and roles for a specific set of data.

Service administrators can also prevent specific users or groups from using the activated social features. Service administrators can give access to certain business groups or users so that they can contribute to the enterprise taxonomy, and they can restrict that function from being accessed by others.

These social features are enabled through either Central Administration or via Windows PowerShell scripts.

Enable Social Features for Usage by Users and Groups

To enable the social features for usage by users and groups, do the following:

1. Browse to Central Administration, Application Management, Manage Service Applications. The Manage Service Application page appears.

2. Scroll down, and in the Type column, click the User Profile Service Application link to select the row.

3. On the management ribbon, click Manage. The Manage Profile Service: User Profile Service Application page appears.

4. In the People section, click the Manage User Permissions link. The Permissions for User Profile Service Application dialog box appears, as shown in Figure 13.18.

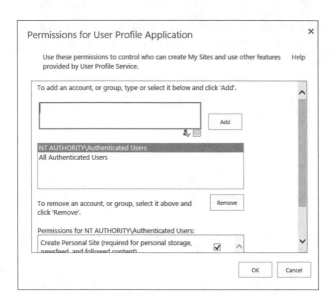

FIGURE 13.18
Permissions for User Profile Service Application dialog box that is used to update user permissions.

5. Type or select a user or group account in the people picker, and then click the Add button.

6. In the Permissions for Users box, select all the relevant social features you want to enable for the given user.

7. Click OK to save, or click Cancel to cancel the operation.

The Permissions in SharePoint 2013 are similar to those of SharePoint 2010 but have a more purposeful description (see Table 13.1).

Table 13.1   **SharePoint Permissions**

Then (SharePoint 2010)	Now (SharePoint 2013)
Create Personal Site	Create Personal Site (required for personal storage, newsfeed, and followed content)
Use Social Features	Follow People and Edit Profile
User Personal Features	Use Tags and Notes

Social Tags and Note Boards

Social features such as tagging and notes allow users to track and remember information, as well as state what information they'd like to share with others. These social features are enabled by default.

Activate or Deactivate Tagging and Notes

To activate or deactivate the tagging and notes social features via Central Administration, perform the following:

1. Browse to Central Administration, System Settings, Manage Farm Features. The Manage Farm Features page appears, as shown in Figure 13.19.

FIGURE 13.19
Manage Farm Features page showing activated features in blue.

2. If the Social Tags and Note Board Ribbon Controls feature has an Activate button, click it to activate the feature.
3. If the Social Tags and Note Board Ribbon Controls feature has a Deactivate button, click it, and the Deactivate Feature Warning page appears, as shown in Figure 13.20.

FIGURE 13.20
Deactivate Feature Warning page.

4. Click the Deactivate This Feature link to confirm the action.

> **Note**
>
> Deactivation of this feature can also be accomplished via Windows PowerShell using the enable-SPFeature disable-SPFeature cmdlets. See http://technet.microsoft.com/en-us/library/ee721062(office.14).aspx#section2.

Delete All Tags or Notes for a Specific User

In addition to controlling the social features at a farm level, the service administrator can also manage the tags and notes directly. Tags and notes can be deleted for a specific link or user, within a date range, or at the even more granular level of the specific tag or note. Functions like this can be particularly useful for multiple scenarios, such as when an employee adds a tag that you might not want to be retained or used within the enterprise. This is a huge improvement of 2013 because many administrators desired this functionality.

To delete all tags or notes for a specific user from within Central Administration, perform the following steps:

1. Browse to Central Administration, Application Management, Manage Service Applications. The Manage Service Application page appears.

2. Scroll down, and in the Type column, click the User Profile Service Application link to select the row.

3. On the management ribbon, click Manage. The Manage Profile Service: User Profile Service Application page appears.

4. In the My Site Settings section, click the Manage Social Tags and Notes link. The Manage Social Tags and Note page appears, as shown in Figure 13.21.

5. From the Type drop-down list, specify either Tags or Notes as the type to search for.

6. Enter a user or group to search for in the User field.

7. Enter a URL to search for in the URL field.

8. Enter a date range to search for in the provided Date Range fields.

9. In the Tag/Note Contains field, enter information about a tag or note that you want to search for.

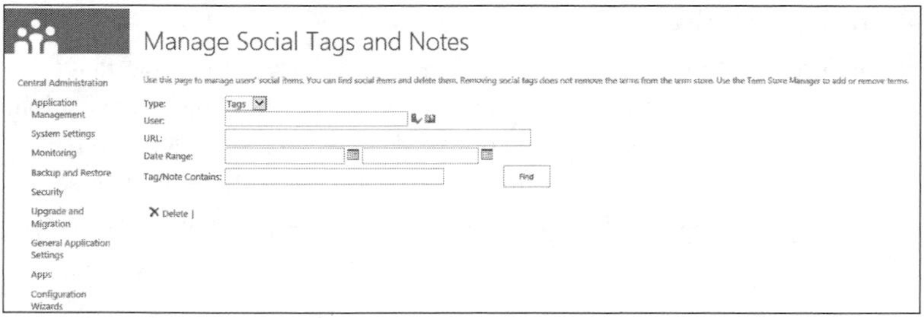

FIGURE 13.21
Manage Social Tags and Notes page located in Central Administration.

10. Click the Find button. The results are displayed in the grid below the search criteria

11. Select the check box of the line item that you want to delete, and then click the Delete link.

12. A confirmation dialog box confirms the deletion operation. Click OK to delete the item, or click Cancel to cancel the operation.

My Sites

Social Features in SharePoint 2013 are driven by two site collections, My Site Host, and the Personal Site (My Site) for the user. The dependence on the My Site Host and Personal Site is important because they rely on each other to either push or pull data to and from a user's personal site. For all social features to work, a personal site for the user must be provisioned.

My Site websites are personal websites that allow users to take advantage of the many social networking features of SharePoint Server 2013 within their enterprise. A My Site website consists of the following:

- **Newsfeed**—Displays information about items followed by a user; it is no longer just about following people, but objects and items. There are even Everyone feeds where the most recent 20 posts and or replies are displayed for all SharePoint users

- **About Me**—A profile page where users can update their profile picture, user profile properties, contact details, and other activity feeds.

- **Microblogging**—Allows users to add messages to content that users may be interested in publicizing and creating further conversation about. Microblogging can make use of URLs, videos, images, and plain text.

Planning My Sites

If your organization wants to enable the social features, it is important to plan for a personal site for each employee or user within your organization. SharePoint 2013 shifts the storage of the My Site data to content databases. This provides the capability to scale out if needed. To provide scalability, SharePoint 2013 allows for you to create multiple content databases for your My Sites.

> **Note**
>
> If your organization has thousands of potential My Sites, remember that each My Site is a site collection, and as such, each content database has a recommended threshold of site collections.

By default My Sites are created with a 100MB storage quota. This should be increased to an acceptable amount based on the organization's capabilities and storage thresholds. Not increasing the storage quota will affect users very quickly. The My Site is stored within the content database, which is also where the user's SkyDrive Pro storage is located. If a user consumes his or her quota, that specific user's social capabilities will be impacted, such as not being able to add a profile picture, posting pictures in feeds, tagging, and adding comments.

> **Note**
>
> If your organization is considering SharePoint 2013 social features and has storage limits that may prevent adequate storage support, consider a cloud solution. Solutions such as Microsoft Office 365 often provide higher default quotas. The current default quota for a My Site in an Office 365 environment is 7GB.

My Sites are highly dependent on the managed metadata service (MMS) application for the term database. My Sites require the MMS to allow users to specify keywords in the Ask Me About portion of their profile pages. The managed metadata service application must be configured as the default keyword term store for the My Site Web Application. My Sites depend on the term store for social tagging capabilities for features such as Tags and Notes. The tight integration with the term store gives the term store administrator the ability to predefine and load the term store with a standard set of hashtags or keywords needed by the organization.

My Sites Governance

It is important when planning to deploy My Sites or other social features, that organizations give plenty of forethought into their social governance plan. Before deploying My Sites or other social features, ensure that they are configured within your organization's policies and procedures and that adherence to any federal or local laws is occurring.

Note

Before setting your My Sites to be created under a "personal" managed path, ensure that "personal" is adequately defined to ensure that privacy laws are followed.

Setting Up My Sites Websites

Configuration of the My Sites websites is accomplished in the My Site host location. To configure the settings of My Sites websites, complete the following steps:

1. Browse to Central Administration, Application Management, Manage Service Applications. The Manage Service Application page appears.

2. Scroll down, and in the Type column, click the User Profile Service Application link to select the row.

3. On the management ribbon, click Manage. The Manage Profile Service: User Profile Service Application page appears.

4. In the My Site Settings section, click the Setup My Sites link. The My Site Settings page appears, as shown in Figure 13.22.

5. The settings in the Preferred Search Center section allow you to dictate what search center is used when a user executes a search from within a My Site page:

   - Enter the URL of the search center into the Preferred Search Center text box.

   - Select the relevant scope in the Search Scope for Finding People drop-down list.

   - Select the relevant scope in the Search Scope for Finding Documents drop-down list.

My Site Settings

Use this page to manage My Site settings for this User Profile Service Application.

Central Administration	
Application Management	**Preferred Search Center**
System Settings	Setting the preferred search center allows you to control which search center users are taken to when they execute a search from the My Site profile page.
Monitoring	
Backup and Restore	
Security	
Upgrade and Migration	
General Application Settings	**My Site Host**
Apps	Setting a My Site Host allows you to use a designated site to host personal sites. All users accessing personal sites for this Shared Services Provider will be automatically redirected to the server you specify.
Configuration Wizards	If there are any existing personal sites, you must manually transfer their contents to the new location.
Site Contents	Note: To change the location hosting personal sites, create a new site collection at the desired location using the My Site Host site template.

Preferred Search Center:

Example: http://sitename/SearchCenter/Pages/

Search scope for finding people:
People

Search scope for finding documents:
All Sites

My Site Host location:
http://my.contoso.com:80/

Example: http://portal_site/

My Site Host URL in Active Directory

Note: This URL will be returned to the client through Exchange Auto Discovery. Use the appropriate PowerShell script to change the My Site host URL in Active Directory.

Personal Site Location

Select the location at which to create personal sites. This should be a wildcard inclusion managed path defined on the web

Location: *
personal

FIGURE 13.22
My Site Settings page showing the ability to specify a search center, My Site Host, My Site Host URL in Active Directory, and the location of Personal Sites.

6. The My Site Host Location box allows you to specify a particular site to host all the My Site websites. Enter the specific URL into the text box.

7. The Personal Site Location section allows you to specify a particular location in which to create My Site websites. Enter the path into the text box.

8. The Site Naming Format section determines the format of a user's My Site website:

   ■ Select the User Name (Do Not Resolve Conflicts) option to use the individual's username—for example, http://<My Site Host Web Application>/<My Site Managed Path>/username/.

   ■ Select the User Name (Resolve Conflicts By Using domain_username) option to use the individual's username. Or, when there's a conflict, use the domain_username format.

   ■ Select the Domain and User Name (Will Not Have Conflicts) option to use the domain_username format at all times—for example, http://<My Site Host Web Application>/<My Site Managed Path>/domain_username.

9. The Allow User to Choose the Language of Their Personal Site check box in the Language Options section determines whether users can choose the language of their My Site website. The list of available languages is determined by the language packs installed.

10. Accounts added in the Read Permission Level section are given read-level access to My Site websites when they are created. Enter the desired accounts here.

11. The text box in the My Site E-mail Notifications section contains the From e-mail address for all My Site notification e-mail messages. Enter a value here.

12. My Site Cleanup provides the option to provide administrative access to a My Site after a user profile has been deleted.

13. Privacy Settings provide administrative control over whether all My Sites, their content, and the users' activities will be publicly available.

14. Click OK to save the settings, or click Cancel to cancel the operation.

My Site Provisioning

Traditionally, in previous versions of SharePoint, users were given a single access point to provision a My Site. In SharePoint this has increased and instead is now provisioned either through an interactive request or an inactive request:

- **Interactive Request** is a request to provision a My Site that was generated by a specific action performed by the user (Newsfeed Link, About Me Link, and SkyDrive Pro Link).

- **Non-interactive Request** is a request that is initiated on the behalf of the user through My Site autodiscovery with either the Office client or from Exchange.

SharePoint 2013 My Sites are now provisioned asynchronously. Asynchronous provisioning lowers the time to provision a new My Site while reducing risk to the server. To reduce the risk to the server and to lower duration times for My Site provision, the SharePoint 2013 architecture accommodates each type of provisioning request using three queues. A single queue is provided to handle noninteractive requests. The remaining two queues are used for interactive requests; because these requests were initialized by the user, they are also given a higher priority and will be accelerated ahead of a noninteractive request.

Adding or Deleting a Trusted My Site Host Location

Trusted My Site host locations are typically used when organizations have multiple UPA Service Applications, such as when geographically dispersed, and you need to target the users' My Site to only one My Site Host. Otherwise, the user could potentially have multiple My Sites.

Add a Trusted My Site Host Location

To add a Trusted My Site host location, do the following:

1. Browse to Central Administration, Application Management, Manage Service Applications. The Manage Service Application page appears.

2. Scroll down, and in the Type column, click the User Profile Service Application link to select the row.

3. On the management ribbon, click Manage. The Manage Profile Service: User Profile Service Application page appears.

4. In the My Site Settings section, click the Configure Trusted Host Locations link. The Trusted My Site Host Locations page appears, as shown in Figure 13.23.

FIGURE 13.23
Trusted My Site Host Locations page.

5. Click New Link to bring up the Add Trusted Host Location page. (See Figure 13.24.)

6. In the Properties section, do the following:

   ■ Enter the URL of a trusted location into the text box.

   ■ Enter the description of the trusted location into the Description text box.

   ■ Enter any target audiences for this location (optional).

7. Click OK to save the location, or click Cancel to cancel the operation.

Add Trusted Host Location

* Indicates a required field

Properties
Apply audiences to identify which user's My Sites are hosted in that location.

URL: *

Title: *

Description:

Image URL:

Target Audiences:

OK   Cancel

FIGURE 13.24
Add Trusted Host Location page.

Delete a Trusted My Site Host Location
To delete a trusted My Site host location, do the following:

1. Browse to Central Administration, Application Management, Manage Service Applications. The Manage Service Application page appears.

2. Scroll down, and in the Type column, click the User Profile Service Application link to select the row.

3. On the management ribbon, click Manage. The Manage Profile Service: User Profile Service Application page appears.

4. In the My Site Settings section, click the Configure Trusted Host Locations link. The Trusted My Site Host Locations page appears.

5. In the list of trusted host locations that appears, select the check boxes of the locations you want to delete.

6. Click Delete Link and a confirmation dialog box appears.

7. Click OK to confirm the deletion, or click Cancel to cancel the operation.

Promoted Sites
Promoted sites are links that are added to the Promoted Link area on the user's Sites page of his or her My Site. These promoted site links appear throughout all the My Site Sites pages. These links may be targeted to a specific group of users by using audiences.

Add a Personalization Link

To add a personalization site link, do the following:

1. Browse to Central Administration, Application Management, Manage Service Applications. The Manage Service Application page appears.

2. Scroll down, and in the Type column, click the User Profile Service Application link to select the row.

3. On the management ribbon, click Manage. The Manage Profile Service: User Profile Service Application page appears.

4. In the My Site Settings section, click the Configure Promoted Site link. The Promoted Sites page appears, as shown in Figure 13.25.

Promoted Sites

Use this list to promote certain sites to users. Sites added here will appear on Sites page in user's My Sites. Use audiences if you want a link

🖼 New Link | ✕ Delete Link

URL	Title	Owner	Target Audiences
The query returns nothing.			

FIGURE 13.25
Promoted Site Links page.

5. Click New Link. The Promoted Sites page appears, as shown in Figure 13.26.

FIGURE 13.26
Add Promote a Site Link page with the properties available for editing.

6. In the Properties section, do the following:

- Enter the address of the link into the URL text box.
- Enter a description in the Description text box.
- Enter a user as the owner of this link. (This is optional.)
- Enter a target audience for this link. (This is optional.)

7. Click OK to save this link, or click Cancel to cancel the operation.

Delete a Promoted Site Link

To delete a promoted site link, complete the following steps:

1. Browse to Central Administration, Application Management, Manage Service Applications. The Manage Service Application page appears.

2. Scroll down, and in the Type column, click the User Profile Service Application link to select the row.

3. On the management ribbon, click Manage. The Manage Profile Service: User Profile Service Application page appears.

4. In the My Site Settings section, click the Configure Promoted Sites link. The Configure Promoted Sites page appears.

5. In the list of promoted site links that appears, select the check boxes of the site links you want to delete.

6. Click Delete Link and a confirmation dialog box appears.

7. Click OK to confirm the deletion, or click Cancel to cancel the operation.

Links to the Microsoft Office 2013 Client Applications

SharePoint Server 2013 and Office 2013 provide a deeper level of integration between the server and client tools. One of those additional integration points is the capability to publish links to SharePoint libraries and lists down to the client application. These links are exposed under the My Places bar that can be found next to the Open and Save dialog boxes. These links offer an additional level of integration when adding or saving items to SharePoint Server 2013.

Add a Link to an Office 2013 Client Application

To add a link to an Office 2013 client application, do the following:

1. Browse to Central Administration, Application Management, Manage Service Applications. The Manage Service Application page appears.

2. Scroll down, and in the Type column, click the User Profile Service Application link to select the row.

3. On the management ribbon, click Manage. The Manage Profile Service: User Profile Service Application page appears.

4. In the My Site Settings section, click the Publish Links to Office Client Applications link. The Published Links to Office Client Applications page appears, as shown in Figure 13.27.

Published links to Office client applications

Use this list to publish links to SharePoint sites and lists when opening and saving documents from Office client applications. Links published here will show up under the My SharePoints tab when opening and saving documents . Use audiences to specify if a link should only be published to a specific set of users.

📄 New Link | ✕ Delete Link

URL	Title	Type	Target Audiences
The query returns nothing.			

FIGURE 13.27
Published Links to Office Client Applications page.

5. Click New Link. The Add Published Link page appears, as shown in Figure 13.28.

Add Published Link

* Indicates a required field

Properties
Use audiences to specify if a link should only be published to a specific set of users.

URL: *

Title: *

Description:

Image URL:

Type:
Process Repository

Target Audiences:

OK   Cancel

FIGURE 13.28
Add Published Link page showing the URL and description fields along with the type of link it is.

6. In the Properties section, complete the following:

   - In the URL text box, enter the address of the location to publish to.

   - In the Description text box, enter a description.

   - Select the type from the drop-down list.

   - Enter a target audience for this link.

7. Click OK to save this link, or click Cancel to cancel the operation.

Delete a Link to an Office 2013 Client Application

To delete a link to an Office 2013 client application, do the following:

1. Browse to Central Administration, Application Management, Manage Service Applications. The Manage Service Application page appears.

2. Scroll down, and in the Type column, click the User Profile Service Application link to select the row.

3. On the management ribbon, click Manage. The Manage Profile Service: User Profile Service Application page appears.

4. In the My Site Settings section, click the Publish Links to Office Client Applications link. The Published Links to Office Client Applications page appears.

5. Select the check boxes of the links you want to delete, click Delete Link in the action bar, and click OK to confirm the deletion or Cancel to cancel the operation.

PART III

OPERATING

IN THIS PART

CHAPTER 14

Backing Up and Restoring SharePoint Server 2013

- ■ SharePoint Farm Backup and Recovery
- ■ Service and Web Application Backup and Restore
- ■ Granular Backup and Restore

Microsoft SharePoint Server 2013 provides robust tools necessary to back up and restore your content and configuration. The overall backup and restore methodology remains unchanged from SharePoint Server 2010. The selection of tools includes Central Administration and the Windows PowerShell backup and restore cmdlets to address the backup and restore needs for SharePoint Server 2013 management. SharePoint 2013 backup and restore tools have been updated to include new functionality, such as changes in the introduction of the App Management Service.

As you read through this chapter, you will notice that the ability to restore at a specific scope, such as a site collection, depends on what tool and method is selected to perform the backup. For example, if you back up a farm using full farm backups via Windows PowerShell, you would not be able to restore a site collection in a single step. Likewise, an export of a site hierarchy does not allow the restoration of an entire site collection; items such as Recycle Bin are not captured via a site export. You should always test your backup and restore plan to ensure you can retrieve the content and configuration dictated by your requirements.

SharePoint Server 2013 provides two primary tools to back up and restore your server farm and components:

- Central Administration
- Windows PowerShell

Many organizations have strict Business Continuity Plans (BCPs) and require a combination of these backup methods to ensure a fully restored and functional server farm in the event of data loss. When determining your recovery plan, be sure to refer to your organization's BCPs and its Recovery Time Objective (RTO) and Recovery Point Objective (RPO). Tools and processes to back up and restore SharePoint Server 2013 are covered in this chapter. However, there are many dependencies for SharePoint Server 2013 to function correctly, such as Microsoft Windows Server, Domain Name System (DNS) Server, Microsoft SQL Server, Active Directory, and more, that are not covered in this chapter. Be sure to keep in mind that all the dependencies of SharePoint Server 2013 must be anticipated, and the recovery plan must be tested.

SharePoint Farm Backup and Recovery

Before performing your first server farm backup, you need to decide where you will store the backup files. SharePoint Server 2013 does not provide a way to back up directly to tape. Instead, SharePoint Server 2013 backs up to a Universal Naming Convention (UNC) file share.

> **Note**
>
> The interface will allow a backup to a file system drive letter. This is highly discouraged because server names and volumes can change, and server drives are often a poor choice for SharePoint Server 2013 backups. It is recommended to connect to a Storage Area Network (SAN) or Network Attached Storage (NAS) for the backup location.

A common backup strategy involves backing up all content and configuration data to a file share and then using classic backup software and media to create offline backups. A good starting place for implementing this strategy is to create weekly full backups and daily differential backups. This approach allows you to quickly and easily restore content in the event of data loss. Unless another backup program is used to manage your data recovery, you should leave the last full backup and all differential backups from that full backup on disk. After you have successfully performed a subsequent full backup, you can then safely archive the last backup sent to tape or other media storage. Figure 14.1 shows an example of a basic SharePoint Server 2013 farm backup plan.

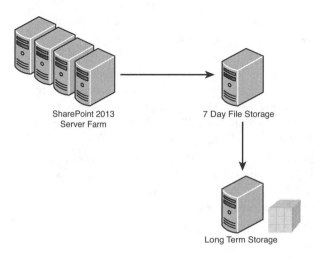

SharePoint 2013
Server Farm

7 Day File Storage

Long Term Storage

FIGURE 14.1
Multitier backup storage.

Preparing for Server Farm Backups

When backing up server farm data to file shares, care should be taken to minimize the access to storage locations. You should give the least amount of access possible for both the NTFS-level and share-level permissions. For the examples in this chapter, the file server is named *APP02* and the file share name is *Backups*. The following accounts need Full Control permissions to the backup location whether you are using Central Administration or Windows PowerShell farm tools:

- SQL Server service account
- SQL Server Machine account
- SharePoint 2013 Timer Log On Account (which can be verified in Windows Server 2012 Services Console)
- User account that is executing the command

Although this file share can, technically, exist anywhere that can be reached from the server farm member servers, it is best to have it on the same local area network.

The following should be considered when planning the physical storage of your backup locations:

- **Capacity**—Verify that you have enough capacity for the planned backups. For example, if you plan to keep one full backup and six differential backups on disk, you need the aggregate size of those backups plus up to 10 percent for logs and indexes.

- **Disk Speed**—Be sure the storage device being used for writing backups supports adequate write speeds so that the backup process can be completed within the required maintenance window. Keep in mind that backup processes consume a significant amount of disk throughput during backups and will affect any users consuming the disks for file sharing.

- **Network Speed**—Ensure that you use the fastest network fabric to avoid delays in backups. For all but the smallest server farms, you need gigabit Ethernet connections or better between all server farm members and the backup destination.

- **SQL Server**—All database backups and configuration data are written directly from SQL Server to the backup destination. Be sure the required network ports are open between the source and destination. If you have backups that are failing, first suspect permissions and next verify network connectivity to SQL Server.

- **Long-Term Storage**—Unless you'll be backing up directly to a long-term storage system, you need to plan for backing up the file share to tape or other media. Be sure you verify that the process for restoring data from tape to the file share is available for SharePoint Server 2013.

After you have prepared the target file share for backups, you need to decide what tool to use to perform farm backups. The following tools are available for performing farm backups:

- **Central Administration**—You cannot schedule a backup via Central Administration. Therefore, the primary use of Central Administration backups is to verify the configuration of the target backup location and to back up server farms before major operations.

- **Windows PowerShell**—The preferred way to schedule backups in SharePoint Server 2013 is by using Windows PowerShell. This method gives you the most options and will be fully supported in the future.

Using Central Administration for Farm Backup and Restores

Central Administration provides the easiest way to begin backing up and restoring SharePoint Server 2013. Regardless of the method or software you use, always verifying that you can perform a backup from Central Administration is a good idea. Doing so confirms all components in your farm can be successfully backed up and that your target device is properly prepared for backups. After a successful installation and configuration of SharePoint Server 2013, you should always perform a full farm backup.

Note

It always prudent to perform a full farm backup before any major farm configuration changes, such as creating and deleting a web or service application, applying cumulative updates, or upgrading to a new Service Pack.

Content and Configuration Backup

To access the Farm Backup and Restore section of Central Administration, either click Backup and Restore from the Quick Launch navigation bar or click Perform a Backup from the main screen (in the Backup and Restore area), as shown in Figure 14.2.

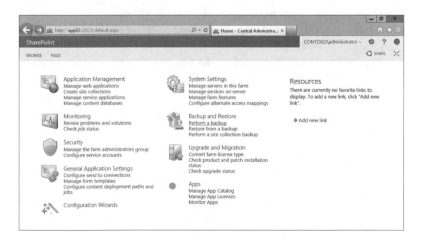

FIGURE 14.2
Click Perform a Backup to begin a full farm backup.

The first backup screen enables you to define what components of the farm you want to back up. You can select items individually or select the check box next to the Farm component, as shown in Figure 14.3.

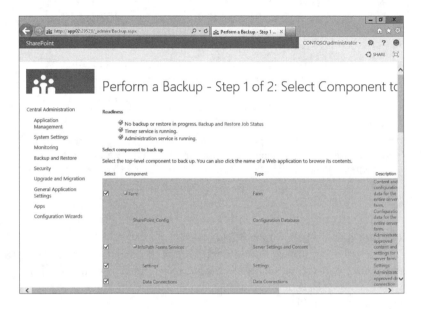

FIGURE 14.3
Select the Farm check box to select all components.

By selecting the Farm check box, you select all components in your farm. Your options will vary depending on the components you have installed, such as Excel Services and PerformancePoint.

After selecting all components, click Next. You will be presented with the second step in farm backups. You have two options when backing up the entire farm:

- **Back Up Content and Configuration Settings**—The default option is to back up content and configuration settings. This option backs up all content databases, service applications, and configuration data.

- **Back Up Only Configuration Settings**—Included in SharePoint Server 2013 is the capability to back up only the configuration settings, as shown in Figure 14.4.

This allows you to restore configuration to a different farm, which might be necessary when building a development server farm.

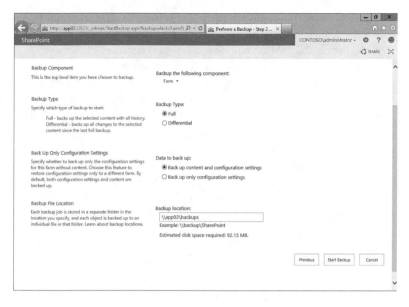

FIGURE 14.4
The default backup setting is selected. Select Back Up Only Configuration
Settings when restoring to a different farm.

Tip

A configuration-only backup can be used for development environments
where the content isn't important or constantly changing. This option
enables you to quickly recover the configuration content without restoring
the content. In the event of custom code crashing the development farm
because of modifications on the farm configuration, you can perform a
configuration-only restore using the same database names.

Last, enter the backup location that you have prepared. An estimated disk
space will be shown, but note that this calculation may underestimate the
actual amount of estimated space. It is best to have ample amounts of
available disk space and not rely on the estimator in this screen. After you
have entered your backup location, click Start Backup.

If you receive errors during your backup, refer to the Windows Event
Logs, the SharePoint Server 2013 trace logs, and the spbackup.log file if
available in the backup UNC path location. Be sure to verify permissions
on the file share in the event of an error. The vast majority of backup errors
are caused by insufficient permissions and network access.

You have the option to configure multiple file shares for backups, however, only a single file share per backup. In the root of the backup file share is an XML file named *spbrtoc.xml*. The filename is short for SharePoint Backup and Restore Table of Contents. It is essentially the catalog for all backups contained in the folder. Because it is unique, you should never have two SharePoint Server 2013 server farms using the same backup file location. You should always use a dedicated file share per server farm. The following is a sample Spbrtoc.xml file:

```
<?xml version="1.0" encoding="utf-8"?>
<SPBackupRestoreHistory>
    <SPHistoryObject>
        <SPId>36d9a605-a8ab-48c5-accf-
16255ad146ba</SPId>

<SPRequestedBy>CONTOSO\administrator</SPRequestedBy>
        <SPBackupMethod>Full</SPBackupMethod>
        <SPRestoreMethod>None</SPRestoreMethod>
        <SPStartTime>09/14/2012 11:21:32</SPStartTime>
        <SPFinishTime>09/14/2012 11:21:52</SPFinishTime>
        <SPIsBackup>True</SPIsBackup>

<SPConfigurationOnly>False</SPConfigurationOnly>
        <SPBackupDirectory>\\app02\backups\spbr0000\
</SPBackupDirectory>
        <SPDirectoryName>spbr0000</SPDirectoryName>
        <SPDirectoryNumber>0</SPDirectoryNumber>
        <SPTopComponent>Farm</SPTopComponent>
        <SPTopComponentId>6665802c-cf99-4128-
b1b7-a9bf509e3b9f</SPTopComponentId>
        <SPWarningCount>0</SPWarningCount>
        <SPErrorCount>0</SPErrorCount>
    </SPHistoryObject>
</SPBackupRestoreHistory>
```

Referencing spbrtoc.xml can quickly show an administrator what was included in the backup and details about the process itself, such as errors and warnings. There is not a way to trim backup history from the Spbrtoc.xml file. Although you can edit the file and remove content, doing so is unsupported. If you need to create a new Spbrtoc.xml file, you should unshare the directory, rename it, and create a new folder for backups. Then share the new folder with the original name, and SharePoint Server 2013 will successfully back up to it. Remember to apply any required permissions.

To further troubleshoot backups, you can open the directory of the backup in question, such as Spbr0002, as shown in the following example. Inside of a backup folder, you will see many .bak files, a log file, and a Spbackup.xml file. Useful for troubleshooting is the Spbackup.log file. Upon opening the log file, you'll see all components that were backed up and the corresponding .bak files they are stored in. This list can assist you if you have backup or restore problems.

Of particular interest are the lines that define the content database backup files. Using the earlier example, the following line is found within the Spbackup.log file:

```
@db_name=WSS_Content_CTHub,
@db_loc=\\app02\backups\spbr0002\000000DA.bak
```

From this line, you can see which .bak file contains the Content Type Hub used for your farm. In a worst-case scenario, you can use SQL Server tools to restore the content database and the site collections contained therein. Always use the Central Administration or command-line tools first. But if the Spbrtoc.xml and Spbr0002.xml files are missing or corrupt, the content databases can still be recovered. If you are unsure about restoring this content, contact Microsoft Support Services.

Content and Configuration Restore

Remember, you can restore only what you have backed up. If you select specific components when backing up SharePoint Server 2013, only those components will be available during restore. To begin a server farm restore, browse to Backup and Restore in Central Administration and click Backup and Restore; then click Restore from a Backup, as shown in Figure 14.5.

> **Note**
>
> Central Administration does not provide a way to back up directly to tape. You must first back up to a file share and then back up the file share to tape.

Additionally, you should always use a UNC path (see Figure 14.4); don't use a file system path, such as C:\.

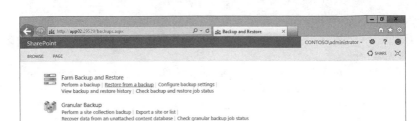

FIGURE 14.5
Click Restore from a Backup to restore content.

On the first of three Restore from Backup screens, you should see all the available backups in the defined Backup Directory Location. In the example shown in Figure 14.6, backups are stored in \\app02\backups. You can expand the backup to see further details, such as the user who began the backup and the error count.

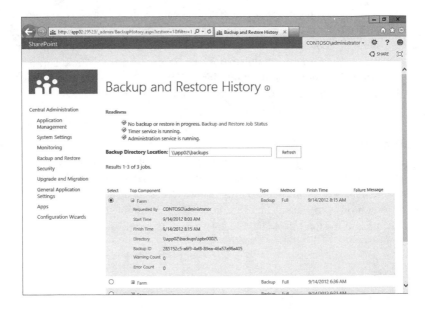

FIGURE 14.6
Expand Top Component to see details about the backup.

Restore from Previous Backup

To restore from a previous backup, perform the following steps:

1. Browse to Central Administration, Backup And Restore.

2. Click Restore from a Backup.

3. Enter the backup directory location and click Refresh.

4. Select the backup to restore from.

5. Click Next.

6. Select the farm component.

7. Click Next.

8. Choose the Restore Content and Configuration Settings option.

9. Optionally, select New Configuration to restore to a different database server or use different database names.

10. Select Same Configuration to overwrite existing content.

11. Enter the password for every application shown, as shown in Figure 14.7. It is not recommended to change the username on this configuration screen.

12. Click Start Restore.

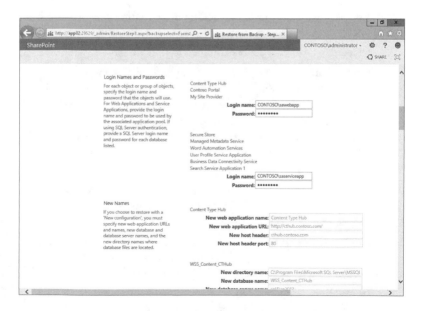

FIGURE 14.7
Enter the password for each application you are prompted about.

Farm Backup and Restore Using Windows PowerShell

Using Windows PowerShell, you can create custom scripts to back up your SharePoint Server 2013 server farm. This allows you to schedule backups during maintenance windows. Before performing the steps in this section, be sure you have prepared the backup location and performed at least one full backup using Central Administration.

Test Backup and Restores Using Windows PowerShell

Tobegin testing backup and restores using PowerShell, enter **Get-Help Backup-SPFarm** to see all farm backup options.

You can use get-help in front of any cmdlet to see the available options. To see detailed help options for any cmdlet, you can add the –detailed switch—for example, **Get-Help Backup-SPFarm –detailed**.

Back Up a Server Farm Using Windows PowerShell

To back up a server farm using Windows PowerShell, enter the following command:

```
Backup-SPFarm -directory \\app02\backups -
BackupMethod Full
```

Several options are available when backing up the farm using Windows PowerShell:

- **Directory**—Defines the backup location previously prepared.

- **BackupThreads**—A definite advantage to using Windows PowerShell for backing up SharePoint Server 2013 is the capability to increase the backup threads for processing. The default thread count is 3. Be sure to test increases in the thread count before implementing the change in a production environment. You can adversely affect the performance of both the SharePoint Server 2013 server farm and the destination storage location.

- **ShowTree**—Displays the objects in the farm that are available to be backed up. If you use this setting in conjunction with Item, it is scoped to the object underneath Item.

- **ConfigurationOnly**—Identical to the Central Administration option; backs up only the farm configuration data. No content will be backed up when you select ConfigurationOnly.

- **Item**—Backs up a farm component, such as a web application, content database, or service application. You cannot back up site collections, sites, list, libraries, or list items using the Item parameter.

- **Percentage**—Specifies the progress increments on the screen. If scripting, you do not need to use the Percentage option.

- **Force**—Bypasses the default behavior of halting the backup if the estimator calculates there is insufficient disk space.

- **Verbose**—Shows the progress of the backup. Otherwise, you won't be presented with current progress information.

- **WhatIf**—Displays the output of running the backup without actually performing the backup.

Restore a Server Farm

An alternative example might include the *-ConfigurationOnly* option, which captures all configuration information without including any content or service application databases. This can be done by entering the following command:

```
Backup-SPFarm -directory \\app02\backups -BackupMethod Full -
ConfigurationOnly
```

Windows PowerShell allows administrators to create backup scripts and execute these by using the Windows Server Task Scheduler. When using scripts to perform backups, the backups created by command-line tools can be restored using Central Administration.

Optionally, you could choose to restore farm components using Windows PowerShell. The command options look similar to the backup commands, but you must know the `BackupId` you want to restore. To find the `BackupId`, you run the following command:

```
Get-SPBackupHistory -Directory <Backup folder> -ShowBackup
[-Verbose]
```

If you have console access, you can also do the following to get the BackupId with additional information, if needed:

1. Open the Spbrtoc.xml in the directory containing your backups. Using the previous example, it would be \\app02\backups\ spbrtoc.xml.

2. Search for the relevant backup date, as shown in the following example.

3. Copy the SPId file. It is 36d9a605-a8ab-48c5-accf-16255ad146ba in the example.

```
<SPHistoryObject>
```

```
        <SPId>36d9a605-a8ab-48c5-accf-
16255ad146ba</SPId>

<SPRequestedBy>CONTOSO\administrator</SPRequestedBy>
    <SPBackupMethod>Full</SPBackupMethod>
    <SPRestoreMethod>None</SPRestoreMethod>
    <SPStartTime>09/14/2012 11:21:32</SPStartTime>
    <SPFinishTime>09/14/2012 11:21:52</SPFinishTime>
    <SPIsBackup>True</SPIsBackup>

<SPConfigurationOnly>False</SPConfigurationOnly>

<SPBackupDirectory>\\app02\backups\spbr0000\
</SPBackupDirectory>
        <SPDirectoryName>spbr0000</SPDirectoryName>
        <SPDirectoryNumber>0</SPDirectoryNumber>
        <SPTopComponent>Farm</SPTopComponent>
        <SPTopComponentId>6665802c-cf99-4128-b1b7-
a9bf509e3b9f</SPTopComponentId>
        <SPWarningCount>0</SPWarningCount>
        <SPErrorCount>0</SPErrorCount>
    </SPHistoryObject>
```

Using the example of APP02 as the backup file server, *Backups* as the share name, and the previously found *BackupId*, execute the following command for a full farm restore:

```
Restore-SPFarm -Directory \\app02\backups -BackupId 36d9a605-
a8ab-48c5-accf-16255ad146ba
```

There are several options when executing the Restore-SPFarm cmdlet:

- **Directory**—Specifies the path to the SharePoint Server 2013 backup location you want to restore from. There must be a valid spbrtoc.xml file in the root of the backup directory.

- **RestoreMethod**—You must choose either New or Overwrite. The New Option restores the selected backup components and configuration using either new database names, a new SQL Server instance, or both. Overwrite is the same option displayed in Central Administration as Same. Using the Overwrite option restores your content and configuration to the same names.

- **BackupId**—The unique backup ID you want to restore from.

- **ConfigurationOnly**—Restores only the farm configuration data, and no content.

- **Confirm**—Requires you to confirm the backup by typing **Y**.

- **FarmCredentials**—You must supply the farm credentials when restoring content and configuration data.

- **Force**—If you change content, as is the case when using overwrite, using force suppresses the prompt for confirmation. This is common when using remote command-line tools for restoring content.

- **Item**—Indicates the part of the backup you want to restore. For example, if you have performed a full farm backup, you might choose to only restore a web application or content database. An item name can be seen in the backup log files or by using the –showtree option.

- **NewDatabaseServer**—If you want to restore to an alternative database server, you can specify that during the restore process.

- **Percentage**—Specifies the progress increments on the screen. Percentage complete is shown only when you use the Verbose option.

- **RestoreThreads**—The default number of process threads is 3. This can be increased to 10 or decreased to 1.

- **WhatIf**—Displays the effect of a command without running an actual restore process.

- **Verbose**—Displays the output of a command.

Be sure to monitor the restore process. When restoring web applications and some service applications, you might be prompted for the application pool password. If this occurs, the restore process pauses until you enter credentials. Although you can change the usernames of these during the restore, doing so is not recommended unless there is no other option.

Automating SharePoint Products and Technologies Backups

SharePoint Server 2013 does not provide an automated method to back up your content and configuration. You can schedule backups using a combination of Windows Server 2012 task scheduling and command-line tools.

Automate SharePoint Backups

Using Windows PowerShell, perform the following steps:

1. Create a batch file containing a tested command-line backup string, as shown previously.

2. Open Task Scheduler from the Administrative Tools program group.

3. From the Action menu, click Create Task.

4. Click New on the Actions tab and browse to choose the batch file you created in step 1.

5. Name the Task; for example, **SharePoint Server Backup**, on the General tab.

6. Click New on the Triggers tab to configure the frequency, usually Daily.

7. Select the start time. Be careful not to set this to overlap with content Indexing or other scheduled system maintenance.

8. Configure the credentials required to execute the scheduled task on the General tab. This user must have write access to the backup share destination and be a farm administrator.

9. Click OK.

Service and Web Application Backup and Restore

If you need to back up service and web applications independently of the entire farm, you can do so using Windows PowerShell. You can also restore individual items, such as a service application, from a full farm backup without restoring the entire backup. This is useful in restoring functionality such as Search or the Secure Store.

Caution

You must back up the Secure Store whenever you change or refresh the master key. The database is encrypted using the master key, and thus older Secure Store backups will not successfully restore.

To back up a service or web application, use the –item option of the Restore-SPFarm Windows PowerShell cmdlet. To get the exact name of the item you want to back up, use the Backup-SPFarm –showtree command. Figure 14.8 shows an example of the output of the –showtree command.

FIGURE 14.8
Example of Backup-SPFarm –showtree command.

From the output, you can see items such as Secure Store and Search
Service. When backing up individual applications, you'll generally back up
the entire service, and not a subcomponent such as a database. But if you
are restoring a subcomponent, such as a Secure Store database, you might
restore only what is required. Restoring the minimal set of content reduces
the possibility that you are overwriting new content that has been added
since the last backup. Using the previous example's server names and
BackupId, the following command restores the Secure Store. Note that the
Secure Store is named Secure Store:

```
Restore-SPFarm -directory \\app02\backups
-backupid 36d9a605-a8ab-48c5-accf-16255ad146ba -item
"Farm\Shared Services\Shared Services Applications\Secure
Store"
```

If you also need to restore the Secure Store Proxy, run the following
command next:

```
Restore-SPFarm -directory \\app02\backups -backupid 36d9a605-
a8ab-48c5-accf-16255ad146ba -item "Farm\Shared Services\Shared
Services Proxies\Secure Store"
```

> **Note**
>
> You can restore individual components from a full farm backup. You do
> not need to back up each component individually to restore a single
> component.

Granular Backup and Restore

There are many times when administering SharePoint Server 2013 servers
that you need to back up and restore only site collections, sites, and lists.
In addition to restoring from granular backups, you also have the option of
restoring site collections, sites, and lists from unattached content databases.
The following granular backup and restore options are available in
SharePoint Server 2013:

- Site Collections
- Sites, Lists, and Libraries

Site Collections

If you need to back up a single site collection, you can use Central
Administration or Windows PowerShell. But you can only restore a site
collection using Windows PowerShell.

Site collection backups are full fidelity. The backup will contain all
content, users, permissions, workflows, alerts, settings, and the Recycle
Bin. Be aware that restoring a site collection to a farm in a different Active
Directory domain might produce suboptimal results with regard to permissions. The Active Directory Security ID (SID) for objects will be
orphaned. If you restore to another Active Directory domain, be prepared
to associate users in the new domain with accounts referenced in the old
domain.

Back Up a Site Collection Using Central Administration

To back up a site collection using Central Administration, perform the
following steps:

1. Open Central Administration.

2. Browse to the Backup and Restore page.

3. From the Granular Backup grouping, click Perform a Site Collection
   Backup.

4. Select a site collection from the drop-down menu. Note that it might appear to be a web application listed, but it is actually the root site collection in the web application. Always verify you are working with the correct site collection.

5. Click Start Backup.

6. Monitor the backup progress, as shown in Figure 14.9.

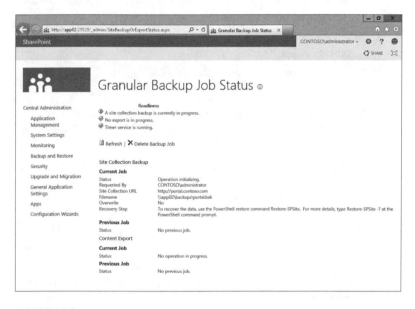

FIGURE 14.9
Backup status can be seen after the backup begins.

> **Note**
>
> There is not a Central Administration interface to restore site collections.

Back Up a Site Collection Using Windows PowerShell

If you are remotely managing a server or building backup scripts for site collections, you can use Windows PowerShell for the task. Windows PowerShell automatically locks the site collection during backup to reduce the risk of SQL blocking and locking errors. If you need to perform site collection backups during business hours, consider using a SQL snapshot to back up the data. **Enter Get-Help Backup-SPSite** to see all site backup options. You can use Get-Help in front of any cmdlet to see the available options. To see detailed help options for any cmdlet, you can add the –detailed switch—for example, **Get-Help Backup-SPSite –detailed**.

The following options are available when backing up a site collection via Windows PowerShell:

- **Identity**—Specifies the URL or GUID of the site collection to back up—for example, http://portal.contoso.com/sites/HR.

- **Path**—Specifies the full backup path, including the filename. An example is \\app02\backups\portal.bak.

- **Confirm**—Requires you to confirm the backup by typing **Y**.

- **Force**—Overwrites an existing file.

- **NoSiteLock**—Backs up the site collection without making it read-only. Be aware that large site collection backups often fail without a site lock.

- **UseSqlSnapshot**—If you need to back up site collections during the day and require users to continue full read/write operations, you'll need to create a SQL snapshot to back up from. Using this option creates a temporary SQL Server database snapshot. After the snapshot is created, the backup will be from the snapshot, not the live database. This is the best method to get a full fidelity site collection backup.

- **WhatIf**—Shows the effects of a command without performing the actual backup.

To back up a site collection via Windows PowerShell, do the following:

1. Open the SharePoint 2013 Management Shell.

2. Decide what options you'll use for the backup, such as SQL Snapshots.

3. Enter **Backup-SPSite -identity http://WebApp/sites/SiteCollection -path \\app02\backups\SiteCollection.bak**. Be sure to include any options you require from the previous list. When you restore a site collection with Windows PowerShell, using the Restore-SPSite cmdlet, you have several options:

   - **Identity**—Specifies the URL where the site collection will be restored.

- **Path**—Specifies the full location of the backup file, such as \\app02\backups\portal.bak.

- **Confirm**—Requires confirmation before continuing the procedure.

- **ContentDatabase**—Specifies the content database the site collection will be restored to. If None is selected, the content database with the greatest remaining capacity will be used.

- **GradualDelete**—If there is a site collection at the location specified by identity, you must use the *Force* option to overwrite. Use of the *Force* option commits the site being overwritten to the Gradual Delete timer job.

- **WhatIf**—If overwriting an existing site collection, you can perform a gradual delete that will be executed by a timer job. This will reduce the impact to the server farm during restoration. Figure 14.10 shows how the timer job will display in Central Administration, Running Jobs.

FIGURE 14.10
During the gradual delete, you will see an Application Server Timer Job option.

Restore a Site Collection Using PowerShell

To restore a site collection using Windows PowerShell, perform the following steps:

1. Open the SharePoint 2013 Management Shell.

2. Enter **Restore-SPSite -identity http://portal.contoso.com/ -path \\app02\backups\portal.bak**, inserting your URL and backup file location. Be sure to include any options, such as force and gradual delete.

3. Verify the site collection has restored. If you are using gradual delete, you need to wait until the timer job completes before verifying a successful restore.

Sites, Lists, and Libraries

You can also use Central Administration or PowerShell to export a SharePoint site, list, or library. As with site collections, however, you cannot use Central Administration to import a site, list, or library.

Export a Site, List, or Library Using Central Administration

To back up a site collection using Central Administration, perform the following steps:

1. Open Central Administration.

2. Browse to the Backup and Restore page.

3. From the Granular Backup grouping, click Export a Site or a List.

4. Select a Site Collection from the drop-down menu.

5. Select a Site; more specifically, you can also choose a list or library within this site

6. Click Start Export.

Export a Site Using Windows PowerShell

You can use Window PowerShell to export a SharePoint site. This task must be completed by using the *Export-SPWeb* cmdlet. To accomplish this, perform the following steps:

1. Open the SharePoint 2013 Management Shell.

2. Enter **Export-SPWeb -identity http://portal.contoso.com/products/ -path \\app02\backups\products.bak**.

3. Verify that the appropriate backup file has been created.

Export a List or Library Using Windows PowerShell

When exporting a list or library, you will also use the Export-SPWeb cmdlet; however, you will also include the ItemURL parameter using the following as an example:

```
Export-SPWeb -identity http://portal.contoso.com/products/ -
ItemURL /products/Shared Documents/ -path
\\app02\Backups\ProductDocuments.bak
```

Import a Site, List, or Library Using Windows PowerShell

When importing a site, list, or library with Windows PowerShell, you use the Import-SPWeb cmdlet. Perform the following steps:

1. Open the SharePoint 2013 Management Shell.

2. Enter **Import-SPWeb -identity http://portal.contoso.com/site/ - path \\app02\backups\portal.bak**, inserting your URL and backup file location. Be sure to include any options, such as force and gradual delete.

3. Verify that the site, list, or library has been restored.

Recovering from an Unattached Content Database

Included in SharePoint Server 2013 is the capability to restore directly from an unattached content database. Unattached does not mean unattached in SQL Server. An unattached database in Central Administration refers to a database that isn't associated with a web application.

This allows for the restoration of site collections directly from SQL Server.

Restore from an Unattached Content Database

To restore from an unattached content database, perform the following steps:

1. Restore the content database that hosts the site collection to be restored.

2. From Central Administration, Backup and Restore, click Recover Data from an Unattached Content Database, as shown in Figure 14.11.

3. Enter the database server and database name.

4. Select Backup Site Collection.

5. Click Next.

FIGURE 14.11
Click Recover Data from an Unattached Content Database.

6. Select the site collection you want to back up.

7. Click Next.

8. Enter the full backup location, including the filename.

9. Click Start Backup.

The interface can be confusing because site collections appear to be under Central Administration. They are not. They should appear in the same relative URL as before, prefixed by the Central Administration URL. This is normal.

CHAPTER 15

Managing Apps and Solutions

- Managing Apps
- Installing and Configuring Web Parts
- Installing and Configuring Features
- Managing Solutions

This chapter covers the interrelated topics of SharePoint Apps, web parts, features, and solutions. Apps have been introduced with SharePoint Server 2013 and provide a new way to integrate web application functionality into your SharePoint environment. In addition to apps, *web parts* continue to be one of the simplest ways of customizing Microsoft SharePoint Server 2013. Web parts are reusable controls that allow users to create pages that solve business problems using only the browser. *Features* are SharePoint Server 2013–specific programming artifacts that work as the control panel for a host of functions. Features have low-level data access within SharePoint Server 2013 to configure the environment as well as copy and provision lists and libraries. They are critical for controlling the deployment and the functionality of SharePoint Server 2013. *Solutions* are the only supported method for deploying fully trusted developer artifacts consistently to multiple servers in a farm. SharePoint apps and solutions, combined with features, provide a mechanism for extending SharePoint Server 2013 functionality to meet changing requirements.

Managing Apps

SharePoint Apps are standalone and isolated functionality that loosely integrate into a SharePoint site. The management of app installations and deployments are managed within a specialized site collection called the App Catalog.

The following sections provide a high-level detail of the app storage model and the supporting SharePoint services that are required to support the apps capabilities.

Cloud App Model

SharePoint Server 2013 brings with it the introduction of the Cloud App Model to enable developers to create apps that can be deployed to your environment. Apps are a new method to deliver functionality to SharePoint through small modular code that can solve specific business needs using familiar programming models. The app model supports a tiered architecture where business logic, data, and the user interface (UI) can be separated into tiers using a variety of different programming languages such as HTML, JavaScript, PHP, or .NET.

This new model provides developers the capability to create apps that integrate into SharePoint leveraging a UI based on HTML and JavaScript, presenting the logic through .NET, and using data hosted within SQL Azure. Apps do not replace the functionality of features and solutions within SharePoint because apps don't have access to the low-level API interfaces that full-trust solutions do. Apps are intended to bring functionality from the Web into SharePoint and to overcome the limitations of using Sandboxed Solutions by providing a rich web application experience without affecting the underlying infrastructure of the SharePoint environment.

Service Applications

The SharePoint Cloud App Model requires the App Management Service, Subscription Settings Service, and Search Service to be configured within your SharePoint environment in order to function properly. The following sections detail the required service applications and the primary configuration steps for each.

App Management Service

The App Management Service is required within your environment in order to be able to use SharePoint Apps. The App Management Service stores and provides information relating to the licenses and permissions for an app. Licenses downloaded from the SharePoint Store or stored within your organization's App Catalog are managed within the App Management Service and accessed each time an app is requested within your environment. Since the App Management Service is necessary to validate the current license status, it would be a performance hit to route all traffic for all apps within the environment through the App Management Service. To increase performance and avoid unnecessary traffic validating the licenses each time an app is accessed, SharePoint provides a caching process for the license data within the web front-end servers of the environment. To cache the license data, the first time a user accesses an app, data traffic flows from the web server to the application server running the App Management Service, where the service validates the current license for the app. When the web front end receives the license data from the App Management Service, it will also receive and maintain a pointer to the location within the service database within SQL Server where the current license state is located. From this point, every time the app is accessed from the web front end (WFE), the WFE accesses the license data directly within SQL Server using the cached data location and validates the license for the app. By allowing the license data location within SQL Server to be cached on the WFE, it is no longer necessary to route all app traffic through the App Management Service, thus reducing the data load on the app server running the service.

Subscription Settings Service

The Subscription Settings Service is required within the environment to provide the tenancy configuration that is necessary for apps within SharePoint to function. As part of the SharePoint App architecture, apps are required to be within a tenancy scope to exist. The Subscription Settings Service is responsible for providing the unique subscription IDs that define a tenancy within your environment. Without the Subscription Settings Service, no tenancies will exist. In a typical on-premises farm implementation, the use of tenancies is not required because the SharePoint farm will be isolated within the organization. By creating an instance of the Subscription Settings Service within your environment, this creates the default tenant for your SharePoint Farm and allows for the use of the App Catalog. The creation of the service must be performed through PowerShell because there is no option to create the Subscription Settings Service through Central Administration.

Configure the Subscription Settings Service and App Management Services Within Your Environment Using PowerShell

To configure the Subscription Settings Service and App Management Services within your environment using PowerShell, perform the following steps:

1. Verify that you have the following memberships:

   - securityadmin fixed server role on the SQL Server instance
   - db_owner fixed database role on all databases that are to be updated
   - Administrators group on the server where you will execute the PowerShell cmdlets

2. Open the SharePoint 2013 Management Shell.

3. Enter the following commands to start the App Management and Subscription Settings Services:

```
Get-SPServiceInstance ¦ where {$_.GetType().Name -eq
"AppManagementServiceInstance"
-or $_.GetType().Name -eq
"SPSubscriptionSettingsServiceInstance"} ¦ Start-
SPServiceInstance
```

4. Enter each of the following commands to create the app pools necessary for the services:

```
$farmAcct = Get-SPManagedAccount "<farm account>"
$appPoolSubSetSvc = New-SPServiceApplicationPool -Name
SettingsServiceAppPool -Account farmAcct
$appPoolAppMgmtSvc = New-SPServiceApplicationPool -Name
AppServiceAppPool -Account $farmAcct
```

Where:

   - *<farm account>* is the name of the Farm administrators account in the SharePoint farm.

5. Enter the following commands to create the service app instances and the service app proxies:

```
$appSubSetSvc = New-
SPSubscriptionSettingsServiceApplication –ApplicationPool
$appPoolSubSetSvc –Name SettingsServiceApp –DatabaseName
<SubSetServiceDB>
$proxySubSetSvc = New-
SPSubscriptionSettingsServiceApplicationProxy
```

```
-ServiceApplication $appSubSetSvc
$appMgmtSvc = New-SPAppManagementServiceApplication -
ApplicationPool $appPoolAppMgmtSvc -Name AppServiceApp -
DatabaseName
<AppMgmtServiceDB>
$proxyAppMgmtSvc = New-
SPAppManagementServiceApplicationProxy -
ServiceApplication $ appMgmtSvc
```

Where:

- <SubSetServiceDB> is the name of the Subscription Settings service database.
- <AppMgmtServiceDB> is the name of the App Management service database.

Search Service

The SharePoint Search Service is required within the environment in order to use the monitoring capabilities of the SharePoint App Model.

Note

For complete provisioning and configuration of the SharePoint Search Service, refer to Chapter 10, "Enterprise Search."

SharePoint Store

The SharePoint Server 2013 App Model includes the addition of the SharePoint Store where Farm Administrators and end users can search, download, and install apps into their organization's SharePoint App Catalog. For apps that were added to the environment from the SharePoint Store, the App Management Service will manage the license data for the app and provide license validation each time the app is used.

App Catalog

In addition to the SharePoint Store, organizations can upload in-house developed apps or apps that were developed and downloaded outside of the SharePoint Store to the organization's App Catalog.

The App Catalog is a special Site Collection within your organization that can be used to store and provide trusted apps for SharePoint and Office.

You can have multiple App Catalogs within your farm, such as one for each web application. The App Catalog is created by a farm administrator through Central Administration and provides an isolated Site Collection within the environment to host the apps. Figure 15.1 is an example of an App Catalog for a SharePoint Server 2013 site.

FIGURE 15.1
Site App Catalog.

The configuration of the App Catalog within your environment requires the addition of an App Catalog administrator. This administrator can determine whether users are able to add apps from the SharePoint Store or whether the addition of apps is restricted to select approved apps. If users are restricted from directly purchasing, downloading, and deploying SharePoint Store apps to their environments, the App Catalog provides the capability to request the addition of an app to the organization's App Catalog. After the user request is made for an app, the App Catalog administrator will review the request and either approve or deny the request. If approved, the requested app will be downloaded from the SharePoint Store where it will then be available for addition to sites within web applications associated with the instance of the App Catalog.

App Isolation

One of the greatest features of the SharePoint App architecture from an IT administrator's perspective is the isolation that is provided to the app from the underlying infrastructure of your organization's SharePoint environment. By isolating the executing business processes of an App, farm administrators have much tighter control of their environments and reduce the overall risk of deploying custom solutions within their environments. This reduced risk not only increases the stability of the environment as a whole, but it reduces the ongoing operating cost and maintenance time for the farm.

Hosting Options

The robustness and isolationist architecture of the SharePoint App Model provides three hosting models for deploying an app within your environment: provider hosted, Windows Azure hosted, and hosted by SharePoint.

Provider-hosted apps is a hosting option where the app and all its resources are hosted on a system within the organization's environment. This hosting architecture allows for a system that contains sensitive or proprietary data to remain secure and within the control and management of the organization yet integrated into your SharePoint environment. A good example is the integration of a payroll or HR system into SharePoint. The data within the external system is highly sensitive but protected with an app used to surface this sensitive data within SharePoint.

SharePoint-hosted apps run within your SharePoint environment and are installed on a website called the Host Web. All resources for the hosted apps reside on an isolated website called the App Web. This site structure allows for the use of SharePoint artifacts such as lists and libraries while providing the isolation necessary to maintain the infrastructure integrity. Access to SharePoint objects such as Lists, Libraries, and Web Parts is provided only through HTML and client-side JavaScript calls with no execution of server-side code allowed.

Windows Azure–hosted apps offer a hosting option that is available only from within an Office 365 environment. Using this hosting option for your solution, apps are hosted within the cloud Azure environment and components for the app are provisioned as necessary when the app is installed. This allows for the isolation of the app from your SharePoint environment but will maintain the full cloud advantage of not having to maintain the app's environment. Another major benefit to this option is that when the app is provisioned, the app is created in what is essentially a scaled-down version of the Windows Azure websites, which will automatically handle any load-balancing, multitenancy, and additional important maintenance tasks for you. The downside to this implementation is that each time an app is provisioned with this hosting option, a new website within the Azure environment is created.

Using Apps

To use a SharePoint app within your environment, it must be available within the App Catalog of the farm. The process for adding apps to the App Catalog is straightforward and will need to be completed before end users are able to deploy the app within their sites. The following sections detail the installation and configuration process for SharePoint apps.

Installing Apps

Installing SharePoint apps to your environment, and provisioning these apps within SharePoint sites is a simple process. As mentioned earlier, SharePoint apps can either be downloaded from the SharePoint Store or added by a system administrator to your organization's App Catalog. Installing directly from the SharePoint Store can be an easy way to provide your users with virtually limitless options for their environments while maintaining stability and security within your infrastructure.

Install a SharePoint App from the SharePoint Store to Your Organization's App Catalog

To install a SharePoint app from the SharePoint Store to your organization's App Catalog, perform the following steps:

1. Verify that the current user is a member of the farm administrator's group.

2. In Central Administration, navigate to the Apps section.

3. In the Apps section, click the Purchase Apps link, as shown in Figure 15.2.

4. Within the SharePoint Store, search for and select the app to install.

5. In the App Details page, click Add It to add the app.

6. From the App Install confirmation page, click Return to Site.

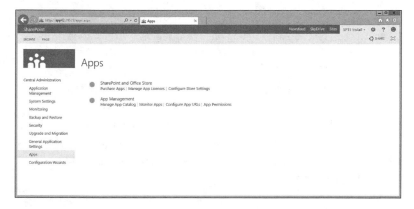

FIGURE 15.2
Central Administration Apps page.

Request a SharePoint App to Your Organization's App Catalog

To request a SharePoint app to your organization's App Catalog, perform the following steps:

1. Verify that the current user is a member of the current site.
2. In your site, select the Settings menu and click the Add an App menu item.
3. Select the SharePoint Store item from the left navigation.
4. Within the SharePoint Store, search for and select the app to install within your organization.
5. In the App Details page, click Request It to add the app.
6. In the App Request dialog box, enter the number of licenses requested and the proper justification for the app purchase; then click Request.

Upload and Install a Custom-Developed SharePoint App to Your Organization's App Catalog

To upload and install a custom-developed SharePoint app to your organization's App Catalog, perform the following steps:

1. Verify that the current user is a member of the farm administrator's group.
2. In Central Administration, navigate to the Apps section.

3. In the Apps section, click the Manage App Catalog link.

4. In the Manage App Catalog page, use the Web Application drop-down to select the appropriate web app; then click the Site URL to navigate to the App Catalog.

5. Within the left navigation, click the Apps for SharePoint link to view a listing of the current apps within the App Catalog.

6. Click the New Item link to display the document upload dialog box.

7. Click the Browse button and locate the .app file to upload to the App Catalog, select the file, and then click Open. Then click OK within the dialog box.

8. In the Apps for SharePoint dialog box, complete the relevant information and click the Save button within the ribbon.

Install a SharePoint App Within Your Environment Using PowerShell
To install a SharePoint app within your environment using PowerShell, perform the following steps:

1. Verify that the current user is a member of the farm administrator's group.

2. Execute the following commands within the SharePoint Management PowerShell console:

```
$spapp = Import-SPAppPackage -Path "<AppPath>" -Site
<Web> -Source <SourceApp>
$app = Install-SPApp -Web <Web>  -Identity $spapp
```

Where:

■ <AppPath> is the full physical path to the .app source file.

■ <Web> is an SPWeb object to which the app will be installed.

■ <SourceApp> is a designation of which type of app is being installed.

Note

The following Technet article describes the different source app types: http://msdn.microsoft.com/en-us/library/microsoft.sharepoint. administration.spappsource(v=office.15).aspx

---

Upgrading Apps

As with any continuously enhanced application, SharePoint Apps are upgraded by their developers to provide additional functionality or resolution to outstanding issues. When an app is upgraded within your environment, there are two options for how to roll out the upgrades to the end users. Farm administrators can roll out the upgrade to all instances of the app within the environment, or they can allow the users to decide on their own whether to install the upgrade for their individual app instances.

To upgrade an app within the App Catalog, have the farm administrator upload the new version of the app to the App Catalog using the same procedure as listed in the previous section on installing a custom-developed SharePoint App to your organization's App Catalog.

Upgrade an App Within Your Site with the User Interface

To upgrade an app within your site with the user interface, perform the following steps:

1. Verify that the current user is a site owner for the current site.

2. In your site, select the Settings menu and click the View Site Contents menu item.

3. In the Site Contents page, hover over the app you want to upgrade, click the ellipses (...) within the pop-up dialog box, and then click the About link.

4. The App Details page will contain a message notifying you that a new version of the app is available. Click the Get It button and then select Trust It in the app authorization dialog box.

Upgrade an App Within Your SharePoint Farm Using PowerShell

To upgrade an app within your SharePoint farm using PowerShell, perform the following steps:

1. Verify that the current user is a member of the farm administrator's group.

2. Execute the following commands within the SharePoint Management PowerShell console:

```
$spapp = Import-SPAppPackage -Path "<AppPath>" -Site
<Web> -Source <SourceApp>
$appInstance = Get-SPAppInstance -Web $Web ¦ where-object
{$_.Title -eq "<AppName>"};
```

```
$app = Update-SPAppInstance -Identity $appInstance -App
$spapp
```

Where:

- <AppPath> is the full physical path to the .app source file.
- <Web> is an SPWeb object that contains the app to be upgraded.
- <SourceApp> is a designation of which type of app is being updated.
- <AppName> is the user friendly name for the app.

Note

See the following Technet article describing the different source app types: http://msdn.microsoft.com/en-us/library/microsoft.sharepoint. administration.spappsource(v=office.15).aspx.

Uninstalling Apps

In certain instances, there can be issues where a SharePoint app is to be uninstalled from your organization's environment. Uninstalling an app from SharePoint completely removes installed artifacts associated with the app to provide a clean environment. For example, if an app includes a page to display list data, that page is removed during the uninstall process; however, the list and its data remain because the list was built using SharePoint resources. If the installed app includes an App Web within the site, that App Web is deleted. This process provides a cleaner and more robust implementation than simply deactivating and removing features that were installed as part of the app.

Uninstall an App from Within Your Environment

To uninstall an app from within your environment, perform the following steps:

1. Verify that the current user is a member of the farm administrator's group.
2. In Central Administration, navigate to the Apps section.
3. In the Apps section, click the Manage App Catalog link.

4. In the Manage App Catalog page, use the Web Application drop-down menu to select the appropriate web app. Then click the Site URL to navigate to the App Catalog.

5. Within the left navigation, click the Apps for SharePoint link to view a listing of the current apps within the App Catalog.

6. Select the app within the app listing that should be deleted. Click the Delete button within the Files tab of the ribbon.

Uninstall a SharePoint App from Your Environment Using PowerShell

To uninstall a SharePoint App from your environment using PowerShell, perform the following steps:

1. Verify that the current user is a member of the farm administrator group.

2. Execute the following commands within the SharePoint Management PowerShell console:

```
$appInstance = Get-SPAppInstance -Web <Web> | where-
object {$_.Title -eq "<AppName>"};
$app = Uninstall-SPAppInstance -Identity $appInstance
```

Where:

- <Web> is an SPWeb object that contains the app to be uninstalled.

- <AppName> is the user friendly name for the app.

Uninstall an App Within Your Site with the User Interface

To uninstall an app within your site with the user interface, perform the following steps:

1. Verify that the current user is a site owner for the current site.

2. In your site, select the Settings menu and click the View Site Contents menu item.

3. In the Site Contents page, hover the app you want to uninstall, click the ellipses (...) within the pop-up dialog box, and then click the Remove link. Click OK within the confirmation dialog box to remove the app.

Managing Licenses

The App Model of SharePoint Server 2013 includes licensing capabilities for individual apps that are acquired through the SharePoint Store. As either farm administrators or end users purchase apps through the SharePoint Store, it is important to note that SharePoint Server 2013 will only maintain and provide access to the license data for apps within your environment; it doesn't enforce licensing agreements for individual apps. It is the responsibility of the individual app developers to retrieve the current license data and appropriately notify users in the event that there are license discrepancies. Because of this designed licensing model, SharePoint Server 2013 provides the capability to either recover or remove the license for an app within the environment's App Catalog. Additionally, farm administrators can add managers to an app license, which will allow the admins to delegate the management of an app to other individuals within the organization. To manage the app licenses, perform the following steps:

Remove an App License

1. Verify that the current user is a member of the farm administrator's group.
2. In Central Administration, navigate to the Apps section.
3. In the Apps section, click the Manage Apps Licenses link.
4. On the App Licenses page, within the listing of apps, click the linked title for an app.
5. On the Manage App License page, click the Actions drop-down menu, click the Remove This License link, and then click OK within the confirmation dialog box.

Recover an App License

1. Verify that the current user is a member of the farm administrator's group.
2. In Central Administration, navigate to the Apps section.
3. In the Apps section, click the Manage Apps Licenses link.
4. On the App Licenses page, within the listing of apps, click the linked title for an app.
5. On the Manage App License page, click the Actions drop-down menu, click the Recover License link, and then click OK within the confirmation dialog box to navigate to the SharePoint Store page for this app.

6. On the SharePoint Store page for this app, click the More Actions drop-down menu and click the Recover License link.

Add Managers to an App

1. Verify that the current user is a member of the farm administrator's group.
2. In Central Administration, navigate to the Apps section.
3. In the Apps section, click the Manage Apps Licenses link.
4. On the App Licenses page, within the listing of apps, click the linked title for an app.
5. On the Manage App License page, click the Add Manager link to display a people picker control.
6. Enter the account name or email address for the new app managers into the people picker control, and then click Add Manager.

Monitoring Apps

SharePoint apps can be monitored by farm administrators through Central Administration and by site owners within their site. It's possible that, within a large environment, the elements of certain apps may need to be monitored. To do so, the app must be added to the Monitor Apps list. Farm administrators have an advanced level of capabilities to add apps to the listing of apps to be monitored, as well as view the error and usage data for apps within the farm. Site owners are limited to only viewing the error and usage data of apps within their site. To view the app monitoring details, perform the following steps:

Configure an App for Monitoring in Central Administration

1. Verify that the current user is a member of the farm administrator's group.
2. In Central Administration, navigate to the Apps section.
3. In the Apps section, click the Monitor Apps link.
4. In the Monitored Apps page, click the Add App button within the ribbon.
5. In the Add an App to Monitor dialog box, select the app to monitor or use the search box to refine the listing of apps available for monitoring; then click Add.

View App Usage in Central Administration

1. Verify that the current user is a member of the farm administrator's group.

2. In Central Administration, navigate to the Apps section.

3. In the Apps section, click the Monitor Apps link.

4. Within the listing of monitored apps, either check the box next to the app and click the View Details button in the App Details group in the ribbon or click the linked app title within the list.

5. Within the app details page, view the Usage details for the app at the bottom of the page.

View App Errors in Central Administration

1. Verify that the current user is a member of the farm administrator's group.

2. In Central Administration, navigate to the Apps section.

3. In the Apps section, click the Monitor Apps link.

4. Within the listing of monitored apps, either check the box next to the app and click the View Errors button within the App Details group in the ribbon or click the linked Runtime Errors (past 72 hours) link within the list for the app.

View App Details in Site

1. Verify that the current user is a Site Owner for the current site.

2. From the Settings drop-down menu of the site, click the View Site Contents link.

3. In the Site Contents page, locate the app that you would like to see usage data on. While hovering over the app, click the ellipse (...) in the upper right of the app title box to view the app menu.

4. Click the Monitor link within the app menu to display the App Details page for the app.

5. View the usage graph for the app located at the bottom of the App Details page.

Installing and Configuring Web Parts

Web parts are modular, reusable pieces of code that allow users to modify their appearance, content, and behavior. For example, users might modify the appearance of a web part by adjusting its height and width. Content might be modified for a web part that displays a table of data by selecting which columns are displayed and in what order. As an example of modifying behavior, a web part could display either a summary or details of certain information. The web part might switch between listing every invoice for every salesperson invoiced for the past 90 days or simply listing a total dollar amount for each salesperson. Web parts are the building blocks for SharePoint Server 2013 web user interface interactions.

Web parts are broadly scoped; they serve as windows in SharePoint Server 2013 to the broader world of IT. They are windows into external data sources, such as Microsoft SQL Server or Oracle databases. Additionally, they allow a glimpse into web services, or they can integrate with business applications. Fundamentally, they serve as windows into SharePoint Server 2013 by allowing interaction with information stored in lists and libraries. Finally, web parts are windows into the users of SharePoint Server 2013. They provide a mechanism for interacting with and empowering users to solve business problems.

Web Part Architecture

Two types of files are associated with web parts: an assembly and an XML file. All web parts require a binary assembly and a dynamic-link library (DLL), which contains the code that the web part executes. The XML file registers the assembly, telling SharePoint Server 2013 that the web part exists and indicating what assembly it uses, and it sets the properties that control how the web part behaves. Web parts have to be deployed using either full-trust or sandboxed solutions.

SharePoint Server 2013 ships with a variety of useful web parts that can be configured to accomplish any number of tasks. Custom web parts, either ones that are purchased or web parts created in-house, will be deployed via solution packages. Deployment does not add the web parts to any pages—it simply puts the web parts' required resources in place on the farm servers so that they can be added to pages.

For a web part to appear as an option to be added to a page, its XML file must be located in either a web application's WPCATALOG folder or the web part gallery of a site collection. Web parts deployed to WPCATALOG are scoped at the web-application level and are available to all Site Collections contained in the web application. Web parts added to a web part gallery are scoped to the site collection that contains the gallery. A site collection's web part gallery can be viewed by navigating to Settings, Site Settings, Galleries, Web Parts. The web part gallery is a document library configured to contain web part XML files. As with any document library, items can be created, uploaded, and deleted from the gallery.

> **Note**
>
> Although web parts added to WPCATALOG are immediately available for use, site collection–scoped web parts require a feature to be activated in order to add the copy of the web part XML file to the web part gallery. The default location for WPCATALOG is C:\INETPUB\WWWROOT\WSS\ Virtual Directories\{WebAppName}{PortNumber}.

Because of the specific nature of the web part gallery, the function of the New button has been customized. The web part gallery New Web Parts page provides a list of web part assemblies that can be used in the site collection. To be included in the New Web Parts list, a web part must be a public assembly that inherits from one of the web part base classes, and it must be marked as safe in a Safe Control entry, in the web application's Web.config file. The following is a sample Safe Control entry:

```
<SafeControl Assembly="System.Web, Version=1.0.5000.0,
Culture=neutral,PublicKeyToken=b03f5f7f11d50a3a"
Namespace="System.Web.UI.WebControls"TypeName="*" Safe="True"/>
```

Safe Control entries function as gate keepers that limit the assemblies that can run in a web application to only those that have been explicitly marked as safe. Any control that is not marked as safe is considered unsafe and will not be allowed to run.

In addition to marking controls as safe to run, safe controls can be useful for denying a specific control from running. Suppose the assembly *TwoParts* contains two web parts named *GoodPart* and *BadPart*. The following two safe control entries allow *GoodPart* to run but explicitly prevent *BadPart* from doing so:

```
<SafeControl Assembly="TwoParts, Version=1.0.0.0,
Culture=neutral,PublicKeyToken=1234567810111213"
Namespace="TwoPartsNS"
TypeName="*"Safe="True"/>
<SafeControl Assembly="TwoParts, Version=1.0.0.0,
Culture=neutral,PublicKeyToken=1234567810111213"
Namespace="TwoPartsNS"
TypeName="BadPart"Safe="False"/>
```

The first entry marks all web parts in the namespace *TwoPartsNS* in the assembly *TwoParts* as safe. The second safe control entry overrides the first entry and explicitly registers *BadPart* as not safe, thus preventing it from running. A web part not marked as safe cannot be added to a page, and a web part already added to a page will cease running if its safe control status is changed.

Web Parts and Pages

Pages enable related content to be consolidated into a unique view of the content that is optimized for a specific purpose. For instance, you can consolidate related information into a single page to provide an overview. Pages collect and organize web parts to create a customized layout and customized functionality.

Creating a Content Page and Adding Web Parts

In previous versions of SharePoint Server, web parts were largely restricted to being placed in predefined web part zones. SharePoint Server 2013 allows web parts to be placed into content areas and positioned using standard markup. Freeing web parts from web part zones allows users greater flexibility in creating and customizing presentations. For the many instances when simple predefined regions are sufficient for organizing web parts, the more structured web part pages are still available. Although the predefined zones of web part pages are less flexible, they also require less effort to organize the presentation.

There are several ways to create the various page types SharePoint Server 2013 has available. The most readily available approach is to select New Page from the Settings drop-down menu. The New Page option from the Settings drop-down menu creates a page that uses the Body Only page layout, also known as a Blank page. The Body Only page layout has a single large content area that can contain web parts and other markup.

Create a Body Only Page and Add Web Parts to It
To create a Body Only page and add web parts to it, perform the following steps:

1. Open the site where you want to add the page.
2. From the Settings menu, select New Page.
3. Enter a name for the new page, and click Create.
4. Click the Insert tab on the ribbon, as shown in Figure 15.3.

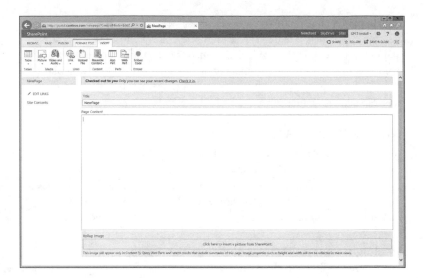

FIGURE 15.3
Selecting the Insert tab on the ribbon.

5. Click the Web Part button.

6. Select a category.

7. Select a web part.

8. Select where to add the web part.

9. Click the Add button.

After the web part is added to the rich content area, you can customize its layout by directly editing the markup of the content area. You can edit the content area's markup by clicking the Format Text tab on the ribbon and selecting Edit HTML Source from the HTML drop-down menu.

Creating Web Part Pages and Adding Web Parts

In many instances, the flexibility of adding web parts directly to the content area is not necessary. Web part pages come with predefined web part zones to provide a default organization for web parts. With some creativity, these web part pages can be adapted to a variety of layout requirements. The first thing to know about web part pages with a pre-defined layout is that after the layout is chosen, it cannot be easily altered. Therefore, the more flexible the layout you choose, the better off you will be.

The second thing to know is that an empty web part zone renders as nothing. If a web part page with three columns is chosen and only two are used, the page renders as two columns. The third, unused column does not use up valuable screen real estate. Therefore, it is best to use a web part page layout with as many web part zones as possible. The unused zones are ignored, taking up no page space, but they are still available for future use. Figure 15.4 shows the page in edit mode and demonstrates the absence of a web part in Row 1. Figure 15.5 shows the same page as users would see it.

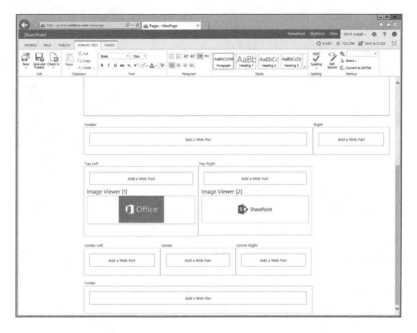

FIGURE 15.4
Web part zones are seen in edit mode when they are empty.

Experience has shown that the Header-Footer-4-Columns page, Left-Column-Header-Footer page, and Right-Column-Header-Footer page are the most useful web part pages because they provide the greatest number of possible combinations.

FIGURE 15.5
Users will not see the empty web part zone.

Create a Web Part Page

To create a web part page, perform the following steps:

1. Open the site where you want to add the page.
2. From the Settings drop-down menu, select Add a Page.
. 3. Enter a name for the web part page.
4. Click the Create button.

When the web part page is created, it will automatically be in edit mode. Because the page is in edit mode, all the web part zones on the page are displayed. After the page is published, only the zones that contain web parts are actually rendered. Any empty zones are ignored. The process for adding web parts to the web part page is somewhat different from the process for content pages.

Add a Web Part

To add a web part, perform the following steps:

1. Click the Add a Web Part button in the zone where you want to add the web part.
2. Select a category.
3. Select a web part.
4. Optionally, select a different zone from the Add Web Part To drop-down menu.
5. Click the Add button.

Deleting and Closing Web Parts

There are two options for removing web parts from a page: Close and Delete. Although the two have similar effects, they are different enough that you need to understand how to use them appropriately. Deleting a web part deletes the web part from the page permanently. Although the same web part can be added to the page again, all customization or configuration of the deleted web part is lost. There is no Recycle Bin capability for web part customizations.

Delete a Web Part
To delete a web part, perform the following steps:

1. Open the page where the web part is located.
2. Select Edit Page from the Settings drop-down menu.
3. Click the web part to be deleted.
4. Click the Web Part Tools tab on the ribbon.
5. Click the Delete button, and then click OK in the warning dialog box.

Closing a web part preserves the web part's configuration and customization by moving the web part to the Closed Web Parts gallery. The web part can be returned to the page from the Closed Web Parts gallery with all of its configuration and customizations intact.

> **Tip**
> Another major benefit of closing web parts is that closed web parts no longer consume the same system resources as open web parts.

Close a Web Part
To close a web part, perform the following steps:

1. Open the page where the web part is located.
2. Click the web part.
3. Select Close from the web part's shortcut menu, as shown in Figure 15.6.

FIGURE 15.6
Select Close to preserve the web part's customization.

Closed web parts can be returned to the page by going through the process
to add a web part, and then selecting a web part from the Closed Web Parts
category. A quick way to see a list of all closed web parts on the page is to
use the Web Parts Maintenance page. The Web Parts Maintenance page
can be opened by appending *?contents=1* to any page that contains web
parts.

For example, *http://portal.contoso.com/Pages/default.aspx?contents=1*
would open the Web Parts Page Maintenance for the Contoso Portal home
page. From the Web Parts Page Maintenance, web parts can be closed,
deleted, and reset. The Web Parts Maintenance page can also be a useful
tool for removing web parts that keep the page from loading.

As an alternative to closing, many web parts can be exported, thus preserv-
ing their customizations without requiring them to be maintained in the
gallery.

Web Part Connections

Web parts support a connectivity model that allows them to interoperate.
Connected web parts can be used to do tasks such as filtering result sets or

providing related parent and details views of data. Not all web parts support connections, and some web parts can be connected only to certain types of web parts, depending on how the web part was developed. Although the web part framework has been greatly improved to ensure *type safe* web part connections, you can still connect web parts in meaningless, but technically valid, ways—for example, supplying a Social Security number in the place of a telephone number. Therefore, always test to verify that web part connections behave in the way they are intended.

Connect to Web Parts

To connect to web parts, perform the following steps:

1. Open the page that contains the web parts.
2. Select Edit Page from the Settings menu.
3. Click Connection in the web part's shortcut menu.
4. Select the type of connection.
5. Select the target web part.
6. Optionally, provide required connection information.

The behavior of connected web parts varies, depending on the types of web parts involved. Some web parts allow unlimited connections, whereas others allow only one connection at a time. Web parts can support multiple types of connections, but many web parts implement only a single connection type. There are some guidelines provided when developing web parts in Microsoft Visual Studio, but a developer can choose to override them.

In general, web parts do not support bidirectional connections. Information can be passed from one web part to another, but not back and forth. Web parts typically provide an unlimited number of connections to other web parts but allow only a single consuming connection. As an example, image web parts can be connected to libraries that contain images. A library can provide a connection to multiple image web parts, but an image web part consumes images from only one library at a time.

Although bidirectional web part connections are not supported, a web part can be both a consumer and provider. To do so, it must provide a connection to one web part and consume a connection from a different web part. After web part connections have been established, they can be terminated easily.

Break a Web Part Connection

To break a web part connection, perform the following steps:

1. Open the page that contains the web parts.
2. Select Edit Page from the Settings menu.
3. Select Connections in the web part's shortcut menu.
4. Select the connection that is to be terminated.
5. Click the connection to be terminated.

Web Part Properties and Personalization

Web parts are configured and customized by modifying web part properties. Although web parts have different properties, almost all web parts share certain common properties. To modify a web part's properties, select Edit Web Part from the web part's shortcut menu, as shown in Figure 15.7. Table 15.1 shows the common web part properties that most web parts possess.

FIGURE 15.7
Editing the web part.

Table 15.1   **Common Web Part Properties**

Properties	Descriptions
Title	Changes the title of the web part on the page.
Height	Either fits the web part to the page or sets a fixed height.
Width	Either fits the web part to the page or sets a fixed width.
Chrome State	Selecting Minimized displays only the web part's title and adds a Restore option to its menu.
Chrome Type	A control displaying the title and border.
Hidden	Specifies that the web part will not be displayed but will still execute.
Zone	Changes the web part's zone.
Zone Index	Changes the order of the web part in its zone.
Allow Minimize	A control that sets the chrome state to minimized.
Allow Close	A control that allows the web part to be closed.
Allow Hide	A control that allows the web part to be hidden.
Allow Zone Change	A control that allows the web part to be moved between zones.
Allow Connections	A control that allows web part connections.

Web part properties have three possible states:

- **Shared**—These properties are the default values shared by all users. They are the values the web part begins with before it is personalized.

- **Personalized**—These properties are created when a user personalizes a page. When a user personalizes a page, the shared value becomes the user's new personalized value. Personalization allows users to reorder web parts on a page and customize the behavior of the web parts on a per-user basis. To personalize a page, click the Welcome User control (where your username is displayed) and select Personalize This Page.

- **Private**—These properties are analogous to Personalized properties, except they apply to private web parts that only you can see.

> **Note**
>
> To view the shared view of the page, repeat the process but click Show Shared View instead of Personalize This Page. There is a quirk that requires you to exit edit mode to allow you to switch to the shared view of a page.

When editing a personalized page, users should see a message that they are editing a personal version of the page. After users personalize a page, they can configure web parts for their individual needs. For example, users can make web parts they frequently work with large, while minimizing web parts that are of less interest to them.

Problems can arise with users inadvertently personalizing web parts with values that need to be shared. A common issue is that users personalize web parts with connection strings. If a web part that shares a connection string is personalized, the web part continues to work normally until the value of the connection string changes. If that happens, the web part continues to work for everyone but the user who personalized the web part. Proper coding techniques will prevent this problem from occurring. Unfortunately, proper coding techniques are not always followed. If a single user has problems with web parts that no one else has, check to make sure that the user does not have problems with a personalized page. If personalization issues are the problem, use the Web Parts Maintenance page to view the personalized copy of the page and reset the web parts on the personalized copy.

In addition to personalizing web parts already on a page, users can add web parts to a personalized page. These web parts are private to the user and have only personalized properties. Private web parts can be helpful in allowing users to integrate information of value to them into the shared version of a page.

Installing and Configuring Features

Features are SharePoint Server 2013 specific declarative (XML) programming elements. Whereas web parts do things *in* SharePoint Server 2013, features do things *to* SharePoint Server 2013. Features configure, associate, define, create, and copy. Features are most commonly used for the following:

- To define the columns that make up list types and the fields that the columns are based on

- To copy web parts and master pages to their respective galleries
- To associate Visual Studio workflows with a list or site
- To modify and extend the configuration of the SharePoint Server 2013 user interface
- To serve as a control panel that allows code and configuration changes to be turned on and off in the browser

> **Note**
>
> Features can affect four different scopes: farm, web application, site collection, and site. Site-scoped and site collection–scoped features can be controlled by information workers, which allows farm administrators to delegate responsibility for them.

Feature Architecture

Features are XML files and must be contained in a folder in C:\Programs Files\Common Files\Microsoft Shared\Web Server Extensions\15\ TEMPLATE\FEATURES.

Feature files not deployed to a subfolder in TEMPLATE\FEATURES will not be recognized as features and will not work. Features are generally composed of two types of files: a feature header file and one or more element files. Because the feature files are simply XML and because they are located in TEMPLATE\FEATURES, they can be easily inspected by browsing to the appropriate folder and examining the contents of the files. Feature header files are generally named Feature.xml. The following is an example of a feature.xml file:

```xml
<Feature
xmlns="http://schemas.microsoft.com/sharepoint/"Id="9965A8BB-
3F03-
448c-A4F1-57C66B13F7A2"
Title="FlyOutMaster"Description="Custom Master Page"
Scope="Web" Hidden="TRUE"
ReceiverAssembly="FeaturesTalk, Version=1.0.0.0,
Culture=neutral,
PublicKeyToken=580b0c2207433027"ReceiverClass="FeaturesTalk.
FlyOutMasterFeatureReceiver"><ElementManifests>
<ElementManifest Location="Elements.xml"/>
</ElementManifests></Feature>
```

The header file specifies the ID, title, description, scope, and whether the feature is hidden. If a feature is hidden, it will not be seen in the browser but can be activated with Windows PowerShell or programmatically in Visual Studio.

A feature receiver, or its dependent features, behave differently depending on the scope of the features involved. If a feature has a dependency on a higher-scoped feature, the higher-scoped feature must be activated before the feature with the dependency can be activated. For example, the site-scoped SharePoint Server Publishing feature requires that the site collection–scoped SharePoint Server Publishing Infrastructure feature be activated first.

If a feature has a dependency on a feature of the same scope, the dependent feature is automatically activated. Higher-scoped dependencies are generally used to guarantee that required resources are available to the dependent feature. Similarly scoped dependencies are generally used to synchronize the activation and deactivation of a number of interrelated and interdependent features. In the case of similarly scoped dependencies, the dependent features are typically hidden, thereby preventing their accidental activation or deactivation.

Feature Life Cycle

There is a four-stage feature life cycle. Features are installed, activated, deactivated, and uninstalled. Features can be manipulated in Central Administration and Windows PowerShell. Features are deployed using solution packages with either full-trust or sandboxed deployment mechanisms. They form an essential part of solution deployment because features provide a mechanism for solutions to deploy physical artifacts to the file system of the SharePoint server.

> **Note**
>
> Solution packages bundle and deploy SharePoint Server 2013 artifacts and use features to control activation, configuration, and replication of those artifacts.

Installing Features

Features are deployed with solution packages and should be automatically installed when deployed. Although it is uncommon to have to manually install features, you should be aware of how this process works.

To install a feature, the necessary feature files must already be deployed to the TEMPLATE\FEATURES directory on all servers in the farm. Installing a feature simply makes it available to be activated. Any installed feature that does not have the property *Hidden=True* can be seen and activated through the SharePoint Server 2013 user interface.

Note

Feature installation does not cause the feature to do anything. It simply makes the features available for activation and visible in the browser.

There is no mechanism for installing features using Central Administration. Central Administration is used only to manage previously installed features. Features must be installed using Windows PowerShell. To install a feature using Windows PowerShell, use the following command:

```
Install-SPFeature -Path <String> [-AssignmentCollection
<SPAssignmentCollection>]
   [-Confirm [<SwitchParameter>]] [-Force <SwitchParameter>]
   [-WhatIf [<SwitchParameter>]][<CommonParameters>]
```

The *Path* parameter can be either the name of the feature's folder in TEMPLATE\FEATURES or a relative path to the feature's header file. The *Confirm* parameter asks for confirmation before executing a command.

Tip

Use the *Force* parameter to force the reinstallation of an already installed feature.

Activating and Deactivating Features

A feature must be activated for it to take effect. Farm-scoped features deployed with full-trust solutions and site collection–scoped features deployed with sandboxed solutions are automatically activated when they are deployed. Deactivation does not necessarily reverse the results of activation. For example, if activating a feature that provisioned a custom list, deactivating the feature probably will not delete the list. This behavior is intentional and follows a general philosophy of SharePoint Server 2013 to do no harm. As a general principle, SharePoint Server 2013 will not destroy or delete information unless explicitly instructed to do so.

> **Tip**
>
> Be aware that when you deactivate features, they might not clean up after themselves and you might need to do the cleanup manually. Many times, deactivated features will leave in place lists and libraries that the feature provisioned during the initial activation. If the feature is then reactivated on the site and the feature is not developed properly, the feature could attempt to re-create lists or libraries that already exist and then fail the activation.

After deactivating any feature with which you are unfamiliar, check the result of the deactivation.

Managing Features from Central Administration

Unlike installation, features can be activated and deactivated through the Central Administration interface in addition to using Windows PowerShell. The location for activating and deactivating features is different for each feature scope.

Activate or Deactivate a Farm-Scoped Feature Using Central Administration

To activate or deactivate a farm-scoped feature using Central Administration, perform the following steps:

1. Browse to Central Administration, System Settings, Manage Farm Features.

2. Click either the feature's Activate or Deactivate button.

3. To deactivate a feature, confirm the deactivation.

Activating web application–scoped features in Central Administration has changed considerably and is now accomplished using the new management ribbon.

Activate a Web Application–Scoped Feature

To activate a web application–scoped feature, perform the following steps:

1. Browse to Central Administration, Application Management, Manage Web Applications.

2. Click the row that contains the web application that the feature should be activated on.

3. Click the Web Application tab in the management ribbon.

4. Click the Manage Features button in the management ribbon, as shown in Figure 15.8.

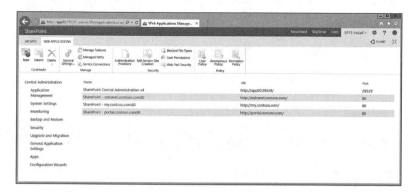

FIGURE 15.8
Select the row of the web application and then click Manage Features.

5. Click either the feature's Activate button or its Deactivate button.

6. To deactivate the feature, confirm the deactivation.

Activating and Deactivating Features in a Site Collection

If a feature has been installed to the farm and scoped to a site collection, a site collection administrator can then either activate or deactivate the feature.

Activate or Deactivate a Site Collection–Scoped Feature

To activate or deactivate a site collection–scoped feature, perform the following steps:

1. Open the appropriate site collection in the browser.

2. From the Settings drop-down menu, click Site Settings.

3. Click the Site Collection Features hyperlink in the Site Collection Administration group, as shown in Figure 15.9. If the Site Collection Administration group contains a Go to Top Level Site Settings hyperlink, click it to go to the top-level site, and then click the Site Collection Features hyperlink.

4. Click the Activate or Deactivate button.

5. To deactivate a feature, confirm the deactivation.

Activate and Deactivate Features in a Site

If a feature has been installed to the farm and scoped to a site, a site owner can activate and deactivate the feature. To activate or deactivate a site-scoped feature, perform the following steps:

1. Open the site in the browser.

2. From the Settings drop-down menu, click Site Settings.

3. Click the Manage Site Features hyperlink in the Settings group, as shown in Figure 15.9.

FIGURE 15.9
Choose to manage features in the relevant scope.

4. Click the Activate button or the Deactivate button.

5. Confirm the deactivation.

Activate and Deactivate Features Using Windows PowerShell

To activate (enable) or deactivate (disable) features with
Windows PowerShell, use the appropriate cmdlet:

```
Enable-SPFeature -Identity <SPFeatureDefinitionPipeBind>
[-AssignmentCollection <SPAssignmentCollection>]
[-Confirm [<SwitchParameter>]] [-Force <SwitchParameter>]
[-PassThru <SwitchParameter>] [-Url <String>]
[-WhatIf [<SwitchParameter>]] [<CommonParameters>]
```

Or

```
Disable-SPFeature -Identity <SPFeatureDefinitionPipeBind>
[-AssignmentCollection <SPAssignmentCollection>]
[-Confirm [<SwitchParameter>]] [-Force <SwitchParameter>] [-Url
<String>]
[-WhatIf [<SwitchParameter>]][<CommonParameters>]
```

When you are enabling or disabling a feature, the *Identity* parameter must
refer to either the name of the folder in which the feature resides in
TEMPLATE\FEATURES or the feature's unique ID. The *Force* parameter
forces the reactivation of an already activated feature, therefore causing
any custom code associated with the feature to be rerun. If the feature is
scoped at the web application, site collection, or site scopes, the *URL* of
the web application, site collection, or site must be provided.

Uninstalling Features

When a feature is uninstalled, its feature files are not deleted. Uninstalling
a feature causes SharePoint Server 2013 only to ignore the feature files
deployed to TEMPLATE\FEATURES. An uninstalled feature will not be
displayed in the user interface, and it cannot be activated with Windows
PowerShell without first being reinstalled. This behavior allows you to
uninstall a problem feature to keep it from affecting farm performance
and stability.

Note

Because features are deployed using solution packages, it is not a good
idea to manually delete the feature files. If a feature needs to be permanently and completely removed from the farm, the appropriate steps are
to retract and delete the solution package that deployed the feature. If
other assets from the solution package are still required, a new version
of the solution package must be created and redeployed.

Uninstall Features via Windows PowerShell

To uninstall a feature via Windows PowerShell, use the following cmdlet:

```
Uninstall-SPFeature -Identity <SPFeatureDefinitionPipeBind>
[-AssignmentCollection <SPAssignmentCollection>]
[-Confirm [<SwitchParameter>]] [-Force <SwitchParameter>]
[-WhatIf[<SwitchParameter>]] [<CommonParameters>]
```

The *Identity* parameter must specify either the name of the folder in TEMPLATE\FEATURES where the feature is located or the feature's unique ID. The *Force* switch causes the feature to be uninstalled even if it's currently activated.

Managing Solutions

SharePoint Server 2013 is both a powerful product and a flexible and extensible platform. Some organizations will be able to accomplish their goals using SharePoint Server 2013 as their only product. When the native functionality of SharePoint Server 2013 is no longer sufficient to fulfill an organization's requirements, SharePoint Server 2013 can be extended and enhanced using custom code. Because of SharePoint Server 2013's multi-server architecture and its ability to delegate administrative tasks to information workers, it has some specific methods for deploying custom developer artifacts. SharePoint Server 2013 has two related technologies for packaging and managing developer artifacts: full-trust and sandboxed solutions. Sandboxed solutions provide a mechanism for allowing information workers to manage extending the native platform while control of the process is maintained by farm administrators. Full-trust solutions are directly managed by farm administrators and principally used to deploy and retract developer artifacts on multiple servers.

Understanding Full-Trust Solutions

The flexible and scalable nature of SharePoint Server 2013 provides some unique deployment challenges. Multiple artifact types—such as web parts, master pages, and features—need to be deployed to multiple locations on multiple servers. As the number of items deployed increases, the number of locations deployed to increases and, as the number of servers in the farm grows, manual deployment rapidly ceases to be an option. It is therefore critical to understand full-trust solutions and how to use them.

Full-trust solutions provide a method for consistently deploying artifacts to all the servers in a SharePoint farm. Full-trust solutions are cabinet (.CAB) files that contain a group of artifacts to be deployed and an XML file named Manifest.xml, and these files have .WSP added as a suffix. The Manifest.xml file defines the deployment locations and other properties of the artifacts contained in the full-trust solution. Full-trust solutions can deploy artifacts to the following locations:

- Global assembly cache (GAC), located at C:\Windows\Assembly

- SharePoint Root Folder, located at C:\Program Files\Common Files\Microsoft Shared\Web Server Extensions\15

- Inetpub, located at C:\Inetpub\WWWRoot\WSS\VirtualDirectories\ [WebAppName][Port Number]

The contents of a full-trust solution can be inspected using the following process:

1. Copy the full-trust solution .WSP file.

2. Change the file extension to .CAB.

3. Open the renamed file to view the contents.

4. Extract the Manifest.xml file to determine where and how the contents of the full-trust solution will be deployed.

Adding a full-trust solution to the store does not deploy, activate, or implement any of the solution package's components. The full-trust solution is simply made available to be deployed across all servers in the farm in a consistent manner. After the full-trust solution is added to the store, it can be deployed immediately, at a scheduled time, or it can be left in the store for future use.

When a full-trust solution is deployed, it is deployed on all servers throughout the farm. Items are copied to each of the servers in the farm, but they still might not be functional. They must be activated either via custom code or manually in site and site collection settings. Deployment simply guarantees that items are copied to their appropriate locations. In addition to providing a mechanism for consistently deploying items, full-trust solutions also coordinate the removal of items that have reached the end of their life cycle. Full-trust solutions pass through the following life-cycle process:

1. Adding a solution to the solution store

2. Deploying the solution's content

3. Upgrading the solution

4. Retracting the content deployed by the solution

5. Deleting the solution from the solution store

Managing Full-Trust Solutions

Central Administration and Windows PowerShell can all be used to manage full-trust solutions, but only Windows PowerShell can add a solution to the configuration store.

Add and Inspect Full-Trust Solutions Using Windows PowerShell

Although it is not possible to add a full-trust solution to the solution store using Central Administration, it is possible to add a solution to the solution store using Windows PowerShell.

Add a Full-Trust Solution to the Solution Store Using Windows PowerShell

To add a full-trust solution to the solution store using Windows PowerShell, perform the following steps:

1. Open the SharePoint Server 2013 Management Shell located at Start, All Programs, Microsoft SharePoint 2013 Products.

2. Type the following command: `Add-SPSolution <FilePath>`. Dragging the file from Windows Explorer into the Windows PowerShell console will copy the path to the Windows PowerShell command line.

You can examine the contents of the solution store from the command line using Windows PowerShell. To display the contents of the solution store using Windows PowerShell, execute the following command from the SharePoint Server 2013 Management Shell:

```
Get-SPSolution
```

Deploying Full-Trust Solutions

Full-trust solutions can be deployed using Windows PowerShell and Central Administration. When a solution is deployed, the solution's Manifest.xml file is inspected, which determines what items will be deployed and where they will be deployed. When the full-trust solution is deployed, it copies files consistently to every server in the farm. The following deployment locations are possible for full-trust solution deployment:

- SharePoint Root Folder, C:\Program File\...\Web Server Extensions\15

- Web Application Directories, default C:\Inetpub\WSS\Virtual Directories\
- Global assembly cache, C:\Windows\Assembly

Deploy Full-Trust Solutions Using Central Administration

Full-trust solutions can also be deployed using Central Administration. To manage full-trust solutions, perform the following steps:

1. Open Central Administration.
2. Click the Systems Settings hyperlink.
3. Click the Manage Farm Solutions link in the Farm Management group.

The Solution Management interface displays a list of all full-trust solutions in the solution store. If a solution isn't displayed, it needs to be added to the solution store from the command line. The summary includes the deployment status of the solution and some of the locations where the solution is deployed. For more information about the solution, click its name to open a details page that lists its deployment status; where it is deployed; the results of the last operation performed on the solution; and whether the solution contains GAC-deployed assemblies, CAS policies, or web application–scoped resources. (See Figure 15.10.) From the details page, you can also retract and deploy solutions.

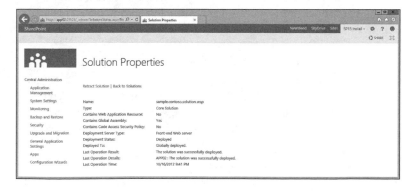

FIGURE 15.10
The solution details page controls deployment and provides deployment information.

Deploy a Solution Using Central Administration

To deploy a solution using Central Administration, perform the following steps:

1. Open Central Administration.
2. Click the Systems Settings hyperlink.
3. Click the Manage Farm Solutions hyperlink.
4. Click the name of the full-trust solution to be deployed.
5. Click the Deploy Solution hyperlink, shown in Figure 15.11.
6. Set a date and time for the deployment, or choose Now.
7. Choose the deployment target, either All Content URLs or a web application to deploy to.
8. Note any warnings, listed in red, about the full-trust solution deploying items to either the global assembly cache or deploying code access security policies.
9. Click OK.

The deployment process is done via timer jobs and might not execute instantaneously, even for immediate deployments. Also, it might be necessary to perform IIS resets on all the servers in the farm to ensure that the solution takes effect immediately. If it is not necessary for the solution to take effect immediately, the web application will refresh after 15 to 20 minutes by default. Remember, all the servers must be handled in the same manner; otherwise, errors will occur when servers begin behaving differently. The full-trust solution deployment interface is shown in Figure 15.11.

Deploy Full-Trust Solutions Using Windows PowerShell

Full-trust solutions can also be deployed using Windows PowerShell. Not all life-cycle names in Windows PowerShell match the names in Central Administration. In Windows PowerShell, the verb *install* replaces the term *deploy*. To deploy a full-trust solution using Windows PowerShell, use the following cmdlet:

```
Install-SPSolution -Identity <SPSolutionPipeBind>
[-AllWebApplications <SwitchParameter>] [-AssignmentCollection
<SPAssignmentCollection>] [-CASPolicies <SwitchParameter>]
[-Confirm [<SwitchParameter>]] [-Force <SwitchParameter>]
[-GACDeployment <SwitchParameter>] [-Local <SwitchParameter>]
[-Time <String>] [-WebApplication <SPWebApplicationPipeBind>]
[-WhatIf [<SwitchParameter>]] [<CommonParameters>]
```

FIGURE 15.11
Schedule deployment in the solution deployment interface.

The *identity* parameter is the name of the full-trust solution in the solution store, including the .wsp file extension. If the full-trust solution contains web application–scoped artifacts, you must specify either *AllWebApplications or WebApplication* and a *URL*. To schedule a deployment, specify a value for the *Time* parameter; otherwise, the deployment will occur immediately. If the *Local* flag is specified, the full-trust solution will be deployed on only the server where the command is being run. The *Force* parameter overwrites items installed by other solutions. To deploy assemblies to the global assembly cache or using code access security policies, you must use the *GACDeployment* or *CASPolicies* flags. If the *Confirm* flag is specified, you will be prompted to confirm the command before it executes. Although this is not very useful when used directly from the command line, it can be useful when scripting.

Retracting Full-Trust Solutions

Over the course of time, resources deployed with full-trust solutions need to be updated and removed. Artifacts deployed via full-trust solution can be retracted from one or all web applications where they are deployed in a manner similar to deploying them. Retracting a full-trust solution removes the deployed artifacts from the servers in the farm, but it does not delete the full-trust solution from the solution store. If a full-trust solution is retracted from some, but not all, web applications where it is deployed, only the web applications being retracted are affected by retracting the solution.

For example, consider a full-trust solution that contains an assembly deployed to the web application *bin* directory and a feature that is deployed to SharePoint Root\TEMPLATE\FEATURES. When the solution is deployed, the GAC assembly is copied to the global assembly cache and the *bin* assembly is copied to the *bin* directory of every web application that it is deployed to. If the full-trust solution is retracted from a single web application, only one copy of the *bin* assembly is deleted from the web application that the solution is being retracted from. The copy of the assemblies deployed to the other web applications and to the GAC are unaffected. It is acceptable and safe to retract a solution from one web application but not another.

Retract Solutions Using Central Administration

Solutions can also be retracted using Central Administration. To retract a solution using Central Administration, perform the following steps:

1. Open Central Administration.
2. Click the Systems Settings hyperlink.
3. Click the Manage Farm Solutions hyperlink.
4. Click the name of the full-trust solution to be retracted.
5. Click the Retract Solution hyperlink.
6. Set when to retract the full-trust solution, or choose Now.
7. Choose which web application to retract the full-trust solution from, either All Content URLs or a single web application.
8. Click OK.

Tip

Because a timer job is used to retract the full-trust solution, it is likely that the status of the solution will be shown as Retracting for several minutes.

Retract Solutions Using Windows PowerShell

You can also retract full-trust solutions using Windows PowerShell. Unlike Central Administration, Windows PowerShell uses the verb *uninstall* in the place of the term *retract*. To retract a solution using Windows PowerShell, execute the following cmdlet:

```
Uninstall-SPSolution -Identity <SPSolutionPipeBind> -
AllWebApplications
-WebApplication <SPWeb ApplicationPipeBind> <SwitchParameter>
[-AssignmentCollection <SPAssignmentCollection>]
[-Confirm [<SwitchParameter>]]
[-Language <UInt32>] [-Local<SwitchParameter>]
[-Time <String>] [-WhatIf
[<SwitchParameter>]][<CommonParameters>]
```

The *Identity* parameter specifies the name of the full-trust solution in the solution store, including the .wsp file extension. If the full-trust solution contains artifacts scoped at the web-application level, you must use either the *AllWebApplications* flag or the *WebApplication* parameter specifying the URL of a web application. To schedule a retraction, use the *Time* parameter; if no time is specified, the retraction occurs immediately.

Deleting Full-Trust Solutions

When full-trust solutions are retracted, they are not removed from the solution store. Full-trust solutions can be deleted using Central Administration and Windows PowerShell.

Delete Full-Trust Solutions Using Central Administration

Although you cannot add full-trust solutions using Central Administration, you can delete them. To delete a full-trust solution using Central Administration, perform the following steps:

1. Browse to Central Administration, System Settings, Manage Farm Solutions.
2. Click the name of the full trust solution to be deleted.
3. Click the Remove Solution hyperlink.
4. Set when to retract the full-trust solution, or choose Now.
5. Confirm that you want to delete the full-trust solution by clicking OK.

Delete Full-Trust Solutions Using Windows PowerShell

To delete a full-trust solution using Windows PowerShell, use the following command:

```
Remove-SPSolution -Identity <SPSolutionPipeBind>
[-AssignmentCollection <SPAssignmentCollection>] [-Confirm
```

```
[<SwitchParameter>]] [-Force<SwitchParameter>] [-Language
<UInt32>]
[-WhatIf [<SwitchParameter>]][<CommonParameters>]
```

The *Identity* parameter specifies the name of the full-trust solution in the solution store. The *Force* parameter deletes the full-trust solution from the solution store even though artifacts from it are still deployed. If the *Force* parameter is used, you will not be able to retract (uninstall) the full-trust solution,

Upgrading Full-Trust Solutions

Upgrading the solution replaces the full-trust solution in the solution store with a new version and deploys the contents of the new full-trust solution. Full-trust solutions can be upgraded using Windows PowerShell.

Upgrade Full-Trust Solutions Using Windows PowerShell

To upgrade a full-trust solution using Windows PowerShell, execute the following cmdlet:

```
Update-SPSolution -Identity <SPSolutionPipeBind> -LiteralPath
<String>
[-AssignmentCollection <SPAssignmentCollection>]
[-CASPolicies <SwitchParameter>] [-Confirm [<SwitchParameter>]]
[-Force <SwitchParameter>] [-GACDeployment <SwitchParameter>]
[-Local <SwitchParameter>] [-Time <String>] [-WhatIf
[<SwitchParameter>]]
[<CommonParameters>]
```

The *Identify* parameter specifies the name of the full-trust solution in the solution store and should include the .wsp file extension. The *LiteralPath* parameter is the path to the new full-trust solution package file that will be used for upgrade. To allow either code access security policies to be deployed or assemblies to be deployed to the global assembly cache, you must use the *GACDeployment* or *CASPolicies* flag. To schedule an update at a later time, use the *Time* parameter. If no value for the *Time* parameter is specified, the update is processed immediately. Including the *Local* flag causes the update to occur on only the server where the command is being run. The *Local* flag is intended for use by developers in a single-server environment.

Just as with deploying artifacts, you must run an IISRESET on every server in the farm for the upgrade to take immediate effect. Unfortunately, there is not an option for upgrading solutions from Central Administration. This means that the process cannot be accomplished using a graphical user interface.

Managing Sandboxed Solutions

Sandboxed full-trust solutions were introduced in SharePoint Server 2010 and were created to provide new levels of flexibility and control when deploying SharePoint Server 2010 artifacts. Instead of deploying items farmwide, sandboxed solutions are contained within a single site collection. Instead of being stored in the solution store, sandboxed solutions are stored in the site collection gallery like web parts and list templates. One advantage of scoping sandboxed solutions at the site-collection level is that it allows site collection administrators, instead of farm-level administrators, to manage solutions packages.

Although allowing information workers to deploy code might seem risky at first glance, sandboxed solutions provide a security enhancement compared to full-trust solutions. Sandboxed solutions are run using a restrictive set of code access security policies and are limited to a specific subset of the SharePoint Server 2013 object model. In addition to running with limited trust, sandboxed solutions are monitored to ensure that they do not affect server performance by consuming too many system resources.

Furthermore, because sandboxed solutions are limited to operation within a single site collection, potential problems are limited to only that site collection.

Sandboxed solutions can also be set to execute on a single dedicated server or group of servers. If the security enhancements present in sandboxed solutions are not adequate for your environment, they can be disabled entirely by farm administrators. When used properly, they provide a more elegant trust solution than code access security because they are monitored, controlled, and adaptable to different requirements using different quotas for each site collection. Additionally, the responsibility for sandboxed solutions can be delegated to information workers.

Table 15.2 shows the allowed and disallowed functions when using sandboxed solutions:

Table 15.2   Allowed and Disallowed Items and Actions in a Sandboxed Solution

Allowed Items and Actions	Disallowed Items and Actions
Custom list templates	Farm-scoped features
Creating lists	Web application–scoped features
Extending the user interface	Hiding and grouping items in the UI
Copying files to lists, libraries, and galleries	Content-type bindings
Web parts not requiring full trust	Web parts that contain user controls
InfoPath Forms not requiring full trust	Running with elevated privileges
Silverlight controls and JavaScript	Accessing external data
Workflow	Interacting with other site collections
List, item, and site event receivers	Timer jobs

Sandboxed solutions have the same basic structure as full-trust solutions. They are cabinet files with the .wsp suffix instead of .cab. They contain an XML file named Manifest.xml that describes the contents of the solution and how to deploy them. As with full-trust solutions, you can inspect the contents of a sandboxed solution by changing the file extension to .cab, as discussed previously in this chapter.

> **Note**
>
> You can upload a full-trust solution to a solution gallery, but if the solution is activated and attempts to violate the partial-trust policy, an error will occur.

For sandboxed solutions to run properly, the Microsoft SharePoint Foundation Sandboxed Code service must be started. The service does not have to be started on every server, only on the servers that will run sandboxed solutions. The recommended configuration is for the service to be started on one, or perhaps more, application servers. Doing so insulates web front-end servers from the performance requirements of running sandboxed solutions. To start the Microsoft SharePoint Foundation User Code service, perform the following steps:

1. Browse to Central Administration, Systems Settings, Manage Services on Server.

2. Select a server to run the Microsoft SharePoint Foundation Sandboxed Code service.

3. Click the Start hyperlink for Microsoft SharePoint Foundation Sandboxed Code service.

4. Repeat steps 3 and 4 if additional servers will be used to run the Sandboxed Code service.

Not surprisingly, sandboxed solutions have a different life cycle than full-trust solutions. Instead of being added, deployed, retracted, and deleted, sandboxed solutions are uploaded, activated, deactivated, and deleted. There is also an upgrade option similar to the one provided for full-trust solutions.

Upload, Activate, and Rename Sandboxed Solutions
To upload a sandboxed solution, perform the following steps:

1. Open the Site Collection where the solution is to be added.

2. Select Site Settings from the Settings menu.

3. Click the Solutions hyperlink in the Galleries group. If Solutions isn't present in the Galleries group, click the Go to Top-Level Site Settings hyperlink in the Site Collection Administration group.

4. Click the Solutions tab on the ribbon as shown in Figure 15.12.

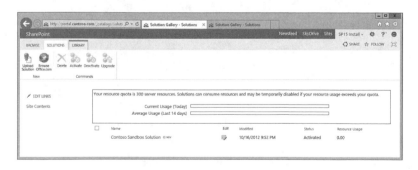

FIGURE 15.12
Managing sandboxed solutions using the ribbon.

5. Click the Upload Solution button on the ribbon.

6. Browse to the location of the solution file.

7. Click OK.

To download a sandboxed solution, click the solution's name. To change the name of a solution, click the edit icon. Upon being uploaded to the gallery, a sandboxed solution does not automatically do anything; it is simply available to be activated. When a sandboxed solution is activated, it automatically activates any Site Collection–scoped features that it contains. Site-scoped features must be manually activated for every site where they are to run. To activate a sandboxed solution, perform the following steps:

1. Open the Site Collection where the solution is to be added.

2. Select Site Settings from the Settings menu.

3. Click the Solutions hyperlink in the Galleries group.

4. If Solutions isn't present in the Galleries group, click the Go to Top-Level Site Settings hyperlink in the Site Collection Administration group.

5. Click the row that contains the full-trust solution, causing it to be highlighted.

6. Click the Activate button on the ribbon, as shown in Figure 15.13.

7. Click the Activate button in the window that opens.

8. Wait for the sandboxed solution to activate and the window to close.

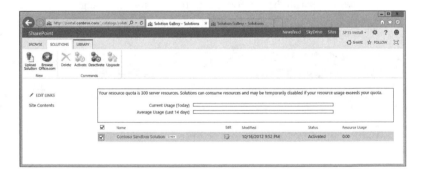

FIGURE 15.13
Activating a sandboxed solution using the management ribbon.

Monitoring Sandboxed Solutions

One of the biggest advantages to sandboxed solutions is the ability to monitor them and terminate execution if they consume excessive system resources. Before sandboxed solutions, the only way to gauge the impact of deployed solutions was by monitoring overall system performance and making comparisons between when solutions were and were not deployed. As the number of solutions deployed in the farm grew and the baseline comparisons became more outdated, pinpointing the source of performance problems became more and more difficult. It was not uncommon to know something was not performing well without the capability to easily pinpoint what the problem was.

To address these problems, sandboxed solutions have been moved entirely out of the standard Internet Information Services (IIS) worker processes and are instead run in a separate process named *SPUCWorkerProcess*. Usage quotas can be set for each site collection, and sandboxed solutions that exceed the quota for a site collection will not be allowed to run. Because the quotas are per site collection, you can assign different values for different site collections based on their intended use. This approach effectively allows for a balance of different sandboxed solution service agreements for different site collections in your organization. To manage sandboxed solution quotas, perform the following steps:

1. Browse to Central Administration, Application Management, Configure Quotas and Locks.

2. Select the site collection to be configured from the Site Collection drop-down menu, as shown in Figure 15.14.

3. Click OK.

The Sandboxed Solutions Resource Quota value specifies a maximum resource utilization for sandboxed solutions for the selected site collection. The value is specified in resource points. Resource points are an abstract concept and not directly related to any specific measure of server perform-ance. Instead, the resource components are themselves based on a set of 14 metrics that measure specific conditions. These 14 metrics, listed in Table 15.3, are then weighted to balance their overall influence on the resource point scale. There is no way to view the actual metrics and their point values within Central Administration. You can use the following short Windows PowerShell script to display the list of metrics and their current weighting:

```
Add-PSSnapin
Microsoft.SharePoint.Powershell[System.Reflection.Assembly]::Lo
ad("Microsoft.SharePoint, Version=12.0.0.0,
Culture=neutral,
PublicKeyToken=71e9bce111e9429c")$s=[Microsoft.SharePoint.Admin
istration.SPUserCodeService]::
Local$s.ResourceMeasures ¦ Select-Object Name,ResourcesPerPoint
```

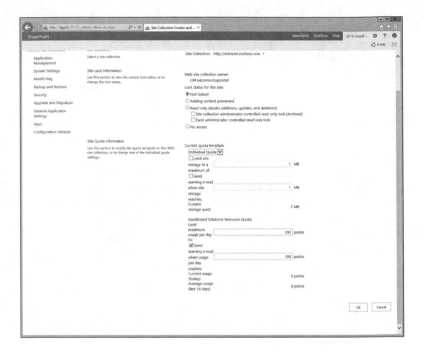

FIGURE 15.14
The sandboxed solution quota management interface.

Table 15.3 **Resource Point Metrics and Weighting**

Name	Resources/ Point	Absolute Limit	Units
AbnormalProcessTermination Count	1	1	Count
CPUExecutionTime	3600	60	Seconds
CriticalExceptionCount	10	3	Events
InvocationCount	100	100	Events
PercentProcessorTime	85	100	%
ProcessCPUCycles	100000000000	100000000000	Cycles
ProcessHandleCount	10000	1000	Items
ProcessIOBytes	10000000	100000000	Items
ProcessThreadCount	10000	200	Instances
ProcessVirtualBytes	100000000	1000000000	Bytes

Name	Resources/ Point	Absolute Limit	Units
SharePointDatabaseQueryCount	20	100	Instances
SharePointDatabaseQueryTime	120	60	Seconds
UnhandledExceptionCount	50	3	Instances
UnresponsiveprocessCount	2	1	Instances

Essentially, the process works like this: each metric, also referred to as *resource measures*, has a *resources per point value*. When a sandboxed solution's resource utilization exceeds one of the resource per point values for a resource measure, one resource point is deducted from the daily quota.

For example, every time an Abnormal Process Termination occurs, it consumes a resource point from the daily quota. Likewise, if the sandboxed solution uses 3600 seconds of CPU time, 1 point from the daily quota is used. The daily quota is cumulative for all sandboxed solutions in the site collection. That is to say, when the quota is exceeded by one or more solutions, no sandboxed solutions can run in that site collection for the remainder of the day. To keep one really badly behaving sandboxed solution from stopping execution of all sandboxed solutions, there is an absolute limit that controls execution of the single offending sandboxed solution. If a single sandboxed solution consumes more than 85 percent of processor time, or if it encounters more than three unhandled exceptions, it is locked. The absolute limit provides fault tolerance in the event a single solution seriously malfunctions.

You can create predefined quotas that can be used repeatedly instead of setting values for each site collection. To create a predefined quota, perform the following steps:

1. Browse to Central Administration, Application Management.
2. Click the Specify Quota Templates hyperlink in the Site Collections group.
3. Select the Create A New Quota Template radio button.
4. Select a template to base the new template on.
5. Give the template a meaningful name.
6. Specify a storage limit for the site collection and an email warning level. An email message will be sent when either value is reached.
7. In the Sandboxed Solutions with Code Limits section, set the maximum daily usage and email warning levels.

Configure Sandboxed Solution Load Balancing

By default, sandboxed solutions run only on servers that have the Microsoft SharePoint Foundation Sandboxed Code Service running. This allows sandboxed solution execution to be offloaded from individual web front-end servers and isolated on one or more servers. You can also have sandboxed solutions execute directly on the web front-end servers. To change the sandboxed solution load-balancing scheme, perform the following steps:

1. Open Central Administration.
2. Click the Systems Settings hyperlink.
3. Click the Manage User Solutions hyperlink.
4. Select either All Sandboxed Code Runs on the Same Machine as the Request or Requests to Run Sandboxed Code Are Routed by Solution Affinity.
5. Click OK.

Block Sandboxed Solutions

To prevent a truly pernicious sandboxed solution from executing, you can implement a list of blocked solutions. Blocked solutions are prevented from executing. To block a sandboxed solution, perform the following steps:

1. Browse to Central Administration, System Settings, Manage User Solutions.
2. Under Add New Solution to Block, click the Browse button, and select the solution.
3. Provide a message that users will see when attempting to use the blocked sandboxed solution.
4. Click the Block button.

CHAPTER 16

Configuring Sites and Site Collections

- Site Settings
- Creating and Managing List and Library Apps
- Navigation and Promoted Links

After you've created your site collection, the configuration and setup of the sites is the next critical step. SharePoint 2013 has added new functionality, such as centralized navigation management, to ease the pain in the configuration and setup of a site or site collection. The configuration of SharePoint sites and site collections is critical to the successful usage and adoption of the platform in any organization. This chapter explores the configuration and management needs after the creation and setup of sites and site collections.

Site Settings

Top-level sites, as well as subsites, are managed through the Site Settings page. In a site collection, each subsite has its own Site Settings page. The top-level site, the root of the site collection, has its own Site Settings page that applies to the site collection itself. To access the Site Settings page for any site, click the Site Settings link on the Settings menu button. From the Site Settings page of a subsite, the site collection settings page can be accessed from the Site Collection Settings section, where there is a link to the top-level Site Settings page. The settings shown on the Site Settings page are filtered based on the user's role within the site collection.

> **Note**
>
> To manage the site collection settings, you must be a site collection administrator. To manage site settings (for the top-level site and subsites), you must be a site owner. If you see site settings only in the top-level site, and not the site collection settings, you are not a site collection administrator.

Regional Settings

Regional settings control how a site behaves, including how lists are sorted and how values such as dates are displayed. Regional settings for a site are based on standards for a particular region of the world. For example, some parts of the world use a 24-hour clock and others, such as the United States, use a 12-hour clock as a general rule. Also, some regions of the world use the Gregorian calendar and other regions use different calendars. Here are the regional settings available to a site:

- **Time Zone**—The standard time zone.

- **Locale**—The locale setting controls numbering, sorting, calendar, and date and time formatting for the website.

- **Sort Order**—The method used for sorting.

- **Set Your Calendar**—The type of calendar used, such as Gregorian or Buddhist.

- **Enable an Alternate Calendar**—An additional calendar to provide extra information about the calendar features.

- **Define Your Work Week**—The standard working days of the week for the region. This includes other settings, such as first day of the week and first week of the year, as well as workday start and end times.

- **Time Format**—Defines either the 12-hour or 24-hour clock.

Regional settings for a site can be managed through the Regional Settings link on the Site Settings page of the site.

Recycle Bin

The Recycle Bin was introduced in SharePoint 2007 and has proven to be a very useful tool by providing the capability to recover the accidental deletion of objects in SharePoint. The Recycle Bin provides similar functionality to that of the Windows Recycle Bin, allowing deleted documents or list items to be preserved for a period of time before being permanently destroyed. At any time while a document or list item resides in the Recycle Bin, it can be restored to its original location.

> **Note**
>
> Sites and site collections can now also be recovered from the Recycle Bin; however, site collections can only be recovered using PowerShell.

End User Recycle Bin

The Recycle Bin in SharePoint 2013 exists on two levels. The first of these levels is the end user Recycle Bin. When a user deletes an item from a list or library, the item gets sent to the end user Recycle Bin where it remains until it is purged by either the user or automatically based on administrative settings.

Site Collection Recycle Bin

When an item is purged from the end user Recycle Bin, it is moved into the site collection Recycle Bin. All objects purged by users in all subsites as well as the top-level site are moved here. This second layer of recoverability allows the administrator to restore files that have been deleted by users and even purged from their Recycle Bins. To restore an item from the end user Recycle Bin, do the following:

1. From the home page of the site, click the Site Contents link in the left navigation pane.

2. On the next page, Site Contents, click Recycle Bin.

3. Select the box next to the item to be restored.

4. Click Restore Selection, as demonstrated in Figure 16.1.

Managing the Site Collection Recycle Bin

The site collection Recycle Bin can be managed from the top-level site settings page. There are two views available for this Recycle Bin: one for viewing items located in end users' Recycle Bins throughout the site collection and the other for managing items that have been purged from users' Recycle Bins and are now located in the administrative Recycle Bin, with the former being the default.

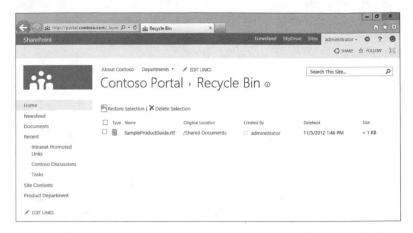

FIGURE 16.1
Restoring an item from the Recycle Bin.

From the site users' view, you can see all the items deleted by users within the site collection. From here, you can delete individual items, sending them to the administrative Recycle Bin, or you can empty the users' Recycle Bins all at once by clicking Empty Recycle Bin. Using either method, the deleted items end up in the administrative Recycle Bin. From there, they can be permanently deleted or restored to their original locations.

Portal Site Connection

A portal provides the capability to aggregate and organize site collections in an organization. It generally provides the capability to browse and search for sites by specified criteria. Any site collection can be linked to from the portal, typically using the Navigation settings under Look and Feel of the Site Settings page, but sites by default don't have a clear path back to the portal. This is the purpose of the portal site connection—it provides a navigational breadcrumb link back to the portal site. The following steps demonstrate how to configure the portal site connection for a site collection:

1. From the Settings menu of the site collection, choose Site Settings.

2. In the Site Collection Administration Section, choose the Portal Site Connection link.

3. Select the option to connect to the portal site.

4. Type the web address of the portal.

5. Type a friendly name for the portal. This will be the name displayed in the breadcrumb link on all pages in the site collection.

6. Click OK.

Note

The Portal Site Connection is not visible in SharePoint 2013 and is available only in SharePoint 2010 mode. To provide similar functionality, but more easily managed, consider using Managed Navigation in lieu of the Portal Site Connection.

Information Management Policies

An Information Management Policy is a container for a set of rules that can be applied to a type of content. Rules within a policy are called policy features. Information management policies allow you to control access to information within your organization and to specify how long it should be retained, what to do when the retention period expires, and so on. Policies can be implemented to enable organizational compliance with legally mandated requirements, such as the Sarbanes-Oxley Act in the United States, or internal requirements within an organization.

Policy features are enabled by a farm administrator and, once enabled, can be used by site collection administrators to create and implement policies. Some available policy features include the following:

- **Expiration**—Allows for the disposal or processing of content based on time, such as a specific date, a date based on columns associated with the content, or a length of time relative to some action involving the content.

- **Auditing**—Allows for logging of actions or events related to content, such as editing or viewing of a document, check-in or check-out of a document, changing permissions of a document, or deleting a document.

- **Labeling**—Enables labels to be formatted and for searchable text areas to be automatically associated with a document or list item.

- **Barcode**—Allows tracking of physical copies of documents using a barcode representation of a unique identifier for the document. By default, barcodes are compliant with the Code 39 standard, but custom barcode providers can be plugged in using the policies object model.

Creating Information Management Policies

These are the default policy features available out of the box, but custom features can be developed or purchased from third-party vendors. To create an information management policy, do the following:

1. Click the Settings menu, and choose Site Settings from the site collection where you want to associate an information management policy.

2. In the Site Collection Administration section, click Site Collection Policies.

3. On the Site Collection Policies page, click Create.

4. On the Edit Policy page, type a name and administrative description. This information will be seen by list managers when associating a policy with a list or content type.

5. In the Policy Statement section, type a policy statement to be shown to users anytime they open an item governed by this policy.

6. In the Retention section, select the Enable Retention check box.

7. Click Add a Retention Stage.

8. In the Stage Properties dialog box in the Event section, choose This Stage Is Based Off a Date Property on the Item.

9. Choose Last Modified + 1 Years for the time period.

10. In the Action section, choose Move To Recycle Bin.

11. Click OK. The completed Stage Properties dialog box is shown in Figure 16.2.

12. In the Auditing section, select the Enable Auditing check box and select all the events to audit.

13. Leave the Enable Barcodes and Enable Labels check boxes cleared.

14. Click OK to save the new information management policy.

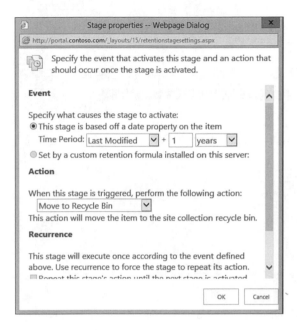

FIGURE 16.2
The Stage Properties dialog box.

Associate an Information Management Policy with a Document Library

After creating a policy, you can then associate it with either a content type or a document library. To associate an information management policy with a document library, perform the following steps:

1. From the document library where the policy will be associated, click the Library tab in the Library Tools area of the management ribbon.

2. In the Settings section of the ribbon, click Library Settings.

3. In the Permissions and Management section of the Document Library Settings page, choose Information Management Policy Settings.

4. Leave the Source of Retention for this library set to Content Types, and click the Document content type.

5. In the Specify the Policy section, choose Use a Site Collection Policy.

6. Choose the site collection policy just created from the drop-down list, as shown in Figure 16.3.

FIGURE 16.3
Specify the site collection policy to apply to all documents or content types in a specific list or library.

7. Click OK to accept the policy association.

SharePoint Designer Settings

SharePoint Designer is a useful tool for designing and managing SharePoint sites. However, an inexperienced or malicious user could do a lot of damage using SharePoint Designer, so its use should be carefully controlled. The following SharePoint Designer–related settings are available for a site collection:

- **Enable SharePoint Designer**—Controls whether SharePoint Designer can be used by anyone other than a site collection administrator. If this setting is enabled, site owners and designers are allowed to use SharePoint Designer.

- **Enable Detaching Pages from the Site Definition**—Controls whether site owners and designers can detach (formerly referred to as unghosting) pages from the site definition.

- **Enable Customizing Master Pages and Page Layouts**—Controls whether site owners and designers can customize master pages and layout pages for a site collection.

- **Enable Managing of Web Site URL Structure**—Controls whether site owners and designers can view and manage the hidden URL structure of a site collection.

Configure SharePoint Designer Settings for a Site Collection

To configure SharePoint Designer settings for a site collection, follow these steps:

1. From any site within the site collection, click the Settings menu button and choose Site Settings.

2. On the Site Settings page, in the Site Collection Administration section, choose SharePoint Designer Settings.

3. On the SharePoint Designer Settings page, enable the SharePoint Designer features by selecting the corresponding check box.

4. Click OK to save the settings. The SharePoint Designer Settings page is shown in Figure 16.4.

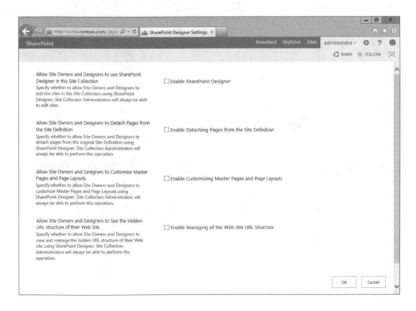

FIGURE 16.4

The SharePoint Designer Settings page is important to determine if SharePoint Designer access will be allowed and what actions can be performed if SharePoint Designer access is allowed.

Site collection administrators will always be able to perform all these actions unless prohibited at the web-application level by a farm administrator. If SharePoint Designer is blocked for the web application, the user will see a message similar to the one shown in Figure 16.5.

FIGURE 16.5
SharePoint Designer settings have been disabled at the web-application level.

Creating and Managing List and Library Apps

Preceding SharePoint 2013, lists and libraries were considered to be the primary storage location for list- and item-level content throughout SharePoint. In SharePoint 2013, the same capabilities that were once referred to as *lists* and *libraries* are now simply referred to as *apps*. In SharePoint 2013, apps are now used to add the same additional functionality to SharePoint sites that lists and libraries provided in previous versions. For more on apps see Chapter 15, "Managing Apps and Solutions."

Creating and Managing Document Libraries

Document libraries provide a central location for storing and managing documents. They can be organized into folder hierarchies as in the traditional network file share model, but with much better management capabilities, such as document check-in and check-out, automatic versioning, and integrated workflow.

Now that lists and libraries are considered apps, the traditional functions such as Creating a New Document Library are done through adding an app. To create a document library, follow these steps:

1. From the Settings button, click Add an App.

2. You will be redirected to the Site Contents, Your Apps page.

3. Under Apps, click Document Library to create a new document library.

4. Type a name for this document library.

5. Click Advanced Options for the following:

   ■ Type a description about the document library.

   ■ Specify whether to turn on versioning for the document library.

   ■ Choose a document template to be used when creating new documents in this library.

   ■ You can adjust these settings in the Library Settings after creation.

6. Click OK to create the document library.

Note

The document template does not limit the document library to storing only a single type of document. This is used to determine the type of document that should be created when a new document is created from the menu. Any types of documents that are not restricted can be stored in the document library.

Configuring Document Library Versioning Settings

One of the most powerful and consistently used document management features of SharePoint is versioning. Versioning tracks changes to a document throughout its life cycle and provides the capability to go back and look at the document as it existed at any previous point where a version was saved. SharePoint provides the capability to track major and minor versions of a document.

Document libraries can be configured to require documents to be checked out before they can be edited. Checking out the document locks it for editing to prevent multiple users from interfering with one another while trying to edit the file. If check-out is required, a user must check in a document before another user can check it out for editing. To configure versioning and check-out requirements for a document library, do the following:

1. From the document library default page, click the Library tab in the management ribbon.

2. In the Library ribbon, in the Settings section, click Library Settings.

3. On the Document Library Settings page, click Versioning Settings.

4. On the Versioning Settings page, in the Content Approval section, select Yes to turn on content approval for the document library. This will cause new items and changes to existing items to remain in a draft state until they are approved.

5. In the Document Version History section, choose whether to implement major versions, major and minor versions, or no versioning. You can also specify how many major versions to keep and how many of those major versions to keep drafts for.

6. In the Draft Item Security section, choose who should be able to view drafts of documents in the library.

7. In the Require Check-Out section, choose whether to require documents to be checked out before editing.

8. Click OK to save the settings. An example of the Versioning Settings page is shown in Figure 16.6.

Configuring Document Library Advanced Settings

The document library Advanced Settings page provides a catch-all for miscellaneous settings related to document libraries. The following list describes the settings available on the Advanced Settings page:

- **Content Types**—Specifies whether to allow the management of content types on this document library. Each content type appears on the new button and can have a unique set of columns, workflows, and other behaviors.

- **Document Template**—Specifies the URL to the template to be used for new documents. If multiple content types are enabled, this setting is managed per content type.

- **Opening Documents in the Browser**—Specifies the behavior that should be used when opening a document—whether to open the document in the client application or the browser. If the client application is unavailable, the browser will always be used.

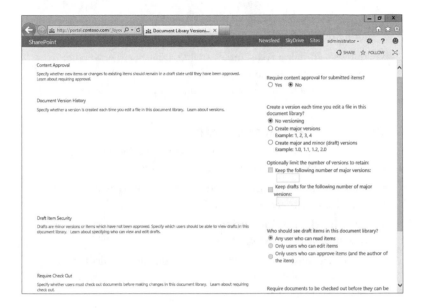

FIGURE 16.6
The Document Library Versioning Settings page.

- **Custom Send To Destination**—Specifies the name and URL of a destination that should appear in the Send To context menu option of documents in the library.

- **Search**—Specifies whether documents in the library should be included in search results.

- **Reindex Document Library**—Flags the current document library to be fully indexed during the next scheduled crawl.

Note

This is a *very* powerful feature to empower you, and perhaps more importantly your users, to influence search results by surfacing content that users feel is important.

- **Offline Client Availability**—Specifies whether the document library should be available to offline clients.

- **Site Assets Library**—Specifies whether this library should be presented as the default location for storing images or other files that users upload to their wiki pages.

- **Datasheet**—Specifies whether datasheet mode is available for bulk editing of this document library.

- **Dialogs**—If dialog boxes are available, this specifies whether to launch the new, edit, and display forms in a dialog box. Selecting No causes these actions to navigate to the full page.

Configuring Other General Settings

Many other settings can be configured for document libraries. The following list describes the most common ones:

- **Validation settings**—Enter validation formulas to be evaluated when documents are added to a document library.

- **Column default value settings**—Administrators can specify default column values for documents added to the library.

- **Rating settings**—Enable ratings for documents in a document library, which will add ratings fields to the content types used by the library and to the default view.

- **Audience targeting settings**—Enabling audience targeting creates a targeting column for the library, which can be used to filter the view of the library by audience.

- **Form Settings**—Specifies the use of custom forms for this document library.

- **Metadata navigation settings**—This page can be used to configure metadata navigation hierarchies and key filter input controls. You can also enable the automatic creation of indices on the library to enhance query performance.

- **Per-location view settings**—This page allows for the management of views available for the library. Views can be specified explicitly here or configured to be inherited from a parent.

Permissions and Management

The following settings are generally used settings for information management as well as to establish the permissions and actions that can be performed with and against a library or list:

- **Save Document Library as Template**—Allows for the document library to be saved as a template for use across the site collection.

■ **Permissions for This Document Library**—Specifies the users and/or groups that have specific permissions for activities on this document library.

■ **Manage Files Which Have No Checked In Version**—Gives the administrator of the document library the ability to manage all files within this document library that are not checked in.

■ **Workflow Settings**—Allows for the association of specific workflows for items that are stored or created inside of this document library.

■ **Information Management Policy Settings**—Allows the administrator to assign the appropriate policy to all documents stored within this document library.

■ **Add Enterprise Key Words**—Specifies the use of Enterprise Key Words in a column within this document library that will enable easier searching and filtering.

■ **Metadata Publishing**—Enables the sharing of the Managed Metadata and Enterprise Keywords columns as social tags.

Managing Acceptable Document Types and Sizes

SharePoint 2013 provides the capability to specify the document types that are allowed to be stored and created in document libraries through the use of the Blocked File Types list. This list is managed through the Central Administration website. Blocked file types are specified on a per–web application basis. To add a file to the Blocked File Types list, do the following:

1. Open SharePoint 2013 Central Administration and click the Security link in the left navigation pane.

2. Select Define Blocked File Types in the General Security section.

3. Choose the web application to define blocked file types for.

4. Add the file extension of the file type to be blocked on a new line in the list, as shown in Figure 16.7.

5. Click OK to save the changes.

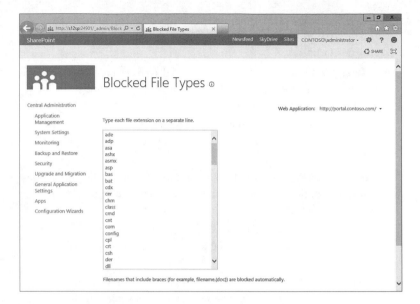

FIGURE 16.7
Adding the file extension of the file type to be blocked on a new line in the list.

Setting Size Limitations on Documents

You cannot limit the size of documents from within the Site settings or Document Library settings. You can only limit the size of files uploaded to a web application. SharePoint 2013 now has a default setting of 250MB for file uploads. This setting is available from the SharePoint 2013 Central Administration website and can be modified in the following way:

1. Open Central Administration, click Application Management, and under Web Applications click Manage Web Applications.

2. Click the web application whose upload size limit you want to modify.

3. In the Manage section of the management ribbon, click the General Settings drop-down menu and choose General Settings.

4. On the Web Application General Settings page, scroll down to the Maximum Upload Size section near the bottom of the page.

5. In the Maximum Upload Size text box, type the maximum allowed size for uploads.

6. Click OK to save the settings.

> **Note**
>
> The Maximum Upload Size setting applies to any single upload, whether it's a single file or a group of files. Therefore, even if the individual files are below the maximum, if the combined size of a group of uploaded files exceeds the maximum, you will receive an error upon attempting the upload.

Using Content Types in Document Libraries

Content types are used to provide a means of encapsulating settings and metadata for a particular type of content. A single document library can host one or more content types simultaneously. When a new document library is created, a content type called Document is provisioned with a document template based on the default document type of the document library. For example, if the default document type is set to be Microsoft Excel, the document template for the default Document content type will be template.xls.

By default, content types cannot be managed for a document library. To perform actions such as adding a content type or modifying the default content type, you must first allow management of content types in the Advanced Settings menu of the document library settings. To add a content type to a document library, perform the following steps:

1. From the document library default page, click the Library tab in the management ribbon.

2. In the Library ribbon, in the Settings section, click Library Settings.

3. On the Document Library Settings page, click Advanced Settings.

4. On the Advanced Settings page, in the Content Types section, choose Yes to allow management of content types.

5. Click OK to save the settings.

6. In the Document Library Settings page, a new section is available called Content Type. Click the Add from Existing Site Content Types link.

7. On the Add Content Types page, choose Document Content Types from the Select Site Content Types From drop-down list because you are adding a content type to a document library. Figure 16.8 shows the Add Content Types page with the Form content type being added to a document library.

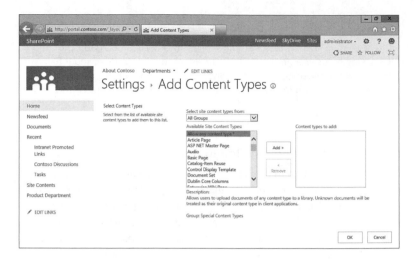

FIGURE 16.8
The Add Content Types page is used when additional content types are needed for a document library.

8. Choose the new content type to add from the Available Site Content Types list, and click the Add button to add it to the document library.

9. Click OK to finish adding the new content type to the document library.

Creating and Managing Lists

Like Document Libraries in SharePoint 2013, lists are also now considered apps and are created using the Add an App option under Site Settings. Lists provide the basic building blocks of SharePoint 2013 products. They allow data to be organized logically and manipulated easily. List creation and management is a fundamental concept to understanding SharePoint 2013 Products. To create a list, follow these steps:

1. From the site where the list is to be created, click the Settings menu and choose Add an App.

2. Choose the type of list to create. For this example, you will create a new Announcements list, so click Announcements.

3. On the Create page, type a name for the list and (optionally) give it a description by clicking More Options.

4. Specify whether to display a link to the list on the Quick Launch toolbar.

5. Click Create to create the list.

Note

The various library types, such as document and picture, as well as discussion boards and surveys are all specialized types of apps.

Creating Site Columns (Field Definitions)

Shared list columns, also called *site columns*, provide a column definition that can be reused among lists without the need to redefine the column in each list. The site column is defined once at the site level and saved as a template from which lists and content types can reference it. When a site column is added to a list, a local copy of the column is created as a list column. Any changes made to that column from the list are local changes, applying only to the list column.

There were a few problematic points in site columns in SharePoint Server 2007 that were resolved in SharePoint Server 2010. In SharePoint Server 2007, there was no out-of-the-box way to specify that a site column should be unique. Also, there was no easy way to provide validation on data entered into a column. These problems were solvable using custom development, and there were certainly some creative solutions developed by the community, but most IT professionals did not have the time or expertise to delve into the world of custom development. Furthermore, these were features that just seemed like they should be available and require minimal effort to implement. In SharePoint 2010, and continuing into 2013, these features are made available out of the box, as you can see when creating a new site column.

SharePoint 2013 has provided additional functionality with the Site Columns to provide better aggregation of content.

To create a new site column, do the following:

1. From the site where the column should be created, click the Settings button, and click Site Settings.

2. In the Web Designer Galleries section of the Site Settings page, choose Site Columns.

3. On the Site Columns page, click Create.

4. In the Name and Type section, type a name in the Column Name box.

5. Choose a type for the column in the type list, as shown in Figure 16.9. Choose Single Line of Text for this example.

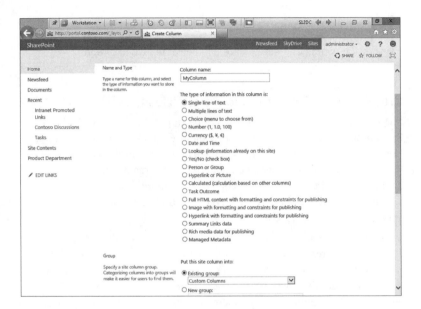

FIGURE 16.9
Choosing a type for the column in the type list.

6. Choose a group for the new column. Groups are simply a means of organizing site columns to make them easier to browse.

7. In the Additional Column Settings section, (optionally) type a description for the column.

8. Choose whether to make the column required by default.

9. Choose whether the column values should be unique.

10. Because you chose Single Line of Text, you are asked to specify the maximum number of characters for the column. The default is 255.

11. You can also provide a default value, either text or some calculated value. If this setting is left blank, no default value will be used.

12. Optionally, in the Column Validation section, enter a formula to be used to validate data in the column. This formula must evaluate to True for the validation to pass.

If you are providing a validation function for the site column, you should also type a user message to explain to those entering data in the column what is considered valid data.

13. Click OK to save the new site column.

After you have created a new site column, you can now add it to a list. To add a site column to a list, do the following:

1. From the list where the site column should be added, click the List tab in the List Tools area of the management ribbon.

2. In the Settings section on the List ribbon, choose List Settings.

3. In the Columns section of the List Settings page, click Add from Existing Site Columns.

4. Leave the Select Site Columns From drop-down list set to All Groups, and find the column you want to add in the Available Site Columns list.

5. Click the column you want to add, and then click the Add button to add it to the Columns to Add list.

6. In the Options section, choose whether to add the column to the default view of the list.

7. Click OK to finish adding the column to the list.

Creating Content Types

Content types are one of the building blocks of lists in SharePoint Server 2013. As stated previously, content types provide a means of encapsulating settings and metadata for a particular type of content in a template that can be reused and is independent of any particular list or library. Content types can include one or more of the following:

■ Content metadata, represented by columns that will be added to the list or library upon addition of the content type.

■ Association with an Information Management Policy, thus ensuring that all similar content types are following the same policies. This is important for organizations that face strict auditing and compliance needs.

■ Custom forms, used for New, Edit, and Display functions.

■ Workflows that can be designed to start automatically based on some event or condition or manually started by a user.

- The document template on which to base the documents created from this type (for document content types only).
- Custom information stored as XML files.

Just like site columns, content types are scoped at both the site and list levels. Content types are created at the site level and then are available to the containing site and any subsites beneath it. When a content type is added to a list or document library, a local copy of the content type is created. This is known as a list content type, and any changes made to it directly apply only to the list where it resides.

Create a New Content Type

To create a new content type, do the following:

1. From the Settings menu, choose Site Settings.

2. In the Web Designer Galleries section, click Site Content Types.

3. On the Site Content Types page, click Create.

4. On the New Site Content Type page, type a name for the new content type in the Name box and (optionally) type a description.

5. Choose the type of parent content type the new content type will be created from, and choose the parent content type. All new content types must be created from a parent content type, as shown in Figure 16.10.

6. In the Group section, specify the group for the new content type. You can either choose an existing group or specify a new group.

7. Click OK to save the new content type.

Adding the content type to a list can be accomplished the same way as adding a content type to a document library. After a content type has been added, the content type will be available on the New Item menu when creating new list items. Figure 16.11 shows the New Item menu of the Task list with a custom content type called Contoso Task added.

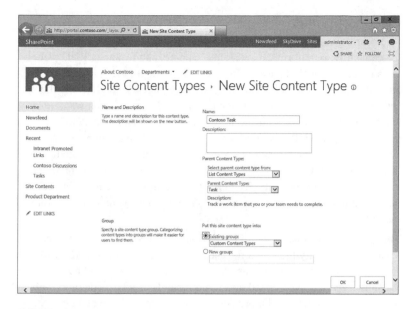

FIGURE 16.10
The New Site Content Type page is used when a new content type is needed.

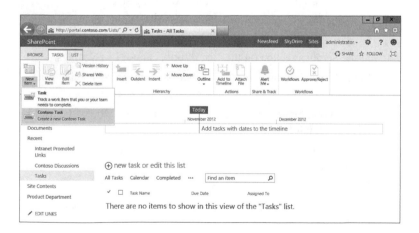

FIGURE 16.11
The New Item menu of the Tasks list.

Using List Forms

One of the great features of SharePoint going back to the very beginning is the capability to perform Create, Read, Update, and Delete (CRUD) functions on lists through the user interface (UI) without having to actually build the UI forms. When a list is created, the pages for performing these actions are automatically provisioned. This works great if you want your users to be able to edit all the columns in the list when a new item is inserted or updated. But what if you want only certain columns to be available through the UI, and you want other columns to be updated through an event handler on the list? In previous versions of SharePoint, this required some creativity. By default, all columns were available on insert and update and there was no easy way to modify the forms for an individual list.

This problem was finally addressed in SharePoint Server 2010 with the capability to modify the forms for each individual list in using Microsoft InfoPath Designer 2010. In SharePoint 2013, InfoPath can still be used for the same capability and to add and remove fields as well as pictures, validation, formatted text, and more. When a list is created, the default forms are provisioned as in SharePoint 2010, but an administrator can build customized forms instead, using InfoPath 2013. To modify a task form using InfoPath Designer 2013, perform the following steps:

1. From the list where the site column should be added, click the List tab in the List Tools area of the management ribbon.

2. In the Settings section on the List ribbon, choose List Settings.

3. In the General Settings section of the List Settings page, click Form Settings.

4. On the Form Settings page, click OK to customize the default Tasks form using InfoPath 2013.

5. In the Design view for the form, right-click inside the Predecessors row and choose Delete and then Rows.

6. Do the same for the Priority row.

7. Click the File tab, and choose Publish to publish the changes to SharePoint.

8. On the Publish page, choose SharePoint List.

9. When you receive the message that the form has been published successfully, click OK.

Figure 16.12 shows the default form for the Tasks list, and Figure 16.13 shows the edited form with the Predecessors and Priority rows removed.

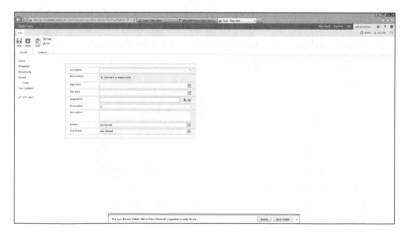

FIGURE 16.12
The default form for the Tasks list.

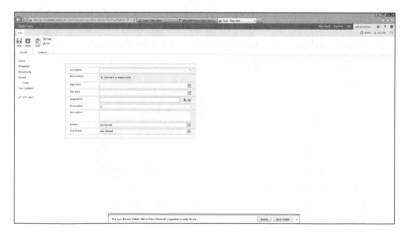

FIGURE 16.13
The edited form.

Deploying Solutions

Solutions originate back to SharePoint Server 2007 and were originally introduced as a way to package functionality for deployment to a server farm. When functionality is deployed using a solution, SharePoint automatically manages the deployment of the functionality on servers that are added to the farm. In SharePoint Server 2007, however, solutions could only be deployed at the farm level by a farm administrator. In SharePoint 2010, this limitation was addressed by using a feature called sandboxed solutions. However, in SharePoint 2013, sandboxed solutions are deprecated. This is largely due to the shift to the App Store for SharePoint as a way to deploy and manage this functionality more efficiently. However, for backward compatibility, sandboxed solutions can still be installed to site collections. For more on apps and solution deployment, see Chapter 15, "Managing Apps and Solutions."

Sandboxed solutions are solutions that can be deployed to a specific site collection and are limited in scope to that site collection. This means that the solution is effectively placed within a "sandbox" that is contained within a site collection. Because the "sandbox" is within the site collection, the solution will affect only the site collection in which it is deployed. In fact, the "sandbox" can be considered the surrogate process that is executed by the SPUserCode service that the custom solution runs within. Sandboxed solutions can also be limited in the amount of resources they can consume and be automatically disabled if resource consumption crosses the defined threshold. To deploy a sandboxed solution, do the following:

1. From the site collection where the solution will be deployed, click the Settings menu button and choose Site Settings.

2. On the Site Settings page, in the Web Designer Galleries section, click Solutions.

3. In the Solutions Library, click the Solutions tab in the management ribbon and choose Upload Solution.

4. In the Upload Document window, click the Browse button, find the solution file to be uploaded, and then click Open.

5. Click OK to upload the solution.

6. On the Solutions tab, click Activate.

Creating User Alerts

As the number of sites, and presumably the number of lists and libraries, in your SharePoint farm grows, it will become a much more difficult task to keep up with the changes to lists and libraries across various sites and web applications. This is where alerts come in. Alerts provide the capability to be notified by email when a particular type of change happens in a list or library, so they can be created and then essentially forgotten until an event occurs on the list that triggers the associated alert action. To create an alert, perform the following steps:

1. From the site containing the list for which you want to be alerted, click the list or library that you want to create an alert for.

2. Select List, or Library, in the ribbon to display the List Settings or Library Settings.

3. In the Share and Track section of the ribbon, left-click Alert Me (see Figure 16.14).

FIGURE 16.14
The Alert Me context menu.

4. In the Context menu, left-click Set Alert on This Library to create an alert for this library.

5. On the New Alert page, in the Alert Title section, type a descriptive title for the alert.

6. In the Send Alerts To section, ensure that your username is listed. Additionally, add the usernames of any other users who should receive the same alert.

7. In the Delivery Method section, choose a delivery method for the alert.

Note

For alerts to be sent by email, outgoing email settings must be configured for the farm. Second, for users to receive alerts, the users must also have a valid email address configured in the user profile service. For alerts to be sent via text message (SMS), the SMS settings must be configured for the farm. All these settings can be configured in Central Administration in the Email and Text Messages (SMS) section of the System Settings page.

---

8. In the Change Type section, choose the types of changes that you want to be alerted to. Choosing All Changes will cause alerts to be sent for any additions, modifications, or deletions that occur.

9. In the Send Alerts for These Changes section, choose whether to filter alerts based on specific criteria, such as who made the changes, who created the original item, and whether an expiration date is associated with the item.

10. In the When to Send Alerts section, choose the frequency with which alerts should be sent. Notifications can be sent immediately or on a daily or weekly schedule.

11. Click OK to save the alert.

Alerts for a user can be managed through the My Alerts page, which is accessed by following steps 1 through 3 in the procedure just shown. To manage your alerts, left-click Manage My Alerts.

Creating Discussion Boards

A discussion board is a specialized list that uses the Thread and Message content types to provide functionality similar to a web newsgroup or discussion board. A new thread is created in the discussion list with a subject and body, and then replies can be added. The topics are displayed by subject, but when a user clicks a topic, the replies can be viewed in a flat or threaded view. An example of the flat view is shown in Figure 16.15.

The other topic is shown in Figure 16.16 using the threaded view.

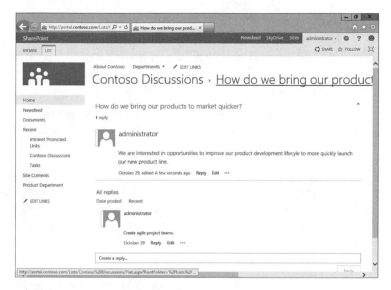

FIGURE 16.15
The discussion topic shown in a flat view so that all of the discussions can be shown on a single page, in chronological order.

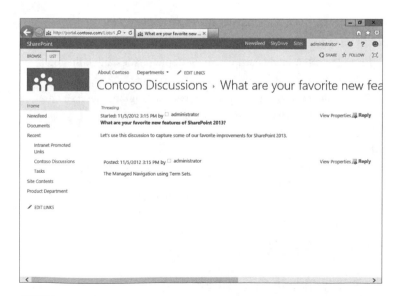

FIGURE 16.16
The discussion topic can also be viewed in a threaded view. This can often make for an easier reading experience for the user.

Create a New Discussion Board

To create a new discussion board, do the following:

1. From the Site Settings menu, click Add an App.

2. On the Your Apps page, choose Discussion Board from the Apps You Can Add section.

3. On the New page, give the discussion board a name and (optionally) a description by clicking Advanced Options.

4. Click Create to create the new discussion board.

Create a New Discussion Topic

To create a new discussion topic, do the following:

1. Navigate to the discussion board where you want to post a new topic.

2. Click New Discussion.

3. Enter a subject and body for the discussion. You may also indicate if your topic is a question for everyone.

4. Click Save to save the new discussion topic.

Post a Reply to a Discussion Topic

To post a reply to a discussion topic, follow these steps:

1. From the discussion board where the topic resides, click the topic link.

2. Choose the message to reply to—either the original message or an existing reply—and from that message click Reply.

> **Note**
>
> Notice that the Subject field is missing from the Reply form. You cannot change the subject of a message when you reply to it. You can only enter text for the body of your reply, which will be appended to the other replies.

3. Click Save to post the reply.

Using Really Simple Syndication

The dynamic nature of SharePoint content makes it a perfect candidate for Really Simple Syndication (RSS). RSS provides the capability to monitor changes to SharePoint content in a simple and straightforward way, with the latest changes being automatically downloaded and bubbled to the top of your chosen RSS feed reader, such as Internet Explorer 10 or Outlook 2012. Just as in SharePoint 2010, RSS feed creation in SharePoint 2013 is accomplished automatically for every list created.

View a List Using RSS

To view a list using RSS, do the following:

1. Navigate to the list you want to view using RSS.
2. Click the List tab in the List Tools area of the management ribbon.
3. In the Share and Track section of the ribbon, choose RSS Feed.

> **Note**
>
> The content of the list will automatically be rendered using RSS, and the output will be formatted via XSLT for most browsers. If you are using Internet Explorer 8, or any other modern browser, you can subscribe to the feed directly from this page.

4. If you are using Internet Explorer 10, you can click Subscribe to This Feed to set up a subscription to the feed.

Managing RSS Settings for a List

The RSS settings for a list can be modified from the List Settings page by clicking the RSS Settings link in the Communications section. Table 16.1 shows the available settings.

Table 16.1   **RSS Settings for a List**

Setting	Description
Allow RSS for this list?	Yes or No
Truncate multiline text fields to 256 characters?	Yes or No
Title	Title channel element of RSS feed definition
Description	Description channel element of RSS feed
Image URL	Image URL channel element of RSS feed
Columns	List columns to be included in RSS feed
Maximum items to include	Integer representing the maximum number of items to be included in the RSS feed
Maximum days to include	Maximum number of previous days to include in RSS feed

Navigation and Promoted Links

SharePoint 2013 has a few new capabilities to help better manage navigation. One of the toughest challenges for many SharePoint environments is not only the creation, but the management of a consistent navigation experience. The Managed Navigation along with Promoted Links in SharePoint 2013 increases not only the administrator's influence, but simplifies the user experience as well.

Enabling Managed Navigation Using the Term Store

The Managed Metadata Service and the use of the Term Store were great additions in SharePoint 2010. In SharePoint 2013 they take yet another significant step forward by being used to manage and facilitate a consistent navigational experience. Using a Term Set now allows SharePoint Administrators to build out and define a navigation structure that maps more directly to enterprise content rather than the URL structure of the SharePoint environment. Managed Navigation is significant for any organization that faces the challenge of centrally managing navigation across the organization's environment. To use the Managed Navigation feature, it will be important to first create a term set using the Term Store Management tool. Managed Navigation essentially brings the capability to integrate the tagging of content with the navigation, ensuring that content is now more easily findable. Friendly URLs are URLs without the /pages/ and .aspx additions.

Real World

For organizations with intranets needing consistent navigation, consider using a Term Set for central management for enterprisewide navigation control.

To make use of the Managed Navigation capability, you will need to have the ability to create the Term Set Structure and have the ability as a site administrator to activate the navigation capabilities.

Enable Managed Navigation

To enable Managed Navigation, follow these steps:

> **Note**
>
> Before adjusting your navigation settings, you will need to determine if you want to use Managed Navigation for your Global Navigation (top), Current Navigation (left), or both. If you choose both, consider using two different term sets for each form of navigation.

1. Left-click the Settings Gear icon.
2. Left-click Site Settings.
3. Under Look and Feel, left-click Navigation.
4. On the Site Settings, Navigation Settings page, left-click Managed Navigation under Global Navigation. The Navigation Settings are shown in Figure 16.17.

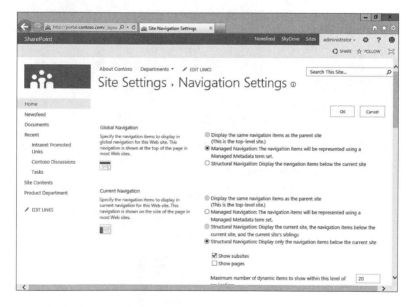

FIGURE 16.17
The navigation settings showing the Managed Navigation option selected.

5. In the Current Navigation Section (not found in publishing sites), left-click Managed Navigation.

Best Practice

If Navigation has not been set up in the Term Store, consider creating a Term Set to centrally manage the Term Sets that your organization will be using before following the remaining steps. The Navigation Term Set must also be enabled under Intended Use for Use This Term Set for Navigation. For more on creating Term Groups and Term Sets, see Chapter 8.

6. To create a New Navigation Term Set, in the Managed Navigation: Term Set section, left-click the link to Open the Term Store Management tool to edit term sets.

7. Under Site Collection, left-click the desired Navigation to open the Term Set menu options.

8. Left-click Create Term, and type **Departments**.

9. In the Main window pane to the right, left-click Navigation (see Figure 16.18).

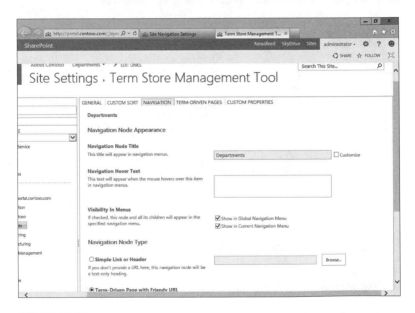

FIGURE 16.18
The Navigation tab of the Term List settings when setting up the Term Set for Managed Navigation.

10. Select the Navigation Node Type, Term-Driven Page with Friendly URL, for the Departments term:

■ **Simple Link or Header**—Allows for the assignment of a specific URL; without it, the navigation node will be a text-only heading.

■ **Term-Driven Page with Friendly URL**—This navigation node will be a friendly URL to a term-driven page. Switch to the Term-Driven Page tab at the top to configure more options for this node type.

11. In the Main window pane of the Term Store Management tool, left-click the Term-Driven Pages tab.

12. Under Configure Friendly URL for this term, click the Customize option to the right of the /departments URL.

13. Change departments to /departments-internal.

14. Left-click Save.

Real World

The use of the Term Store to drive Managed Navigation also provides the capability to have multiple levels of navigation, as shown next.

Managing Promoted Links

New to SharePoint 2013 are Promoted Links. These links provide the animation and a similar feel that resembles the Windows 8 Tiles. Similar in concept to Managed Navigation, the Promoted Links are centrally managed in a Promoted Links app (see Figure 16.19). The Promoted Links are a great way to a direct a user's focus on the page.

Real World

To sustain the Promoted Links effectiveness, it is important to not overuse the Promoted Links capability. Also of equal importance is to make sure that your Promoted Links are not stale and are regularly updated and changed to reflect what your users need.

Before you start creating and customizing Promoted Links for your users, you will need to create your own Promoted Links app.

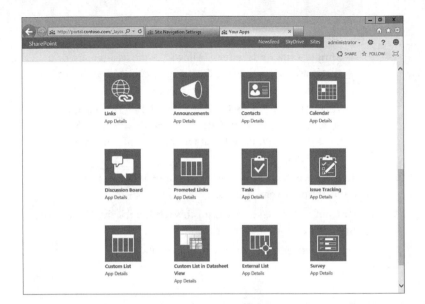

FIGURE 16.19
Promoted Links app added to the Contoso Portal.

Add Your Own Promoted Links App
To add your own Promoted Links app, do the following:

1. Left-click the Settings Gear icon.
2. In the drop-down menu, left-click the Add an App menu option.
3. On the next page, Your Apps, left-click the Promoted Links App.
4. Click Add It.
5. Enter a name for the new list and click Create.

   The Promoted Links list has now been created. The list should now be in the Quick Launch underneath the Recent grouping.

Add New Promoted Links
To add new promoted links, you will need to do the following:

1. Left-click Intranet Promoted Links.
2. On the next page, left-click All Promoted Links.
3. In the Intranet Promoted Links list, click the New Item link to create the new Promoted Link

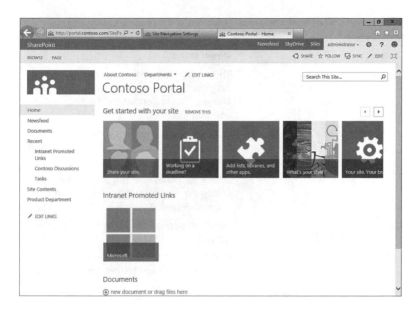

FIGURE 16.20
Available list of apps showing Promoted Links as an app to be created.

Table 16.2 shows the standard columns used for a Promoted Links List.

Table 16.2   **Standard Columns Used for a Promoted Links List**

Column	Description
Title	Enter a meaningful title that the user will understand. This title will be displayed on the Tile of Promoted Links App.
Background Image Location	Enter the URL of the location of the background image for the tile.
Type the Description	Enter a description of the background image. This is important for Section 508 compliance.
Description	The description is shown when a user places the cursor over the Promoted Link Tile.
Link Location	This is the web address that the user will be redirected to after the user left-clicks the link.

Table 16.2 **Standard Columns Used for a Promoted Links List (continued)**

Column	Description
Type the Description	This is the description of the link that is displayed when a user hovers over a link. This is also important for Section 508 compliance.
Launch Behavior	In page navigation, this redirects the current page being browsed to the target link.
	Dialog launches the target location in a dialog box window within the current browser session.
	New Tab opens the target location in a new browser tab.
Order	Use numbers to specify the order in which the tiles will be displayed from left to right.

CHAPTER 17

Upgrading from SharePoint Server 2010

- Planning and Preparing
- Database Attach Upgrades
- Upgrading Sites and Site Collections
- Upgrading My Sites

Depending on the level of complexity and customization of your current system, there are many variables to take into consideration when upgrading to Microsoft SharePoint Server 2013. If your current system isn't highly customized or complex, the upgrade process will be fairly painless. However, if you have deployed custom code and made multiple Internet Information Services (IIS) modifications, your implementation will require significant planning and testing. The in-place upgrade option has been removed in SharePoint Server 2013. Instead, Microsoft focused a large amount of energy and time into separating the database upgrade and the site collection upgrade processes from one another.

Because version-to-version in-place upgrade is not an option, if you are planning to upgrade to SharePoint 2013, you will need an additional set of hardware. The hardware requirements have significantly increased; therefore, new hardware should usually be planned for.

Follow these steps when you upgrade from SharePoint Server 2010 to SharePoint 2013:

1. Study and understand the upgrade process and the upgrade options available to you.

2. Thoroughly document your current system, including databases, features, solutions, shared services, authentication providers, email settings, Internet Information Services settings such as SSL bindings, Port binding, Host headers, and any other customizations made outside of SharePoint, and SQL Server, hardware, and farm-level customizations, such as alternate access mappings and host headers.

3. Communicate with users and stakeholders about potential system outages and changes.

> **Note**
>
> The upgrade changes made by Microsoft were intended to reduce end-user downtime and provided SharePoint administrators the capability to manage IT requirements for downtime as well as the needs of the user population.

4. Plan your upgrade, and verify that it aligns with a supported upgrade scenario. More upgrade planning information can be found at http://technet.microsoft.com/en-us/library/cc303429.aspx.

5. Make sure that your environment is clean and ready for upgrade by making sure that your logs are as error free as possible.

6. Test your upgrade in a nonproduction environment using a copy of production data.

7. Create and test your rollback plan in the event of upgrade failure.

8. Upgrade your server farm or farms, deploy custom code, and execute a test plan.

9. Validate a successful upgrade by testing all components detailed in your system documentation. Be sure to test any customizations in features and solutions as well as new features (such as visual upgrades), and get plenty of user feedback.

It's possible your first attempt will not be 100 percent successful. Always prepare for the worst and hope for the best by having multiple, reliable backups of all systems and databases. Good planning and testing performed in advance will greatly reduce the chance of a failed upgrade.

> **Note**
>
> For information on planning and documenting your current environment for the purposes of upgrading, download the Upgrade Worksheet for SharePoint Server 2013 at http://www.microsoft.com/en-us/download/details.aspx?id=30370.

Planning and Preparing

SharePoint 2013 has a single version-to-version (v2v) upgrade scenario—the database attach. Despite the database attach being the sole method for a SharePoint v2v upgrade, there will still be a few decision points that must be considered as well as items that will need to be documented and fleshed out before the upgrade should begin.

Communicating to Stakeholders

It is so often the case with new technology and server environments that technology and systems are updated with minimal communication to the stakeholders and end users. As you begin planning and preparing to upgrade, do not forget about the end users of your SharePoint environment. The users' success will ultimately be your success.

When communicating to the stakeholders, do not consider all end users as being created equal; they are not. Prior to upgrading, it is worth the time and resource investment to document a high-level plan for communicating with your users. Your pre-upgrade communication plan should be tailored to your organization but cover the SharePoint 2013 changes and improvements and, ultimately, accomplish the goal of reducing the fear and resistance that may consume the upgrade approach.

As a part of the communication plan, consider a training plan as well. Providing your stakeholders the opportunity to learn about the tool through training will not only aid in your governance, but further demonstrate your commitment to a successful SharePoint 2013 upgrade.

Reviewing Topology and Environment

Before moving forward in the upgrade path, it is important that you, as an administrator, know the topology and the environment that you will be upgrading. It is important to first start with the topology of the farm by knowing which servers are running which services. Also, ensure that you know any service accounts, regardless of whether you will be changing domains.

> **Note**
>
> SharePoint 2013 uses Claims-based authentication. If the existing environment that you will be upgrading from is currently not Claims enabled, strong consideration should be made to migrating toward Claims prior to upgrading.

Document Customizations

As part of the upgrade planning, document and record all the customizations currently running in your environment. When looking for customizations, these are the items and areas that must be closely inspected:

- Customizations and Solution packages (WSP)
- Service Applications
- Web Applications
- Large Lists
- Configurations
- Language Packs
- InfoPath Forms
- Event Handlers
- Master Pages
- Page Layouts
- CSS
- Proxy Groups
- Authentication Providers

> **Note**
>
> Document all customizations for each server in your environment.

Web Enumeration

One additional command is useful when planning an upgrade:
Stsadm.exe -o enumallwebs.

Although it isn't an upgrade command specifically, it provides information that is useful for planning an upgrade and can help locate customizations throughout your SharePoint farm.

Stsadm.exe -o enumallwebs can provide a list of all site collections and sites in a content database in addition to site definitions in use. Remember that in the object model the term *sites* is equivalent to site collections and the term *webs* is equivalent to sites. For example, running stsadm.exe -o enumallwebs -databasename WSS_Content_Portal_Root might produce the following output for a content database with a single publishing site:

```
<Sites Count="1"> <Site Id="cb88eb37-395d-4bb2-
9941-
fff291a1eb34"OwnerLogin="CONTOSO\administrator"
InSiteMap="True">
 <Webs Count="1">    <Web Id="f4d0c333-c883-4888-
9f34-
2b1eefdb75a5" Url="/"LanguageId="1033"
TemplateName="STS#0"
TemplateId="1" />  </Webs> </Site>
```

Clean Up

Every upgrade should always be considered an opportunity to start fresh with a clean environment. Some general clean-up steps should be performed.

Before upgrading, do the following:

1. As a part of the cleanup and preparation, document all your service applications and their assigned databases and database names.

2. Check your SharePoint server logs; if errors exist, take the necessary steps to clean them.

3. Check your database for errors, and put forth any effort needed to remove them.

4. Remove orphaned items. To do this, you will need to check your databases for duplicate or orphaned sites and site collections.

5. Assess your content for stagnation. If there is content that can be removed before upgrade, do so.

Note

Before deleting a site collection, ensure that there are no subsites that are needed or are being used. Also, *always* back up the site collection before deletion.

---

6. To delete sites collections or subsites, use the following PowerShell Commands:

- Site Collection: Use Remove-SPSite.

- Subsite: Use Remove-SPWeb.

7. For lists with many columns, consider either trimming them or removing the wide list entirely.

8. Test for wide lists or large lists with large amounts of data by using the Test-SPContentDatabase command.

9. Before migration, consider reorganizing not only your sites, but also your content databases. If you have some site collections that are very large in size, consider moving them to their own content database prior to migration.

> **Note**
>
> Attaching multiple content databases does not necessarily increase your upgrade time. In fact, it may decrease the time by running multiple content database upgrades in parallel if you don't add additional disk resources and CPU resources on SQL to support multiple, simultaneous database attaches.

10. After inventorying customizations, catalogue them as templates, features, or web parts. After cataloging, identify whether these items are used throughout your environment. If they are not used at all, remove them.

> **Tip**
>
> Use the **Stasdm -o EnumAll Webs - include features** or **-includewebparts** to find the location of these items and where they are being used.

11. Remove FAST Search Center sites; the existing FAST Search Center will continue to work in the 14 mode (SharePoint 2010), but it is not upgradeable. If you want to use a Search Center in SharePoint 2013, you will need to use the Enterprise Search Center in SharePoint 2013.

Test Your Upgrade

Testing your upgrade is an important step prior to actually living through the experience of an unrehearsed upgrade. The steps are simple:

1. Set up and configure a test farm that can be removed without detriment.

2. Install all the customizations that you identified in the planning phase discussed in this chapter.

3. Move live data to this environment by upgrading the databases using a database attach.

4. Use a backup and restore of your content database.

5. Review the logs and results of the database upgrade. Logs will be located here:

   `%COMMONPROGRAMFILES%\Microsoft Shared\Web server extensions\15\LOGS`. Named `Upgrade-YYYYMMDD-HHMMSS-SSS.log`.

6. Resolve any logs or issues during the database upgrade.

7. Identify and upgrade a site collection.

8. Review the results of the site collection upgrade.

   Logs of the site collection upgrades are stored in an upgrade document library located in the _catalogs\Upgrade document library.

9. Test the My Sites upgrade.

10. Upgrade the My Site Host site collection.

11. Visit your My Site to queue the upgrade of your Personal Site migration. Note that you'll get only one opportunity to migrate to SkyDrive Pro.

12. After several minutes, validate the migration of your Personal Site.

Test-SPContentDatabase

If you are attaching a SharePoint Server 2010 database to a SharePoint Server 2013 server farm for upgrade, you have the option of using the Windows PowerShell cmdlet Test-SPContentDatabase. This Windows PowerShell cmdlet checks to see whether all the server infrastructure customizations are present for the site collections in a SharePoint Server 2010 content database.

Tip

You can also execute the Test-SPContentDatabase cmdlet against a SharePoint Server 2010 content database. It will verify that all server-side customizations are present for site collections contained in the database.

This cmdlet should be run before attaching the content database to a SharePoint Server 2013 web application. You should not attempt an upgrade before running this cmdlet. Although you certainly can upgrade without running the Test-SPContentDatabase cmdlet, you cannot run the cmdlet after attempting a database attach upgrade. The cmdlet provides the following information about site collections in a given content database:

- Reports server-side customizations that are missing and required by site collections
- Compares the site collections contained in a content database against a specific web application
- Identifies current or potential data orphans
- Identifies missing site definitions
- Identifies missing features
- Identifies missing assemblies
- Shows table sizing metrics

The following is an example of executing Test-SPContentDatabase with a SharePoint Server 2010 database named WSS_Content_Portal and a SharePoint Server 2013 web application named http://portal.contoso.com:

```
Test-SPContentDatabase -name WSS_Content_Portal
-WebApplication http://portal.contoso.com
```

The following example is for a content database that hosts a team site collection using Excel Services. The target SharePoint Server 2013 web application does not have Excel Services available. Notice that the error will not prevent (block) an upgrade. However, you should configure Excel Services in your SharePoint Server 2013 server farm before a production deployment:

```
Category: MissingSetupFileError     :
TrueUpgradeBlocking : FalseMessage     :
File[Features\ExcelServerSite\Microsoft.Office.Excel.
WebUI.dwp] is
referenced[1] times in the database
[WSS_Content_Portal], but is
not installed on the current farm. Please install any
feature/solution which contains this file. Remedy
: One
or more setup files are referenced in the
```

```
database[WSS_Content_Portal], but are not installed
on the current farm.
Please install any feature or solution which contains these
files.
```

The following options are available for the Test-SPContentDatabase cmdlet:

- **Name**—The name of a content database. It must be online in SQL Server Management Studio before you attempt a test.

- **WebApplication**—The web application to test the content database with, which is a process also known as *pairing*. Pay close attention to the web application you are testing against. For example, if the web application you are using to test does not have an Excel Services service application associated with it, you'll get errors in the test.

- **DatabaseCredentials**—If you are using SQL Server authentication, you should include the username and password. Most administrators will not require this option. However, you need to verify that the SharePoint Server 2013 farm account has sufficient access to the content database when using Windows Authentication.

- **ServerInstance**—The SQL server and instance name. If you are using the default instance, this will be the SQL server name.

- **ShowRowCounts**—Displays the total row count in the database.

Farm Planning

If you have a medium or larger server installation or many customizations, you need to do planning that is beyond the scope of this book. Only the basics of upgrade farm planning are covered in this section.

Tip

Before you begin the upgrade planning and testing process, remove all unnecessary content—unused sites and customizations, such as Web parts and workflows—from your current server farm. Doing so will speed up the migration of content and lessen the impact of customizations during the upgrade process.

Before beginning your upgrade, you must first meet all prerequisites for installing SharePoint Server 2013. It's possible that you currently meet the prerequisites for SharePoint Server 2013, but that same hardware and software—either the SQL Server build or the Windows Server version—is not compatible with the new version. Also, you cannot perform an In-place Upgrade and need to plan accordingly. Refer to Chapter 1, "Installing SharePoint Server 2013," for details on requirements.

> **Note**
>
> You must have 64-bit Windows Server 2008 R2 Service Pack 1 or the 64-bit Windows Server 2012 Standard or Datacenter to install SharePoint Server 2013. Additionally, remember you need, at a minimum, SQL Server 2008 R2 with Service Pack 1 or SQL Server 2012.

The benefit of the database attach option is that it allows you to build a new SharePoint Server 2013 farm and leave your SharePoint Server 2010 farm intact. This provides a fallback platform in case the upgrade fails. Verify that you have the following software installed in your SharePoint Server 2013 environment (for a complete and updated list, visit http://technet.microsoft.com/en-us/library/cc262485.aspx#section4):

- Database Server
  - The 64-bit edition of Windows Server 2008 R2 Service Pack 1 (SP1) Standard, Enterprise, or Datacenter or the 64-bit edition of Windows Server 2012 Standard or Datacenter.
  - The SharePoint parsing process crashes in Windows Server 2008 R2 (KB 2554876).
  - FIX: IIS 7.5 configurations are not updated when you use the ServerManager class to commit configuration changes (KB 2708075).
  - Hotfix: ASP.NET (SharePoint) race condition in .NET 4.5 RTM:
    - Windows Server 2008 R2 SP1 (KB 2759112)
    - Windows Server 2012 (KB 2765317)
  - The Microsoft SharePoint Products Preparation Tool installs the following prerequisites for front-end web servers and application servers in a farm:
    - Microsoft .NET 4.5

The following are minimum requirements for front-end web servers and application servers in a farm (source http://technet.microsoft.com/en-us/library/cc262485.aspx):

- Front-end and application server.

- The 64-bit edition of Windows Server 2008 R2 Service Pack 1 (SP1) Standard, Enterprise, or Datacenter or the 64-bit edition of Windows Server 2012 Standard or Datacenter.

- The SharePoint parsing process crashes in Windows Server 2008 R2 (KB 2554876).

- FIX: IIS 7.5 configurations are not updated when you use the ServerManager class to commit configuration changes (KB 2708075).

- Hotfix: ASP.NET (SharePoint) race condition in .NET 4.5 RTM:

  - Windows Server 2008 R2 SP1 (KB 2759112)

  - Windows Server 2012 (KB 2765317)

The Microsoft SharePoint Products Preparation Tool installs the following prerequisites for front-end web servers and application servers in a farm:

- Web Server (IIS) role

- Application Server role

- SQL Server 2008 R2 SP1 Native Client

- Microsoft WCF Data Services 5.0

- Microsoft Information Protection and Control Client (MSIPC)

- Microsoft Sync Framework Runtime v1.0 SP1 (x64)

- Windows Management Framework 3.0, which includes Windows PowerShell 3.0

- Windows Identity Foundation (WIF) 1.0 and Microsoft Identity Extensions (previously named WIF 1.1)

- Windows Server AppFabric

- Cumulative Update Package 1 for Microsoft AppFabric 1.1 for Windows Server (KB 2671763)

Ensure that any additional language packs used in your SharePoint 2010 environment have been configured in the new SharePoint 2013 environment.

Removing Pre-upgrade Checks

When you were upgrading from SharePoint Server 2007 to SharePoint 2010, you had the capability to perform a pre-upgrade check to scan your existing SharePoint Server 2007 environment for problems. The pre-upgrade checker is not needed to migrate from SharePoint 2010 to SharePoint 2013. Instead, when the database attach begins, any errors that are thrown are captured using an error log. This will be your source of information to resolve any errors for the upgrade. Because SharePoint now separates the site collection upgrade process from the database upgrade process, you can now run pre-upgrade checks against the site collection—a more meaningful approach toward issue mitigation.

Many planning and execution variables can affect database attach upgrade. For example, many administrators will ask, "How long will it take?" This depends on both your current software configuration and target hardware configuration. The current number of site collections, subsites, document libraries, lists, custom lists with numerous columns, number of documents, document size, version history, and site collection size will significantly impact both the time and complexity of an upgrade. A benefit of doing a dry run test is that the test will provide you with metrics, such as length of upgrade time and expected downtime periods.

Note

If you are not presently running Claims-based authentication, it is highly recommended to convert to Claims prior to upgrading.

Likewise, the hardware that you perform the actual upgrade on will affect the time for upgrading. Items affected include the processor speed and disk speeds of your SQL Server hardware, the SharePoint Server 2013 web server memory and processor, the application server memory and processor, and the speed and complexity of your network environment.

Note

Always back up your current system and test system restores before attempting an upgrade. The latter, an adequate system restoration plan, is a key requirement before attempting an upgrade. Many administrators fail to test the ability to completely restore a server farm in the event of a disaster. See http://technet.microsoft.com/en-us/library/ee662536(v=office.15) for information on creating a SharePoint Server 2013 disaster recovery plan.

The system upgrade steps are performed in serial. Therefore, the more objects you have to upgrade, the longer the upgrade will take. This is especially important if you are upgrading hundreds or thousands of sites.

The upgrade process will handle each site in turn and not in parallel. The single exception to the rule is that you can attach multiple databases simultaneously, depending on your hardware. Many SQL Server instances will not perform well on simultaneous database upgrades unless they have multiple, fast disk volumes and extra CPU and memory.

After you have adequately planned for the upgrade and cleaned your environment, it is safe to begin the preparation steps needed. First, we need to ensure we have the information for two service applications. After the installation and configuration of your SharePoint 2013 environment, it is important to perform these steps:

1. Document the passphrase for the Secure Store Service.

2. Export the encryption key for the User Profile Service if you intend to include the sync DB in the attach process.

> **Note**
>
> You will need to perform each step one time per instance of that service application in the farm.

> **Note**
>
> If you are upgrading multiple farms that are federating services, you must *always* update the services farm first.

Prior to moving forward, the target farm must be installed and configured. For more information on installation and configuration, refer to Chapter 1 and Chapter 2, "Configuring Farm Operations."

Setting Databases to Read-only

A key component of the database attach and upgrade is the backup and restoration of the databases. As mentioned earlier, the database attach upgrade method allows for the original source farm location to remain active for users to continually access their information. During the upgrade, if continual access is needed by the organization, set all previous SharePoint 2010 content databases to read-only. This will enable the users to view content but not update it.

Backing Up and Restoring Databases

In the database attach upgrade are several service applications that will be configured when their respective databases are upgraded. The following service applications must have their databases, along with *all* content databases, backed up and copied to the target SharePoint 2013 environment. Table 17.1 shows the service applications and their respective databases.

Table 17.1   **Service Application Databases**

Service Application	Default Database Name
Business Data Connectivity	BDC_Service_DB_ID
Managed Metadata	Managed Metadata Service_ID
PerformancePoint Application_ID	PerformancePoint Service
SharePoint Search	Search_Service_Application_DB_ID
Secure Store	Secure_Store_Service_DB_ID
User Profile: Profile, Social, and Sync databases	User Profile Service Application_ProfileDB_ID
	User Profile Service Application_SocialDB_ID
	User Profile Service Application_SyncDB_ID

Best Practice

In an upgrade scenario, *do not* use the Farm Configuration Wizard for services listed in Table 17.1.

After performing each database backup, the next step will be restoring them to the target SharePoint 2013 environment; these databases will be restored to the SQL Server being used to host the SharePoint 2013 databases. Follow these steps:

1. Restore the databases from backup.

2. After the databases are restored, set them to read/write.

3. Configure the SQL Server logins for the service accounts.

Note

You must set the databases to read/write or the database attach upgrade will fail.

Upgrading Service Application Databases

Prior to performing the database attach upgrade, it is important that the farm have all the needed services started and their respective databases upgraded.

Each of the following services shown in Table 17.2 may be started from Central Administration or by using PowerShell. Of the six listed in the table, the Search service application must be started by using PowerShell.

Table 17.2   **Service Application Grades**

Application	Use PowerShell to Create Service Application and Upgrade Database	Create Proxy and Add It to Default Group	Special Instructions	Repeat for Each Service App
Secure Store	Yes	Yes	Restore the passphrase from the SharePoint 2010 environment.	Yes
Business Data Connectivity	Yes	No	None.	Yes
Managed Metadata	Yes	Yes	Must upgrade managed metadata service application before you can upgrade the User Profile Service application.	Yes
User Profile Service	Yes	Yes	Import the Microsoft Identity Integration Server Key. Start the user profile synchronization service.	
PerformancePoint Services	Yes	Yes	None.	Yes
Search Service	Yes	Yes	None.	Yes

Creating New Service Applications

Before upgrading, you will need to create the following service applications:

> **Note**
>
> Although not essential, it is useful to create the WSS Usage Service app first to shorten the Search Services Application provision time.

- **State Service**—Allows various components of SharePoint 2013, such as InfoPath Services, to communicate across HTTP requests.

- **App Management Service**—This lets admins manage SharePoint apps, which you can buy from the SharePoint Marketplace or create yourself and deploy in the Internal App Directory. The service manages the permission settings and ensures the licensing is up-to-date before letting the user access the app.

> **Service Applications Without Upgradeable Databases**
>
> The following service applications are not associated with upgradeable databases. For more on the configuration of these services see Chapter 4, "Creating and Configuring Service Applications":
>
> - Excel Services
> - Visio Graphic Services
> - Word Automation Services
> - InfoPath Forms
> - Office Web Apps

> **Note**
>
> If you have deployed InfoPath templates that you want to continue using from your SharePoint 2010 environment, you will need to export any administrator-approved form templates (.xsn files) and their corresponding .udcx data connection files.
>
> Use the Export- SPInfoPathAdministrationFiles Windows PowerShell cmdlet.
>
> If the URLs are different in your new environment, use the Windows PowerShell cmdlet Update- SPInfoPathAdminFileURL to update the links in the templates.

Database Attach Upgrades

The upgrade approach to SharePoint 2013 is broken into five major phases:

1. Create the SharePoint 2013 farm that you will be attaching your databases to.
2. Back up your content databases and copy them to your new farm.
3. Upgrade service applications.
4. Upgrade content databases.
5. Upgrade site collections.

Before we can successfully perform the database attach upgrade, there are a series of steps, detailed in each section that follows, that you must ensure have been followed. These steps are:

1. Create web applications in your new SharePoint 2013 farm.
2. Apply customizations from SharePoint 2010 farm or new customizations as required.
3. Verify customizations.
4. Attach database to web application.
5. Upgrade database.
6. Verify database upgrade success.
7. Attach the remaining content databases for this web application and upgrade each.

Creating Web Applications

The database attach upgrade method requires that web applications already be created in the target SharePoint 2013 environment. If you are using the same URL as your source location, it is important to make sure that your alternate-access mappings, along with the port and host headers, have all been configured.

> **Note**
>
> If you use Windows classic authentication in your original SharePoint 2010 environment, unless you convert to Claims prior to the upgrade, you will need to configure your target SharePoint 2013 web application to use classic mode authentication. You cannot accomplish this from the UI and will need to use PowerShell to create this web application. For more on this topic, see http://technet.microsoft.com/en-us/library/gg276326.aspx.

Applying Customizations

After your web application has been created, ensure that all the customizations you documented during the pre-upgrade phase have been applied in the new environment. All customizations must be applied to each web front end before you can move forward with the upgrade. Although solution deployment should be automatic, it should always be checked before moving on to the next upgrade task. Unlike SharePoint 2010, SharePoint 2013 has the capability of being able to host the previous version alongside itself. Because of this it is important that any customizations from the SharePoint 2010 environment are installed in the /14 directory and not the /15—the /15 directory is for SharePoint 2013.

After the customizations have been installed, perform the Test_SPContentDatabase PowerShell command to validate that the database has all the needed customizations in the target farm.

To test the content database, perform this Windows PowerShell cmdlet:

```
Test-SPContentDatabase -Name DatabaseName - WebApplication URL
```

Performing the Database Attach Upgrade Method

The database attach upgrade method allows you to build a new, pristine SharePoint Server 2013 server farm. Many items, such as Excel Services, cannot be upgraded with the database attach method. If you need to upgrade a service, such as Excel Services, you will need to reconfigure that service application.

> **Note**
>
> Before you begin a SharePoint Server 2013 database attach upgrade, you must first have your SharePoint Server 2013 server farm configured. You must also have the databases you want to upgrade available on a SQL Server instance that is both accessible from the SharePoint Server 2013 server farm and that will be the permanent host.

Content databases contain most of your valuable user data in the form of site collections. When upgrading a content database, you must attach it to a SharePoint Server 2013 web application. Unlike SharePoint 2010, in SharePoint 2013 when a database is attached to a site collection, the upgrade process does not upgrade the site collections.

> **Note**
>
> Always attach the root site collection content database first for every web application. This rule applies only to web applications that have multiple content databases. Don't forget to remove the database that was created when you created the new web application.

To update a content database, you will need to use the PowerShell cmdlet Mount-SPContentDatabase. For upgrading purposes, you cannot use the Central Administration approach to upgrade the content database.

Before attaching the content database, the administrative account that is being used must have a few important memberships:

- SQL Server securityadmin
- SQL Server db_owner
- Association with server administrators group

To perform the database attach with PowerShell, follow these steps:

1. Launch the SharePoint PowerShell Management Shell.

2. At the PowerShell prompt, enter the following:

   ```
   Mount-SPContentDatabase -Name [DatabaseName] -
   DatabaseServer [ServerName] -WebApplication URL
   ```

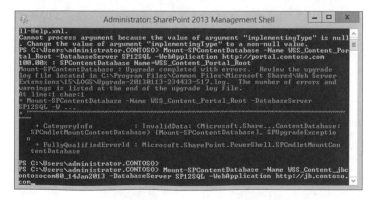

Figure 17.1
PowerShell cmdlet showing the commands used to attach and upgrade a SharePoint 2010 content database.

To test a SharePoint Server 2010 content database before attaching it to a web application, you can first run the Windows PowerShell cmdlet, Test-SPContentDatabase. This was detailed earlier in the chapter, and it's similar to the following:

```
Test-SPContentDatabase -name WSS_Content_Portal -
WebApplicationhttp://portal.contoso.com
```

This command tests the WSS_Content_Portal SharePoint Server 2010 content database against the http://portal.contoso.com SharePoint Server 2013 web application. Be sure to resolve any errors that would cause a blocked upgrade before attaching a content database to the web application. Upon attaching the database to a web application, it will automatically upgrade unless you use the add-spcontentdatabase or mount-spcontentdatbase cmdlets.

Because Stsadm.exe was deprecated in SharePoint 2013, Windows PowerShell is the preferred method to attach a content database to a SharePoint Server 2013 server farm for upgrade. To attach a content database using Windows PowerShell, you use the Mount-SPContentDatabase cmdlet. The following options are available for the cmdlet:

- **Name**—Specifies the SharePoint Server 2010 content database to be attached to SharePoint Server 2013.

- **WebApplication**—Specifies the SharePoint Server 2013 web application where the site collection will be attached. This is often referred to as associating a content database with a web application.

- **AssignNewDatabaseId**—Creates a new database ID when the database is attached. This is usually not required.

- **Confirm**—Requires you to confirm the command before executing.

- **ClearChangeLog**—Clears the change log when the database is attached. If you have not trimmed the change log in SharePoint Server 2010, you should consider doing so to reduce the size of the content database.

- **DatabaseCredentials**—If using SQL authentication, you must enter the database credentials.

- **DatabaseServer**—Specifies the database server if it is not the default database server specified in Central Administration.

- **MaxSiteCount**—Specifies the maximum number of site collections the database can contain. It must be at least the current number of site collections.

- **WarningSiteCount**—Specifies the number of site collections created before a warning is generated. A value of 0 turns the warning off.

- **WhatIf**—Shows what the effect of the command will be before modifying any content.

An example of running the Mount-SPContentDatabase cmdlet for a web application named http://portal.contoso.com, a content database named WSS_Content_Portal, a warning site count of 0, and a maximum site count of 1 is as follows:

```
Mount-SPContentDatabase -name WSS_Content_Portal -
WebApplicationhttp://portal.contoso.com -MaxSiteCount 1 -
WarningSiteCount 0
```

The output of the command should look similar to the following with a single site collection:

```
Id          : ad9ddb61-867b-47db-93c5-be61691fe21aName       :
WSS_Content_PortalWebApplication   : SPWebApplication
Name=Contoso PortalServer        : app01CurrentSiteCount : 1
```

Figure 17.2 shows the output of a successfully upgraded content database.

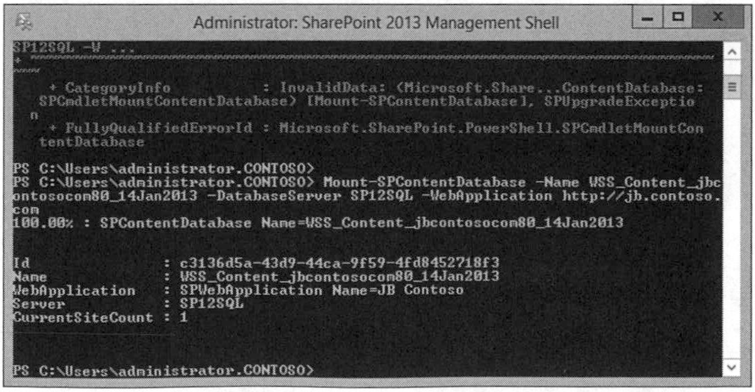

Figure 17.2
The output of a successful content database attach PowerShell cmdlet that was executed against a SharePoint 2010 content database.

If the upgrade process does not upgrade the site collection, you can manually restart the upgrade process using the Windows PowerShell cmdlet

Upgrade-SPContentDatabase. The unique option for this command is
-ForceDeleteLock. This forces the deletion of all locks on the database
before the upgrade starts.

Upgrading Sites and Site Collections

Upgrading the server farm to SharePoint Server 2013 is the first step to the
upgrade process. However, that is only the first step. After you have
configured the server farm and service applications, you must still upgrade
the sites. Many site collection administrators have been empowered in
SharePoint 2013 with the Site Settings option to upgrade their sites. In
fact, site administrators also will be given the capability to manage the
upgrade process separately from the site collection administrators.

To begin, open the legacy URL in a browser window. For this example, the
site collection is located at http://jb.contoso.com (see Figure 17.3). Upon
opening the site collection, it should look almost identical to how it
appeared before the upgrade.

Figure 17.3
The root site of the http://jb.contoso.com site collection as it appeared immediately after the database attach upgrade.

The first change you'll notice is that the Site Actions menu has changed. There will still be some SharePoint Server 2010 items in the menu.

> **Note**
>
> To perform the site collection upgrade, the user account must be a site collection administrator.

1. Click the Site Actions menu.
2. Select Site Settings.
3. On the Site Settings page, under the Site Collection Administration Section, click Site Collection Upgrade (see Figure 17.4).

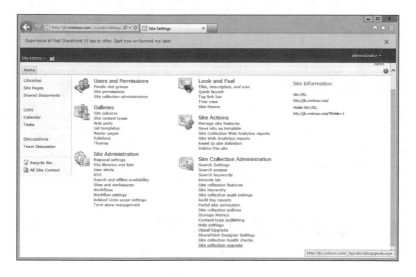

Figure 17.4
The settings available for Site Collection Administration on the Site Settings page now have the option to perform the Site Collection Upgrade.

After clicking the Site Collection Upgrade option, you will be directed to the page shown in Figure 17.5.

4. Click I'm Ready on the verification dialog box (see Figure 17.6) to begin the upgrade.

Immediately after you click the I'm Ready button, the Site Collection upgrade runs through a series of health checks (see Figure 17.7) prior to performing the upgrade.

Table 17.3 describes the health checks performed.

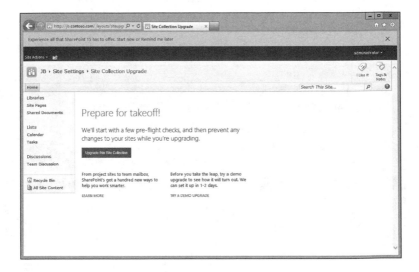

Figure 17.5
The Site Collection Upgrade page provides the site collection administrator the option to upgrade the site collection or to request a demo site collection.

Figure 17.6
The "Just checking..." dialog box appears immediately after selecting Site Collection Upgrade from Site Settings. Click I'm Ready to begin the upgrade process.

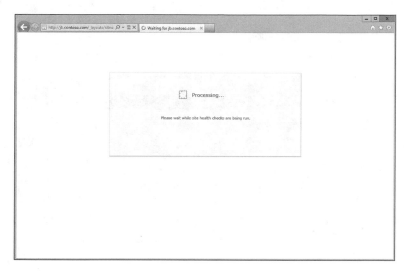

Figure 17.7
After clicking I'm Ready, you will see the health checks processing dialog box appear.

Table 17.3 **Health Checks**

Rule Name	Description
Customized Files	This rule checks for any files that were customized (or unghosted) in the site collection or subsites. When run in repair mode, it can reset the page to the default (reghost the file).
Missing Galleries	This rule checks for all default galleries and reports if any are missing from the site collection or subsites.
Missing Site Templates	This rule checks to make sure that the template the site is based on is available and reports if any elements are missing.
Unsupported Language Pack References	This rule checks to make sure that the language packs that are used by the site collection exist and are referenced correctly by the site collection.
Unsupported MUI References	This rule checks to make sure that the multiuser interface elements that are used by the site collection exist and are referenced correctly by the site collection.

Source: http://technet.microsoft.com/en-us/library/jj219720(v=office.15))

5. After the upgrade starts, you will be directed to the Upgrade Status page (see Figure 17.8).

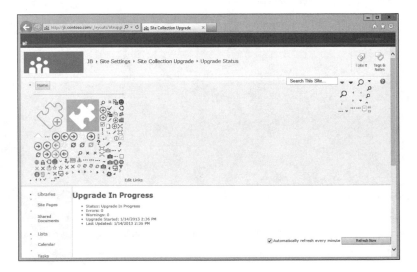

Figure 17.8
The upgrade status page is refreshed by default every 1 minute. It provides detailed information as to the upgrade process for the site collection.

6. When the upgrade is completed successfully, the upgrade status is changed to Upgrade Completed Successfully (see Figure 17.9).

7. To see the output log of the current site collection upgrade, click the blue .txt file next to Log File (shown in Figure 17.10).

8. Click the Let's See the New Site button shown in Figure 17.9 to go to the newly upgraded site (see Figure 17.11).

Instead of the Visual Upgrade Option, SharePoint 2013 allows for the site collection administrator to request an upgrade evaluation of the site collection. This evaluation is advantageous to the site collection administrator because it creates a fully functional site running SharePoint 2013 separate from the original SharePoint 2010 site. Unlike SharePoint 2010's Visual Upgrade option, this Demo Site is a fully functional, independent site.

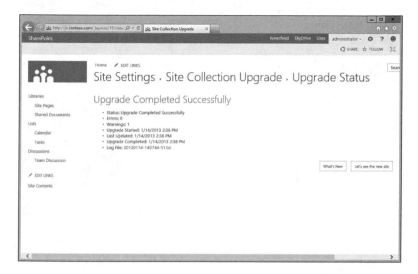

Figure 17.9
When the site collection is upgraded successfully, you will be directed to the page
shown with a link to the corresponding log file.

Figure 17.10
The .txt log file will appear in the browser after the site collection administrator
clicks the link.

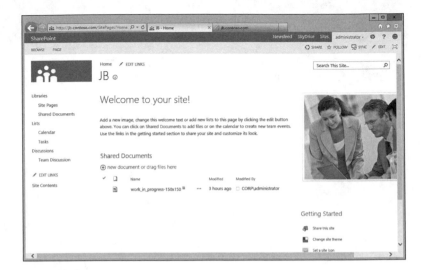

Figure 17.11
The default root site collection for the jb.contoso web application after the site collection upgrade completed successfully.

> **Note**
>
> Use the demo site only for the validation of current capabilities. Do not do any custom configurations or edits to this site collection because you will not retain them when you perform the Site Collection upgrade.

When you request an upgrade evaluation site collection, the request can take up to 24 hours depending on the number of site collection administrators requesting evaluations. This delay depends on the size of the site. Also, if you have SQL Server Enterprise edition, the upgrade uses SQL snapshots.

When a request is made by the site collection administrator, a request is added to the Create Upgrade Evaluation Site Collections timer job. This timer job is set to run only one time per day. When the timer job is run, it will email the requesting site collection administrator a notification of completion.

Upgrading My Sites

To upgrade My Sites from SharePoint 2010 to SharePoint 2013, the SharePoint farm administrator must upgrade the My Site host first. After the My Site host has been upgraded, each user will be provided the option to upgrade his or her My Site.

To upgrade the My Site host, you need to create the My Site web application. When the web application has been created, you need to perform the database attach upgrade to the target web application. When the database attach has completed, the My Site will be automatically upgraded on the first visit by the user. Users have the option to get SkyDrive Pro but will not have the option to upgrade.

> **Note**
>
> Because My Sites have dependencies across multiple service applications, it is best to not attempt to upgrade My Sites until all service applications and features have been deployed.

A user's My Site will be upgraded when the user visits his or her own My Site.

> **Note**
>
> Users may not upgrade their My Sites until the My Site Host has been upgraded. My Sites are not available in SharePoint Foundation 2013.

Index

A

M

BEN CURRY
JASON BATCHELOR
SHANE KING
JAY SIMCOX

Microsoft®
SHAREPOINT
2013

POCKET GUIDE

SAMS

FREE
Online Edition

Safari.
Books Online

Your purchase of *Microsoft® SharePoint® 2013 Pocket Guide* includes access to a free onlin
edition for 45 days through the **Safari Books Online** subscription service. Nearly every Sam
book is available online through **Safari Books Online**, along with thousands of books and
videos from publishers such as Addison-Wesley Professional, Cisco Press, Exam Cram, IBM
Press, O'Reilly Media, Prentice Hall, Que, and VMware Press.

Safari Books Online is a digital library providing searchable, on-demand access to thousands
of technology, digital media, and professional development books and videos from leading
publishers. With one monthly or yearly subscription price, you get unlimited access to learning
tools and information on topics including mobile app and software development, tips and tricks
on using your favorite gadgets, networking, project management, graphic design, and much
more.

Activate your FREE Online Edition at
informit.com/safarifree

STEP 1:   Enter the coupon code: QVJMOGA.

STEP 2:   New Safari users, complete the brief registration form.
           Safari subscribers, just log in.

If you have difficulty registering on Safari or accessing the online edition,
please e-mail customer-service@safaribooksonline.com